Contents

Part 1

Introduction to Today's Physical Education   1

Part 2

A Basic Physical Education Curriculum   69

Part 3

Refining Physical Education Teaching Strategies   225

Part 4

Creating a Safe Physical Education Environment 285

Acknowledgments

A special thanks to Peter Werner, Debbie Vigil, Lauren Lieberman, Deborah Wolf, Rae Pica, Mike Sutliffe, Eloise Elliott, David Belka, and Wendy Mustain for contributing their knowledge and experience to help make this book a truly unique and usable guide for the classroom teacher.

Also thanks to the following authors whose ideas and published work added to this book to ensure its usability and to better illustrate concepts: Craig A. Bushner, Thomas Ratliffe, Laraine Ratliffe, Theresa M. Purcell Cone, Stephen L. Cone, Amelia Mays Woods, George Graham, Shirley Holt-Hale, Melissa Parker, Christine Hopple, Bette Logsdon, Luann M. Allman, Sue Ann Straits, Dawn Clark, Stephen J. Virgilio, Linda L. Griffin, Stephen A. Mitchell, Judith Oslin, Sue Schiemer, D. Gallahue, Lois Carnes, Madge Ashy, Steve Grineski, Margaret J. Safrit, Joseph P. Winnick, C. Sherrill, Susan Lowy, Barbara Cadden, Kathy Harris, Joe L. Frost, Robin C. Moore, Susan M. Goltsman, Daniel S. Iacofano, and Richard A. Simmons.

And finally, thanks to the staff, faculty, and students at Dr. Howard School and Carrie Busey School, in Champaign, IL, and the staff, faculty, and students at Leal School in Urbana, IL for their cooperation in allowing us access for the photo shoots.

Macey, 5

Brooke, 12

Credits

Chapter 7

Sample Unit Sequence For First Grade Games reprinted, by permission, from Logsdon, B., 1997, *Physical Education Unit Plans for Grades 1-2*, (Champaign, IL: Human Kinetics), 1.

Dribbling, Passing, and Trapping reprinted, by permission, from Logsdon, B., 1997, *Physical Education Unit Plans for Grades 1-2*, (Champaign, IL: Human Kinetics), 2-5.

Leap for Life reprinted, by permission, from Buschner, C., 1994, *Teaching Children Movement Concepts and Skills*, (Champaign, IL: Human Kinetics), 101-103.

Chapter 8

Fitness Checklist reprinted, by permission, from Wikgren, S., 1993, "Fitness—What's the right approach for children," Teaching Elementary Physical Education, 4(1):7.

Stretching Yourself and Heart Pump Circuit reprinted, by permission, from Ratliffe, T., *Teaching Children Fitness*, (Champaign, IL: Human Kinetics) 77-80, 96-98.

Chapter 9

Sample Unit Sequence for Second Grade Games reprinted, by permission, from Logsdon, B., 1997, *Physical Education Unit Plans for Grades 1-2*, (Champaign, IL: Human Kinetics), 77.

Throwing and Catching reprinted, by permission, from Logsdon, B., 1997, *Physical Education Unit Plans for Grades 1-2*, (Champaign, IL: Human Kinetics), 95-98.

Defend the Shots reprinted, by permission, from Belka, D., 1994, *Teaching Children Games*, (Champaign, IL: Human Kinetics), 67-68.

Chapter 10

Sample Unit Sequence for Kindergarten Gymnastics Units reprinted, by permission, from Logsdon, B., 1997, *Physical Education Unit Plans for Preschool-Kindergarten*, (Champaign, IL: Human Kinetics) 103.

Traveling on Different Body Parts reprinted, by permission, from Logsdon, B., 1997, *Physical Education Unit Plans for Preschool-Kindergarten*, (Champaign, IL: Human Kinetics), 104, 107.

A Roll by Any Other Name reprinted, by permission, from Werner, P., 1994, *Teaching Children Gymnastics*, (Champaign, IL: Human Kinetics), 121-123.

Chapter 11

The Cat reprinted, by permission, from Purcell, T., 1994, *Teaching Children Dance*, (Champaign, IL: Human Kinetics), 97-99.

Sample Unit Sequence for Sixth Grade Dance reprinted, by permission, from Logsdon, B., 1997, *Physical Education Unit Plans for Grades 5-6*, (Champaign, IL: Human Kinetics), 133.

Altering Body Shape Using Partners reprinted, by permission, from Logsdon, B., 1997, *Physical Education Unit Plans for Grades 5-6*, (Champaign, IL: Human Kinetics), 134-137.

Chapter 12

Chapter 12 adapted, by permission, from Cone, T., P. Werner, S. Cone, A. Woods, 1998, *Interdisciplinary Teaching Through Physical Education*, (Champaign, IL: Human Kinetics), 4-6, 35-40, 42, 59, 85-89, 96, 97, 154, 195.

Chapter 13

Human Obstacle Course, Wand Grabbing, Sportball Juggle, Bump Over, Thunderstorm Dance, Tinikling, and Routines "Let's Do it Together" reprinted, by permission, from Grineski, S., 1996, *Cooperative Learning in Physical Education*, (Champaign, IL: Human Kinetics), 58-59, 63, 76-77, 86, 92-93, 98, 105.

Chapter 16

Fitness Field Day reprinted, by permission, from Virgilio, S., 1997, *Fitness Education for Children*, (Champaign, IL: Human Kinetics), 194, 196.

Other

Sidebars in chapters 1, 3, 4, 6, 7, 8, 9, 10, 11, 13, 14, 16, 18, and 19 reprinted from *Developmentally Appropriate Physical Education Practices for Children* (COPEC 1992) with permission from the National Association for Sport and Physical Education (NASPE), 1900 Association Drive, Reston, VA 20191-1599.

Teddy, 6

Rachel, 5

Sarah, 4

Editor's Preface

The idea for a physical education text written specifically for classroom teachers came to me after I gave a talk to elementary education majors who were about to start their semester of student teaching. These student teachers had been assigned to schools in a district that had no physical education specialists and therefore would be responsible for teaching physical education. Because a majority of these student teachers had not taken a physical education methods course, I had been asked by the adviser at their university to help provide some "pointers."

During the hour I had with these student teachers, several things became obvious to me. First, the majority thought of physical education in terms of the "gym class" they had endured as elementary students. Several horror stories were shared, and many nodded in agreement with the statement of one person who commented, "Gym seemed to be more harmful than beneficial to the students who needed help the most."

Second, these student teachers cared about what they were doing and wanted to be the best teachers they could for their students. They asked insightful questions and seemed quite excited about the prospects of the "new" physical education I described to them.

Third, their educational courses in elementary methods provided a basic understanding of children and teaching methods, so by discussing physical education in terms that they were familiar with, they quickly caught on to many of the concepts I was trying to share.

During a concluding discussion, we all agreed that physical education is, without a doubt, ideally taught by a specialist, but a classroom teacher could provide a quality experience if armed with the appropriate information and resources. That is the purpose of this text—to supply you with the basics so that you can provide the best possible physical education experience for your students, whether you have full responsibility for the program or you are working with a part-time or full-time specialist.

The information in this text is based on the very best physical education teaching methods, gleaned from current research and the experience of our many contributors. However, we do not simply provide you with information. Instead, we share it with you through the eyes of a classroom teacher, with many illustrative stories that help bring the concepts to life. In addition, we have provided plenty of cross-curricular ideas that not only will teach important physical education concepts but also will enhance the learning of other subjects.

Further, this book is written with the understanding that you may not be a gifted athlete. Indeed, if you consider yourself to have been a "clumsy child who hated gym class," you might have even more to offer your children because you understand how physical education that is taught poorly can turn off children. Now, in this book, we will show you how well-taught physical education can provide the knowledge, experience, and motivation *every* child in your class needs to live a physically active, healthy life.

Scott Wikgren
Director
Academic Book Division
Human Kinetics

Introduction

Me? Teach physical education? I'm a classroom teacher with several other subjects to cover! Why not just let the kids have an extra recess? I always hated physical education when I was growing up. I'd be doing the kids a favor by not trying to teach it. Why can't we hire a specialist? I resent losing yet another planning period—and having to plan for another subject! Okay, the district curriculum guidelines say I have to teach physical education. So where should I start? Help! I haven't a clue!

That's what I used to think, and maybe it's what you're thinking right now. But teaching physical education can be worthwhile, practical, and—most of all—fun! In this book, we'll show you how to develop a realistic approach to teaching physical education as a regular classroom teacher.

But first, you may be relieved to hear about what we won't do: We won't expect you to be the next Michael Jordan or Mia Hamm or to lose 10 pounds before starting this program; we won't expect you to buy loads of expensive equipment or build a new gym; we won't expect you to change into a sweat suit (although comfortable shoes will be a plus); and we won't expect you to produce future professional athletes.

What we will do, however, is provide you with a basic physical education curriculum and concrete, realistic, user-friendly suggestions as to how to implement this curriculum.

Table 1 lists the content of a basic curriculum.

Even if your students meet with a specialist once or twice a week, they will benefit from an organized program five days a week. This means you as a classroom teacher need to understand what makes a quality physical education program, its purpose, and how to effectively teach such a program. And in order to provide students with maximum benefits, both you and the specialist need to work together to plan, instruct, and assess the program. As we explore these issues, we'll focus on what works for real classroom teachers, teaching physical education to real kids, under realistic circumstances.

In part 1, we'll provide you with a concise overview of physical education today, including research on the value of structured physical activity, physical education and the elementary school mission, authentic assessment, behavior management, and instruction, demonstration, and motivation. In part 2, we'll outline strategies for actually teaching physical education, including the various curricular areas of physical education, and integrating physical education across the curriculum. In part 3, we'll help you refine your physical education instruction by explaining how you can employ cooperative learning, inclusion, and peer-tutoring strategies to enhance all students' learning. Also in part 3, we'll explain how to collaborate with fellow teachers, physical education specialists, and community resources to assist you in your program. Finally, in part 4, we'll discuss safety in relation to liability, equipment, facilities, and playgrounds. In addition, we'll show you how to help kids get the most out of free play.

As you use this book, we encourage you to adapt our suggestions to fit your situation

Table 1   Sample Physical Education Curriculum for Dribbling

Proficiency level	Utilization level	Control level	Precontrol level
❑ Small-group basketball	❑ Dribbling against an opponent: one on one	❑ Moving switches	❑ Dribbling and walking
❑ Dribble/Pass Keep Away	❑ Dribbling and passing with a partner	❑ Dribbling and traveling	❑ Bouncing a ball down (dribbling) continuously
❑ Dribbling and throwing at a target	❑ Mirroring and matching while dribbling	❑ Dribbling in different places around the body while stationary	❑ Bouncing a ball down and catching it
❑ Making up fancy dribbling/passing routines	❑ Dribbling around stationary obstacles	❑ Dribbling with the body in different positions	
❑ Dribbling and passing in game situations	❑ Dribbling in different pathways	❑ Switches	
❑ Dribbling while dodging	❑ Starting and stopping while changing directions	❑ Dribbling and looking	
❑ Dribble Tag	❑ Dribbling while changing directions	❑ Dribbling at different heights	
❑ Now You've Got It, Now You Don't	❑ Dribbling and changing speed of travel	❑ Dribble like a basketball player	
❑ Dribbling against opponents: group situations		❑ All the time dribble	

Reprinted, by permission, from Graham, G., S. Holt/Hale, and M. Parker, 1987, *Children Moving*, (Mountain View, CA: Mayfield), 524.

while staying within the developmentally appropriate curriculum and methods we'll outline. Moreover, we encourage you to always put individual needs first in a sensitive and supportive teaching-learning environment; we'll show you how to do this in simple and realistic ways so all your students will learn the basic skills they'll need both to improve in physical activity and to enjoy physical activity for its own sake. We believe these

two gifts are some of the best you can give your students!

Note: As this book was a group project, we have used "we" to mean the collective input of Bonnie as a classroom teacher and the many physical education specialists who provided research data, advice, and feedback (see "Acknowledgments"). "I" narratives represent Bonnie's personal experiences as a classroom teacher.

Disclaimer

Human Kinetics believes strongly that physical education should be taught by physical education specialists. All classroom teachers should have a full understanding of physical education, as provided in this book, so the classroom teacher can support the physical education program.

Part 1

Introduction to Today's Physical Education

The competent and sensitive physical education instructor of today is probably quite different from the physical education instructor you grew up with. Moreover, the physical education program a physical educator would consider well designed is quite different today. Indeed, no longer should physical education be allowed to function as a completely separate activity or as merely a way to keep kids busy and allow them to blow off steam so they can come back to "important" work. Quite the contrary! Today's physical education enhances academic learning, helps meet the overall elementary school mission, employs authentic assessment strategies, treats students with dignity and respect, and applies instructional and motivational techniques rooted in the latest research. In part 1 we'll examine all these factors and explain why physical education is an important, integral part of the elementary school curriculum, then show you how to assess, manage, and instruct effectively.

In chapter 1, we'll introduce you to the latest research on the benefits of physical education and physical activity. In chapter 2, we'll explain how a physical education program can support the elementary school mission. Next, in chapter 3, we'll outline how authentic assessment applies in physical education. Then, in chapter 4, we'll describe how to manage the physical education class effectively. Finally, in chapter 5, we'll discuss the best techniques for instructing, demonstrating, and motivating in physical education.

Chapter 1

Physical Education Today

Laura, 9

"Not only was I chosen last, but the captains argued over who would have to take me."

—Bob, age 44

Hardly a week goes by that I don't hear another adult lamenting over the humiliation of being chosen last for a team in physical education. Where are those adults who were chosen first? I suspect that many of them have the good grace not to rub it in to the rest of us. I also think that even one experience of being chosen last burns such a painful scar into the memory that perhaps the more positive experiences are forgotten.

Fortunately, the definition of quality physical education has changed. Today, we know—often from personal experience—the damage choosing sides and other insensitive practices can cause. As classroom teachers, we want better for our students' emotional and physical well-being. And so does the physical education profession today!

In this chapter, after first defining the term *physical education* and discussing its benefits, we will examine what physical education specialists consider to be *best practices* by answering the question, "What is good physical education?" Specifically, we'll look at the national standards for physical education. Then, we'll see how all these components fit together in a developmentally appropriate, progressive curriculum. Finally, we'll discuss practical ways to create individual instruction so that each child can get the most out of

physical education—and feel good about his physical self at the same time.

Physical Education: A Contemporary Definition

What is *physical education*? Before reading on, take a moment to think about how you would define this term. . . . Now let's look at how the physical education specialists define it. *Physical education* prepares students to live physically active, healthy lives by providing a carefully planned scope and sequence of learning experiences. These experiences must be designed to foster the developmentally appropriate acquisition of motor skills, health-related fitness, health-related fitness knowledge, confidence in being physically active, and an appreciation of the benefits of physical activity. In other words, physical education provides a rare venue in which to educate the whole child—her affective, cognitive, and psychomotor selves. Thus, the classroom teacher can use this avenue to promote not only physical development but also social, emotional, and cognitive development. Figure 1.1 shows how the National Association for Sport and Physical Education (NASPE) defines a physically educated person.

A Physically Educated Person

- Has learned skills necessary to perform a variety of physical activities
    1. moves using concepts of body awareness, space awareness, effort, and relationships.
    2. demonstrates competence in a variety of manipulative, locomotor, and nonlocomotor skills.
    3. demonstrates competence in combinations of manipulative, locomotor, and nonlocomotor skills performed individually and with others.
    4. demonstrates competence in many different forms of physical activity.
    5. demonstrates proficiency in a few forms of physical activity.
    6. has learned how to learn new skills.
- Is physically fit
    7. assesses, achieves, and maintains physical fitness.
    8. designs safe, personal fitness programs in accordance with principles of training and conditioning.
- Does participate regularly in physical activity
    9. participates in health-enhancing physical activity at least three times a week.
    10. selects and regularly participates in lifetime physical activities.
- Knows the implications of and the benefits from involvement in physical activities
    11. identifies the benefits, costs, and obligations associated with regular participation in physical activity.
    12. recognizes the risk and safety factors associated with regular participation in physical activity.
    13. applies concepts and principles to the development of motor skills.
    14. understands that wellness involves more than being physically fit.
    15. knows the rules, strategies, and appropriate behaviors for selected physical activities.
    16. recognizes that participation in physical activity can lead to multicultural and international understanding.
    17. understands that physical activity provides the opportunity for enjoyment, self-expression, and communication.
- Values physical activity and its contributions to a healthful lifestyle
    18. appreciates the relationships with others that result from participation in physical activity.
    19. respects the role that regular physical activity plays in the pursuit of lifelong health and well-being.
    20. cherishes the feelings that result from regular participation in physical activity.

Figure 1.1 Characteristics of a physically educated person.
Reprinted from *Outcomes of Quality Physical Education* (1992) with permission from the National Association for Sport and Physical Education (NASPE), 1900 Association Drive, Reston, VA 20191-1599.

NASPE's definition of a physically educated person includes mastering motor skills, being physically fit, regularly participating in physical activity, understanding the benefits and risks of physical activity, and valuing physical activity as a lifelong pursuit.

Benefits of Physical Education

Simply by stating what a physically educated person is, we have touched upon the major benefits of physical education. Figure 1.2 lists several health benefits of physical activity (and therefore physical education) as summarized by the Centers for Disease Control and Prevention (USDHHS 1996). In this section, we will look more closely at the specific benefits of physical education to students, benefits that can and do contribute to an individual's quality of life—for life. Then we'll look at how you as a teacher can benefit from including physical education in your curriculum.

Student Benefits

Do students really benefit from physical education? After all, they have regular recesses.

The Centers for Disease Control and Prevention has stated that "regular physical activity that is performed on most days of the week reduces the risk of developing or dying from some of the leading causes of illnesses and death in the United States." Regular physical activity

1. reduces the risk of dying prematurely,
2. reduces the risk of dying prematurely from heart disease,
3. reduces the risk of developing diabetes,
4. reduces the risk of developing high blood pressure,
5. helps reduce blood pressure in people who already have high blood pressure,
6. reduces the risk of developing colon cancer,
7. reduces feelings of depression and anxiety,
8. helps build and maintain healthy bones, muscles, and joints,
9. helps older adults become stronger and better able to move without falling, and
10. promotes psychological well-being.

Figure 1.2 Benefits of regular physical activity. USDHHS 1996, 1997.

And aren't the "three Rs" more important? In this section, you'll see how children and their academic endeavors benefit from physical education.

Physical Fitness

An obvious benefit of physical education is physical fitness. Children have an innate need to move, and given the chance and encouragement, they will be physically fit through physical education and other movement opportunities. And while you may consider physical fitness to only involve endurance (e.g., the ability to run for an extended period of time), it involves five major aspects: cardiorespiratory fitness, muscular strength, muscular endurance, flexibility, and body composition (the ratio of body fat mass to lean tissue mass).

When we speak of these components of physical fitness, we are defining *health-related physical fitness* as opposed to *sport-* or *skill-related physical fitness*, which involves the specific skills and strengths needed to excel at a particular sport. Thus, in today's physical

education, students benefit from a broad approach to physical fitness that seeks to encourage a lifelong quest for physical health, not just sport-specific skill mastery.

Psychomotor Skills

I remember the amazement I felt when I learned early in my teaching career that the physical educator at my school could and did teach ballhandling skills in a logical, predetermined sequence. I had thought that either you could handle a ball or you couldn't. But today's physical education benefits children by systematically teaching them basic motor concepts and skills that they can apply to a variety of situations in and outside of the physical education setting. For example, hand-eye coordination developed in physical education can carry over to classroom and household tasks, and increased fitness allows the child to respond more effectively to emergencies. Moreover, today's physical education teaches children *how* to learn new skills. In this way, physical education gives children practical skills that will benefit them the rest of their lives.

Regular Physical Activity

The American Heart Association (1992) found physical inactivity to be the fourth most prevalent risk factor for coronary heart disease (after smoking, high blood pressure, and high cholesterol). An adequate physical education schedule provides children with regular physical activity and all its benefits in a way that recess simply cannot provide. Although recess, of course, has its place in the school day, children need to experience physical activity in a structured physical education setting as well in order to derive the most benefit from it (see also chapter 19). For example, cardiovascular benefits may only be obtained through activity that elevates the heart rate sufficiently for at least 20 minutes three times per week. This 20 minutes does not include time spent warming up, cooling down, or listening to instructions, but it can accumulate throughout the day, rather than occur all at once. This may or may not happen during recess or other free times, depending on the child's activity choices.

Furthermore, a physical education program conducted in a sensitive, caring setting promotes the desire within children to be physically active outside of school time. Returning to our opening vignette, ask yourself, "Is the child who suffered the humiliation of team captains fighting over who had to take him likely to participate in physical activity after school?" Probably not. But the approach to physical education you choose to take can encourage children to enjoy physical activity so that they are more likely to pursue it after school—and after graduation. So they need to learn basic skills to perform and enjoy physical activity, have positive physical activity experiences, and understand the benefits of physical activity. In these ways, children benefit from physical education because they learn to seek physical activity as a way of life.

Emotional Wellness

When physical education promotes physical activity as a way of life, it also promotes emotional wellness. Specifically, those who exercise regularly—no matter their age—are less likely to feel depressed or anxious (USDHHS 1997). Thus, they are more likely to enjoy psychological well-being. And positive physical activity experiences can enhance the self-esteem of students who are primarily kinesthetic learners. These positive experiences are sure to benefit your entire curriculum, because kids who feel right will act right and are more ready to learn in all areas.

Social Skills

Physical education teaches, develops, and reinforces social skills. Whether working together to develop a new game to practice

Figure 1.3 Physical education promotes more than just healthy bodies—it promotes social skills as well.

ballhandling skills, offering sincere encouragement to one another, or designing a creative dance in a small group, children learn social skills in physical education that can carry over to the rest of their school experiences and daily lives. Indeed, the practices of accepting others' physical abilities and limitations and of working as a team to enhance each individual's success can lend itself to accepting diversity in other school settings. Thus, in a supportive teaching-learning environment, children develop and hone social skills as much—or more—in the physical education setting as in the regular classroom. In fact, many specialists assert that physical education is the perfect arena in which to develop social skills.

Personal Responsibility

As in other areas of the curriculum, your students can gain essential practice taking responsibility for themselves in physical education. You can structure your program to allow students to gradually assume more and more personal responsibility for their physical well-being and their activities in and stemming from the physical education setting. Eventually, you may be able to guide students toward trying new activities without complaining, engaging in physical activity outside of school voluntarily, and working cheerfully with anyone in the class (Masser 1990).

We will explore more about responsibility when we discuss class management in chapter 4.

Cognitive Skills

By creating opportunities for problem solving and questioning, you can use physical education to engage your students cognitively. Can't imagine how? Try having your students create a game to practice racket skills, discover solutions as to how to balance on three body parts, or use their natural curiosity to explore general movement possibilities. Or use physical activity to enhance academic learning (see chapter 12). Through

Step by Step

Sarah had learned several different dance steps in physical education class. Her teacher asked her to create an original dance. Sarah put together several different steps and added music to create her own dance. This experience helped her to understand and follow sequences in other areas as well, including in science experiments and reading comprehension.

Effects of Movement

An active body sets the stage for an active mind. Let's look at what Carla Hannaford (1995), a researcher on this topic, has to say:

- Physical movement, from earliest infancy and throughout our lives, plays an important role in the creation of nerve cell networks, which are actually the essence of learning.

- Movement activates the neural wiring throughout the body, making the whole body the instrument of learning.

- It takes a physically fit body to supply the massive oxygen needs of the brain. Movement is essential not only for nerve net development and thought but also for adequate heart and lung development to support brain function.

- Movement helps develop blood vessels that carry learning-essential water, oxygen, and nutrients to the brain.

As you can see, movement directly benefits the nervous system, including the brain.

Hearts and Minds

A class of fifth graders was learning about the heart. The teacher had given the students a textbook with information and pictures, but her attempts to explain the opening and closing of the valves and how blood moved through them were failing miserably. Finally, one student asked the teacher if the students could "do" the actions. The student then arranged his classmates into three groups: one valve opening as the other was closing and the blood rushing through them. Because they saw *and* experienced *this science concept, the students finally* understood *it!*

a bodily-kinesthetic approach, you can reinforce and extend the *habit* of problem solving in your students, thereby enhancing their achievement across the curriculum.

Knowledge of the Benefits of Physical Activity

An effective physical education program teaches children the specific benefits we have been discussing. They then carry this knowledge with them after they leave your classroom. In addition to learning the specific benefits of physical activity, your students can learn the specific risks of certain activities and how to minimize the chance of injury. Indeed, no matter how enthusiastic a child is about physical activity, if he is injured, he cannot participate fully. Finally, through physical education, students learn the risks of inactivity, not to scare them into becoming active but to arm them with accurate information in a society that does more to encourage TV-watching than physical fitness.

Teacher Benefits

The benefits of physical education aren't just for students! You, too, can benefit from regularly scheduling and conducting physical education classes, because physical education can make classroom management and assessment easier and give you a chance to get exercise, too.

Enhanced Class Management

Movement facilitates classroom management. Children certainly don't like to sit still, and expecting them to do so for long periods of time is asking for trouble. Indeed, as concentration wanes, wiggling prevails and learning suffers. But when you allow children frequent, purposeful "fitness breaks," you help develop a sense of community and an atmosphere of cooperation (Pica 1995; see also chapter 19). Thus, children who have appropriate chances to move in an organized manner are easier to teach.

Of course, not all this movement must come from physical education, but some of it can. For example, you can incorporate physical education concepts into dramatizing stories (e.g., dance, gymnastics, body control) or illuminating science principles (e.g., balance, leverage). See also chapter 12.

Enhanced Assessment

Movement activities give you an effective means of evaluation in other subjects. Although traditional academic assessment methods may not always quickly show who doesn't understand an academic concept or skill, movement experiences allow you to immediately detect those students who do not understand (Gilbert 1977). For example, having children act out how an electrical circuit operates instead of talking about it will quickly show you whose wires are crossed!

Personal Fitness

No time to work out? Join your students in their physical activities. Not only will you be a more effective leader, you'll also get some exercise and all its many benefits. In addition, you'll model the importance of physical activity and the need to try even if you're not good at something. You may be surprised by how supportive your students are. Of course, you should not get so involved that you violate the basic principles of classroom management that we'll discuss in chapter 4.

Best Practices

What, then, is good physical education? In other words, what components does a physical education program need to have to be effective, providing the benefits children need and deserve? As with any other curriculum area, national standards provide both credibility and guidance. In this section, we'll outline the National Association for Sport and Physical Education's (NASPE) National Physical Education Standards (NASPE 1995) and the Council on Physical Education for Children's (COPEC) "Developmentally Appropriate Physical Education Practices for Children" (COPEC 1992). Then we'll put it all together and outline how you can use these documents to create a cohesive program.

NASPE Standards

In 1992 NASPE, the largest professional association of physical educators in the United States, published specific physical education standards for kindergarten, second, fourth, and sixth grades (as well as up through high school). Along with these standards, NASPE offered sample benchmarks for measuring achievement and assessment examples to help the teacher determine a child's level of mastery. The following is a summary of the NASPE Content Standards in Physical Education. These are exit standards that a student should achieve by the time he finishes sixth grade:

1. Demonstrates competency in many movement forms and proficiency in a few movement forms
2. Applies movement concepts and principles to the learning and development of motor skills
3. Exhibits a physically active lifestyle
4. Achieves and maintains a health-enhancing level of physical fitness
5. Demonstrates responsible personal and social behavior in physical activity settings
6. Demonstrates understanding and respect for differences among people in physical activity settings
7. Understands that physical activity provides the opportunity for enjoyment, challenge, self-expression, and social interaction

Like NASPE's definition of a physically educated person, this list of exit standards speaks to the whole child: the affective, cognitive,

COMPONENT— Development of Movement Concepts and Motor Skills

Appropriate Practice

Children are provided with frequent and meaningful age-appropriate practice opportunities that enable them to develop a functional understanding of movement concepts (body awareness, space awareness, effort, and relationships) and build competence and confidence in their ability to perform a variety of motor skills (locomotor, nonlocomotor, and manipulative).

Inappropriate Practice

Children participate in a limited number of games and activities in which the opportunity for individual children to develop basic concepts and motor skills is restricted.

Reprinted from COPEC/NASPE 1992.

and psychomotor development of the individual.

Against this backdrop of national standards, teachers can analyze and assess student progress in an authentic manner (see chapter 3). Thus, the NASPE National Physical Education Standards provide an important framework within which actual physical education programs should take place.

Developmentally Appropriate Physical Education

Certainly, we need standards to know where an individual should be functioning at a particular age or grade. But we also need to know specific information to be able to plan the scope and sequence of a developmentally appropriate program. And just as we do not begin teaching reading with a book written at the sixth-grade reading level, we cannot expect students to meet the exit standards without following a logical sequence for physical development. COPEC has published a pamphlet titled "Developmentally Appropriate Physical Education Practices for Children" (1992). This document lists several components of physical education and examples of appropriate and inappropriate practices, based on the following three major premises:

1. **Physical education and athletic programs have different purposes.** Athletic programs are for children eager to specialize in a sport. In contrast, physical education programs are for all children, providing them with a foundation of movement experiences that will eventually lead to active and healthy lifestyles.

2. **Children are not miniature adults.** Children need, and learn from, programs designed specifically with their needs and differences in mind.

3. **Children in school today will not be adults in today's world.** Contemporary programs help children learn how to learn—and to enjoy—the process of discovering and exploring new and different challenges in the physical domain. This prepares children to cope with our rapidly changing world effectively.

Adapted from COPEC 1992.

In the next section and at various points throughout this book, we will examine the specific examples COPEC has set forth.

Appropriate Versus Inappropriate Physical Education

Most of us can probably provide an extreme example of a physical education practice of the past that we would call "inappropriate," such as having team captains choose teams. But there are many other practices that physical education experts would like to see eliminated. The following examples from COPEC provide acceptable alternatives.

As you can see, good physical education takes organization and planning to avoid inappropriate practices. Throughout this book,

COMPONENT— Regular Involvement of Every Child

Appropriate Practice

Children participate in their regularly scheduled physical education class because it is recognized as an important part of their overall education.

Inappropriate Practice

Children are removed from physical education classes to participate in classroom activities, as a punishment for not completing assignments, or for misbehavior in the classroom.

Reprinted from COPEC/NASPE 1992.

COMPONENT—
Active Participation for Every Child

Appropriate Practice

All children are involved in activities that allow them to remain continually active.

Classes are designed to meet a child's need for active participation in all learning experiences.

Inappropriate Practice

Activity time is limited because children are waiting in lines for a turn in relay races or to be chosen for a team or because of limited equipment or playing of games such as Duck, Duck, Goose.

Children are organized into large groups in which getting a turn is based on individual competitiveness or aggressive behavior.

Children are eliminated from an activity with no chance to reenter, or they must sit for long periods of time.

Reprinted from COPEC/NASPE 1992.

An Appropriate Approach

Thirty sixth graders practice sets and bumps in small groups, using beach balls. Their teacher is constantly circulating among the groups, offering feedback.

An Inappropriate Approach

Sixty sixth graders are having physical education in one gym with one teacher. The students are serving a regular volleyball back and forth across two nets. The teacher is visiting with a colleague with her back to the class.

A student teacher reported the following incident: On one particular day, the cooperating teacher was absent, and the substitute teacher decided to have each class play kickball. During a game with a class of second graders, one boy was rounding third base and on his way toward home plate when he was suddenly struck by the ball, knocking him to the ground. The teacher himself had thrown the ball! Not only was the child robbed of the feelings of success and exhilaration of getting "home," he was also physically hurt and so was reduced to tears.

we will point out further examples of inappropriate practices and show you how you can employ appropriate practices instead.

A Well-Designed Program

Naturally, a well-designed physical education program avoids inappropriate practices and relies on appropriate ones. Simply put, a well-designed physical education program teaches developmentally appropriate skills and concepts in a logical sequence, responding to the individual needs of each student in a caring, compassionate, supportive manner.

The scope and sequence of a physical education program should be set for kindergarten through 12th grade at the district level. Thus, the elementary program prepares the student for the middle school program, and the middle school program prepares the student for the high school program. In this way, the scope and sequence you follow fits into an overall scheme that prepares your students for subsequent learning. Likewise, in general, your students should come to you prepared to learn the content you are expected to teach.

If your district does not provide you with a set scope and sequence to follow, try lobbying for one. Encourage your district to create a temporary team of physical education specialists, classroom teachers, administrators, and parents to develop a basic scope and sequence for every teacher to follow. In this way, students have a better chance of receiving a balanced physical education program, despite the lack of physical education specialists. At the same time, this committee should create a policy statement regarding the atmosphere of the physical education teaching-learning environment. Figure 1.4 provides an example of such a statement.

If all else fails, obtain a listing of your state-mandated scope and sequence for physical education, encourage the colleagues in your building to follow it, and be especially careful to plan for individualization.

Individualizing Instruction

Although directly addressing the whole class has its place, individualization is as vital to effective physical education as it is to effective reading instruction. Developmental appropriateness is the key to individualizing your program. Throughout this book, we will provide you with examples of how to individualize each type of lesson to better serve each student. For now, however, let's look at three students and their individual needs. Use these examples to help you start thinking about how to individualize in the physical education setting.

Statement of Philosophy

1. The learner is an individual, and his or her individuality varies from day to day, task to task, and moment to moment.

2. As teachers, we must respect the integrity of the learner and accept responsibility for the education of this whole being.

3. We need to dedicate our talents, time, and energy to each child, permitting him or her to become an increasingly independent learner, and thereby helping him or her to achieve full potential.

4. The learner is capable of making decisions; therefore, we are responsible for helping the learner develop the ability to make reasoned choices so that he or she can adjust to his or her role appropriately as his or her social and physical surroundings change.

5. Each child may develop the understanding and skills essential to progression at different times through different experiences.

6. To be meaningful to the child, physical education teachers must provide experiences that improve his or her ability to move, that engage thought processes, and that contribute positively to both his or her developing value system and to the esteem with which he or she regards self and others.

Figure 1.4 Statement of Philosophy.
Reprinted, by permission, from Logsdon, B., 1997, *Physical Education Unit Plans for Preschool-Kindergarten*, (Champaign, IL: Human Kinetics).

• **The skillful child.** Johnny is a "natural" athlete and seems to pick up skills easily.

Examples of how to individualize: You must challenge Johnny. Expect him to do more repetitions of a particular skill, move from point A to point B in less time, or hit a target with greater accuracy. To avoid making him feel punished for doing better, privately say to him, for example, "Looks like you're a real pro at this, Johnny. Let's see if you can do this like the older kids—I bet you can!" Work together to set individual goals, then design individual task cards or a contract to help him reach those goals.

• **The small, awkward child.** Victor is small for his age and somewhat shy and uncoordinated.

Examples of how to individualize: Allow Victor to experience success by modifying the number of repetitions, time limit, and degree of accuracy, making these parameters more realistic for him. Then gradually increase your expectations.

• **The child with physical challenges.** Julie has the full use of her arms but uses a wheelchair. An aide accompanies her at all times.

Examples of how to individualize: When the other students are walking, running, and the like, Julie can use her wheelchair to move. She can use her arms instead of her legs to "kick" a ball for example.

Note that none of these suggestions involves a great deal of teacher effort—only thoughtfulness and foresight. Because of slight modifications, each of these children will experience success, gaining the confidence, skill, and intrinsic motivation to continue to be physically active, thereby becoming more physically fit and competent. Moreover, the social interaction possible through physical education is enhanced by participating at a greater capacity. Individualization helps each child develop to his or her fullest affective, cognitive, and psychomotor potentials.

Summary

Physical education pedagogy today is different from physical education 20 or 30 years ago. Nowadays, physical education experts emphasize sensitive, caring practices carried out in a developmentally appropriate sequence. The field has set national standards,

Figure 1.5 Slight modifications in games can allow every child the chance to participate.

and practitioners are expected to strive to help their students meet these standards. But within the context of striving for the national standards, today's physical educators work to meet the individual's needs. The overall goal is not athletic prowess but rather individual skill development and health-related fitness as well as psychological well-being. In this way, each student can learn to enjoy physical activity for its intrinsic value so that he or she will continue to be physically active throughout his or her life.

Although it is best for children to have the benefit of a physical education specialist, as a classroom teacher, you can help each of your students reach his or her full potential by individualizing instruction and planning for personal success. Furthermore, you can create a supportive teaching-learning environment that encourages each student to want to be physically active for life.

Alex, 8

Sara, 4

Anthony, 8

Chapter 2

Meeting the Elementary School Mission

Jason, 13

Mr. Wilkes' fourth graders are learning about desert environments. Using a map, they calculate how many miles it is from their school to the nearest desert. As a fitness activity, they decide to "run" to the desert during their physical education and recess time. Every lap around the gym counts as one mile, and every lap around the playground counts as two miles. Mr. Wilkes requires students to run for five minutes at the beginning of each physical education class, and many choose to run extra "miles" during recess. They practice addition and subtraction by recording how far they run collectively and how far they have to go. Meanwhile, the students study the geography, history, and cultural influences of the desert they are running toward. They practice their writing skills by writing letters to pen pals living in a desert community. The physical activity in which they are participating is more meaningful to them because their teacher has related it to knowledge across similar curricular areas. At the same time, they may increase their cardiorespiratory fitness levels as well as have more fun running than they might otherwise. They are proud when they finally reach their destination.

What is the overall mission of the elementary school and how can physical education help accomplish it? Enhancing the growth of the whole (cognitive, affective, and psychomotor) child through education is the mission of the elementary school. Education is a "process of human growth by which one gains greater understanding and control over oneself and one's world. It involves our minds, our bodies, and our relations with the people and the world around us" (Ryan and Cooper 1992). Moreover, it is important for schools to produce individuals who can stay healthy under changing circumstances, meet their personal needs, and contribute to society. This process begins in elementary school. The following objectives of an effective physical education program enhance the elementary school's ability to achieve its mission (IAHPERD 1995; U.S. Department of Education 1986). Physical education must help

- improve the total health of the individual in various ways;
- increase cognitive capacity, enhancing readiness to learn, academic performance, enthusiasm for learning, and the ability to make knowledgeable choices regarding health and life in general; and
- enhance the self-esteem of the individual as well as positive interpersonal relationships, responsible behavior, and independence.

As you can see, the goals of physical education dovetail completely with the goals of elementary education in general. Furthermore, physical education addresses the development of the whole child in a way no other subject can—through movement. No matter the subject or setting, the chance to move enhances learning. Therefore, physical education should be a fundamental component of the elementary school curriculum.

As you study this chapter, keep in mind this oft-quoted research (Fauth 1990): We retain

- 10 percent of what we read,
- 20 percent of what we hear,
- 30 percent of what we see,
- 50 percent of what we hear and see at the same time,
- 70 percent of what we hear, see, and say, and
- 90 percent of what we hear, see, say, and *do* (dramatizing, painting, dancing, drawing, touching, constructing—*moving*).

Given children's innate desire and need to move, heeding this research is even more important to their learning than to adults'. Unfortunately, the typical school curriculum offers precious few kinesthetic learning opportunities and techniques (Hannaford 1995).

You can change this trend. How? In this chapter, we'll discuss the various ways you can make physical education a fundamental component of your curriculum. First, we'll explore physical education and cross-curricular learning. And while a multiple-intelligence approach and a theme-based approach can be interrelated, for the purposes of discussion, we'll show you how to apply Gardner's Theory of Multiple Intelligences in the physical education setting, then how you can integrate physical education into other subject areas based on themes. Next, we'll examine the concept of a comprehensive school health and wellness program. Finally, we'll investigate how physical education can help enhance your school's culture and community relations.

Cross-Curricular Learning

Many have traditionally viewed physical education and "academics" as being on opposite sides of the educational fence. Increasing evidence, however, reveals that because a child's earliest learning is based on motor development, so too is the learning that follows (Pica 1996). Indeed, "body, thought, and emotion are intimately bound together through an intricate nerve network, and function as a whole unit to enrich our knowing" (Hannaford 1995). Therefore, today's physical education integrates other subjects into its curricula whenever possible.

Certainly, given the limited time we have with our students compared with the demands placed upon us, it simply makes sense to get "more for our money" out of every lesson. For example, a physical education lesson on spatial awareness for kindergartners could include having the students form letters with their bodies, thereby integrating prereading skills. Likewise, movement can be integrated into other subjects. For example, a lesson on the letter "C" could include the challenge to demonstrate three bodily-kinesthetic ways to make a letter "C" (e.g., draw the letter on

the floor with a finger or foot and form the letter by curling the entire body or the fingers of one hand). Although such integrations cannot substitute for a solid physical education program, they can enhance learning in many subject areas.

Keep in mind, however, that you must make logical and natural connections between subject areas. To be effective, the cross-curricular approach must make sense to everyone, especially the students. Otherwise, the two most important reasons for using a cross-curricular approach—deepening understanding through making logical connections and simulating a real-world approach to problems—are lost.

In this section, we'll look closely at how you can integrate physical education across your curriculum. Specifically, we'll dissect Gardner's Theory of Multiple Intelligences from the physical education point of view, then we'll look at the theme-based approach to planning.

Gardner's Theory of Multiple Intelligences

By now you've most likely come across Gardner's Theory of Multiple Intelligences (1983, 1993) in several different contexts as well as how important it is to teach to all eight types of intelligence. Here, of course, we will focus on how this popular and relevant theory applies to physical education.

Bodily-Kinesthetic Intelligence

Individuals with high bodily-kinesthetic intelligence create or solve problems with their bodies or body parts. They prefer to learn through mime, crafts, hands-on science, dramatics, physical education, and other creative movement opportunities. They are the actors, dancers, athletes, surgeons, and craftspeople among us. Naturally, this type of intelligence is the most obvious that physical education addresses and fosters. But too often even the biggest advocates of cross-curricular teaching neglect the moving part of the child.

Even if a child is not among the 15 percent of the population who learns best through bodily-kinesthetic experiences, he can benefit

Figure 2.1 Individuals with high bodily-kinesthetic intelligence solve problems with their bodies or body parts.

greatly from movement experiences. Remember, we retain 90 percent of what we hear, see, say, and *do*. In the rest of this section on multiple intelligences, you'll see how the bodily-kinesthetic approach enhances each other type of intelligence.

Spatial Intelligence

Individuals with high spatial intelligence understand how objects orient in space. They have a strong sense of direction and are able to visualize end products accurately. They prefer to learn through sketching ideas and using charts, graphs, maps, diagrams, and graphics software and through building models. Architects, sculptors, and navigators have strong spatial intelligence.

Movement is about orientation in space. So you can use physical education, especially dance and gymnastics, to strengthen a child's understanding of how her body and body parts orient in space. This understanding can transfer to other areas in which she needs to use these concepts on paper.

An interesting study illustrates this point. Since the early 1990s, Dr. Marjorie Corso (1993) has researched ways in which body-space awareness transfers to paper-space awareness. She discovered that if a child fails to use a quadrant of his body space, he also

fails to use the same quadrant of a sheet of paper when writing or drawing. So, for example, if the child does not use his left arm in space, he tends to not use the upper left quadrant of his paper. Moreover, a child who has trouble finding his personal space (e.g., lining up too closely to others) usually writes his letters in a similar pattern. And a child who cannot cross midline in movement activities tends to stop reading at the middle of a page. You can use movement experiences, then, to directly intervene in spatial problems you observe in the regular classroom.

Interpersonal Intelligence

Interpersonal intelligence helps individuals understand and relate well to others. Psychologists and social workers are strong in interpersonal intelligence. Individuals strong in this area prefer to learn through group brainstorming, cooperative activities, peer tutoring, simulations, and community-based activities.

Certainly, cooperation should not stop at the gym door. Thus, today's physical education incorporates cooperative learning to foster interpersonal intelligence. In cooperative physical education activities, students work together to achieve a movement or skill goal. You can accomplish this by having students

Figure 2.2 Individuals with high spatial intelligence understand how objects orient in space.

Figure 2.3 Interpersonal intelligence helps individuals understand and relate well to others.

play a traditional game for which you keep a cooperative, rather than a competitive, score. Simply add up all points scored by all teams to find a class total. In this way, students can focus on helping everyone sharpen movement skills. In chapter 13, we'll explain more about how you can use physical education to develop and reinforce the cooperative approach you use in the rest of your curriculum.

Musical Intelligence

Musically intelligent individuals are fascinated with sound and are able to interpret, transform, and express musical forms. They are, of course, the musicians and dancers among us. They prefer to learn through raps, chants, songs, rhythms, and musical concepts.

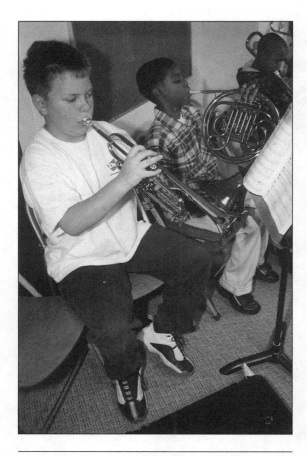

Figure 2.4 Musically intelligent individuals are fascinated with sound and are able to interpret, transform, and express musical forms.

Music and movement are practically inseparable. Certainly, music involves movement. And you can easily and effectively combine music with many movement activities. This approach enhances listening and body control skills that may transfer to other curricular areas.

Linguistic Intelligence

Individuals high in linguistic intelligence use words very effectively. These children often become writers, poets, and public speakers. They prefer to learn through reading, storytelling, lectures, small and large group discussions, debate, and writing activities. Traditional education favors these learners. But you can expand the linguistic intelligence of all students through physical education activities. For example, you might require students to keep a written log of their physical education activities. Or you can use stories and poetry to inspire movement.

Logical-Mathematical Intelligence

Individuals high in logical-mathematical intelligence are governed by reason and can use numbers very effectively. They tend to grow up to be scientists, mathematicians, and engineers. They prefer to learn through science demonstrations, math problems, sequential presentation of subject matter, critical-thinking activities, and problem-solving exercises.

You can speak to this type of intelligence when you challenge students to solve movement problems, such as, "Find four different ways to balance on three body parts." If the students work in small groups, this activity also enhances interpersonal skills. You can have younger children explore math vocabulary through body shapes, such as *long* and *short*, *high* and *low*, *big* and *little*, and *wide* and *narrow* (Pica 1996). This approach also reinforces linguistic and spatial intelligence.

Intrapersonal Intelligence

Individuals high in this intelligence know both their strengths and weaknesses well. Self-reliant and independent, those strong in this area prefer to learn through making personal connections, using interest centers and self-paced activities, reflecting, and setting goals.

A high positive relationship exists between physical movement and self-acceptance. As a child learns to move more skillfully, she also tends to develop a stronger self-concept (U.S. Department of Education 1986). This and the self-confidence she gains solving problems and otherwise succeeding in a supportive, developmentally appropriate physical education program can transfer to other areas of learning.

Naturalist

The latest addition to Gardner's Theory of Multiple Intelligences identifies people who are adept at identifying flora and fauna. You can address this intelligence through physical education by using themes from nature as well as stories and poems about nature to inspire movement experiences that get children thinking along these lines.

Figure 2.5 Individuals high in linguistic intelligence use words very effectively.

Now that you have seen how physical education can speak to each type of intelligence, we'll look closely at another angle on cross-curricular planning: the theme-based approach.

Theme-Based Approach

Most of us are familiar with the concept and practice of choosing a central theme, such as "Outer Space" or "Spiders," and then planning lessons across the curriculum through which to teach the theme. This approach is also called a *webbed curriculum* or *threaded curriculum*, depending on how, and the degree to which, the various subject areas are integrated (Placek 1996).

Webbed Curriculum

In a webbed curriculum, themes can be topics, such as oceanography; concepts, such as caring; categories, such as poetry; problems, such as "How do desert animals survive?"; or ideas, such as "Friendship is important" (Placek 1996). You can integrate ideas for physical education into each type of theme. For example, many teachers teach

Figure 2.6 Individuals high in logical-mathematical intelligence are governed by reason and can use numbers very effectively.

Figure 2.7 Individuals high in intrapersonal intelligence know both their strengths and weaknesses.

Figure 2.8 Naturalists are people who are adept at identifying flora and fauna.

the dances of the time or place students are studying in social studies. This is a content-based approach through which the teacher seeks to overlap the content across the curriculum (see figure 2.9).

Threaded Curriculum

In a threaded curriculum, the theme is more abstract and is threaded throughout a metacurriculum involving all subject areas. Such an approach may, for example, focus on social or critical thinking skills. Gardner's Theory of Multiple Intelligences and the whole language approach are primary examples of this type of curriculum. In contrast to the webbed curriculum, the threaded curriculum is a learner-based rather than a content-based approach. The teacher actively seeks to overlap the teaching of skills and concepts in the subjects involved, based on the needs of the individual learner (Placek 1996). For example, if the theme is problem solving, one way to apply this approach in physical education is to ask each individual, "What is the best way for *you* to get through this obstacle course?"

A Comprehensive School Health and Wellness Program

Guiding students toward more healthful lifestyles is the job of the entire school, not merely the physical education program. This concept is a natural outgrowth of viewing each individual as a whole person rather than a sum of distinct, unrelated parts. You can work with administrators, the school nurse, school social worker or psychologist, other teachers, students, and parents to promote healthier, more active lifestyles through a comprehensive school health and wellness program.

Physical Education

Naturally, physical education plays a vital role in a comprehensive school health program. Whether developing fitness or skills on a schoolwide basis, physical education makes a large contribution to student health. Moreover, as we mentioned in chapter 1, the physical activity that physical education provides contributes to psychological well-being, which, of course, affects overall health. Finally, don't forget that physical activity increases blood and oxygen flow to the brain (Hannaford 1995) enhancing learning. With this in mind, some schools have instituted regular fitness breaks—in addition to physical education—during which teachers and students take short breaks for aerobic exercise, one or more times per day, to rejuvenate their bodies and brains (see also chapter 19).

Health Education

It is as important to provide a formal health education curriculum as it is to provide formal math and physical education curricula. And as with other subject areas, a health program must be organized in a developmentally appropriate sequence. Furthermore, it must empower children with the knowledge they need to advocate for their own health needs. To this end, to be effective, a health education program must not only promote positive health behaviors, it must also sharpen critical-thinking and problem-solving skills related to health issues.

Health Services

Your school nurse is the natural starting point for school-based health services. Begin by asking him or her to help a committee of teachers, administrators, and parents define "wellness" in the context of your school population's needs. In this way, your school can go beyond merely providing emergency care and move into the realm of actively and systematically identifying health issues that may hamper student learning. This approach includes annual screening for hearing, dental, height and weight, vision, blood pressure, and posture problems.

The school nurse should also help you educate students and their parents about preventative health care, that is, how to avoid health problems from occurring in the first place.

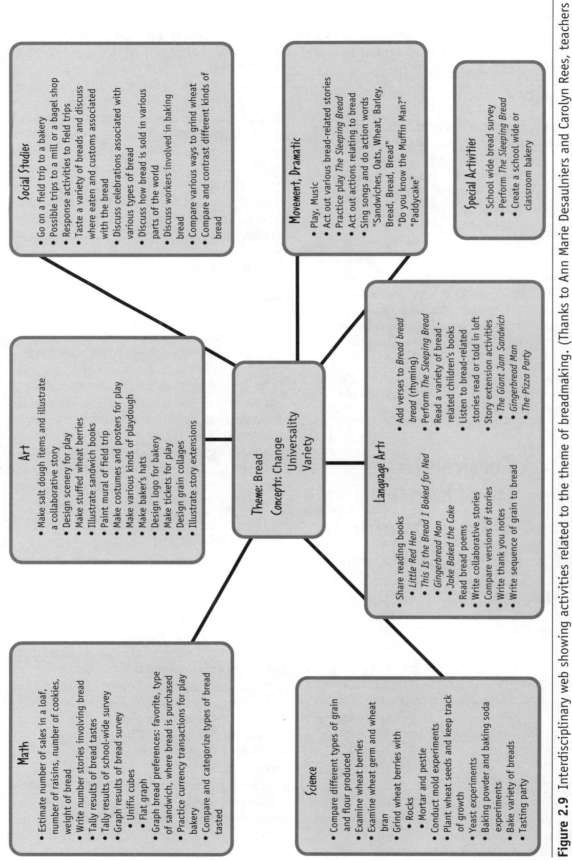

Social Studies

- Go on a field trip to a bakery
- Possible trips to a mill or a bagel shop
- Response activities to field trips
- Taste a variety of breads and discuss where eaten and customs associated with the bread
- Discuss celebrations associated with various types of bread
- Discuss how bread is sold in various parts of the world
- Discuss workers involved in baking bread
- Compare various ways to grind wheat
- Compare and contrast different kinds of bread

Art

- Make salt dough items and illustrate a collaborative story
- Design scenery for play
- Make stuffed wheat berries
- Illustrate sandwich books
- Paint mural of field trip
- Make costumes and posters for play
- Make various kinds of playdough
- Make baker's hats
- Design logo for bakery
- Make tickets for play
- Design grain collages
- Illustrate story extensions

Math

- Estimate number of sales in a loaf, number of raisins, number of cookies, weight of bread
- Write number stories involving bread
- Tally results of bread tastes
- Tally results of school-wide survey
- Graph results of bread survey
  - Unifix cubes
  - Flat graph
- Graph bread preferences: favorite, type of sandwich, where bread is purchased
- Practice currency transactions for play bakery
- Compare and categorize types of bread tasted

Science

- Compare different types of grain and flour produced
- Examine wheat berries
- Examine wheat germ and wheat bran
- Grind wheat berries with
  - Rocks
  - Mortar and pestle
- Conduct mold experiments
- Plant wheat seeds and keep track of growth
- Yeast experiments
- Baking powder and baking soda experiments
- Bake variety of breads
- Tasting party

Theme: Bread

Concepts: Change
Universality
Variety

Movement, Dramatic

- Play, Music
- Act out various bread-related stories
- Practice play *The Sleeping Bread*
- Act out actions relating to bread
- Sing songs and do action words "Sandwiches, Oats, Wheat, Barley, Bread, Bread, Bread"
  "Do you know the Muffin Man?"
  "Paddycake"

Special Activities

- School wide bread survey
- Perform *The Sleeping Bread*
- Create a school wide or classroom bakery

Language Arts

- Share reading books
  - *Little Red Hen*
  - *This Is the Bread I Baked for Ned*
  - *Gingerbread Man*
  - *Jake Baked the Cake*
- Read bread poems
- Write collaborative stories
- Compare versions of stories
- Write thank you notes
- Write sequence of grain to bread
- Add verses to *Bread bread bread* (rhyming)
- Perform *The Sleeping Bread*
- Read a variety of bread-related children's books
- Listen to bread-related stories read or told in loft
- Story extension activities
  - *The Giant Jam Sandwich*
  - *Gingerbread Man*
  - *The Pizza Party*

Figure 2.9 Interdisciplinary web showing activities related to the theme of breadmaking. (Thanks to Ann Marie Desaulniers and Carolyn Rees, teachers at Beauvoir, The National Cathedral Elementary School, Washington, D.C.)

Reprinted, by permission, from Logsdon, B., 1997, *Physical Education Unit Plans for Preschool-Kindergarten*, (Champaign, IL: Human Kinetics).

Nutrition Services

Good nutrition is more than teaching students about the Food Guide Pyramid. For starters, it's making healthful food choices the norm in the school cafeteria. This is where your students can see a model of a balanced and healthy diet, low in sugar, fat, and salt. In addition, encourage healthy snacks at school parties by having students plan a balanced menu of snack items from each food group. Finally, be an advocate of healthy fund-raisers. For example, instead of selling candy,

- hold a neighborhood park cleanup day and take pledges,
- sell fresh fruit,
- hold a "dance-a-thon,"
- have a "bowl-a-thon," or
- hold a "play day" with lots of activities in which students, teachers, and parents can participate.

Counseling and Psychological Services

A comprehensive school health and wellness program promotes emotional, social, and mental health among students. First and foremost, your school social worker, counselor, or psychologist provides a forum through which students may express their emotional needs. In turn, this professional should work to help troubled students get the help they need. Finally, he or she should offer staff training to help you detect the warning signs of a student in need.

Parent and Community Involvement

It's easier to get parents and the community involved in a comprehensive school health and wellness program than in a physical education program that stands alone. For one thing, it's easier to make the school's health and wellness goals and needs known to parents and the rest of the community if the message comes from a team effort. We'll ex-plore effective ways to elicit such support later in this chapter.

A Safe and Healthy School Environment

Children do not learn to their maximum potentials if they do not feel psychologically or physically safe. They have a right to learn in a fear-free and clean environment. Moreover, your school should meet legal standards for heating, lighting, and ventilation.

Health Promotion Among Staff

Let's not forget ourselves! It's only too true that you can't take care of others unless you take care of yourself. Thus, a comprehensive school health and wellness program should provide opportunities for staff to develop fitness, manage stress, benefit from health screening, control weight, and improve nutrition. In addition, staff should strive to be good examples of healthful lifestyles. You may consider designing your own health and fitness "club" so you can exercise on-site. Your school's parent-teacher association may be willing to help you buy equipment if you share it with parents, or you can write a grant proposal and appeal for funds elsewhere. Donated equipment is also an option.

Most of the components of a comprehensive school health and wellness program may already exist in your school. The idea is to systematically work together across disciplines, job descriptions, and areas of concern to create a unified approach to providing students with the health care they need and deserve. This is an unusual but exciting and beneficial way to be "cross-curricular" in approach.

School Culture

Physical education can foster positive interactions among students, teachers, and administrators. It should be an extension of a positive school environment in which students feel safe enough to try new skills. Moreover, the attitude of accepting diverse abilities in physical education can carry over to other areas of school life. Finally, you can champion multiculturalism through physical education. For example, you can integrate movement activities from other cultures by including games, dances, and customs from a variety of cultures. (See more about physical education and inclusion in chapter 14.)

School–Community Relations

There's nothing like good public relations to help your physical education program grow and thrive. The following is a list of specific ways you can both enhance school-community relations and elicit the support your physical education program needs and deserves (see also chapter 16).

- Publicize any special events (e.g., fitness days or evenings, health fairs, play days) through all media.
- Involve community members in school events as often as possible.
- Publicize any honors earned by students in physical education.
- Develop and expand physical education programs that use community facilities to more broadly expose students to lifetime activities.

- Open school facilities to community members at appropriate times throughout the week.

Got a good thing going? Don't be shy—tell the world.

Summary

You can integrate movement and physical education across your entire curriculum as you address each type of intelligence or plan theme-based units. Your students will not only benefit from increased meaningful physical activity, they'll also learn better across the curriculum.

But your physical education program should not take place in isolation. A comprehensive school health and wellness program is a natural outgrowth of viewing each child as a whole person, rather than as a sum of distinct, unrelated parts. By involving the entire school community in planning and carrying out a comprehensive approach to health and wellness, each student will have a better chance of adopting and leading a healthy lifestyle. What better way to enhance school culture than to show respect and concern for each individual's health and wellness?

Finally, let your broader community know what you and your school are doing to promote physical education, health, and wellness. The community support you elicit will be well worth the effort.

Chapter 3

Assessing Students in Physical Education

Steffy, 8

Mr. Jaxon's second grade class was practicing throwing at progressively smaller targets. Partners worked together analyzing each other's throws by checking for the lesson's focus component of a good throw. Students self-assessed their own readiness to move on to the next smaller target by counting when they could hit a target 7 out of 10 times.

As in any other subject area, you are responsible for assessing what students have learned in physical education, based on set goals and objectives. You cannot achieve authentic assessment based solely on traditional written tests. To be authentic, assessment needs to take place in a context as similar to real life as possible. For example, you would probably never assess a child's ability to write a poem, say in limerick form, based on his ability to describe in writing how it is done—you would probably simply assess the actual product of your instruction. Then you might compare this attempt to an earlier attempt at following a poetic form and assess the student's progress. Likewise, in physical education, you should assess the actual attempts your students make in the psychomotor, cognitive, and affective domains by observing their actual performances.

Fortunately, the very nature of physical education lends itself to performance-based assessment. This is not to say, however, that a written rules or other cognitive test is never appropriate, but in physical education as in creative writing, you need to look more at the process than the product, gathering evidence of progress over time. For example, helping a student learn to throw a ball well is more important than finding out how far she can throw it (Hopple 1995).

In this chapter, we will examine the unique applications of the authentic assessment movement to the physical education setting. First, we'll discuss the role of assessment in physical education. Then, we'll outline the four major areas of assessment in physical education: physical fitness, psychomotor skills, cognitive understanding, and affective performance. Next, we'll describe practical assessment strategies and offer you assessment management tips. Finally, we'll explore the relationship between assessment and grading.

The Role of Assessment in Physical Education

The role of assessment in physical education taught by a classroom teacher is fourfold. First, assessment forces you to focus on the individual student who might otherwise be lost in the crowd. Second, assessment gives you the necessary data to see how the class as a whole

COMPONENT— *Success Rate*

Appropriate Practice

Children are given the opportunity to practice skills at a high rate of success adjusted for their individual skill levels.

Inappropriate Practice

Children are asked to perform activities that are too easy or too hard, causing frustration, boredom, or misbehavior.

All children are expected to perform to the same standards with no allowance for individual abilities and interests.

Reprinted from COPEC/NASPE 1992.

is progressing. Third, assessment offers you valuable feedback on how you are doing as a physical education instructor and how your physical education program is doing. Fourth, when designed and conducted appropriately, assessment itself is a valuable teaching tool (adapted from Freeland and Moore 1996 and Graham 1992). In the following sections, we'll discuss each of these aspects in detail.

Focusing on the Individual

Returning to our poetry analogy, you cannot look closely at 30 students' poems all at once, nor can you assess 30 students' physical education performances simultaneously. Periodically, then, you must find ways to focus in a meaningful way on each individual. You can do this in a variety of ways from journal entries to rubrics, which we'll discuss in detail later in this chapter.

Once you determine how a student is doing in a selected aspect of physical education at a particular time, you can use the data to better tailor your program to meet this individual's needs. For example, if you observe that a child is excelling in the overhand throwing technique, you should now challenge her to throw farther. But if you observe

a child struggling with this technique, you should find ways to give her more helpful feedback during physical education class. In this way, you will be meeting two of COPEC's (1992) parameters for providing developmentally appropriate physical education.

Determining Class Progress

Once you have assessed each individual in a particular skill or area, you should use the data to assess how your class is doing as a whole. If you find that most of your students are doing well, you'll know you're probably on the right track for the skill or concept. But if you determine that a significant number of students have failed to grasp the skill or concept, you will know that you must spend more time on this area and find other ways to approach it. Assessment data will allow you to group students appropriately so that each individual is challenged appropriately by each lesson.

Or you may simply determine that your students are not ready for the skill or concept. If this is the case, you can either back up and do more basic work related to the area you have assessed or move on to an entirely different area for the time being.

COMPONENT— Assessment

Appropriate Practice

Teacher decisions are based primarily on ongoing individual assessments of children as they participate in physical education class activities (formative evaluation) and not on the basis of a single test score (summative evaluation).

Assessment of children's physical progress and achievement is used to individualize instruction, plan yearly curriculum and weekly lessons, identify children with special needs, communicate with parents, and evaluate the program's effectiveness.

Inappropriate Practice

Children are evaluated on the basis of fitness test scores or on a single physical skill test. For example, children receive a grade in physical education based on their scores on a standardized fitness test or on the number of times they can continuously jump rope.

Reprinted from COPEC/NASPE 1992.

Assessing Your Physical Education Instruction and Program

How effective are you as a physical education instructor? How effective is your physical education program? You can use assessment as helpful feedback on your teaching and your program. If, over time, you find that your class as a whole does not do well on assessments, you should not be discouraged, but rather you should seek ways to improve your instruction. Perhaps you and a colleague can take turns observing each other's physical education classes. Likewise, videotaping and then viewing a physical education class you teach can give you invaluable information on your techniques and approach. Or maybe you can request that an elementary physical education specialist observe and offer constructive criticism and pertinent inservice training (see also chapter 16).

This is also a good time to evaluate your overall physical education program to see where you can improve it. Indeed, assessment makes program evaluation more efficient and objective (Strand and Wilson 1993). You can then decide which components of your physical education program to emphasize and deemphasize.

If, on the whole, you find your students do well on assessments, give yourself a pat on the back but still seek to learn and grow as a teacher of physical education. Your students will benefit greatly.

Assessing as a Teaching Tool

Assessment need not take away from valuable instructional time. If you involve the students in the assessment process, whether through self- or peer assessment or by encouraging reflection, assessment time doubles as practice and thinking time. It also enhances the cognitive aspect of physical education learning as students learn to think about *how* to learn, focusing on the process, not simply the product. Moreover, seeing their own progress is a great motivator.

In addition, assessment should determine future instruction as you respond to your new knowledge of student needs. How do you know if you should adjust your curriculum based on assessment? Consider the concept of *mastery learning*, which assumes that all children can learn to a certain standard if given enough time and support. The following principles underlie the concept of mastery learning (Carnes 1997):

- Children do not necessarily experience success at the same time.
- Assessment must be based on what each child has mastered.
- Assessment must be linked directly to curriculum (students know what you expect them to learn, you teach this, and you assess what you taught).
- Assessment should take the form of realistic or applied ("real-world") learning.
- Assessment should be based on improvement over time.

If you follow these basic principles, assessment will truly be a learning tool. (Find more on the relationships of curriculum, instruction, and assessment in chapter 6).

Assessment Areas

Language arts has many components to both teach and assess, of which creative writing is only one; likewise, physical education has several areas to both teach and assess. The following describes the various areas in which you should assess your students in physical education:

- Physical fitness tests measure each aspect of health-related fitness: cardiorespiratory fitness, muscular strength, muscular endurance, flexibility, and body composition (ratio of body fat mass to lean tissue mass).
- Psychomotor skill assessment includes specific performance tests of specific motor skills, for example, the ability to skip with a mature movement pattern.
- Cognitive assessment includes monitoring students' understanding of how to

perform, for example, the motor skills correctly, how to increase muscular strength, how to dribble a ball against a defender, among others.

- Affective assessment monitors students' social development and attitudes in the physical education setting.

An appropriately designed and taught physical education program teaches and assesses each of these four areas in a balanced, progressive curriculum. In the next section, we'll outline various strategies you can use to assess your students' physical education learning in these areas.

Assessment Strategies

Many of the physical education assessment tools and tips we'll mention in this section probably parallel those you use in the regular classroom. Look for these parallels as you read and study this section to help you better understand and adapt them to your situation.

Portfolios

To help you track and assess student progress over time, you should set up a separate physical education portfolio for each student. As with other subject areas, the physical education portfolio gives you a handy reference for assessment, grading, and parent-teacher conferences. To create sturdy portfolios, you can use a traditional three-hole folder, a piece of folded 12- by 18-inch construction paper, a flat box, or another appropriate container.

What should go into these portfolios? In the following sections, we'll outline many different possible assessment strategies that will produce assessment products for the physical education portfolio. As you read, note how the various strategies address the different types of intelligence, thereby making them cross-curricular in nature as well as teaching tools themselves.

Fitness Testing

Gone are the days (we hope!) when fitness tests were used to separate the fit from the unfit—humiliation optional. Today's physical education uses fitness testing as only one component of an approach to health-related fitness that promotes self-improvement and good attitudes toward physical activity and health-related fitness. COPEC (1992) states our philosophy regarding fitness testing very succinctly (see sidebar below).

Thus, in developmentally appropriate physical education, better understanding of fitness should be the goal of fitness testing—not displaying physical prowess or incompetence for someone else's benefit.

You should record the results of these tests on a form stapled or glued inside each child's portfolio so that you, the child, and the parents can see progress over time (see figure 3.1). We'll look at the specific appropriate tests and how to conduct them in chapter 8.

COMPONENT— *Physical Fitness Tests*

Appropriate Practice

Test results are shared privately with children and their parents as a tool for developing their physical fitness knowledge, understanding, and competence.

Inappropriate Practice

Children are required to complete a physical fitness battery without understanding why they are performing the tests or what the implications of their individual results are as they apply to their future health and well-being.

Reprinted from COPEC/NASPE 1992.

Date	Performance task in unit	Rubric level O*	Rubric level A*	Rubric level D*	Comments

Student _____ Class _____

Grade _____

*O = outstanding, A = acceptable, D = deficient

Figure 3.1 Performance assessment record.
Reprinted, by permission, from Hopple, C., 1995, *Teaching Outcomes in Physical Education: A Guide for Curriculum and Assessment*, (Champaign, IL: Human Kinetics), 29.

Knowledge Tests

Another traditional approach to assessing both within and outside of physical education is the use of knowledge tests. And although the pencil and paper tests have their place and may belong in the physical education portfolio, there are many other ways to more quickly assess student knowledge so that you can adjust your lesson plans accordingly. Graham offers the following suggestions (1992):

Checking for Understanding Ask the children to show you their understanding of a particular cue (critical component) or concept you have taught. For example, when the children are assembled around you, ask them to "Show me one good way to stretch your lower back muscles. . . ."

Poker Chip Survey For example, a teacher might demonstrate a stretch incorrectly (bouncing rather than stretching statically). As the children leave the class, they are asked to put a red poker chip (or checker) in a box if the stretch was done correctly or a blue poker chip (or black checker) if the stretch was done incorrectly. A quick survey of the color of the chips will tell the teacher how well the children have understood the concept.

Another way to receive immediate feedback on student understanding is to ask true or false questions and have students signal thumbs up for true and thumbs down for false.

If you do opt for a written test, consider a quick quiz of only three to five central questions that will not take too much instructional or teacher time. Figure 3.2 is an example of such a quiz.

Journals

Journals are an effective way to monitor both student understanding and feelings regarding physical education. Moreover, journaling involves linguistic intelligence, tying language arts learning into your physical education curriculum. The following is a list of possible journal assignments:

- "Help your friend. . . ." Have students describe in writing how to do a particular skill (see figure 3.3).

1. To throw a ball farther, you should
   a. keep your back very straight as you throw
   b. turn your body to the side before you throw
   c. jump off the ground with both feet as you throw
   d. I don't know

2. You should do warm-up exercises before physical activities so that
   a. you will not get cold during the activities
   b. you will be less likely to get sore muscles
   c. your bones will not get tired as quickly
   d. I don't know

3. When you are trying to jump over a bench, what should you do to help you jump higher?
   a. Keep your legs straight before you jump
   b. Stand on your toes before you jump
   c. Bend your knees before you jump
   d. I don't know

4. To lift a heavy object from the floor safely, you should
   a. bend your knees
   b. bend your back
   c. keep your legs straight
   d. I don't know

5. To catch a ball correctly you should
   a. bend your elbows
   b. keep your arms straight
   c. turn your head to the side
   d. I don't know

Figure 3.2 Examples of questions teachers might develop to assess children's cognitive understanding.
Reprinted, by permission, from Graham, G., 1992 *Teaching Children Physical Education*, (Champaign, IL: Human Kinetics), 157.

- Recording feelings. Occasionally or regularly have students record how they feel physically and emotionally after physical education class.

- Recording performance. Have students record the number of trials they made for the lesson's skill or skills by making check marks. They can record a smiley or frowny face next to each check mark to indicate how successful they felt each performance was (adapted from Schiemer 1996).

1. To use the finger pads of your hand not the palm
2. Not to <u>hit</u> the ball down
   push it so you will stay in control
3. Don't have your wrist like a peice of metel but
   don't have it so loose you can't keep control of it
4. Keep your eyes looking in front of you to make
   sure you don't run into anything
5. Don't bash the thing so hard it go's above your
   head keep it at your waist

Figure 3.3 Children's written description of how to perform an activity can tell you whether they understand.
Reprinted, by permission, from Graham, G., 1992 *Teaching Children Physical Education*, (Champaign, IL: Human Kinetics), 157.

• Analyzing performance. Have students record what they feel they did correctly and incorrectly on a particular skill and what exactly they will work on to improve their performances.

Self-Monitoring Sheets

An easy and effective way to keep students on-task is to have them record their physical education activity on a self-monitoring sheet such as that shown in figure 3.4.

Requiring students to analyze their performances by putting a smiley or frowny face in each attempt space and by writing in a "Thinking About Learning" box turns this class management tool into an assessment tool. By encouraging reflection, you encourage learning. Furthermore, you can tell at a glance who is struggling and who is succeeding. Be sure, however, that it's safe to be honest, or you will not get the information you need (Schiemer 1996).

Rubrics

Another authentic assessment tool is the rubric. As with assessing hands-on science, the best rubrics limit the levels to three to five, making it easier for you to make judgments. The points listed can be as simple "Excellent," "Acceptable," and "Needs Improvement" (see figure 3.5). Brief descriptions of what constitutes each level for that skill or port-

folio task will turn the rubric into a teaching tool if you discuss the descriptions with the students.

Self Evaluating You can collect valid and reliable data by students through self-assessment techniques if you train students and hold them accountable for accurate information and good management (Rink and Hensley 1996). You can make a self-monitoring sheet a self-evaluating sheet by simply asking an evaluative question. Or you can give students more specific rubrics to fill out. Whenever you ask a student to evaluate himself, you are stretching his cognitive and intrapersonal skills.

Peer Assessing The same rubrics students use for self-assessment will work well for peer assessment. And as with self-assessment, if you train students to use rubrics properly, you will gather helpful data. Moreover, peer assessment enhances both cognitive and interpersonal skills, providing valuable experience in these areas.

Teacher Use At times it will be appropriate for you to perform a more formal assessment using a rubric. You can use the same rubrics that your students use for themselves and peers or you can use an abbreviated form such as the checklist shown in figure 3.6.

As you can see, this checklist is a simple form of a rubric, keeping the student's performance information in one place.

Videotaping

If you have the equipment available to you, videotaping is a good way to track student progress over time. You can require each student to bring in a blank videotape as part of his school supplies at the beginning of the school year. Then you can periodically videotape each student performing "event tasks," which are "culminating, relevant activities that require the student to demonstrate skills and abilities in real settings rather than contrived settings" (Rink and Hensley 1996). Examples include a dance, game, or gymnastics routine. Parent volunteers can help with videotaping (Clark and Sanders 1997).

You can assess such a performance as you replay the video for the class or in private,

Name _____

Date _____

1 ◯	2 ◯	3 ◯	4 ◯	5 ◯	6 ◯
7 ◯	8 ◯	9 ◯	10 ◯	11 ◯	12 ◯
13 ◯	14 ◯	15 ◯	16 ◯	17 ◯	18 ◯
19 ◯	20 ◯	21 ◯	22 ◯	23 ◯	24 ◯
25 ◯	26 ◯	27 ◯	28 ◯	29 ◯	30 ◯
31 ◯	32 ◯	33 ◯	34 ◯	35 ◯	36 ◯

Thinking about learning:

Critical elements _____   Record sheet score _____

Independent working skills _____   Concept knowledge _____

Figure 3.4 Self-recording worksheet.
Reprinted, by permission, from Schiemer, S., 1996, "A positive learning experience," *Teaching Elementary Physical Education*, 7(2): 5.

Excellent

- Student clearly described the elements critical to the performance of the skill.
- Student used the appropriate terminology and vocabulary.
- Student provided at least two appropriate examples.

Acceptable

- Student provided partial information on the elements critical to skill performance.
- Student's responses reflected weak or non-existent use of appropriate terminology and vocabulary.
- Student provided at least one appropriate example for each category.

Needs Improvement

- Student displayed minimal use of critical elements, terminology, and vocabulary, or did not respond at all.
- Examples provided by the student were not appropriate.

Figure 3.5 Example of scoring rubric for a portfolio task.
From "Beyond the Traditional Skills Test" by S. Schiemer, 1993, *Teaching Elementary Physical Education*, 4(2), p. 10. Copyright 1993 by Human Kinetics. Reprinted by permission.

freeing you to concentrate on management during class. Moreover, you can have students self- or peer assess via videotape, perhaps at one station on a circuit (see chapter 4). Furthermore, you can use video to help both you and your students see how the class and individuals are doing affectively. Finally, video records of student performance provide a visual record of personal growth over time, which can help you communicate better with both students and parents regarding each individual's progress (Clark and Sanders 1997).

Interviews

Although conducting simple interviews may not be as sophisticated as using video technology, you can gain valuable information through simply listening to student responses to leading questions. Privately ask individu-

als or small groups how they are feeling about physical education and physical activity, what their favorite and least favorite activities are, and what they think they need to be working on. You can do this at one station in a circuit, during an appropriate time in the classroom, or through a simple "Smiley-Face Exit Poll" (Graham 1992). To take an exit poll, pose one question before closing class and have students place a smiley or frowny face into a bin in response. For example, ask, "How do you feel about your ability to balance on three body parts?" Interviews and exit polls can give you vital affective information.

Projects

Projects are more involved modes of assessment than the others we have discussed so far. A project should take the student beyond demonstrating basic knowledge and comprehension into higher levels of thinking (e.g., application, analysis, synthesis, and evaluation [making judgments based on set criteria]). The following make excellent project ideas:

- Designing and teaching a game that applies new skills
- Keeping a log of physical activity times and choices for one week
- Making an art collage that illustrates, for example, the components of health-related fitness
- Researching and reporting on the folk dances of another culture or on an athlete's life story
- Evaluating a completed unit and giving the teacher helpful feedback

Assessment Management Tips

Videos! Journals! Rubrics! How can you manage it all? In this section, we'll discuss ways to put the theory of authentic assessment into practice by offering you practical tips for managing this important aspect of teaching.

Formal Versus Informal Assessment

Most assessment can be informal: self-assessment, peer assessment, and quick visual scanning by you during class. Not only

Stunts Checklist #1						
Rating scale: 1 = poor, 2 = fair, 3 = good						
Heel slap feet	Knees to elbows	Turk stand	Front fall knees	Thread the needle	Half turn	Full turn

Figure 3.6 Stunts checklist.

does this save teacher time, it also encourages students to take responsibility for their own learning. At times, however, you should make more formal assessments using rubrics as discussed earlier in this chapter. You should also periodically review each student's portfolio as a whole to determine individual progress.

If you are particularly concerned about one student's lack of psychomotor, affective, or cognitive progress, be sure to consult with the appropriate specialist in the affected area. Then work with this specialist to further individualize the student's physical education program. Your district should provide this type of support by law (see chapter 14).

Selecting Portfolio Pieces

As with a language arts portfolio, you may wish to have students collect all physical education papers for a time, perhaps for a week or month, then self-select certain items to remain in the portfolio permanently. You may choose to mandate that students retain certain assessments. Or you may select certain pieces while allowing students to select other items. At any rate, ensure that physical education portfolios reflect progress over time so that this assessment tool provides you with adequate data to evaluate achievement and demonstrate to students, parents, and administrators the strengths of your physical education program.

Finding Time to Assess

The gap between theory and practice in authentic assessment can, unfortunately, be wide in any subject area simply because of time constraints. Thus, you must find ways to streamline your assessment procedures so that you can perform this important function efficiently.

First, you should train students to help you manage assessment tasks. For example, take the time to teach students how to file their papers for themselves. Or train just a few capable students to complete this task (or perhaps parents or older students "borrowed" for this purpose if you teach in the younger grades). Then, as we've already discussed, teach students to periodically select representative pieces to retain in their portfolios. This will leave fewer items for you to review. In addition, take the time to ensure that students understand how to self- and peer assess, perhaps through role-playing and group discussion.

Furthermore, make sure that assessment tasks double as learning tasks so that class time is used fully. Encouraging students to think about their own learning through peer and self-assessment is a good way to accomplish this, while saving your time and effort for working with individuals who are really struggling.

In the gym or on the playground, you can formally assess students at one station in a physical education circuit. This will keep the other students actively learning until it is their turn to be assessed. You can also have the other members of the group at the station peer assess and discuss the performance as a small group. This is an excellent opportunity to offer encouragement and teach peers to offer encouragement as well. Back in your classroom, you can have students make a journal entry while rows or groups take turns getting drinks after physical activity. You can also send home some assessments as homework (e.g., self-assessments, journal entries, and the like).

Hopple (1995) offers two additional management tips. If you are assessing a student-developed game or sequence, have students write down the rules or steps before you assess them so that you can use this information to assess their actual performances. Finally, rather than your writing down information for each student, simply list those who can't do a skill (see figure 3.7a and b).

Grading

As you probably know, assessing and grading are not the same. Indeed, they have very different purposes. Assessment tells you and your students how they are improving or what they need to work on. Grading attempts to communicate, primarily to parents, all that the individual has done in your physical education program in a single letter or number (Graham 1992). Moreover, grading can help you recognize the strengths and weaknesses of your physical education program.

To grade students fairly, you must develop criteria for testing and grading, including the weight you will give to each component of the grade. Then you must communicate these parameters to students and parents—before collecting data. Finally, you must collect explicit documentation to maintain accountability.

But a grade in physical education doesn't do much to tell students and parents how an individual is doing. For example, a student who cannot hit, catch, or throw a ball may receive a "Satisfactory" simply for behaving in physical education class and trying hard (Graham 1992). You can overcome this problem by providing separate grades for affective, psychomotor, and cognitive performance. Develop and use your own form, such as the one in figure 3.9, to send home with the rest of the report card. On this form, note areas of improvement and offer hints as to how the student can overcome problem areas. You can also use such a form at the end of each unit, whether it's grading time or not. Even if you must still enter a total grade on the regular report card, by offering students and parents specific information, you will help students learn through grading, thereby making it a more worthwhile use of your time.

Indeed, objective and thorough grading should do the following:

• Help the student understand where he can improve

• Help the teacher recognize if program objectives are being met

• Show the teacher where changes in the program should occur

• Promote the physical education program to the school and community

• Justify the ongoing need for physical education in the curriculum

Unit	Kicking		
Rubric level	Class: *Peebles*		
Outstanding	*Larry* *Sue* *Rosie* *Dianna* *Mark* *Scott* *George* *Vicky* *Manny* *Harriet*		
Acceptable	*(fill in all other names of students in class later, if desired)*		
Deficient	*Trent* *Lisa*		
Absent	*None*		

Figure 3.7a Sample form for recording class performance assessments.

Reprinted, by permission, from Hopple, C., 1995, *Teaching Outcomes in Physical Education: A Guide for Curriculum and Assessment*, (Champaign, IL: Human Kinetics), 25.

Unit			
Rubric level	Class:		
Outstanding			
Acceptable			
Deficient			
Absent			

Figure 3.7b Form for recording class performance assessments.

Reprinted, by permission, from Hopple, C., 1995, *Teaching Outcomes in Physical Education: A Guide for Curriculum and Assessment*, (Champaign, IL: Human Kinetics), 26.

Figure 3.8 Assessing students can keep them actively learning.

Summary

Assessment is an indispensable component of all effective teaching; physical education is no exception. Specifically, assessment plays four main roles in physical education. First, it forces the teacher to focus on the individual student. Second, it gives the teacher the necessary data to see how the class as a whole is progressing. Third, assessment offers the teacher valuable feedback on how he is doing as a physical education instructor and how his physical education program is doing. Fourth, assessment can be a valuable teaching tool in itself.

You can and should use a variety of assessment strategies across the physical education curriculum to gather data on each student's achievement. As in other subject areas, portfolios provide the foundation of an authentic assessment approach. You can have students fill portfolios with journal entries, rubrics, and videotapings, among other components. Managing assessment takes thought and planning but is well worth the effort.

Finally, when you give a physical education grade, you should offer specific data,

well-documented in each of the four main areas of physical education learning: physical fitness, psychomotor skills, cognitive understanding, and affective performance. In this way, you will demonstrate that you do, in fact, provide a balanced physical education curriculum. You never know—your attention to this important area may lead to more administrative support of physical education in your school as you document its worth.

Michael, 10

Student _____	Date _____	

The following lists your child's achievement levels in our physical education program. Please contact me if you have any questions.

Area of learning	Grade	Comments
Psychomotor skills We worked on		
Physical skills We worked on		
Social skills We worked on		
Knowledge of physical education We worked on		

Parent comments, suggestions, and questions: _____

_____

_____

_____
Parent's Signature

Key to grades:
O = Outstanding
S = Satisfactory
N = Needs improvement

Figure 3.9 Sample physical education report card form.

Chapter 4

Managing the Physical Education Class

Rachel, 12

Miss Johnson had a unique style for getting her students' attention.

Suzi is the star of her local select soccer team. She was bored and frustrated and therefore disruptive when she had to work on soccer skills in physical education. Then her teacher had an idea: Suzi could teach the soccer skills to the class! Now Suzi is developing leadership skills while giving her classmates top-notch soccer instruction.

"An ounce of prevention is worth a pound of cure" is an old but still true saying. It certainly applies to discipline, which must be proactive, not reactive. When discipline is planned with prevention as the main goal, it is truly proactive class management; but if discipline is reactive, it is probably a formula for chaos. So remember: plan and prevent!

In the physical education setting, any classroom management problems may well be magnified. It's a whole different ball game (no pun intended!) managing students on the move compared with those sitting at desks. And considering that many of your students may have already decided they do not like physical education or feel anxious about it because of past experiences, you may have a bit of a challenge. But the good news is that students who are allowed adequate chances to move are generally easier to manage back in the classroom. And those students who are strong in bodily-kinesthetic intelligence will be in the realm in which they can feel truly successful, which may lead to increased cooperation.

In this chapter, we'll discuss how you can manage your class effectively in the physical education setting. Specifically, we'll outline how to create a positive class atmosphere, minimize and discipline off-task behavior, set helpful class protocols, and develop effective physical education learning centers and stations. You may discover that many of the things you're doing in the classroom will serve you well in the gym and on the playing field. Moreover, you may discover techniques in this chapter that will help you elsewhere in your curriculum. Perhaps, for example, you'll find a hint that will make hands-on science lessons go more smoothly. Let's turn, now, to the foundation of any effective classroom management system: a positive learning atmosphere.

Creating a Positive Learning Atmosphere

The positive learning atmosphere you set in the regular classroom should carry over to the physical education setting. Although the direct style of teaching is often appropriate in physical education, resist the urge to become a harsh drill sergeant because you are nervous about allowing your students to move. Instead, examine how you react to student physical education behavior—perhaps on video—and ensure that you offer a warm but firm demeanor that creates an emotionally and physically safe and supportive learning environment.

Examine Your Approach

As you think about and perhaps see yourself teach a physical education lesson on video, ask yourself the following questions (Lavay, French, and Henderson 1997):

- Am I tuned-in? If you're tuned in, you know what's going on at all times and act immediately to stop misbehavior before it spreads. Graham (1992) calls this "with-it-ness."

- Am I enthusiastic? Your enthusiasm about physical education learning will spread to students—and even parents, making management easier with their support.

- Am I flexible? Adapt each behavioral strategy to your situation. Although you must be consistent, if something simply isn't working, you must be willing to change your approach. Even mid-lesson, remember to "think on your feet," adjusting your lesson to meet the needs of your students instead of allowing it to be too easy or too hard.

- Am I personable? Or do I turn into a drill sergeant in the gym?

If you find that your answers to these questions are negative in the physical education setting, work to change them to the positive.

Being Positive

Physical education offers an excellent opportunity to develop class spirit and camaraderie that will carry over into the regular classroom. Therefore, encourage your students to make everyone feel special, valued, and needed by setting a good example. The following lists several strategies for being positive (Lavay, French, and Henderson 1997; Graham 1992):

- **Catch students being good.** While it's easy to focus on off-task behavior, focusing on student successes through sincere and specific praise, especially new positive behavior, will reinforce desired behavior.

- **Expect students to follow your directions.** Give instructions in a positive yet assertive voice, then quietly maintain eye contact and wait for compliance. Resist the urge to repeat yourself unless students are so absorbed in following your last instruction you feel they did not hear you. Otherwise, the more you give an instruction, the less likely students are to follow it. After all, why should students jump if they know they have five more requests coming?

- **Keep your cool and address problems quickly.** Do not add to the problem by modeling angry, out-of-control behavior. Make sure you know what happened before judging a situation, then act quickly but calmly to keep misbehavior from spreading.

- **Focus on the behavior not on the person.** Don't say, "You are lazy." Instead, say, "I need to see you participating more." Note, too, that an "I" statement is more likely to engender cooperation than a "You" statement (Faber and Mazlish 1995).

- **Be consistent.** Say what you mean, mean what you say, and do what you say you're going to do. Always ensure that students comply with what you say and, no matter your mood, respond the same way to the same behavior every day.

- **Use a continuum of teaching styles.** As students prove they can behave properly in the physical education setting, try becoming less directive, gradually allowing students more choices as to activities and giving them more responsibility for their own learning.

- **Use positive tools.** Vary tasks when interest wanes by adding a new twist to the original task or moving on to the next task. Play music. Use physical activity to help students relax. After warming up, have students do a few minutes of vigorous activity so they can burn off their pent-up energy and frustration and be more ready to focus on the physical education lesson. Graham calls this "instant activity" (1992).

The last point warrants further discussion. Many children are simply too excited about being in the physical education setting to concentrate on instructions until they have had a chance to move; so instead of fighting this natural reaction, use it as part of your lesson. Plan to allow the students to move immediately. And give instructions before leaving the classroom so they know exactly what you expect—before they get too excited. Then expect those who forget to ask another student, not you. More on helpful lesson protocols shortly.

Helping Students Be Positive

Being positive isn't only for teachers. Expect your students to be positive with one another. Do not tolerate put-downs, teasing, and exclusion. Set the tone for teamwork and insist that everyone be a good teammate. Share your own physical activity experiences, especially memories from childhood, both the triumphs and the defeats. Let your students know that it's okay to take chances, make mistakes—and learn!

Avoid Negative Methods

Avoid canceling your positive approach with negative methods. First, do not make comparisons between children. Comparing is a form of putting down and therefore not appropriate (Lavay, French, and Henderson 1997). In addition, refrain from making idle threats. Remember, say what you mean, mean what you say, do what you say you're going to do. Furthermore, never be sarcastic. Hurt feelings never lend themselves to a healthy learning environment. The same goes for humiliating by making fun of a student or using her as a negative example. Discuss problems privately, keeping an eye on everyone else. Do not use physical activity as a punishment. Finally, avoid overreacting and saying something you can't, won't, or

shouldn't follow through on, such as, "You will sit out of physical education activities the rest of the week" (Lavay, French, and Henderson 1997). Keep in mind that lack of activity is likely to contribute to misbehavior in the regular classroom, so don't compound the problem by applying unreasonable consequences.

Minimizing and Disciplining Off-Task Behavior

If you use positive methods and avoid negative ones, you will prevent most misbehavior. In addition, for consistency's sake, you should use the same discipline system you use the rest of your school day. In this section, we'll look at specific tools for preventing and dealing with misbehavior in the physical education setting. In addition to thorough planning, Graham (1992) describes these tools as back-to-the-wall, proximity control, selective ignoring, overlapping, and positive pinpointing. As you read and study these pointers, look for how you can adapt your regular discipline system to physical education.

Plan Thoroughly

As you probably well know, effective planning can prevent most off-task behavior. Lavay, French, and Henderson (1997) list many simple factors that you should consider when planning physical education lessons:

- While your basic classroom rules should also apply during physical education, have students work with you to set rules specific to your physical education needs. Including students in the process will make them more likely to comply.
- Select curriculum with your particular students in mind. Build in degrees of difficulty from which students may choose. See the teaching by invitation discussion in chapter 5.
- Make sure students have enough equipment so they do not have to wait in long lines for turns. For example, rotate a

COMPONENT—
Active Participation for Every Child

Appropriate Practice	Inappropriate Practice
All children are involved in activities that allow them to remain continually active.	Activity time is limited because children are waiting in lines for a turn in relay races, to be chosen for a team, or because of limited equipment or playing games such as Duck, Duck, Goose.
Classes are designed to meet a child's need for active participation in all learning experiences.	Children are organized into large groups in which getting a turn is based on individual competitiveness or aggressive behavior.
	Children are eliminated with no chance to reenter the activity, or they must sit for long periods of time.
	Reprinted from COPEC/NASPE 1992.

group of three through three related pieces of equipment so that all are actively involved the entire time. Note that this alleviates some problems caused by lack of equipment as well. See also chapter 18.

- Allow room to adjust the activity as needed during the lesson if students are performing better or worse than expected.
- Don't require students to continue practicing a skill they've already mastered. Move on!
- Explain the relevance of the activity.
- Give very brief instructions, then stop activity periodically (but briefly!) to give further instructions.
- Space students far enough apart to prevent friction between students and groups. For example, set up groups so that projectiles such as balls or Frisbees fly into open space or walls. Then plan how you will teach students to retrieve them safely.
- Plan how you will teach students to use equipment properly. Jump ropes and bats are two potentially hazardous types

of equipment. Demonstrating and role-playing are two effective ways to teach safety.
- Plan for transitions. Lay out boundaries and traffic patterns so transitions proceed smoothly. Develop signals such as "When you hear the music stop . . ."

No detail is too small for planning. Remember: *prevent* off-task behavior before it can start.

Keep Your Back to the Wall

Although your students may think you have eyes in the back of your head (and you dare not correct them!), it is best to ensure that you can see the entire class the entire lesson—not only for discipline reasons but also for safety's sake. If you're standing in the middle of the class, you will not be able to see at least 50 percent of your class. This, of course, invites off-task behavior. Thus, stand along a wall in the gym or at the edge of the playground so you can see what is going on in the class better (Graham 1992). But don't stand still! Move along the perimeter, paying equal attention to each group.

Figure 4.1 Proper spacing and rotation of equipment can ensure safety and allow everyone to play.

I find this to be one of the hardest management strategies to plan for. How do I keep my back to the wall and have all the kids throwing at the wall around the perimeter of the gym and still not get hit by a ball? Sometimes it's not possible, but thinking ahead does help prevent problems.

Use Proximity Control

Simply walk toward an off-task student to let him know you see him. Your proximity will often be enough to bring him back on-task. If not, give him "the look," which is simply a nonverbal way of saying "You're off-task; now get back to work" (Graham 1992). The look should not, however, be a "dirty" look. Tilting your head slightly to the side with a twinkle in your eyes, perhaps raising your eyebrows a bit, is a warm but firm way to

communicate that you mean business. Work on using proximity control without losing sight of everyone else in the class. Just be sure to orient yourself so that you can still see the rest of the class.

Ignore Selectively

Ignore misbehavior that is truly minor or really isn't interfering with anyone's learning (Graham 1992). When I was a new teacher, a seasoned veteran told me that she ignored minor misbehavior so students "didn't get more creative in their misbehavior." In the physical education setting, for example, if Johnny is running instead of walking between learning stations, and as long as he isn't hurting himself or anyone else, be grateful for the opportunity for him to burn off some extra "steam."

Overlap Your Attention

Related to having eyes in the back of your head and being tuned-in, you must be able to focus on several things that are happening at once and still move the lesson in the direction you intended (Graham 1992). It's a given: teachers must be able to effectively deal simultaneously with many different situations. And just as you must be able to juggle reading groups and students coming and going for pull-out classes all while the public address system interrupts precious quiet, you must be able to overlap your attention in the physical education setting. For example, practice explaining the day's activity while conducting the warm-up. And work on giving individual feedback while keeping an eye on the rest of the class. With experience, you can master this critical skill in all your teaching.

Pinpoint Positive Behavior

Point out students who are doing what you want the rest of the class to do. Say, for example, "I like the way Lindsey and Julio are helping each other." This works better with younger children who care more about pleasing the teacher. Graham (1992) warns, however, that it can be overused, causing the children to ignore it.

Helpful Lesson Protocols

In the classroom, you need many protocols for various tasks so that little instructional time is wasted on transitions and other noninstructional tasks. For example, you may set procedures for picking up and returning portfolios, using the rest room, and sharpening pencils. Likewise, in the physical education setting, it is essential to train students to follow certain protocols to reduce or prevent injury, wasted time, and misbehavior.

Starting Lessons

Like every good lesson, the physical education lesson needs to get off to a good start. So be sure *you* know what you are doing, then pass the information on to the children when they are able to listen (*after* instant activity). In addition, train your students to follow certain procedures to make equipment dis-

tribution and warming up proceed more smoothly.

Giving Directions

As mentioned earlier in this chapter, most children arrive at physical education bursting with pent-up energy, ready to move—not listen to instructions. Therefore, it is helpful to give initial instructions, including what equipment will be necessary, and briefly explain the purpose of the lesson before lining up to leave the classroom. Moreover, remember to motivate the children to be enthusiastic about the upcoming lesson. This can be part of the lesson's *set induction*, priming the pump so students know what they will be learning about (see chapter 6).

You may also wish to post written instructions upon arrival in the gym or on the playground. Then, encourage students to help one another remember and follow the instructions rather than repeating them yourself.

Distributing Equipment

Having a class of 25 to 30 children try to each get a ball from the same bin at the same time is inviting management problems. Instead, use one of the following methods of equipment distribution:

- Appoint group leaders to gather enough equipment for their groups once in the physical education setting. Direct them to set up the work areas. Train others to wait quietly in assigned areas. Rotate the leadership responsibilities among those who have earned them.
- If possible, distribute equipment to group leaders while still in the classroom. If you keep it in mesh bags or big buckets, you'll reduce the likelihood that it'll be played with on the way to your lesson site.

Finally, as we mentioned earlier, have enough equipment to prevent boredom and frustration. More on this in chapter 18.

Warming Up

Make use of that initial burst of energy work as an effective warm-up by having students do a simple activity related to the lesson. To ensure it is truly instant activity be sure it is a familiar activity that requires little teacher direction. For example, if you are working on a basketball skill, such as dribbling, have students challenge themselves to dribble a ball as continuously as possible or around cones as appropriate, allowing them to choose the type of ball with which they feel they can succeed. In addition to warming up, you'll be able to see at a glance who is having the most trouble with this skill. Moreover, you'll peak interest in the skill. Don't, however, allow students to become bored; a few minutes is generally long enough for a warm-up.

During the Lesson

Establish protocols to keep each physical education lesson running smoothly. Choose groups efficiently, handle emergencies (great and small) effectively, and signal students to stop and listen effectively.

Assigning Groups

You can do this in the classroom, perhaps by keeping rows or groups already established in the classroom in physical education class. Or you can use any one of the many creative ways of assigning groups during physical education. The following ideas should create fairly heterogeneous and equally sized groups:

- **Pick a card, any card.** As each student enters the gym or playground, show her a playing card (remove the face cards), requiring her to memorize it. Then during the course of the lesson, if you need four groups, you can ask all the hearts, all the spades, and so on to group themselves together. If you need two groups, you can ask for all the red cards and all the black cards (Lambdin 1989).
- **Choose a partner.** Have everyone choose a partner. Then have one partner stand on one line, facing the other on another line (or have one stand and one kneel

"Mrs. Johnson's class was determined to make warming up more exciting."

Zzzzzz

Avoid boring warm-ups such as calisthenics and running laps (Graham 1992). Get students immediately involved in an activity appropriate to the particular lesson. Then alter the warm-up slightly to prevent boredom. Finally, using music can give warm-ups some "zip" and signal the warm-up's start and end. Remember, boredom invites off-task behavior.

wherever they are). You can then split the partners, forming two teams. The advantage of this method is that children tend to choose a partner of equal ability so your groups end up being fairly evenly divided (Graham 1992).

- **Gather by birth months.** Ask students to form groups by when they were born. For two teams, divide by January through June birthdays and July through December birthdays. Divide into ever smaller groups by asking for fewer and fewer birth months per group.
- **Are you blue?** Ask students wearing anything blue (or whose favorite color is blue) to work together. Use as many colors as you need.

If one of these methods leaves you with lopsided groups (either by ability or size), quickly shift a few students.

Handling Equipment

Establish a protocol for handling equipment while listening to instructions. For example, have students place equipment on the floor at their feet. Don't allow students to sit on balls, however, as this practice can cause the balls to deflate more quickly.

Teach students how to handle equipment and retrieve projectiles safely. For example, always have students place rather than throw equipment when returning it (Graham 1992). Insist on safety at all times (see also chapter 17).

Handling Emergencies

As always, you are responsible for all students at all times, so don't get so absorbed in a situation that you fail to see and deal with off-task behavior. This is why, whether a child is injured or needs to use the rest room, you should train your entire class to respond to these situations appropriately.

You may wish to bring your classroom passes and post them in the gym or playground and follow your normal classroom procedures for trips to the rest room (an ounce of prevention is worth . . . sending everyone through the rest room *before* physical education).

On a more serious note, be sure you know your students' medical problems and medications and their impact on physical activity. If someone should become ill or injured in physical education, his classmates should know what to do to prevent further problems while you deal with the situation. Have students practice this protocol *before* someone gets hurt or sick (see chapter 17 for more safety information).

Signaling for Attention

Perhaps you flip the light off briefly in the classroom to signal for attention; this may not be possible or safe in the physical education setting. Moreover, a hand signal will be hard for students to notice while turned away from you, following your last instruction. Instead, have students develop an acceptable signal to get their attention when you need to give them further instructions. The signal should mean "freeze" (including voices and equipment) so that you can speak without shouting. When choosing a signal, remind students that bouncing balls and active feet can be hard to hear over, so the signal—and not your valuable voice!—needs to be loud enough to be heard. Students who are allowed to help choose the signal are more likely to cooperate when they hear it.

Ending Lessons

As with any lesson, ending the physical education lesson properly makes the lesson more effective. To do so, you must set and enforce appropriate protocols.

Putting Equipment Away

As you did when students collected the equipment they needed at the beginning of the lesson, you cannot allow chaos to reign when students return equipment. So have students practice performing the reverse process properly. For example, if you use group leaders, when giving your final practice instructions announce that upon the next signal for attention you need groups to gather (where you indicate) and group leaders to quickly and quietly return equipment to its proper place.

Cooling Down

It's important to allow the body to slow down gradually after vigorous activity. So set protocols for shifting gears appropriately. This may be a good time to practice simple relaxation exercises such as breathing in to a count of five and breathing out to a count of seven (if this makes anyone dizzy, suggest lower counts). Consider playing soothing music. Relaxing will help students make the transition back to the regular classroom more smoothly. So ensure that students understand that cooling down is serious business.

Debriefing and Closure

Briefly discussing the lesson and offering words of praise and affirmation for a job well done are as necessary in physical education as in the regular classroom. Indeed, effective closure helps students process what they've learned. Check for understanding as well.

You should also try to mention what they will be working on next in physical education, helping them see the continuity and logic of the sequence of lesson content for themselves. This will also help students come prepared to stay on-task and learn during the next physical education class, so train students on your closure procedures, making those last few moments count (see also chapter 6).

Learning Stations

Learning stations aren't only for the regular classroom! You can use them to reinforce many physical education skills and concepts—both in and out of the physical edu-

Figure 4.2 Allowing students to cool down after physical activity will ease the transition back into the classroom.

cation setting. They also help when equipment or space is limited. One of the most effective ways to use learning stations in physical education is to set them up in a circuit. Grineski (1996) writes that a "learning station circuit is a series of activities, usually centered around a particular theme or skill." He goes on to offer several hints for designing and using them successfully:

- Use learning stations to reinforce and allow students to practice what they've already learned—not to introduce new skills or concepts.

- Use pictures, diagrams, and written description cards as aids for teaching and remembering.

- Use some student-designed activities.

- Focus each station on one specific skill, concept, or fitness component.

- Vary physical demands from station to station.

- Direct traffic flow with signs or have students make maps as per your instructions.

- Have students use different locomotor skills (e.g., running, skipping, hopping, and so on) when moving between stations, and use music as a cue for rotating or as a background.

- Assign a peer-coach to each group, giving these students training and instructions before the lesson.

- Mandate that students must be responsible or lose the privilege of fully participating.

- Allow for individual needs, building in ranges of instructions, such as a range of required repetitions and levels of difficulty.

You can more easily assess student performance when you designate one learning station for this purpose. Those not being assessed will have meaningful work and those being assessed will have the privacy of a small, supportive group.

You can develop a physical education learning center for students to visit back in the regular classroom setting as well. This helps you follow up on key concepts. For example, students can write a description of a game that reinforces the cues on a psychomotor skill checklist or rubric. Or a center can reinforce a science- or math-related physical education concept, such as, when learning about cardiovascular fitness in physical education, how to calculate heart rate when you've only counted your pulse for 10 seconds or investigating the structure of the heart.

Finally, keep students on-task at any learning station by using self-monitoring sheets such as those discussed in chapter 3. Such sheets help students stayed focused and actively involved.

When All Else Fails

Finally, get help if your basic approach does not work with a particular child. Ask the school counselor, principal, or special education teacher for guidance if a student simply cannot seem to function well in the physical education environment. Elicit support from the parents as well. They may have insights into their child's physical education problems that you have overlooked. In fact, the child herself may have helpful insights, so take the time to listen privately to her physical education concerns and feelings.

Then, work to develop and carry out a plan to help the child improve her physical education behavior. To this end, keep in mind that a behavior contract might be easy to write with the child's choice of physical activity as a reward. Some extra one-on-one attention might motivate a child, too. For example, promise to play a game of "H-O-R-S-E" during recess if the child's behavior improves.

Summary

Many basic actions can help you prevent off-task behavior in the physical education setting. Planning, creating a positive class atmosphere, and setting clear protocols for common procedures are only a few. Use and adapt your regular classroom discipline procedures for physical education. This approach provides continuity and consistency, eliminating or reducing many problems you may encounter. Use learning stations to reinforce skills that students have already learned. Finally, get help if all else fails. Remember, discipline is a hard area for all teachers, so don't hesitate to reach out for help and advice when a tough case arises.

Chapter 5

Instructing, Demonstrating, and Motivating

Anthony, 12

I hear and I forget. I see and I remember. I do and I understand.

—Chinese Proverb

Your students need to have a clear idea of what you want them to try to do in order to learn. Moreover, they need to be motivated to learn. In this chapter, we'll discuss effective instructional strategies, demonstration, observation, analysis, feedback, and motivational techniques.

Effective Instructional Strategies

You must make the most of the time you have for physical education for your students to learn as much as possible. In this section, we'll offer information about how to maximize instruction while minimizing time subtracted from children's actually moving and doing. Specifically, we'll discuss important organizational issues and guide you as you strive to provide information and adjust for individual needs.

Organizing the Teaching– Learning Environment

As we said in chapter 4, "Plan and prevent!" When your students know your basic lesson protocols for starting and ending lessons, distributing and putting away equipment, and stopping to listen to you when signaled, you will save most of your physical education time for the day's lesson. So be sure to take the time to establish and practice these protocols from day one. If you find yourself into the school year without a vital protocol, slow down and teach it—it'll be well worth the time it'll save in the long run.

Day to day, however, you will have to make organizational adjustments to fit each particular lesson. Students need to know "what to do, with whom, where, and with what equipment" (Graham 1992). It's as simple as that. To save physical education time, give these instructions in the classroom ahead of time

and expect students to remind one another. Or post a short list of instructions for students to read as you leave the classroom or enter the gym or playing field (prop on a chair or have the first child in line hold the instructions if outside). If the activity is a familiar one, these approaches can provide the "instant activity" that allows students to blow off the steam they've saved all day in a constructive way and can free your time to set up equipment for the physical education class. If the activity is new to the children, simply walk a few students through it to model it for the others. Although a walk-through may seem a waste of valuable time, it can actually save time by helping children visualize how the activity needs to be organized (Graham 1992). In short, "students learn more when they practice more" (Rink 1996), and an organized teaching-learning environment facilitates efficient use of class time.

Providing Information

Now that your students know what they'll be doing, they need to know how. Graham (1992) offers four guidelines to follow when providing skill-related information:

- Limit your instruction to one idea at a time. Even for an adult, more than one focus at a time is overwhelming and defeating.

- Keep your instruction brief. Don't repeat yourself! Get your students back to practicing as fast as possible.

- Use a cue word or phrase. Choose or have your students choose a word or phrase to remind them what the focus of the lesson is—for example, "elbow on shelf" or "ball behind ear" for bending the elbow and bringing it high enough for an effective overhand throw.

- Base your instruction on observation. If you observe that your students know a skill or part of a skill, move on to another skill or refinement!

As you can see, each point will help keep students on-task and behaving as they experience success through effective teaching (see also chapter 4).

Adjusting for Individual Needs

Effective instruction must include adjusting tasks for the individual. This prevents the boredom and frustration that can come from making everyone do the same thing (Graham 1992). In this section, we'll look at two simple ways to make tasks harder or easier.

Teaching by Invitation

Teaching by invitation (Graham 1992) is an instructional strategy that involves allowing students to choose their own level of difficulty. For example, you might offer students a choice of a larger or smaller ball when practicing catching. Or you might offer students two or more tasks from which to choose or two organizational approaches to an activity, such as allowing them to work alone or with a partner or to keep score or not. The key to offering a choice is to avoid making one option sound better than another. Simply allow students to make a choice so they feel comfortable, successful, and challenged (Graham 1992). This empowers students to take responsibility for their own learning.

Intratask Variation

In teaching by invitation, you allow students to vary a task for themselves. But at times you will need to step in and adjust a task so that it is more appropriate for an individual or small group, making it harder or easier. Graham (1992) calls this strategy *intratask variation*. This may, for example, involve sending a small group of more capable students off to one end of the playing field to design a game to apply the basic skills the other students are practicing (keep an eye on everyone, however). Be sure you vary who gets to participate in such activities, at least by unit. But keep in mind that the less capable students may be relieved to have the more capable students off somewhere else. Intratask variation may also involve privately making a task easier for a frustrated child. For example, you might insist that such a child move closer to a target so he can hit it with a beanbag. Or this may involve challenging an individual student to balance on one or three instead of two body parts, depending on ability.

Indirect Instructional Strategies

Thus far, we have concentrated on direct methods of teaching—those that clearly tell students exactly what, where, with whom, with what, and how. And this approach is often appropriate in physical education. But there are times when you can effectively guide students into discovering a point or an entire lesson for themselves. Let's look more

Barry knew his professor would approve of his instructional approach.

closely, now, at two ways to take a more child-directed, problem-solving approach: guided discovery and exploration.

In *guided discovery*, the teacher asks questions to guide students to the one right answer to the problem but never provides the answer. This process is also known as *convergent problem solving*. Through questions, the teacher helps the students converge on the one right answer. In contrast, *exploration* is an open-ended, or *divergent*, problem-solving process. There are many possible answers to the problem the teacher poses (see figure 5.1).

Although these critical-thinking, problem-solving approaches take more time than a direct approach, they are well worth it because they bring the cognitive domain into play. You, however, must set the parameters under which the students are working. For example, you can offer an exploration movement challenge that specifically lists what, where, with whom, with what, but not how: move through the space alone, traveling on three body parts. Or, find as many ways as possible to balance on two body parts. Many times in part 3 we will offer examples of

Sample Activities

The Direct Approach

Follow the Leader, mirroring, finger plays, and Simon Says (played without the elimination process, of course) are examples of developmentally appropriate activities taught with a direct style of instruction. Also in this category are songs accompanied by unison clapping or movement, and rituals like the Mexican Hat Dance and the Hokey Pokey. If these activities are to be performed in a traditional manner, with all children doing the same things at the same time, the only expedient way to teach them is with a Direct Approach using demonstration and imitation.

Guided Discovery

The ultimate goal of the following questions and challenges is a forward roll. However, because guided discovery allows students to respond to challenges at their own developmental level and rate, even if children don't manage to perform the desired forward roll, their responses should be accepted. Ultimately all children can be led to the "correct" answer through convergent problem solving.

Specific challenges and questions will vary according to the responses elicited, but the following is an example of the process:

• Show me an upside-down position with your weight on your hands and feet.
• Show me an upside-down position with your weight on your hands and feet and your tummy facing the floor.
• Can you put your bottom in the air?
• Can you look behind yourself from that position?
• Can you look at the ceiling? Try to look at even more of the ceiling.
• Show me you can roll yourself over from that position. Can you do it more than once?

Exploration

Any challenge that results in a number of responses falls under the heading of Exploration, or divergent problem solving. For example, a challenge to the children to make a crooked shape can result in as many shapes as there are students. A challenge to balance on two body parts can result in one child balancing on the feet, another on the knees, and still another, who may be enrolled in a gymnastics program, doing a handstand. Teachers must encourage children to continue producing divergent responses, but that encouragement should take the form of neutral feedback (e.g., "I see your two-part balance uses one hand and one foot").

Figure 5.1 Sample activities for teaching with different methods.
Reprinted, by permission, from Pica, R., 1995, "Exploration guided discovery and the direct approach," *Teaching Elementary Physical Education*, 6(5): 5.

problem-solving challenges appropriate for the various physical education content areas. Don't be afraid to adapt them to your purposes if you feel your class is ready for a less direct approach. Figure 5.2 shows more examples of alternatives to the direct style of teaching. Note how the critical thinking examples progress through levels similar to Bloom's Taxonomy, eliciting higher and higher levels of thinking. As in any other subject area, children who must process information at a higher level learn more (Rink 1996).

How to Demonstrate—or Have Others Demonstrate

If a picture is worth a thousand words, then a moving model is worth a million in physical education. But no one expects even a

Direct Style

1. Hop forward five times. Then jump sideways three times.

2. Run straight across the room. Hop on one foot back.

3. Bounce the ball with your fingerpads.

4. Rise suddenly, directly, and with a lot of power (explode up), then slowly, directly, and gently sink as you make your body come to rest on the floor.

5. Balance on one foot in a scale position. Then do a forward roll.

6. Hit the ball with a flat racket as you hit your tennis forehand.

7. When dribbling the ball against an opponent, protect the ball by keeping your body between it and the opponent.

Indirect Styles

1. **Select:** Travel around the gymnasium using the steplike weight transfer actions. Each time you hear the drum, change the way you travel. . . . Now each time you hear the drum, change the direction of your travel. . . . Finally, change both your method of travel and direction when you hear the drum.

2. **Classify:** Today we are going to work on different ways to use our feet to travel as we move in general space. You may use only your feet to travel. Ready, go . . . stop. Who can tell me one way? Yes. Walk, run (one foot to the other, alternating). Hop (one foot to the same). Can you try other ways? Yes, I see two to two (jump) . . .

3. **Compare:** Try bouncing the ball with stiff fingers and slap at it with your palm (made lots of noise). Now try pushing the ball down with your fingerpads. Keep your fingers spread and try not to make any noise as you push the ball down to the floor. Which way seems to give you the most control?

4. **Explain, compare, contrast:** Try different rising and sinking actions. Vary the way you use time, force, and effort. Make the way you rise very different from the way you sink. Perform your sequence for a partner by taking turns. Then, compare and contrast your solutions. How were they the same? Different?

5. **Sequence:** Use a roll of your choice to smoothly link two balances.

6. **Apply:** I'm noticing that as you hit your forehand strokes, a lot of balls kind of pop up and go high into the air. Others often hit their ball down into the net. What can you do to change this and hit the balls over level but close to the net? How would this change your grip? Swing?

7. **Analyze:** Dribble a ball against an opponent in this space (15' x 40'). Start at one end and try to get to the other end without your opponent stealing the ball from you. How can you best protect the ball while dribbling down the court?

Figure 5.2 Examples of alternative ways to address issues of critical thinking.
Reprinted, by permission, from Werner, P., "Moving out of the comfort zone to address critical thinking," *Teaching Elementary Physical Education*, 6(5): 7.

physical education specialist to be able to demonstrate every skill, so don't feel bad if you lack the physical know-how to demonstrate in physical education. In this section, we'll explain how to demonstrate and have others demonstrate effectively.

Choosing a Cue Word
The secret to effective demonstrations, observations, and feedback is to focus on the one learnable piece and give it a succinct name. Students can help you choose this one- or two-word cue to remind them and yourself of the lesson focus.

Demonstrating

When you demonstrate a skill, you focus the children's attention on the lesson's objectives. Then after they can visualize this focus, the verbal instruction you give will take on en-

hanced meaning. When breaking down a task into its components, demonstrate it in sequence and demonstrate it more than once (Rink 1996). To demonstrate effectively (Graham 1992),

1. make sure everyone can see you by checking that no one is blocked by another child, too far away, or blinded by sunlight;

2. show the whole action first, then feature the one part you're focusing on for the lesson, and, finally, show the whole action again;

3. show the skill at normal speed, then in slow motion; and

4. be sure to tell the students what they should focus on while watching (the cue word or phrase).

If you don't feel your skills are adequate to demonstrate, tell your students! Let them know it's okay to try, make mistakes, and try again. Tell them the part (learnable piece) you're focusing on and have them analyze your motion to help you do better. They'll appreciate your honesty—and learn from the

Figure 5.3 Demonstrating a skill focuses attention on lesson objectives.

process as well. You just might find yourself becoming more skillful as time goes on. This is far better than presenting an unskillful performance as the "correct" way to do something. Show part of a motion in slow motion, but try to find ways to show students the whole motion correctly.

Having Others Demonstrate

If you know your students' skill levels well, you may be able to select a few students who can demonstrate a particular skill or part of a skill effectively. They will probably even be able to demonstrate in slow motion and one part at a time. Beware, however, of always selecting the motor elite or the same students. Even a low-skilled student can demonstrate a part of a skill (e.g., pointing at a target for throwing accurately). By selecting students of all abilities to contribute, you send the invaluable message that all can succeed in your program. Don't know whom to pick? When using an indirect style of teaching, you can use positive pinpointing (see chapter 4) to select students to demonstrate after allowing time to explore a challenge. Keep in mind that most children prefer to demonstrate as part of a small group of demonstrators rather than as a solo act. Remember, too, that children should have the option to decline to demonstrate.

Finally, you can use video to show students the skill the lesson focuses on. For example, using our overhand throw lesson again, tape part of a baseball game, cue it up to an overhand throw, and show it in the classroom as part of your set induction (see chapter 6),

Never use student demonstration to focus class attention on and embarrass a student who is doing a skill incorrectly. This humiliating form of "teaching" has nothing to do with helping all students succeed at their own level. Always and only highlight correct movement in front of peers.

pointing out the one learnable piece you're highlighting (slow motion can really help). Then refer to this clip when cueing students in physical education class.

How to Observe, Analyze, and Provide Feedback

When you focus a lesson on one learnable piece, you create the foundation for easy and effective observation, analysis, and feedback. In this section, we'll discuss each of these aspects of effective physical education instruction.

Observing

There are several components of each physical education lesson and each movement skill. What do you look for? Graham (1992) suggests you ask yourself the following four questions:

1. Are the children working safely?
2. Are the children on-task?
3. Is the task appropriate?
4. Are individuals using the critical component (which the cue word targets)?

If you answer "no" to any of these questions, immediately adjust the lesson to create a "yes." Keep in mind, too, that you should ask yourself these questions continually throughout each lesson.

Graham (1992) offers the following effective techniques for observing in physical education:

- Keep your back to the wall. You can't observe if you can't see everyone.
- Scan the play area by constantly sweeping your eyes back and forth. Avoid developing "tunnel vision."
- Pretend a visitor is present. How would the lesson look to the PTA president or school principal? This can help you notice problems you might otherwise overlook.
- Focus on one skill component (learnable piece) at a time. This, of course, should

be the one critical component you planned the lesson around and told the students to focus on. Don't get sidetracked by switching your focus to another component or skill. Always focus on the cue!

By observing effectively and adjusting accordingly, you create a child-centered, rather than a subject-centered, program. In other words, you are not only aware of individual performances and needs, you also tailor your teaching to meet those needs.

Analyzing

So how do you know how to tailor your teaching to meet individual needs? You have to process what you observe, "think on your feet," and adjust the lesson accordingly. When you focus on the cue, you can easily tell whether students are "getting it" or not. Then ask yourself the following questions:

- Does most of the class (or an individual) lack a prerequisite skill? If so, back up and teach that skill. Ensuring that students have prerequisite skills is part of offering a developmentally appropriate program (Rink 1996).
- Does most of the class (or an individual) already know this skill or part of the skill? If so, add a challenge or move on.

Providing Feedback

Feedback is as important—if not more so—in physical education as it is in the regular classroom. Whereas children can see what they're doing on a paper or project, they cannot do so with a movement skill or activity—unless they're in front of a mirror or viewing themselves on videotape. So, in general, feedback must come from you and peers. The following are guidelines for offering effective feedback (Graham 1992):

- Be specific. "Good" and "great" can keep a child practicing, but they really don't tell the child anything about what he's doing right. Tell the child exactly what he's doing right, what he needs to focus on, or both. Help him focus on the lesson's cue.

For example, when jumping you might say, "Good bending your knees when landing" (reinforcing the cue from a previous lesson); "now concentrate on landing on the balls of your feet" (reinforcing the cue for today's lesson).

- Ensure congruence. While as in the previous example, you might praise a student by mentioning a previously learned cue, your feedback should focus on the cue or refinement the current lesson focuses on. Don't get sidetracked by talking about an unknown cue, confusing the child. Remember, one focus at a time when observing; this will channel your feedback in the right direction.
- Keep it simple. Always and only giving congruent feedback forces you to keep your feedback simple.
- Be positive or neutral. In general, praise or give helpful information. Save negative feedback for when a child simply does not understand after repeated cues that she is not performing the target action correctly or for the child who thinks she doesn't need help. If you do use negative feedback, administer it privately with an equal or greater dose of encouragement.
- Include everyone. Be careful to make each child aware that you're watching what he's doing. Not only does this encourage time on-task and therefore learning, but it also makes every child feel he's important to you, thereby bolstering his physical activity self-esteem. Of course, certain children will need more attention than others, so be sure to individualize your approach.

You can teach peers to give helpful feedback simply by asking them to watch a partner to see whether he or she is following the lesson's cue. If necessary, role-play acceptable ways to state feedback.

Motivating Children in Physical Education

Several key factors motivate children to practice and do their personal bests in physical education. In this section, we'll discuss extrinsic motivation and intrinsic motivation and look more closely at how building in a high success rate and ensuring developmental appropriateness can motivate children.

Extrinsic and Intrinsic Motivation

Extrinsic motivation involves working for praise or rewards from an outside source. Intrinsic motivation involves trying hard for the sake of the personal satisfaction self-improvement brings. Although giving a sticker or certificate for effort sometimes has its place in physical education and elsewhere, encouraging the desire to participate in physical activity for the pure enjoyment of it should be a major focus of your physical education program. Remember, this is a gift that can last a lifetime.

To develop intrinsic motivation, help your students set realistic personal goals and encourage them to practice hard to reach these goals. Help them compare past and present performances and *never* compare them with other students or some "norm." Although, of course, children will inevitably compare themselves with others, this practice should not come from the "top." Instead, noting progress through a physical education journal or portfolio can be invaluable (see chapter 3). Task sheets (see chapter 4) kept in the portfolio not only keep students on-task but also help them see their own development over time. Finally, child-designed activities intrinsically motivate children (especially older children) as they enjoy working with peers to apply a skill in a relevant context.

Providing Variety

"Variety is the spice of life" is not just a cliché, it's a vital survival tool in your motivational kit! Learning stations are a common way to provide variety to keep students practicing the same skill in new and interesting ways. The following is a list of stations for practicing the underhand throw with primary grade students (see figure 5.4 for a sample setup). You might, for example, hold an "Underhand Throw Carnival." Direct students in small groups to allow each student to try each skill five times and help one another retrieve balls and beanbags before the next person throws:

Station 1: Bins and boxes labeled as "Gold Mines." Throw the beanbag into the gold mine, and it turns to gold. Count how many gold nuggets you make in five tries. (Smaller boxes will challenge the more skillful child.)

Station 2: Paper target made from butcher paper. Count your own points.

Station 3: Rope river. Decide whether you're going to throw the sock ball into or over the river. Give yourself a point every time you do what you say you will. (A narrow point in river will challenge the more skillful child.)

Station 4: Castle floor. Throw the yarn ball onto a tile in the King and Queen's Castle, and it will turn into a diamond. Count how many diamonds you make. (Use 12- by 18-inch construction paper and 12- by 12-inch construction paper "tiles" to vary the difficulty.)

Station 5: Hoopscotch. Throw a ball into a hoop farther and farther away. Count

Praise Sandwich

Help a child listen to your guidance by offering him or her a "praise sandwich." State positive specific praise first (e.g., "I like how you moved into position to catch"), next offer specific corrective information (e.g., "Now, 'give' by pulling your arms and hands toward your chest as you catch"), then finish with another statement of general or specific praise (e.g., "I am pleased with how well you're concentrating").

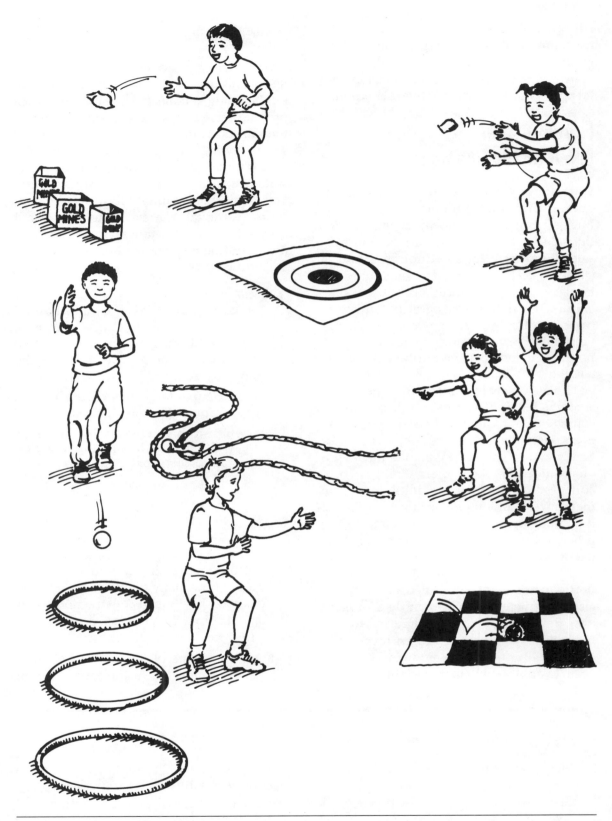

Figure 5.4 Diagram of station setup.

how many times you get the ball into the hoop you're aiming for.

Younger children may need to be introduced to each station as a whole-group activity before rotating through stations in a review lesson. Older students can read instructions and even help you develop new stations. (See also chapter 4.)

Building in Success

Children who are allowed to practice at a reasonably high level of success learn more (Rink 1996). And we have talked all along about tailoring each activity so that students can make choices based on their own abilities. Applying intratask variations and teaching by invitation are big motivators because these strategies reduce the risks of boredom and frustration.

Ensuring Developmental Appropriateness

We've also talked a lot about developmental appropriateness thus far in the book. Naturally, if an activity is developmentally appropriate, it is more motivating to children to participate. Too hard, they get discouraged. Too easy, they get bored. Either way, off-task behavior is sure to ensue. Therefore, pay close attention to the COPEC (1992) recommendations regarding this issue that we quote throughout this book. Furthermore, keep in mind that you cannot always allow or count on children to know when they should make a task harder or easier for themselves as in teaching by invitation. At times, you will need to provide "intratask variation" and make the decisions as to how to adjust an activity to better meet a child's needs (Graham 1992).

Summary

As you can see, much of this chapter provides not only instructional guidelines but also class management strategies. Indeed, the two cannot ever be totally separated. For example, you can't teach if students are unmotivated and therefore off-task. And children work harder and so learn more if you help them focus properly because *you* are focused properly. In short, effective teaching involves effective management created by making wise and sensitive choices in how you present, observe, analyze, give feedback, and motivate students.

Emily, 7

Franklin, 8

A Basic Physical Education Curriculum

Perhaps you still think of physical education as a series of games and activities to keep the kids busy. As we discussed in part 1, however, research into physical education theory and practice reveals that, as in other subject areas, children learn best when they progress through a developmentally appropriate curriculum at their own rates. Thus, in part 2, we'll show you how to design and implement a well-rounded curriculum that does just that.

In chapter 6, we'll outline the basics of curriculum development and unit and lesson planning in the physical education realm. Then in chapters 7 through 11, we'll discuss each of several physical education curriculum areas. In chapter 7, we'll show you how to teach the basic movement skills and concepts, those building blocks of all other physical education learning. Then in chapter 8, we'll discuss how to teach health-related physical fitness and maximize physical activity in your physical education program. Next, in chapters 9 through 11, we'll show you how to teach games, gymnastics, and dance effectively. Finally, in chapter 12, we'll give you more information and examples of how to integrate academic areas into your physical education curriculum.

You'll also notice in chapters 7 through 12 that we've provided sample lessons for each physical education curricular area we touch upon. Why? We recommend that as you read and study this material, you practice the principles we're espousing with real kids in a real school. Use and adapt these plans to the particular class you're working with. Then come back to this text with the questions that arise as you strive to put this material into practice. Review part 1 as necessary and get the most out of parts 3 and 4 by trying out these sample lessons.

Developing a Physical Education Curriculum

Mrs. Kim really wants to be able to offer tennis to her students but only has access to one court, and the weather is unreliable. However, she has plenty of badminton nets and gym space. After contacting the United States Tennis Association for free help (see appendix), she decides to teach her students "short court" tennis using the equipment she has.

Every teaching situation is, of course, unique. Thus, we cannot offer a cut-and-dried curriculum that fits every situation, every teacher, every class, all the time. Instead, in this chapter we will outline the processes of choosing a curriculum emphasis, setting objectives and goals, developing a developmentally appropriate scope and sequence, selecting specific content, and writing unit and lesson plans. Then we'll examine the ongoing nature of curriculum development by discussing how curriculum, instruction, and assessment are interrelated.

Choosing a Curriculum Emphasis

As with every other subject area, your physical education curriculum will have a certain emphasis whether you consciously choose one or not. Indeed, your own experience, expertise, and preferences will influence your curricular choices. In this section, we will outline four possible curricular emphases.

Skill Development

A curriculum that emphasizes skill development focuses on *movement skills*, the basic locomotor, nonlocomotor, and manipulative skills that a person uses in games, gymnastics, dance, sports, bike riding, and so on. *Locomotor skills* include running, skipping, hopping, walking, jumping, leaping, gallop-

ing, and sliding. *Nonlocomotor skills* involve any activity of the body that occurs while remaining in one place: balancing, counterbalancing, spinning, swinging, hanging, twisting, rising, sinking, bending, gesturing, and the like. *Manipulative skills* include the actions of sending away (e.g., kicking, striking, throwing), gaining possession (e.g., catching, collecting), and traveling with (e.g., dribbling, carrying). (See also chapter 7.)

Buschner (1994) calls the locomotor, nonlocomotor, and manipulative skills the "letters" of the "Movement Alphabet." Using the skills in context creates "sentences," and applying the skills to complex movements, as in sports, games, or dance, makes "compositions." An individual can only form meaningful movement sentences and compositions based on his knowledge and possession of the basic letters. A physical education curriculum that emphasizes skill development attempts to give students as many letters as possible to create movement "literacy." Thus, those who espouse skill development as the core of their physical education curriculum believe elementary level students should spend most of their physical education time learning movement skills.

Health-Related Fitness Concepts

As we mentioned in chapter 1, health-related fitness includes five distinct components: muscular strength, muscular endurance, body composition (the ratio of body fat mass to lean tissue mass), cardiorespiratory fitness, and flexibility. A curriculum that emphasizes health-related fitness concepts focuses on explaining why physical fitness is important and how students can achieve it as a way of life. Thus, students spend most of their physical education time learning about health-related fitness concepts (see also chapter 8).

Physical Activity

A physical education curriculum that emphasizes physical activity focuses on facilitating many opportunities to move, to gain health-related fitness benefits. Actually achieving physical health-related fitness through as continual as possible physical activity is most important, and students concentrate on improving each area of health-related fitness. Therefore, they spend most of their physical education time working out and learn many ways to do so. Many teachers have made this approach more relevant by combining it with a health-related fitness concept curriculum, for example, teaching students to monitor their heart rates and other components of health-related fitness while exercising so they can see some of the health-related fitness concepts applied.

Integrated Curriculum

An integrated physical education curriculum attempts to integrate skill development, health-related physical fitness, and physical activity into one cohesive program. Furthermore, it seeks to integrate other subject areas. For example, students work on movement skills in such a way as to stay highly physically active. Then in teachable moments, the instructor briefly points out health-related fitness concepts or the relationship of another subject area to the lesson as an aside. An instructor must plan for these teachable moments to maximize their effectiveness.

We believe that thoughtful, integrated planning can maximize student learning. Moreover, we believe an integrated curriculum is the best way to meet the National Association for Sport and Physical Education's (NASPE) National Physical Education Standards. Therefore, we recommend the integrated approach to planning a physical education curriculum as the most efficient way to use valuable instructional time.

Setting Desired Outcomes

Once you choose your curriculum emphasis, you can set your objectives and goals. In other words, you can decide where you are headed in your physical education program. The National Standards for Physical Education (NASPE 1995) should be the exit standards for elementary students (i.e., for sixth graders). Then by looking at what the National Standards expect of kindergartners and

Figure 6.1 Teaching students to check their heart rates makes a physical activity curriculum more relevant.

second and fourth graders, you can work backward to set yearly, unit, and lesson objectives and goals. This is known as *designing down*. As mentioned in chapter 1, you should not go through this process in isolation; desired outcomes should be set at the district level. So if this has not been done in your district, request that a team of physical education specialists, administrators, parents, and classroom teachers be formed to do so. Of course, if you have a physical educator assigned to your school, this individual should oversee this process for your program. Your state guidelines should be helpful in this process as well.

Setting a Developmentally Appropriate Scope and Sequence

Once you know where you're headed at your grade level, you can decide exactly how you'll get there. To do so you must next decide how much time and in what order you will teach the physical education content to reach your objectives. *Sequence* involves the order of the progression of curriculum from year to year, reflecting the timing and depth of the program from grade to grade (Gallahue 1996). Then you must define your grade level's *scope*, the content of the program

in terms of its breadth or range throughout the academic year (Gallahue 1996). Figure 6.2 outlines a sample scope and sequence guide.

As in any academic subject, the skills covered in any scope and sequence must progress in a developmentally appropriate manner. Children cannot learn more advanced skills before they learn the basic skills—the words before the letters. For example, to learn to juggle, it would be best to first juggle one balloon, then two, and so on. After becoming successful with balloons, a child may progress to yarn or Nerf balls, then to tennis balls—choosing his own rate of progress. Thus, when you set your own scope for the year within the sequence set by your state or district, you must ensure that your students possess the necessary skills to learn what you have planned and that you make room for students to progress at their own rates. If necessary, rewrite your plans to facilitate more basic learning and to allow for teaching by invitation (see chapter 5). But before the school year begins, you can outline your physical education scope, then tailor your actual unit and lesson plans to meet your particular students' needs as you discern them.

As with any other subject area, a cohesive K-12 program makes planning, teaching, learning, and assessment easier, more productive, and more valuable.

COMPONENT— *Curriculum*

Appropriate Practice

The physical education curriculum has an obvious scope and sequence based on goals and objectives that are appropriate for all children. It includes a balance of skills, concepts, games, educational gymnastics, and rhythm and dance experiences designed to enhance the cognitive, motor, affective, and physical fitness development of every child.

Inappropriate Practice

The physical education curriculum lacks developed goals and objectives and is based primarily on the teacher's interests, preferences, and background rather than on those of the children. For example, the curriculum consists primarily of large group games.

Reprinted from COPEC/NASPE 1992.

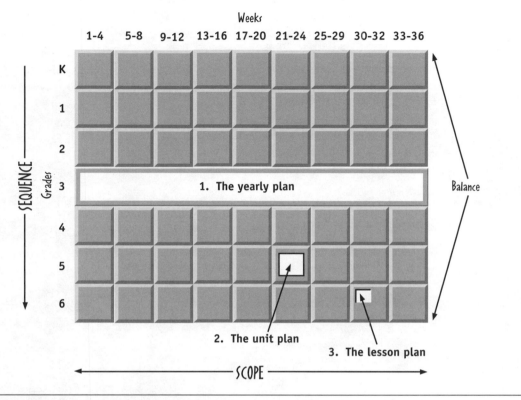

Figure 6.2 Sample scope and sequence chart.
Reprinted, by permission, from Gallahue, D., 1998, *Developmental Physical Education for Today's Children*, 4th ed., (New York, NY: McGraw Hill).

Selecting Specific Content

Exactly what physical education content you select will depend upon many factors, including—among others—your school and physical education objectives and goals, school and community environment and cultural influences, size of your class, student abilities, equipment and facilities available to you, and your own likes, dislikes, strengths, and weaknesses. If one is available, work with your building's physical educator to coordinate content for the year and unit by unit. For example, if your students only see the specialist once or twice a week, work as a team to plan the other three or four lessons each week. In this section, we'll discuss general factors to consider and then outline the final criteria each activity should meet when you're selecting physical education content.

General Factors to Consider

We cannot emphasize enough that no two teaching situations are the same. You must tailor the specific content you choose to your unique situation so as to maximize learning for all students, given the parameters you must work within (see figure 6.3a and b). Thus, beyond your grade-level physical education objectives, take the following factors into consideration before selecting specific units and activities:

- Number of students in your class—Can you manage the unit or activity given the number of students you have?

- Developmental levels of your students—Does the unit or activity meet *all* your students' needs?

- Cultural orientation(s) of your school—Does your choice of unit or activity respect the cultural needs and interests of your students? Does it have the potential to stretch your students' cultural awareness?

- Facilities—Do you have access to a gym, all-purpose room, outdoor space, or community facility appropriate for conducting the unit or activity?

Figure 6.3 Methods for managing a large class will be significantly different from those used to manage a smaller class.

- Equipment—Do you have or can you borrow or make the equipment you need to conduct the unit or activity so that all students are actively involved in learning all the time?

- Amount of time per physical education class period—How much time are you able to set aside for each lesson? Is it enough to accomplish each lesson's objectives?

- Number of physical education class periods per week—How many class periods per week are you able to mandate for physical education? Is the total time enough to accomplish your objectives?

- Safety issues—Given your facilities, training, equipment, and individual students, can you conduct the unit or activity safely?

- Overall value—Is the content meaningful, challenging, and motivating to *all* your students?

Choose only units and activities for which you can answer "yes" to most or all of these questions.

Final Criteria for Selecting Content

No matter what content you select, you should then ensure that each component of a lesson meets the following criteria (Rink 1993). The learning experience

- must have the potential to improve the motor performance and movement skills of the students;

- must provide maximal activity or practice time for all students at their individual ability levels;

- must be appropriate for the experience level of each student; and

- should have the potential to integrate psychomotor, affective, and cognitive educational goals whenever possible.

Given that across your curriculum you have so much to teach in so little time, it is vital that the content of each learning activity be both meaningful and efficiently chosen and organized; this is certainly true of physical education. Thus, if an activity does not meet the criteria outlined here, find another, more beneficial activity.

Developing Physical Education Plans

Whether you're a seasoned veteran or a teacher in training, you probably have some experience either planning lessons or studying how. Thus, in this section, we will assume you have some basic planning know-how and focus on the specific application of this knowledge to the physical education realm. First, we'll outline how to design an effective physical education unit plan, and then we'll show you how to design an effective physical education lesson plan.

Unit Plans

Many physical educators consider three weeks to be an appropriate length of time for a physical education unit. Some students may become bored with the unit's theme if it lasts longer than three weeks. In contrast, a shorter time period would prevent many students from making meaningful gains in their knowledge. You should not, however, be so rigid that your students' needs go unmet. For example, if you are only able to dedicate the minimum of time your state mandates for physical education, you may need to use four rather than three weeks per unit to ensure that your students learn what they need to. Figure 6.4 shows a sample unit plan for the movement skills and concepts themes of body and spatial awareness.

Just as you should follow a developmentally appropriate scope and sequence for kindergarten through sixth grade and on your own grade level, you should organize each unit in a logical, developmentally appropriate progression.

Lesson Plans

Each unit consists of the lessons you will be able to devote to the particular theme you have chosen. The theme, of course, must lend itself to your chosen curriculum emphasis.

Body and Spatial Awareness Unit for Kindergarten and First Grade

	Lesson 1	Lesson 2	Lesson 3
Week 1	**Lesson 1** Body Part Identification, Awareness of Personal Space, Listening Skills Fitness Component: Flexibility	**Lesson 2** Awareness of Personal Space and Body Shapes, Experience With Nonlocomotor Skills of Bending and Stretching, Understanding Levels in Space Fitness Component: Flexibility	**Lesson 3** Personal Space Continued, Compared With Other Objects' Movements and Sport Movements Fitness Component: Flexibility
Week 2	**Lesson 4** More Bending and Stretching, Body Shapes in Personal Space Fitness Component: Muscular Strength	**Lesson 5** Body Shapes Continued, Leading With Particular Body Parts Fitness Component: Muscular Strength	**Lesson 6** More Nonlocomotor Skills in Personal Space, Mirroring a Partner Fitness Component: Muscular Strength
Week 3	**Lesson 7** Personal and General Space Compared, Locomotor Skills Explored Fitness Component: Cardiorespiratory Endurance	**Lesson 8** General Space, More Locomotor Experience (Creating Sequences), Problem Solving, and Respecting Personal Space of Others Fitness Component: Cardiorespiratory Endurance	**Lesson 9** Moving Through General Space in Pairs, Synchronizing Movements Fitness Component: Cardiorespiratory Endurance

Figure 6.4 Sample unit plan.

For example, if you choose a movement skills and concepts theme as in our sample unit plan (figure 6.4) and you are striving for an integrated curriculum, you must plan activities that will not only teach the skills and concepts outlined but also build in plenty of actual physical activity as well as touch upon health-related fitness concepts at appropriate points in the unit (note how each week specifically targets a different health-related fitness component to emphasize). Moreover, if you teach, for example, interpersonal skills across your entire school curriculum, you should design your individual lessons to include cooperative learning activities (see chapter 13). Figure 6.5 shows an example of a lesson plan (Lesson 7) in the unit plan shown earlier in figure 6.4. (See also chapter 4 for effective behavior management planning ideas.)

As you can see in figure 6.5, the physical education lesson plan has the same distinct

Objective, Please!

Mrs. Ryan planned a lesson for which the objective was, "The student will be able to perform three steps of a folk dance in sequence." During class, she introduced the music and outlined the background of the dance. Then several students shared stories from their own ethnic backgrounds. Out of respect for these students, Mrs. Ryan allowed this sharing to continue until the time to practice the folk dance steps ran out. The students, of course, did not meet the objective.

Lesson 7: Personal and General Space

Objectives

- Exploration of nonlocomotor skills
- Experience with general space
- Consideration of others moving through space

Materials

1 hoop per child (optional)

Setup

Have students scatter throughout activity area for the first three activities (7.1-7.3) and line up single-file behind you for the last activity.

7.0 Set induction: We're going to warm up by exploring all the different ways we can move while in one spot—performing nonlocomotor—and then we're going to take our personal space with us, moving in different ways throughout the room. Who can show us a nonlocomotor movement? (Elicit responses from several students to review previous lessons.)

7.1 Challenge the students to see how many different ways they can perform each of the following skills: bending, stretching, sitting, shaking, turning, rocking, swaying, and twisting.

7.2 Take a moment to focus on the health-related fitness component of cardiorespiratory fitness. Have each student place her right hand over her heart to feel how fast or slow her heartbeat is.

7.3 Play The Shrinking Room. Have each child hold a hoop around his waist (or hold his arms out to his sides if hoops aren't available) and move throughout the room *without* touching anyone else's hoop or arms. After a few minutes, hold your hands out to the sides, pretending to be a wall. Move the "wall" a few steps closer to the children, shrinking the area in which they can move. Continue this process as long as the students are still able to move without touching one another.

7.4 Play a game of Follow the Leader with the children in line behind you. Be sure to explore straight, curved, and zigzag pathways; forward, backward, and sideway directions; and low, middle, and high levels.

7.5 Cardiorespiratory fitness concept: Have the children check their heart rates once again and discuss how these compare with the way their heartbeats felt earlier in the lesson (should be faster). Explain that physical activity can raise the heartbeat and that this is good for the heart.

Closure and assessment: Call out various nonlocomotor movements for small groups of children to perform to ensure that they can identify and perform a large variety. Have a small group of students demonstrate how to move through general space safely. Play a quick mirroring game. Note students who have trouble replicating your movements. Tell students to be thinking about how they can combine movements to create sequences in the next lesson.

Figure 6.5 Sample space and body awareness lesson.

components any lesson in any other subject area should have to ensure maximal learning: set induction, core lesson content, and closure. Of course, these parts are known by several different names, but for the purposes of discussion, we'll stick with these for now.

Set induction, also known as *cognitive set* or *anticipatory set*, involves "priming the pump"—preparing and motivating students to learn by offering a brief explanation of the lesson's content and purpose in an enthusiastic manner. An effective set induction helps students see how and why the current lesson's learning fits into the unit's content, enticing students to want to learn through today's activities.

The *core lesson content* includes explanations, demonstrations, and student activities. Remember, each component of the core lesson content must pass the criteria we have outlined so you don't waste precious instructional time. Moreover, these activities must build one upon another. As with your overall physical education scope and sequence, don't expect students to "run" with a skill before they have the opportunity to practice "crawling." Finally, you must ensure that you do not go off on a tangent and end up not teaching what you set out to teach.

Closure summarizes the day's learning and allows you to do a quick check for understanding. An effective lesson closure should solidify student learning by reminding students of the lesson's purpose within the context of both the unit and everyday life. In addition, your closure activity should allow the body to cool down after activity. Furthermore, a closure activity can give you an opportunity to quickly check for understanding. Finally, use closure to prime the pump ahead of time for the next lesson, making it a "pre–set induction" whenever possible.

The Interrelationships of Curriculum, Instruction, and Assessment

To be truly effective, you must not blindly follow a set scope and sequence—no matter how thoroughly it was researched and planned. You must, in reality, "read" your students and not your curriculum or even this book. In other words, always be willing to tailor your plans to your students' needs. This flexibility does not mean, however, you should allow yourself to wander aimlessly through your physical education program. Instead, to remain effective as you strive to meet individual needs, you must understand and use the interrelationships of curriculum, instruction, and assessment.

This concept of interrelationships is known as *instructional alignment* (Carnes 1997). After designing down from your desired outcomes, you have your curriculum. Next, you provide the instruction you feel is necessary for students to reach the desired outcomes. Then, you assess student performance. Finally— and this is vital—you must alter curriculum and instruction as appropriate based on the results of your assessment of student learning. Thus, "curriculum, instruction, and assessment work together in a 'continuous loop of learning'" (Carnes 1997). Indeed, Carnes asserts that assessment must drive instruction, and the purpose of assessment is to "enhance learning, not just document it." Figure 6.6 illustrates instructional alignment.

Also tied to curriculum design and instructional alignment is the concept of mastery learning. Remember, you must give all students time to reach your goals, helping them succeed and grow through either enrichment or remediation at their individual rates.

Summary

Effective curriculum development is an ongoing, never-ending process as you strive to meet the needs of each student. Once you

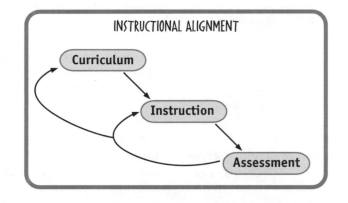

Figure 6.6 Continuous loop of learning.
Reprinted, by permission, from Carnes, L., 1997, "Using models to direct curriculum," *Teaching Elementary Physical Education*, 8(3): 4.

know your desired grade-level outcomes, you must design down (work backward) to create a logical, progressive scope and sequence of units, lessons within units, and activities within lessons that will help your students achieve these outcomes. Then, when assessment reveals learning deficits, you must be flexible enough to alter your curriculum and instruction to better meet your students' individual needs.

In the rest of part 2, we will outline how you can be an effective teacher of movement skills and concepts, health-related physical fitness concepts, and games, gymnastics, and dance based on what you have learned thus far.

Another Word About Individualization

Remember, while some students' needs may require great creativity on your part (see chapter 14 regarding inclusion issues), individualization does not have to be a planning nightmare. Consider the following activity and the simple, yet effective way its creator individualized instruction as well as empowered students to take personal responsibility for their own learning:

Mrs. Cortez noticed Nabeel, a skillful fourth grader, horsing around with his small group. She quietly took him aside and offered him a greater challenge. Instead of serving a tennis ball into the proper service court, she had him hit various targets (e.g., cones, boxes) within the court and record his rate of success on a sheet of paper.

Merry, 6

Aaron, 6

Brooke, 12

Chapter 7

Teaching Movement Skills and Concepts

Lindsey, 11

If you can't fly, run. If you can't run, walk. If you can't walk, crawl. But by all means keep moving.

—Dr. Martin Luther King Jr.

Just as we do not expect a child to speak in sentences before first learning to speak words, we cannot expect students to learn complex motor skills before learning the basic ones. Movement skills and concepts are the foundation of all other physical components of physical education: games, gymnastics, dance, sports, and health-related physical fitness. In this chapter, we'll examine the key issues in teaching movement skills and concepts, outline the basic content and appropriate teaching methods for teaching movement skills and concepts, discuss how to plan effective units and lessons, and describe how to authentically assess student knowledge of movement skills and concepts.

Key Issues

As with any area of learning, the content of movement skills and concepts curricula must be developmentally appropriate. But many teachers have to get past some harmful false assumptions before they teach movement skills and concepts enthusiastically and effectively. In this section, we'll examine developmental appropriateness as it pertains to movement skills and concepts, dispel the common myths surrounding children's learning in this area, then show you how to attain physical education goals through teaching movement skills and concepts.

Developmental Appropriateness

In chapter 6, we described the individual basic locomotor, nonlocomotor, and manipulative skills as being the letters of the "Movement Alphabet" (Buschner 1994). Using the skills in context creates "sentences," and applying the skills in complex movements, as in sports, games, or dance, creates the "compositions." An individual can only form meaningful movement sentences and com-

positions based on his knowledge and possession of the basic letters. A physical education curriculum that emphasizes skill development attempts to give students as many letters as possible to create movement "literacy" (Buschner 1994).

As letters in the "Movement Alphabet," movement skills and concepts are the foundation of a developmentally appropriate curriculum. Then taking this analogy further, if we instead think of the movement skills and concepts as "words" in a "Movement Language," we can say that the movement skills are the "verbs," or the actions (e.g., walking), and the movement concepts are the "adverbs," or the way the actions are performed (e.g., in general space). Table 7.1 lists the motor skills and movement concepts of the "Movement Language."

False Assumptions

As important as basic movement skills and concepts are to future learning, physical education specialists and classroom teachers alike often skip over most or all of the words in the "Movement Language" because of three false assumptions. The following lists and describes each misconception:

1. **Learning how to move develops naturally through maturation.** Although babies learn to walk without any teaching, motor skills beyond the most rudimentary movements and basic reflexes and reactions must be learned. And although children attempt more advanced skills, most cannot master them without developmentally appropriate, progressive intervention (Buschner 1994).

2. **Most children are skilled enough to engage in advanced sports, games, and dances.** This is simply not true. Most need the intervention we just mentioned as well as age-appropriate versions of adult games (see also chapter 9). For example, many children are expected to play soccer in preschool and the primary grades, yet eye-foot coordination is not fully developed until age 9 or 10.

3. **Learning basic skills does not motivate children.** When children are allowed to

Table 7.1   The "Movement Alphabet"

Motor skills—verbs		Movement concepts—adverbs			
Locomotor patterns	**Manipulative patterns**	**Body awareness**	**Space awareness**	**Effort**	**Relationships**
Walking	Throwing	Body parts	General space	Speed	Objects
Jogging	Catching	Shapes	Self-space	Force	Partner
Running	Kicking	Curved	Directions	Flow	
Hopping	Punting	Twisted	Levels		
Skipping	Dribbling	Narrow	Pathways		
Galloping	with feet	Wide	Extensions		
Leaping	Dribbling	Symmetrical			
Chasing	with hands	Asymmetrical			
Dodging	Striking	Nonlocomotor			
Fleeing	Volleying	Swing and sway			
Faking		Twist and turn			
Jumping		Bend and curl			
Landing		Stretch			
Sliding		Sink			
		Push and pull			
		Shake			
		Base of support			

Reprinted, by permission, from Buschner, C., 1994, *Teaching Children Movement Concepts and Skills*, (Champaign, IL: Human Kinetics), 10.

work within a developmentally appropriate, progressive curriculum, they are more motivated and less bored. Indeed, children enjoy learning what meets their needs. For example, if you expect your students to do algebra calculations before they learn the basic math skills (the equivalent of expecting them to play adult-rules basketball before they acquire basic ballhandling and motor skills), they will not only be bored, they'll also be frustrated and restless. Teaching children the basics they need to know increases feelings of competence and confidence, thereby increasing participation. And keep in mind, children who feel competent and confident behave better (see also chapter 4).

To summarize, most children do not learn movement skills and concepts without systematic intervention. Moreover, teaching movement skills and concepts enhances development and confidence, potentially encouraging participation and good behavior.

Attaining Physical Education Goals Through Movement Skills and Concepts

In chapter 6, we recommended that you develop a curriculum that integrates all areas of physical education into each unit so that your students are becoming physically fit and practicing basic movement skills and concepts while learning more specific content. Obviously, working directly on movement skills and concepts automatically addresses a major physical education goal. In addition, when planning movement skill and concept units, keep in mind the following components of an effective program: physical activity and cognitive and social development.

Physical Activity

Keep students moving! Minimize time spent on organization, instruction, and demonstration so that students are moving during most of physical education class.

Cognitive Development

Challenge students to solve movement problems. For example, mark two points on the floor several feet or yards apart. Ask students to find the least and most steps possible to go from one point to the other. What types of steps will they use? What will other parts of their bodies do? In addition, have students analyze both their own movement and that of their peers by using self- and peer assessment sheets (see figures 7.1 and 7.2).

Social Development

There are many ways to develop social skills while teaching a movement skills and concepts unit. Peer tutoring provides opportunities for students to work together (see chapter 15). Cooperative activities and problem solving in small groups also enhance social skills while enhancing the learning of movement skills and concepts.

Movement Skills and Concepts: Curriculum Content

In this section, we will define each motor skill and movement concept that makes up the "Movement Language." Study the figures of mature patterns and the tables outlining components closely to help guide you in your teaching.

Movement Concepts

Movement concepts help children understand how to move efficiently, talk about movement, and apply movement learning to multiple situations. Remember, movement concepts are the adverbs in the "Movement Language." Understanding movement concepts can help you give students specific

---

Directions: The children receive a copy of this assessment form, and the teacher reads these directions to them: "Today you will be evaluating your ability to throw. We just finished practicing this motor skill in our lesson called *Spring Training*. Think about all of the throws you made and how well you can throw a ball. How do you feel about your ability when you use your whole body to throw? [Read other tasks to the children.] You have three choices. You may feel you need more practice. You may feel you are getting better. Or you may feel you are good at throwing, for your grade level. Please draw a baseball in the category that represents your feeling. Please write your name, grade, and today's date at the top of the page and take 3 minutes to think about your throwing ability. Be honest and take this assessment seriously. I do."

Student name _Eric_ _____ Date ___9/15___ Grade ___3rd___

Tasks	Student self-assessment		
	I need more practice to be okay.	I am getting better.	I am good for my grade.
When I use my whole body to throw . . .		O	
When I step with my opposite foot . . .			O
When I throw from a distance . . .		O	
When I throw to the target (baseball glove) . . .		O	
Other notes about how well I throw: _____			
_____			
_____			

Figure 7.1 Student self-assessment using a sample Spring Training learning experience.
Reprinted, by permission, from Buschner, C., 1994, *Teaching Children Movement Concepts and Skills*, (Champaign, IL: Human Kinetics), 52.

Directions: Each child receives a copy of this form. Children are then paired to do the assessment. The teacher discusses the importance of peer assessment, asking the children to fill out the partner's name, date, and grade. The children read over and discuss the throwing tasks with the teacher to prevent misunderstandings. Each child will attempt 15 throws against a wall in designated areas. Partners will stand behind the lines on the floor designating appropriate distances. "You are to carefully watch your partner and check yes or no for each task they perform. If your partner is a good thrower in your estimation, also check the category. If you feel your partner needs my help, check the last category. Any questions? At the bottom of the page you can write down suggestions that may help your partner become a better thrower."

Partner's name ___Sally_____   Date ___11/17___ Grade ___3rd_____

Your name _Mary_____

Tasks		Partner self-assessment		
	Yes	Is a good thrower	No	Needs teacher help
My partner keeps his or her side to the target when throwing.				
—Throw #1 against the wall	✓			
—Throw #2 against the wall	✓			
—Throw #3 against the wall	✓	✓		
My partner steps with the opposite foot.				
—Throw #4 against the wall	✓			
—Throw #5 against the wall	✓			
—Throw #6 against the wall	✓	✓		
My partner was able to hit the wall in the air from				
—10 yards (#7)	✓	✓		
—15 yards (#8)	✓			
—20 yards (#9)			✓	✓
—25 yards (#10)			✓	✓
—Over 30 yards (#11)			✓	✓
My partner hit the target (baseball glove) from				
—5 yards (#12)	✓			
—10 yards (#13)			✓	✓
—15 yards (#14)			✓	✓
—20 yards (#15)			✓	✓

Other suggestions for my partner to become a better thrower: _____

_____

_____

Figure 7.2 Partner assessment using a sample Spring Training learning experience.
Reprinted, by permission, from Buschner, C., 1994, *Teaching Children Movement Concepts and Skills*, (Champaign, IL: Human Kinetics), 53.

feedback, analyze student movement proficiency, and plan comprehensive lessons. Let's turn, now, to examining the specific content of the four movement concepts: body awareness, space awareness, effort, and relationships.

Body Awareness: What the Body Does

Body awareness is an individual's ability to understand what the body does while moving. With body awareness, an individual can demonstrate many ways to move individual body parts while controlling other body parts (Buschner 1994). An individual with strong body awareness can identify body parts, balance on different bases of support, create body shapes and positions in a defined area, and perform the nonlocomotor movements. Table 7.2 lists the content areas and descriptors and cues to help you teach your students the vocabulary and meaning of body awareness aspects.

Space Awareness: Where the Body Moves

Children must be aware of both general and self-space to avoid colliding with a teammate

Cross-Curricular Teaching Tips: Language Arts

Naming, defining, and giving the spelling of movement concepts and skills can aid language development (Buschner 1994). Enhance movement vocabulary by

- giving verbal instructions,
- offering and eliciting verbal descriptions of movement, and
- having students describe a movement or sequence of movements in writing.

Table 7.2   Movement Concepts for Body Awareness

Content areas	Descriptors/cues
Body parts	Head, shoulders, torso, arms, legs, toes, and others
Shapes	
Curved	Round like a tire
Twisted	Part of the body remains still while another part turns away from it, like a pretzel
Narrow	Arms and legs are close together and look thin
Wide	Arms and legs are stretched out
Symmetrical	If you cut your body in two, both sides would be the same
Asymmetrical	If you cut your body in two, both sides would look different
Base of support	Balance and support of the body's weight
Nonlocomotor	
Swing	Big, free, rhythmic movements of the body part(s)
Sway	A controlled swing using smaller movements, side to side or front to back
Twist	See above
Turn	Circular movement of the body or parts; quarter, half, three-quarter, 360 degrees or full
Bend/curl	Flexing, closing the body up, bringing body parts together
Stretch	Extending your arms and legs away from torso
Sink	Gradually moving downward
Push	Moving an object away from you
Pull	Drawing an object toward you
Shake	Shivering; you feel an earthquake

Reprinted, by permission, from Buschner, C., 1994, *Teaching Children Movement Concepts and Skills*, (Champaign, IL: Human Kinetics), 25.

Table 7.3 Movement Concepts for Space Awareness

Content areas	Descriptors/cues
General space	The empty or open space other than one's personal space
Self-space	The space in the immediate area where you don't touch anyone or anything
Directions	
Forward	The front of your body leads
Backward	The back of your body leads
Sideways	Your right or left side leads
Up	Your body goes toward the sky
Down	Your body goes toward the ground
Levels	
Low	Below the waist
Middle	Between the shoulders and waist
High	Above the shoulders
Pathways	
Curved	Bent line
Straight	Same direction, no curve or bend
Zigzag	Straight lines with sharp turns
Extensions	
Near	Arms and legs move a little from the body
Far	Arms and legs move away from body

Reprinted, by permission, from Buschner, C., 1994, *Teaching Children Movement Concepts and Skills*, (Champaign, IL: Human Kinetics), 26.

and to move in a game, sport, or dance. Space awareness also involves directions, levels, pathways, and extensions. Table 7.3 lists the content areas and descriptors and cues for the concept of space awareness (Buschner 1994).

Effort: How the Body Moves

Effort involves the speed, force, and flow of the moving body. For example, to control force, you must know how to efficiently tense and relax the muscles. Effort is also sometimes called the "quality" of the movement. Table 7.4 lists the content areas and helpful descriptors and cues for the concept of effort (Buschner 1994).

Relationships: With What or Whom the Body Moves

Children need to understand the relationship of their bodies to objects and other people. For example, children who understand relationship concepts notice the position of a hoop in relation to the arms and legs or of the body in relation to lines on the gym floor or to a partner or several teammates. In

Table 7.4 Movement Concepts for Effort

Content areas	Descriptors/cues
Speed	
Fast	Quick; sudden; explosive; aerobic; muscles tight
Slow	Careful; drawn out; sustained; aerobic; muscles relaxed
Force	
Strong	Strong; intense; heavy; muscles tight or tense
Light	Easy; weak; buoyant; slight; muscles loosened up
Flow	
Bound	Controlled; jerky; robotic; restricted; muscles tight
Free	Smooth; fluid; continuous; muscles move easily

Reprinted, by permission, from Buschner, C., 1994, *Teaching Children Movement Concepts and Skills*, (Champaign, IL: Human Kinetics), 26.

Cross-Curricular Teaching Tips: Art

Use art to reinforce movement concepts:

- Have partners draw each other on butcher paper (Buschner 1994); this emphasizes awareness of the various body parts and their relationships to one another—at least in two-dimensional space. Encourage creative poses.

- Have children mirror each other by physically replicating what their eyes see as an artist must.

- Have students paint while accompanied by slow then fast music.

- Have students draw themselves or a partner performing a favorite physical activity. Or have them draw an animal whose movements they admire.

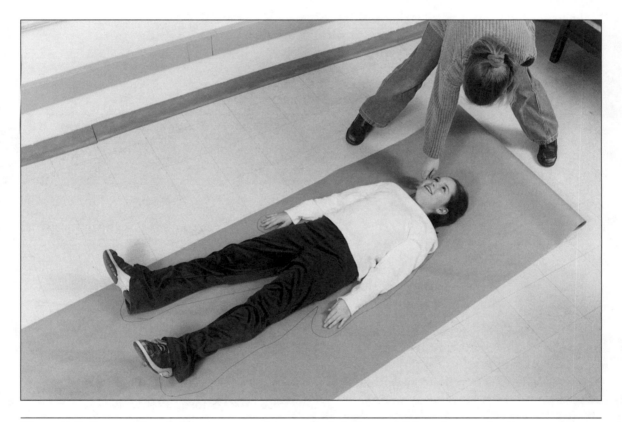

Figure 7.3 One way to reinforce movement concepts is to have children draw each other.

addition, these children understand and anticipate that these relationships are dynamic, or always changing. A child who does not understand relationship concepts will find advanced games, sports, dance, and exercises very difficult. Table 7.5 lists the content areas for the concept of relationships and helpful cues you can use (Buschner 1994). Begin with relationships to objects before working on relationships to other people because objects are less dynamic than people.

Motor Skills

Both locomotor and manipulative patterns comprise what we call "motor skills." Let's look closely, now, at each basic locomotor and manipulative pattern.

Table 7.5 Movement Concepts for Relationships

Content areas	Examples of cues
Objects or others	
Between/inside/outside	Find a way to move inside the hoop.
Around/through	Circle around your partner to catch the ball.
In front of/behind/beside	Place your body beside the target.
Under/over	Move your body under the rope.
On/off	Jump on the box and roll off.
Across	Travel across the mat; you choose the way.
Above/below	Strike the balloon above your head; now hit it below your knees.
Partners	
Leading	Run ahead of and lead your partner.
Following	Slide behind and follow your partner.
Meeting	Move toward the net when striking.
Parting	Move away from your partner.
Matching	Skip in unison, side-by-side to match your partner.
Mirroring	Perform opposite movements with your partner, like being a mirror.

Reprinted, by permission, from Buschner, C., 1994, *Teaching Children Movement Concepts and Skills*, (Champaign, IL: Human Kinetics), 27.

Locomotor Patterns

Although we may take these modes of getting from point A to point B for granted, a child must learn to perform them correctly and therefore efficiently so she can effectively apply them to real-world movement settings. In this section, we'll define each locomotor pattern, provide practice challenges and teaching tips, and list movement combinations and applications.

Buschner (1994) defines each of the following locomotor patterns:

- **Walking**—Walking is placing one foot in front of the other (called "weight transfer") while keeping one foot in contact with the ground at all times (see figure 7.4). The heel contacts the ground first, transfers the body weight to the middle of the foot, and then to the ball of the foot.

- **Running and jogging**—Running and jogging are like walking, but both add a period of suspension (both feet off the ground at the same time), while leaning forward farther and bending the knee higher (see figure 7.5). Jogging involves the same foot placement as walking (heel, midfoot, ball of foot). But sprinting involves running on the balls of the feet for short distances (less than

200 yards). And, obviously, running is faster than jogging.

- **Jumping and landing**—Three ways to jump are to (1) take off with two feet and land on two feet (see figure 7.6), (2) take off with one foot and land on two feet, and (3) take off with two feet and land on one foot. Landing should occur in toe-ball-heel order, with the heel coming all the way down. The knee or knees should bend to absorb the shock of the landing.

- **Sliding**—This pattern combines a step and run to change direction quickly (see figure 7.7). An efficient slide moves from side to side, with the same foot always leading the movement.

- **Galloping**—Galloping is similar to sliding, but one foot leads and the other follows, moving forward (see figure 7.8). Galloping is a clever way to change direction.

- **Leaping**—This pattern is an exaggerated run, in which the individual transfers weight from one foot to the other but with a period of suspension (see figure 7.9). Simply put, leaping is taking off with one foot and landing on the other.

- **Hopping**—This pattern involves taking off with one foot and landing on the ball

Figure 7.4 Mature walking pattern.
Reprinted, by permission, from Buschner, C., 1994, *Teaching Children Movement Concepts and Skills*, (Champaign, IL: Human Kinetics), 27.

Figure 7.5 Mature running pattern.
Reprinted, by permission, from Buschner, C., 1994, *Teaching Children Movement Concepts and Skills*, (Champaign, IL: Human Kinetics), 28.

Figure 7.6 Mature jumping pattern.
Reprinted, by permission, from Buschner, C., 1994, *Teaching Children Movement Concepts and Skills*, (Champaign, IL: Human Kinetics), 28.

Figure 7.7 Mature sliding pattern.
Reprinted, by permission, from Buschner, C., 1994, *Teaching Children Movement Concepts and Skills*, (Champaign, IL: Human Kinetics), 29.

Figure 7.8 Mature galloping pattern.
Reprinted, by permission, from Buschner, C., 1994, *Teaching Children Movement Concepts and Skills*, (Champaign, IL: Human Kinetics), 30.

of the same foot, keeping the knee of the inactive leg bent behind the body and using the arms to help gain height, distance, and balance (see figure 7.10).

- **Skipping**—This combines a step and hop using one side of the body, then the other side (see figure 7.11).

- **Chasing, fleeing, dodging, and faking**—These movements are combinations of the previous eight locomotor patterns, and children must learn to decide which is best to use in which situations. Chasing is attempting to overtake a moving person or object; fleeing is avoiding a chaser; dodging is changing direction; and faking is trying to deceive someone by moving the shoulders,

Figure 7.9 Mature leaping pattern.
Reprinted, by permission, from Buschner, C., 1994, *Teaching Children Movement Concepts and Skills*, (Champaign, IL: Human Kinetics), 30.

Figure 7.10 Mature hopping pattern.
Reprinted, by permission, from Buschner, C., 1994, *Teaching Children Movement Concepts and Skills*, (Champaign, IL: Human Kinetics), 31.

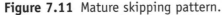

Figure 7.11 Mature skipping pattern.
Reprinted, by permission, from Buschner, C., 1994, *Teaching Children Movement Concepts and Skills*, (Champaign, IL: Human Kinetics), 31.

head, eyes, or other body parts (see figure 7.12).

Manipulative Patterns

Using your hands or feet to manipulate an object is one of the hardest skills you can learn. Yet children love to, so you can build on this natural enthusiasm if you include ample chances for success. In general, ensure success by providing equipment that is

- smaller for throwing,
- larger for catching,
- soft enough to prevent fear of injury, and
- plentiful enough so that each child or pair has one object.

This last point deserves further emphasis: In the classroom, we would never expect stu-

dents to stay on-task—let alone learn maximally—if they didn't have their own pencils. So let's not expect more than two children to share a manipulative object in physical education! (See chapter 18 for creative suggestions for finding or making equipment.)

The following lists and defines each main type of manipulative pattern (Buschner 1994):

- **Throwing**—There are three basic throws (in order of least to most difficult): underhand, overhand, and sidearm. A child should face the target for the underhand throw and turn the side of the body toward the target for the overhand and sidearm throw (left side if the child is right-handed). A backswing of the throwing arm helps all three throws. To throw proficiently,

Figure 7.12 Mature chasing, dodging, and faking patterns.
Reprinted, by permission, from Buschner, C., 1994, *Teaching Children Movement Concepts and Skills*, (Champaign, IL: Human Kinetics), 32.

1. lead each throw with the elbow away from the body;

2. transfer the weight from the back foot to the front foot, twisting at the hips;

3. step with the foot opposite the throwing hand; and

4. follow through or extend the arm toward the target (see figures 7.13, 7.14, and 7.15).

• **Catching**—To catch proficiently,

1. make eye contact with the ball (the most often forgotten pointer),

2. move toward the object,

3. catch with the hands (instead of the body),

4. bend the arms and relax the fingers, and

5. absorb the ball by "giving" with the ball (pulling hands into the body) or taking a step backward.

See figure 7.16.

• **Striking**—For a proficient strike, an individual

1. turns one side of the body toward the object, preparing for a backswing;

2. shifts the body weight from back to front foot;

3. twists the trunk; and

4. keeps the striking arm and leg opposed, extending the arm upon contact with the object.

In addition, the striker keeps the knees bent, keeps a solid grip on the striking implement, makes contact with the

Figure 7.13 Mature underhand throw.
Reprinted, by permission, from Buschner, C., 1994, *Teaching Children Movement Concepts and Skills*, (Champaign, IL: Human Kinetics), 33.

Figure 7.14 Mature overhand throw.
Reprinted, by permission, from Buschner, C., 1994, *Teaching Children Movement Concepts and Skills*, (Champaign, IL: Human Kinetics), 33.

Figure 7.15 Mature sidearm throw.
Reprinted, by permission, from Buschner, C., 1994, *Teaching Children Movement Concepts and Skills*, (Champaign, IL: Human Kinetics), 34.

center of the striking implement, and swings along a level horizontal or vertical plane. (See figure 7.17.)

- **Volleying**—This is a specialized striking skill, which can be done overhand or underhand with the hand, head, knee, or foot. Remind children to bend their knees and keep their wrists stiff, contact

the object solidly enough to control the direction of the object, turn the body toward the object, and follow through with the striking body part (see figure 7.18).

- **Dribbling with the hands**—This manipulative pattern involves continuous bouncing or striking downward, with one or both hands. The child should

Figure 7.16 Mature catching.
Reprinted, by permission, from Buschner, C., 1994, *Teaching Children Movement Concepts and Skills*, (Champaign, IL: Human Kinetics), 34.

Figure 7.17 Mature striking pattern.
Reprinted, by permission, from Buschner, C., 1994, *Teaching Children Movement Concepts and Skills*, (Champaign, IL: Human Kinetics), 35.

- push rather than slap the ball,
- keep the wrists firm but flexible,
- bounce the ball waist-high,
- create a consistent force and rhythm,
- maintain good body balance,
- lean the body slightly forward,
- keep the knees bent, and
- refrain from looking at the ball.

(See figure 7.19.)

- **Kicking, dribbling with the feet, and punting**—A good kick follows the patterns of throwing and striking, that is, it is a whole-body movement. To kick effectively,

  - lead the kicking motion with the hip while bending the support leg and leaning the trunk back slightly, and

  - contact the ball slightly below its center, using the inside of the foot for

Figure 7.18 Mature volleying.
Reprinted, by permission, from Buschner, C., 1994, *Teaching Children Movement Concepts and Skills*, (Champaign, IL: Human Kinetics), 35.

Figure 7.19 Mature dribbling pattern.
Reprinted, by permission, from Buschner, C., 1994, *Teaching Children Movement Concepts and Skills*, (Champaign, IL: Human Kinetics), 36.

short kicks and the instep (shoelace-area), not the toes, for long kicks.

Dribbling with the feet and punting are more complex variations of kicking. (See figures 7.20, 7.21, and 7.22.)

Movement Skills and Concepts: Instructional Strategies

Although we have outlined basic instructional strategies for you to use in the physi-cal education setting, here we will give you tips specific to the teaching of movement skills and concepts. We'll describe how to organize the teaching-learning environment, adjust activities for the individual, and encourage problem solving. Refer to chapter 5 as well.

Organizing the Teaching-Learning Environment

Create motor tasks that challenge children, but that do not frustrate them. To do so, arrange tasks from simple to complex and allow for each child's unique style while striving

Figure 7.20 Mature kicking.
Reprinted, by permission, from Buschner, C., 1994, *Teaching Children Movement Concepts and Skills*, (Champaign, IL: Human Kinetics), 36.

Figure 7.21 Mature dribbling with the feet.
Reprinted, by permission, from Buschner, C., 1994, *Teaching Children Movement Concepts and Skills*, (Champaign, IL: Human Kinetics), 37.

for mastery. As you increase motor demands, increase mental challenges. For example, have students work with more people to challenge their minds (work alone, then with a partner, then, finally, with a small group). In general, keep the following organizational principles in mind when teaching movement skills and concepts (Buschner 1994):

- Focus on only one part or segment of a movement at a time, a learnable piece (see tables 7.6 and 7.7). Give feedback

Figure 7.22 Mature punting.
Reprinted, by permission, from Buschner, C., 1994, *Teaching Children Movement Concepts and Skills*, (Champaign, IL: Human Kinetics), 37.

only on the learnable piece. Not only does this help children learn, but it also helps them feel successful.

- Incorporate more than one locomotor pattern per lesson so as not to overly tire the children.

- Insist that children listen as they move, communicating only when necessary.

- Use a mass formation to teach motor skills because lines and squads limit spatial awareness and movement options.

- Whenever possible use partner and small group work; stations and centers help develop social and cooperative skills because students help one another learn.

Tables 7.6 and 7.7 offer summaries of learnable pieces for each motor skill, teaching tips, and common movement combinations and applications. Note that the locomotor and manipulative patterns are listed roughly in order of least to most difficult. In addition, use the information concerning common applications to help you show children how to connect their physical education learning to the real world, not as a suggestion that they should participate in advanced activities before they're ready.

Adjusting for Individual Needs

The following lists ways to tailor your movement skills and concepts lessons to individual needs (Buschner 1994):

Cross-Curricular Teaching Tips: Art

Younger students with cognitive challenges might benefit from art projects that reinforce the vocabulary of the movement language. The following are a few ideas to get you started:

- Make fingerprint pictures with tempera paint or ink to emphasize the need to use fingerpads only with dribbling with the hands. Have students "dribble" their hands across a large sheet of paper.

- Use crayons or markers on paper or chalk on asphalt to draw pathways (zigzagging, curved, and so on).

- Glue small objects on paper (e.g., large seeds, buttons) to show "people" staying in personal space or not.

- Make collages of magazine pictures of sports figures applying the basic movement skills and concepts.

- Share and discuss activities as a class. As additional benefits, your students will both get valuable public speaking practice and increase their general vocabulary power.

Table 7.6 Teaching Locomotor Patterns

Locomotor pattern	Learnable pieces	Combine with	Sample real-world applications	Teaching tips
Walking	Swing your arms in opposition to your legs. Keep your feet pointed straight ahead as you walk along straight lines. Stay relaxed. Keep your head erect and shoulders straight.		Physical fitness pursuits Activities of daily living Warm-ups and cool-downs March-walk in step aerobics	Encourage children to use a fluid and relaxed walk.
Running and jogging	Keep arms and legs in opposition. Keep arms and upper body relaxed. When sprinting, stay on the balls of your feet. When jogging, follow walking sequence: heel, midfoot, ball of foot.	Almost every manipulative and locomotor pattern	Games Sports Physical fitness pursuits Low organization games Aerobics Outdoor play at home	Help children choose and use the correct technique (sprinting versus jogging), depending on the activity.
Jumping and landing	Take off from the ball of your foot; land either the same or differently. Use your arms while jumping and landing (swinging up and forward). Practice buoyant landings. Vary knee bends for landing.	Hopping Sliding Dodging Leaping	Jumping rope for cardiovascular fitness Gymnastics sequences Basketball Volleyball Other games and sports Step aerobics	Have children practice all three forms extensively. Have children use a short run to increase height and distance. Emphasize swinging the arms for height and distance, bending the knees to land, and landing on the ball of the foot.
Sliding	Stay on the balls of your feet. Try extending your arms and legs, near and far, when sliding.	Galloping Leaping Jumping Each manipulative skill	Most sports Dance Aerobics Slide aerobics	Dispel the common myth that sliding means diving on the ground feet first because this is dangerous.

(continued)

Table 7.6 *(continued)*

Locomotor pattern	Learnable pieces	Combine with	Sample real-world applications	Teaching tips
Sliding *(continued)*	Bend your knees while sliding. Swing your arms to gain speed while sliding.			Check to be sure the same foot leads until you signal practicing leading with the other foot.
Galloping	Lead with your right foot, then the left. Bend your knees to absorb force when you're moving quickly. Stay on the balls of your feet. Maintain a smooth, rhythmic motion.	Running Leaping Jumping	Fencing Many other sports and games	Once they have practiced with the dominant foot, encourage children to lead with the nondominant foot.
Leaping	Stretch your legs as wide as possible while you're airborne. Create momentum by swinging your arms. To help you take off and fly longer, bend your knees. Practice landing on the ball of your right foot and then on your left.	Running Sliding, galloping, then leaping	Dance Hurdles Football Other games and sports Outdoor play at home	Emphasize vertical lift, created by bending the knees, vigorously swinging the arms, and landing on the ball of the foot. Ensure that children do not confuse with jumping or hopping.
Hopping	Practice on each foot, in turn, then alternate your feet rhythmically. To take off and land, stay on the ball of your foot. Create momentum by swinging your arms. Flex your ankles and bend your knees.	Any other loco-motor skill	Aerobics Hopscotch Outdoor play at home Step aerobics	The child who cannot balance on one foot will have more trouble hopping than the one who can. Hopping is quite tiring, so (1) have children hop forward instead of upward and (2) alternate with other activities.

Locomotor pattern	Learnable pieces	Combine with	Sample real-world applications	Teaching tips
Skipping	Keep your arms in opposition to legs. Stay up on the balls of your feet. Keep your arms and upper body relaxed. Try skipping to a beat.	More vigorous forms of locomotion as a "breather" Music	Warm-ups and cool-downs Dance Outdoor play at home	Commonly difficult at primary level; skipping on one side is a normal developmental stage. Have a proficient child demonstrate. Try holding child's hand while skipping with him.
Chasing, fleeing, dodging, and faking	Try making quick pathway and directional changes while traveling. Watch a partner's waist while chasing her. Change speeds while fleeing from a partner. Make quick movements while traveling to fake your partner.	Most other loco-motor and manipulative patterns	Most team sports Outdoor play at home Low organization games	Have students practice each individually, then in combinations. Explain that the head should lead each action and the body should follow.

Adapted, by permission, from Buschner, C., 1994, *Teaching Children Movement Concepts and Skills*, (Champaign, IL: Human Kinetics) and Pica, R., 1995.

- Attempting a motor skill is different from learning it. Children need practice applying each skill in a variety of situations to truly master it.
- Plan for the fact that synchronizing the legs and arms to hop, skip, jump, leap, and slide takes a *lot* of practice. Be sure everyone gets this practice.
- Have children advanced in a motor skill use mental imagery before and during the movement to reinforce it.
- Challenge students who have mastered a basic manipulative skill to try using their nondominant hand or foot (e.g., kicking, throwing, catching, striking) and to lead with both sides of the body for hopping, galloping, and leaping.
- Teach movement concepts in the context of teaching motor skills. For example, when working on the locomotor skill of skipping, have students work on using general space safely. Or, when working on the manipulative skill of throwing, focus on the effort concept of force (strong or light).
- Encourage children to compete only with themselves, not their classmates, especially when learning something new. Even with these basics, champion the idea of "personal best."

Table 7.7 Teaching Manipulative Patterns

Manipulative pattern	Learnable pieces	Combine with	Real-world applications	Teaching tips
Throwing	Turn your body correctly in relation to the target (face it for underhand; sideways for sidearm and overhand). Place the leg opposite your throwing-arm side forward. Shift your body weight from the back foot to the front foot. Point your fingers toward the target to help you follow through to the target.	Catching Running Jumping Leaping Sliding	Many team and individual games and sports	Emphasize using the whole body, not only the shoulder, arm, and hand. Have advanced children add a step and sideways hop at the beginning of a throw to create greater force.
Catching	Move to the object from all directions. Watch the object all the way to your hands to judge where it will land. Relax your hands and arms upon impact. Work on hand positions for both low- and high-level catches.	Throwing Kicking Striking Dribbling Volleying	Many games and sports	Encourage children to keep pinkie fingers together for low catches (below the waist) and thumbs together for high catches. Emphasize keeping an eye on the object and moving toward it. Use light, colorful, and soft equipment until proficiency develops. Group good throwers with poor catchers or use the wall and catch on rebound.
Striking	Turn your hips and shift your body weight. Keep your wrist and elbow firm with short implements. Always follow through toward the target.	Jumping, running	Racket sports Baseball	You'll probably note great variation in striking abilities as this is a very difficult skill. Encourage a free, swinging movement (free flow, an effort concept).

Manipulative pattern	Learnable pieces	Combine with	Real-world applications	Teaching tips
Striking (continued)	Turn the side of your striking arm toward the object; step toward the object to swing.			Striking implements (hands, rackets, paddles, bats, clubs, sticks) can be short or long, but their weight and length should be appropriate to the children.
Volleying	Try stepping forward with your opposite foot and volleying. Move under the ball. Point the striking body toward the target. Bend your knees throughout the movement to keep your legs ready for action.	Striking practice	Volleyball Tennis and other racket sports Table tennis	Point out how striking and volleying are related.
Dribbling with the hands	For better control, use the fingerpads of your hand. Keep your head up and eyes looking right and left. Push with your arm and hand; don't slap. Keep the ball away from your feet but close to your body.	Walking Running Other locomotor patterns	Basketball Games children invent	Emphasize pushing rather than slapping the ball. Challenge advanced students to vary force and level.
Kicking, dribbling with the feet, and punting	Step into the kick, first with one step, then two. Contact the ball with your instep (shoelace area). Make your kicking foot follow through until high and toward the target. Keep your eyes on the ball and contact it below its center.	Running	Football Soccer Games children invent	Emphasize kicking with the shoelace area for distance or the inside of the foot for shorter kicks. Use plastic milk jugs or deflated balls to increase success and decrease retrieval time. Skip while dribbling with the feet to learn alternation of feet.

Adapted, by permission, from Buschner, C., 1994, *Teaching Children Movement Concepts and Skills*, (Champaign, IL: Human Kinetics) and Pica, R., 1995.

- Use individualized task sheets. These guide students by helping them focus on learnable pieces of the skill or concept.
- Teach by invitation, allowing children to choose their own level of difficulty (see chapter 5). Here are a few ideas specific to this area:
  —Allow students to choose to jump rope one, two, or three times consecutively.
  —Offer high, medium, and low baskets for shooting baskets and allow students to choose which one to aim for.
  —Allow students to choose a form of locomotion (e.g., run or skip) and move their at own comfortable speed.
- Devise intratask variations; after allowing children to become familiar with a basic task, add a new aspect to it that creates interest without making the task noticeably harder. For example,
  —work on locomotor skills without, then with, music;
  —dribble a ball without, then to, music;
  —throw to a different target (e.g., into a box instead of at a paper target on a wall); and
  —make general space smaller when traveling, chasing, fleeing, or dodging.

Encouraging Problem Solving in Movement Skills and Concepts

Discuss and then apply possible movement combinations with the children when they're ready (Buschner 1994). Encouraging children to think about movement enhances movement literacy. The following is a list of possible combinations and movement challenges to practice problem solving in this physical education area:

Cross-Curricular Teaching Tips: Music

According to Buschner (1994), music helps children "become more aware of the internal body, giving them a sense of internal timing and the underlying rhythm and beat for various movements." Integrate music by

- using a drum, metronome, or music to enhance sustained and deliberate movements when emphasizing speed (part of effort),
- playing soft music for tiptoeing and loud music for stamping (varying force),
- playing a game of statues (moving while music is playing and freezing when it stops) to reinforce the concept of bound movement, and
- accompanying skills with uneven rhythms (e.g., galloping and skipping) with appropriate music or drumbeat.

COMPONENT— *Development of Movement Concepts and Motor Skills*

Appropriate Practice	Inappropriate Practice
Children are provided with frequent and meaningful age-appropriate practice opportunities that enable individuals to develop a functional understanding of movement concepts . . . and build competence and confidence in their ability to perform a variety of motor skills. . . .	Children participate in a limited number of games and activities where the opportunity for individual children to develop basic concepts and motor skills is restricted. Reprinted from COPEC/NASPE 1992.

COMPONENT—
Cognitive Development

Appropriate Practice	Inappropriate Practice
Physical education activities are designed with both the physical and the cognitive development of children in mind.	Instructors fail to recognize and explore the unique role of physical education, a role that allows children to learn to move while also moving to learn. Reprinted from COPEC/NASPE 1992.

- Add on to an action, such as shake one body part, shake one body part and twist one body part, and so on.

- Move a prop, such as a streamer, in the opposite direction or at another level; for example, move the body high and the streamer low. Add traveling.

- Creative imagery can be a big help in teaching the movement concepts (Buschner 1994). Create or have the children create mental images of what they're doing. For example, instead of asking students to move with bound (interrupted) versus free flow (e.g., illustrating effort concepts), ask them to move like a robot, then a butterfly. Use the descriptors and cues in tables 7.2-7.5 to help you start thinking about how to create the image that will help your particular students.

Planning Movement Skill and Concept Units and Lessons

You should keep the guidelines from the Council on Physical Education for Children (COPEC 1992) in mind as you plan movement skill and concept units and lessons (see sidebars on this and the next page).

Of course, whatever you plan, learning must take place in a "supportive, motivating, and progressive manner" (COPEC 1992) in which all children are continually involved with physical activity at their own individual ability levels.

Setting Priorities

Table 7.1 (page 85) lists several motor skills and 15 basic movement concepts, plus subconcepts. Given time constraints, how should you prioritize when planning your curriculum? The answer depends on your students' level of experience. In general, you should consider students in kindergarten through third grade to be inexperienced no matter their physical education background. With intermediate level students, you should carefully note the type of program they have experienced before joining your class. If they have been in a developmentally appropriate, progressive curriculum since kindergarten (which has been taught consistently), you may be able to consider such a class as experienced. If not, however, you should consider the class to be inexperienced and plan core content as you would for primary level students.

With an inexperienced class, it is best to teach motor skills in isolation and spend extra time stressing the movement concepts, before adding simple combinations. Buschner (1994) offers these tips for planning units and lessons for students inexperienced in movement skills and concepts. In general,

- address the whole class for instruction,

- use the gym wall as a partner as much as possible so that all children are participating maximally,

- make fewer classwide equipment changes so as not to waste class time,

- demonstrate motor skills more often,

- refrain from moving on to combinations before individual skills are mastered, and

- rely heavily on pinpointing, which is selecting two or more children to demonstrate motor skills, emphasizing what they're doing right (Graham 1992; see also chapters 4 and 5).

To this list, we add the following:

- In an approach similar to providing high interest, low vocabulary books for older students in remedial reading groups, make sure you adapt lessons for intermediate level students so that even though you are teaching very basic skills, you are meeting their emotional and social needs. For example, for dribbling practice, use basketballs instead of oversized playground balls, and emphasize helping one another succeed through more peer assessment and problem-solving challenges than you might with younger students (see also chapter 5).

For more experienced students, Buschner (1994) recommends the following. In general,

- work more quickly through learning or reviewing the motor skills,

- integrate movement concepts with more refined motor skills (e.g., the basic throw is similar to the motions used in a tennis serve and the overhead shot in badminton),

- use more combinations of movement concepts and motor skills,

- eventually put the combinations students have mastered into movement sequences that resemble the actions they will use for complex movements in games, sports, gymnastics, and the like, and

- plan to have children who demonstrate more mature movement patterns learn through the play-teach-play method for which you periodically stop the action (e.g., in a game) to cue students in such a way as to refine their learning, then allow them to return to play (Graham 1992).

Thus, your plans should depend on how proficient your students are in the movement language. Tables 7.8 and 7.9 list primary and secondary movement words, respectively, to help you further prioritize.

Creating Variety

As in any other subject area within and outside of physical education, varying teaching methods and types of activities helps keep students interested, motivated, and therefore on-task. Graham (1992) and Buschner (1994) recommend the following approaches:

- Videotaping
- Individualized task sheets
- Teaching by invitation
- Devising intratask variations
- Providing ways for children to experiment with problem-solving challenges

Table 7.8   Primary Alphabet

Body awareness	Space awareness	Effort	Relationships	Locomotor patterns	Manipulative patterns
Body parts	General space	Force	Objects or others	Jogging/ running	Throwing
Shapes	Self-space				Catching
Nonlocomotor movements	Directions			Leaping	Kicking
Twist and turn	Levels			Jumping and landing	Striking
Bend and curl				Sliding	

Reprinted, by permission, from Buschner, C., 1994, *Teaching Children Movement Concepts and Skills*, (Champaign, IL: Human Kinetics), 18.

Table 7.9   Secondary Alphabet

Body awareness	Space awareness	Effort	Relationships	Locomotor patterns	Manipulative patterns
Nonlocomotor movements	Pathways	Speed	Partner	Walking	Punting
Swing and sway	Extensions	Flow		Hopping	Dribbling with feet
Stretch				Skipping	Dribbling with hands
Sink				Galloping	Volleying
Push and pull				Chasing	
Shake				Dodging	
				Fleeing	

Reprinted, by permission, from Buschner, C., 1994, *Teaching Children Movement Concepts and Skills*, (Champaign, IL: Human Kinetics), 18.

Refer often to the instructional strategies listed earlier in this chapter to ensure that you are offering enough variety.

Double-Checking Your Plans

Buschner (1994) offers the following helpful checklist for planning movement skill and concept lessons. Use it to ensure that each lesson in a unit will help students reach the unit's goals and objectives.

✓ What movement concept and/or motor skill will I teach today?

✓ How does today's theme coincide with NASPE's outcomes of a physically educated person (see chapter 1), the curriculum, . . . and tomorrow's lesson?

✓ What learnable piece will I focus on?

✓ What will I say to give specific and useful feedback to children?

✓ How will I modify tasks to accommodate individual children?

✓ Have I arranged for a visual model(s) of the movement concept or motor skill?

✓ What will I say and do to stress good movement?

✓ How many practice opportunities will there be for each child for each skill?

✓ Will at least 85 percent (about 21 of 25) of the children be engaged in the concept or skill?

✓ Will I emphasize process or product today?

✓ How will I tie together what the children learn in class today?

You can adapt this checklist to any type of lesson, but it is especially important for movement concept and skill lessons because these are the foundation of the rest of the curriculum.

Assessing Movement Skill and Concept Learning

To assess movement concepts and skills, you can use the learnable pieces, teaching tips, descriptors, and cues listed in tables 7.2 through 7.7 to create performance checklists. Figures 7.23 and 7.24 are examples of two such checklists. In addition, you can use a task sheet as a rubric to have students assess themselves or one another. Finally, figures 7.25 and 7.26 show how to check for cognitive and affective development, respectively.

Summary

When teaching movement concepts and skills, keep in mind that the process is more important than the product. Giving children a movement language will enhance their physical education learning, no matter the physical education content area they are studying. To this end, use the same terminology whenever possible when teaching other topics. Moreover, work to ensure that

Date _5/5_____   Class _Mr. Wheeler_____   Grade _5th_____

Directions: Observe each child jumping and landing at least five times. Check the learnable piece(s) used by the child in attempting a mature pattern. C = consistently demonstrates this learnable piece; O = occasionally uses this learnable piece; N = never uses this learnable piece.

		Learnable pieces				
Names of children	Trials	Takeoff (ball)	Knees (bend)	Arms (strong)	Land (buoyant)	Land (ball)
1. Traci	ℍℍ	C	C	C	O	O
2. Bryan	ℍℍ II	C	O	C	N	N
3. Jeff	ℍℍ	N	N	O	N	N
4. Brett	ℍℍ III	C	C	C	C	C
5. Crystal	ℍℍ I	O	O	O	N	O

Figure 7.23 Jumping and landing checklist.
Reprinted, by permission, from Buschner, C., 1994, *Teaching Children Movement Concepts and Skills*, (Champaign, IL: Human Kinetics), 50.

Date _4/14_____   Class _Mr. Duffy_____   Grade _4th_____

Directions: Observe each child performing an appropriate task that emphasizes a motor skill(s). This record can be compared from year to year. The teacher should establish criteria for assessing the child's level of learning. For example: B = beginning level (initial attempts at the motor skill that result in an inconsistent pattern or learning product); T = transitional (the child is beginning to control his/her body and/or the object; however, the child expends great energy thinking through and performing the movement); M = mature pattern (a good quality movement that can be applied in a variety of situations; the movement appears fluid and the child accomplishes the motor skill with minimal effort).

	Motor skills		
Names of children	Kicking 9/1/93	Striking 11/9/93	Running 12/6/93
Fred	B	T	T
Sally	T	T	M
Samuel	M	T	M
Natalie	B	B	B
Matilda	T	B	T

Figure 7.24 Developmental checklist.
Reprinted, by permission, from Buschner, C., 1994, *Teaching Children Movement Concepts and Skills*, (Champaign, IL: Human Kinetics), 51.

Understanding Kicking

Directions: Circle the best answer.

1. When learning to kick a ball, you should
   a. move only your legs
   b. step into the kick
   c. wait for the ball to hit your foot
   d. I don't know

2. When learning to become a better kicker, you should use the
   a. toe of the foot
   b. instep (shoe laces)
   c. heel of the foot
   d. I don't know

3. Watching the ball when kicking will
   a. improve your accuracy and direction
   b. prevent your foot from hitting the ground
   c. show that you follow teacher directions
   d. I don't know

4. When kicking for distance, you should "swing through," using the
   a. hip
   b. ankle
   c. knee
   d. I don't know

5. When punting, it is important to
   a. throw the ball in the air and kick it
   b. drop the ball slightly
   c. move your body forward very quickly
   d. I don't know

Figure 7.25 Multiple choice assessment. Reprinted, by permission, from Buschner, C., 1994, *Teaching Children Movement Concepts and Skills*, (Champaign, IL: Human Kinetics), 55.

Lesson Theme: Throwing and Catching

Directions: Circle or shade in the best answer.

1. Throwing and catching are my favorite skills.   Y N
2. Throwing is easy for me.   Y N
3. Practicing my catching is enjoyable.   Y N
4. I practice throwing in my free time.   Y N
5. Throwing will help me when I get older.   Y N
6. How do you feel about your ability to catch a ball?
7. How do you feel about your ability to throw a ball?
8. How do you feel about your ability to throw a ball under pressure?
9. When the ball is thrown to me in a game, I feel . . .
10. Learning to be good at throwing is important to me.

Figure 7.26 Affective paper-and-pencil survey. Reprinted, by permission, from Buschner, C., 1994, *Teaching Children Movement Concepts and Skills*, (Champaign, IL: Human Kinetics), 56.

children see the connections between the basic movement concepts and skills.

Sample Movement Concepts and Skills Lessons

The following are sample lessons in movement concepts and skills. Note that although a grade level or range is given, you can adapt a lesson to use with older or younger students, according to their needs.

The first lessons reprinted here by permission form a first grade games unit in *Physical Education Unit Plans for Grades 1-2* (Logsdon et al. 1997). As you will see, games units at this level should focus primarily on basic motor skills (in this case, dribbling, passing, and trapping with the feet) and basic movement concepts (in this case, moving through space safely). These lessons create a fun, gamelike atmosphere by providing appropriate challenges such as dribbling around cones and working with a partner. The following list shows the context in which this unit takes place as this particular program strives to cover basic skills in a systematic and enjoyable way:

Sample Unit Sequence for First Grade Games (Logsdon et al. 1997)

Unit 1
Dribbling, Passing, and Trapping

Dribbling, passing, and stopping a ball with the feet

Unit 2
Overhand Throw

Developing a forceful overhand throw with a small ball

Unit 3
Traveling and Stretching to Catch

Traveling and stretching to catch a ball

Unit 4
Tapping a Ball With the Hand

Tapping a bouncing ball with the hand(s)

Unit 5
Dribbling, Changing Directions, and Stopping

Dribbling with either hand, changing directions, and stopping

Unit 6
Throwing, Striking, and Kicking

Sharing self-selected throwing, striking, and kicking activities with others

Unit 7
Passing and Trapping

Passing and trapping a soccer ball
    Reprinted from Logsdon 1997.

Unit 1: Dribbling, Passing, and Trapping

3 to 5 lessons

Focus: **Dribbling, passing, and stopping a ball with the feet**

Motor Content

Introduction to Basic Body and Manipulative Control

Body

Manipulative activities—dribbling, passing, and stopping a ball with either foot

Objectives

In this unit, children will (or should be willing to try to) meet these objectives:

- Dribble, looking for empty spaces by taking short running steps and pushing the ball lightly with the feet to keep the ball close in front of them
- Place a supporting foot at the side of the ball with toes pointed toward the direction of the pass and swing the kicking leg toward the target
- Learn how to stop the ball by placing the bottom of the nonsupporting foot lightly at the back of the ball
- Avoid others while dribbling by looking for and traveling into empty spaces

Equipment and Materials

One 8.5-inch vinyl, foam, or partially deflated playground ball; traffic cones, beanbags, rubber disks, or plastic bottles for each child; receptacles for the balls

Learning Experiences

(If class is taught outdoors, be sure to mark off the working area with cones or other markers. Table 7.10 shows a sample assessment.)

1.0 Let's see if you can keep up with a ball as you dribble the ball by pushing it sometimes with one foot and then with the other. Stop the ball with one foot when you hear two claps. Carefully get a ball and begin to dribble with your feet, being very careful to avoid others. (Start and stop them many times, changing the length of time the children dribble before giving the stop signal.)

1.1 Try dribbling and stopping again. This time, take short running steps when dribbling. Push the ball very lightly with the inside and outside of your feet while looking for and traveling into empty spaces.

1.2 Stop the ball by placing the sole of your foot very gently on the back of the ball. (Demonstrate by placing the stopping foot behind the ball with your heel close to the ground and the sole wedging the ball between your foot and the ground. To prevent falling, place little or no weight on your stopping foot.)

1.3 Let's travel again and see if you can stop the ball quickly. Each time I clap, have your ball with you. (Check spacing often to develop and maintain a safe working environment.)

1.4 See if you can dribble into empty spaces for 30 seconds without letting your ball touch another ball or person. (Repeat several times.)

1.5 Now change your pathway each time I clap.

1.6 Everyone remember to stay on the balls of your feet and take quick, short running steps, pushing the ball lightly ahead of you. (Look for children who are staying on the balls of their feet and have them show the class how easily they can maneuver the ball.)

1.7 I just noticed (Christopher) lifting his arms out to his sides to help him keep good balance as he dribbles. Give it a try and see how your arms can help you be a better dribbler.

1.8 Running lightly on the balls of your feet and letting your arms help you balance, let's see if you can dribble into empty spaces for one minute without you or your ball touching anyone or another ball. (Repeat several times to sustain practice.)

2.0 (Place cones all about the space.) Dribble your ball about all the cones in the room without letting it touch anyone else, a cone, or another ball. Look for empty spaces as you dribble.

2.1 Each time you come to a cone, dribble around it. If necessary, stop the ball to keep it from touching the cone. Keep looking for an empty space and then dribble to a new cone.

2.2 Control your ball by staying close to your ball and pushing it with quick, short taps with different parts of your feet. You are the boss of your ball. Take the ball where

Figure 7.27 Proper foot placement for stopping the ball.

Reprinted, by permission, from Logsdon, B., 1997, *Physical Education Unit Plans for Grades 1-2*, (Champaign, IL: Human Kinetics), 3.

Table 7.10   Assessing Dribbling and Stopping Balls

Class list	Dribbles, pushing ball with either foot while running (scale, date)	Uses different parts of foot to stop ball (scale, date)	Points nonkicking foot in direction of intended pass (scale, date)	Aligns body to path of ball when receiving a pass (scale, date)
Ables, Chris	2 9/10 4 9/24	2 9/10	1 9/24	3 9/24
Brenning, Pat	5 9/10	4 9/10	3 9/24	5 9/24

Scale: 5 = consistently; 4 = two-thirds or more of the time; 3 = half of the time; 2 = one-third of the time; 1 = rarely or not at all.

Reprinted, by permission, from Logsdon, B., 1997, *Physical Education Unit Plans for Grades 1-2*, (Champaign, IL: Human Kinetics), 5.

you want to go rather than letting the ball take you where it wants to go.

2.3 You each have five points to start our game. Whenever your ball touches a cone or another ball, you lose one point. If you stop your ball with your foot or shin (touch shin) when I clap my hands, you add one point to your score.

2.4 This time, see if you can dribble your ball to one cone and, just as your ball is about to touch the cone, quickly change the direction of the ball. Sometimes change directions with your left foot and sometimes with your right foot.

2.5 This half of the class take a seat near the wall and observe the dribblers as they look for empty spaces. Observers, see if you can find dribblers who are looking for empty spaces and not bumping into other balls or classmates. (Be sure to give the observers something specific to observe.) Observers, who dribbled without bumping anyone? (Answer: Children who dribbled with their heads up and eyes looking for open spaces. Change roles several times.)

3.0 You are all controlling the ball and getting to be pretty good dribblers. Are you ready for another challenge? This time, try to pass the ball to the wall (or your partner) with the inside of your foot and stop it with any part of your foot. (If working with a partner, put one ball away and begin.)

3.1 Turn your passing foot sideways to contact the ball with the inside of your foot. Always stop the ball before you pass it back. (Have a child demonstrate.)

3.2 Swing the inside of your foot straight toward the wall (partner) after you contact the ball to help your pass go right where you aimed.

3.3 If one foot is getting good at passing, give your other foot practice so you can pass accurately with either foot.

3.4 Practice stopping the ball with different parts of your feet. Can you try using the inside, the outside, the bottom (sole), and the top (instep) of your feet?

3.5 Try pointing your supporting (non-kicking) foot in different directions as you pass the ball. Sometimes point it to the left and sometimes to the right. See how often your ball goes where the supporting foot points?

3.6 Count and see how many times you can send your ball to the wall (partner) and stop it when it comes back without chasing it or touching it with your hands.

4.0 If you have been practicing passing the ball to the wall, join with a partner now and put one ball away. Let's all find a good working space and pass the ball back and forth. Remember to stop the ball only with your feet.

4.1 Some of you are passing accurately. You are sending the ball right to the stopping foot of your partner. Let's see if everyone can pass the ball 10 times without touching it with their hands.

4.2 Receivers, move to a different place in your work space and see if your partner can send the ball straight to you each time.

4.3 If you want a greater challenge, ask your partner to pass the ball a little faster and see if you can still stop it with your foot.

4.4 Remember how you moved your feet quickly to get in front of the ball to catch it with your hands? Let's see if you can move quickly to get in front of the ball to stop it with your foot. Passers, send the ball to the side to make your receiver travel two or three steps to stop the ball.

4.5 Receivers, move quickly to get your body in front of the ball. Reach your foot out in front and wedge the ball between the sole of your foot and the floor to stop the ball. After you stop it, pass it straight back to the front of your receiver, making your kicking leg swing toward the spot where you are aiming.

4.6 Count the passes you and your partner complete while making each other travel a bit to receive each pass. Remember to control your passes to keep the ball in your own working space.

Reprinted from Logsdon 1997.

This final lesson, reprinted by permission from Buschner's *Teaching Children Movement Concepts and Skills* (1994), is most appropriate for third and fourth graders. Use the "How Can I Change This?" and "Teachable Moments" sections to help you extend this lesson into a complete unit. Use the "Look For" section to help you assess student understanding.

Leap for Life*

Objectives

As a result of participating in this learning experience, children will improve their ability to

- leap, taking off and landing on the ball of the foot;
- combine a run with a leap to hurdle an object; and
- rotate cooperatively among stations.

Suggested Grade Range

Intermediate (3rd-4th)

Organization

Two open playing areas for station work (set up before class) (figure 7.28), warm-up, activity, and closure

Equipment Needed

4 medium cones; 2 large cones or chairs for hurdles; extra cones to designate space; drum; 10 jump ropes; 10 hula hoops; chalk or tape to make pathways; 5 dowels; 4 small cones

Description

Find your self-space in our open area and show me you are ready by making a statue of a frozen runner. (Wait for children to make statues.) Great, You can relax now. You have been working as a whole class on running and leaping in different ways. Today you are going to work on running and leaping together. Who can tell me some of the things that are important for running? Good—lean your body forward. Yes, move your arms opposite to your legs and push off with the balls of the feet. Everyone show me which part is the ball of the foot. Great! Now who can tell me some of the things we need to remember when we leap? Yes, really spread your legs forward and backward to get more distance. Use your arms to create momentum and land on the opposite foot. Great, you know something about how to run and leap. Let's put the two together. Warm up now by running and leaping in general space. (Start signal; stop signal.)

Now leap, leading with the other foot. (Stop signal.) Now, each time you hear the drumbeat, leap once through the air. When you hear it two times, stop. (Practice; stop signal.) Great, I see that you can all run and leap keeping control and without bumping into others. Quickly find a partner and stand back-to-back. Now we will practice leaping over our friends. One person crouch down in a small ball, like a watermelon. The other partner, be very careful to leap all the way over your watermelon! On the signal your partner will practice leaping over you, taking off and landing on the ball of the foot, with a running start. When you hear the drum once, quickly change places. On two beats, stop. (Stop signal.) Any accidents? This time, run and leap over all the watermelons. Again, on one beat, those leaping will drop to the floor and become watermelons, and the watermelons will become leapers. (Switch a few times; stop signal.)

Now we will practice running and leaping in different ways, as far as we can, as high as we can, and using different pathways. Sit down with your partner for a moment, so I can show you the different stations you will try. (Model and explain each.) With the

---

*This learning experience was contributed by Rebecca Kaiser, an elementary/adapted specialist at Colusa County Schools, Colusa, California.

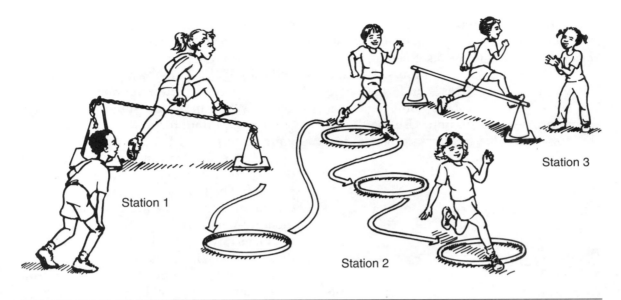

Figure 7.28 Stations for Leap for Life.
Reprinted, by permission, from Buschner, C., 1994, *Teaching Children Movement Concepts and Skills*, (Champaign, IL: Human Kinetics), 101.

slanted ropes, start at the small end and see if you can run and leap across to the greatest distance. With the cones and dowels, see if you can jump over the different heights. Find the one that is the most comfortable for you. Finally, run the pathways and leap over the hoops. Are there any questions? Yes, you will get to use all the stations, but don't change until you hear the signal to stop. Then I will give you directions where to go. Remember to wait your turn if someone is in front of you, and replace the equipment for the next person if you bump it. (Send pairs to a station to practice.) You may start as soon as you get to your equipment. (Practice five minutes; stop signal. Repeat rotation until children have worked on each of the three stations.)

You have done a great job of running and leaping. In a minute we will try putting the different ways together. First let's practice just running in general space where all the equipment is without bumping or touching any of it. Can you go over the equipment? No, that's right, because we are just practicing running—if we went over we would have to leap. (Stop signal.) Now let's try running and leaping over all the equipment. (Stop signal.) Why do you think it's important to take off and land on the ball of the foot? Yes, you then can spring up and absorb the force of landing. Now, try to find just three different pieces to

leap over as you run around the general space. (Stop signal.) Run and leap over your favorite equipment. (Stop signal.) Run and leap as *high* as you can over a piece of equipment. You can use any piece. (Stop signal.) Run and leap as far as you can along a rope or a pathway. You did wonderfully. I saw really high leaps, long leaps, and landing on the ball of the foot. Come sit down together in our open space.

When might you use a run and a leap together in a sport? How about in football, could you use it there? Yes—to run, leap, and catch a pass. How about in basketball? Good—to run and leap for a rebound. We also use the combination in some other sports, like running the hurdles in track. In this event you have to run as fast as you can over a whole bunch of obstacles in a row. Did anyone see this in the Summer Olympics? We also use running and leaping in dance, including ballet. Let's have a PE cheer before we go. Count in Spanish this time. *Uno, dos, tres!* (Everyone shouts together.) All right, PE! Get a drink if you need one, and then leap all the way back to class.

Look For

- Do the children stay on the balls of the feet for takeoff and landing?

- Can the children run and leap over successive objects at the same height? At different heights and distances?
- Are the children replacing equipment when they accidentally bump into it?

How Can I Change This?

- Try leaping in unison with a partner.
- Have one partner make a shape (e.g., wide, narrow) while the other leaps over.
- Run and leap in small groups.
- Run and leap, making a shape in the air.
- Run and leap with soft landings.
- Run and leap over a series of obstacles in a straight line.

- Combine running and leaping with catching.

Teachable Moments

Show a videotape of running with leaping in different sports. Have the children run and leap, and then measure their distances. Mark takeoff and landing, measuring the distance between the two marks. Have the children create running and leaping sequences to perform together with two or more other students. Have the children create their own obstacle courses for running and leaping patterns.

Reprinted from Buschner 1994.

Sarah, 4

Jamie, 8

Brooke, 12

Chapter **8**

Teaching Health–Related Physical Fitness and Physical Activity

The growing urbanization and mechanization of modern life have made it easier for us to become physically lazy and sedentary. We drive rather than walk; we take an elevator rather than climb stairs; we push a button on an electric dryer rather than bend down and reach up to hang clothes on a clothesline. Whereas exercise was once an inevitable part of living, today we must consciously plan to get the exercise needed to maintain good health.

—John Farquhar (1987)

An obvious benefit of physical education is physical fitness. Or can this be assumed? A recent survey reveals that although one in three children go to physical education class every day (grades 4 through 12), almost one in four do not have physical education at all, and fewer than one in four participate in vigorous physical activity for at least 20 minutes seven days a week. At the very best, physical education class time accounts for less than one and three-quarter hours of physical activity per week (ILSI 1997).

But you can improve this situation for your students. And more importantly, you can learn to teach health-related physical fitness and physical activity in such a way so as to

Benefits of Physical Activity

Physical activity leads to many benefits. It

- reduces the risk of heart disease, diabetes, and high blood pressure,

- promotes emotional wellness,

- enhances neural development,

- helps an individual perform non-physical activities better,

- saves society money through improved health,

- enhances skeletal health, muscular strength, and cardiorespiratory fitness,

- and improves posture.

(USDHHS 1996; 1999).

encourage children to seek a healthful, active lifestyle long after they leave your classroom. It's important to remember that fitness is temporary: becoming fit in class will not have lasting benefits if your students elect to be sedentary as adults. In this chapter, we'll examine the basic issues that affect the teaching of health-related physical fitness and physical activity, effective teaching strategies, appropriate ways to assess this area, and tips for planning effective fitness units and lessons.

Key Issues

First, it's important to understand the differences in the terms *health-related physical fitness*, *physical activity*, and *exercise*. Pratt (as quoted in USDHHS 1999) differentiates among these three terms: "In a nutshell, *physical activity* is something you *do*. *Physical fitness* is something you acquire—a characteristic or an attribute one can achieve by being physically active. *Exercise* is structured (physical activity) and tends to have fitness as its goal." A physically fit individual has enough energy and vitality to do daily tasks and pursue active recreation without feeling undue fatigue (USDHHS 1999).

What is the ultimate objective of physical activity? Good health, which means far more than simply the absence of disease. Physical activity can improve not only physical health but also mental health and social and spiritual well-being. In short, physical activity is not just good for athletes—it's an important factor in improving the well-being of every person regardless of occupation or interests.

The Power of Positive Wording

Researchers (CDC 1995) have found that the word "exercise" has a negative connotation among Americans, so they recommend that you use the term "physical activity" and emphasize fun and variety rather than regimen.

It is also important to recognize that even moderate physical activity is beneficial: "Even a little physical activity can go a long way to improve overall health and sense of well-being" (USDHHS 1999). Moreover, working together, the Office of the Surgeon General and the President's Council on Physical Fitness and Sports have stated the following (USDHHS 1996):

- Inactive people can improve their health and well-being by becoming moderately active on a regular basis.

- Physical activity does not need to be strenuous to attain health benefits.

Keep in mind as you study this chapter that our major goal is not to force children to get into shape but to "educate children through active, hands-on learning experiences" (Ratliffe and Ratliffe 1994). Remember, we retain 90 percent of what we hear, see, say, and *do* (Fauth 1990).

Finally, don't confuse health-related fitness with *skill-related fitness*, which is excelling at sport-specific skills, such as hand-eye coordination and ballhandling skills. To avoid confusion, for the rest of this book, we will use the term "health-related fitness" as a short way to embody health-related physical fitness concepts and the physical activity that leads to such fitness.

You must take into consideration a number of issues when teaching physical activity as a way of life. In this section, we'll look at the issues that affect the teaching and learning of physical fitness, including understanding genetic factors, enhancing the learning atmosphere, finding time for physical activity. Think about how you can encourage the lifelong pursuit of physical activity as you read and study this information.

Genetic Factors

Genetics does play a significant role in the health-related fitness scores your students will achieve, and you obviously can't do anything about this. It is important to remember, however, that your emphasis should not be on fitness scores, but rather on how staying active will be important to staying fit and healthy for a lifetime. For example, most of us have seen accounts of former star professional athletes dying of heart attacks in their 50s. Why? In many cases, these athletes stopped exercising after they finished their professional careers, failing to take up any other physical activity while continuing to eat as if they were still active. And once a person stops being physically active, he or she loses the health benefits of physical activity.

As you can see, simply because a person was born with "athletic genes" doesn't mean that person is immune from the hazards of not being physically active. In contrast, a person who tests very poorly in the mile run but who is very physically active as a life-long habit will enjoy the benefits of physical activity despite having "nonathletic genes."

Creating a Positive Atmosphere

We cannot emphasize enough the importance of a positive learning atmosphere in reaching our major goal of encouraging children to seek physical activity as a way of life. In this section, we'll look closely at this issue in relation to the teaching of physical fitness.

A Positive Approach

To encourage lifelong regular physical activity, physical education activities must leave each individual feeling competent and confident. Naturally, criticizing, embarrassing, shaming, and boring students will turn them off. But offering praise, encouragement, and meaningful and varied activities will help motivate them to seek physical activity on their own.

The Obese Child

As you probably well know, a child who is overfat is most likely self-conscious about his or her body, making him or her reluctant to attempt to participate in physical activity. This attitude, of course, perpetuates the obesity and compounds the complications that can arise from obesity. Apply the following guidelines to help the obese child:

- Create a fun physical education program to entice all children to participate and to send the message that physical activity is worth engaging in.

- Always build in ways to individualize physical education lessons so that all children, including the obese child, can succeed.

- Approach family members privately and diplomatically and point them in the direction of professional help, such as the family physician.

- Privately recognize and reinforce small improvements in lifestyle choices such as eating fruit with lunch instead of potato chips or walking to school instead of riding in a car.

- Encourage all children to focus on how individual choices can lead to a healthy lifestyle instead of focusing on weight or body composition as the sole or most important indicator of health and fitness.

- Let the obese child choose his or her own intensity level, as even mild exercise is beneficial in such cases. This approach increases the likelihood the child will continue to participate in physical activity outside of school.

A Child-Centered Curriculum

One major way to promote feelings of competence and confidence is to individualize both your concept lessons and the actual activities you choose. Teaching by invitation (chapter 5) is an easy way to do this. Make it your goal to create such choices for your students so that they feel good about physical activity. The following are some ideas to inspire you:

- Instead of assigning a predetermined number of exercises, give students a range to complete—for example, a choice of doing 10 to 25.
- List several exercises for one component and allow students to choose the ones they want to do (can set up as stations).
- Instead of having all students run a mile, time the run, asking all students to keep moving (running or walking) for 12 minutes while they keep track of how far they go. With this approach, each student can work to the best of his or her ability, and no student will suffer the embarrassment of being the last to finish as all students will finish at the same time.

Improvement-Oriented Emphasis

Another important way to create a positive fitness atmosphere is to focus on the personal effort and improvement of all students, rather than on the prowess of a few elite students. This is one area where cooperative learning rather than competition can be of great benefit to your students. For example, encourage students to cheer one another on in small groups, instead of having them compete to see who can do the most or run the fastest. As the teacher, praise and reward individual effort and improvement as well as group cooperation, thereby inspiring confidence and competence in each student.

Avoiding Negative Attitudes and Practices

You probably well know what bothered you as a physical education student. Always empathize with your students' potential and actual feelings, and you will probably avoid the negative attitudes and practices that can turn students off to physical activity.

Figure 8.1 Instead of constant competition, encourage students to cooperate and cheer each other on in their accomplishments.

Effort *Does* Count

When it comes to health-related fitness, effort does count. For example, a student who works as hard as possible to complete two laps during a 12-minute run will benefit more from that run than a student who completes four laps with a minimal effort.

COPEC (1992) addresses one of the most damaging practices in the box below.

The following lists other attitudes and practices you should also avoid (Ratliffe and Ratliffe 1994):

- Avoid lecturing when teaching fitness. Get students actively involved in fitness concepts.

- Avoid making negative comments about a poor performance. Instead, privately discuss a poor performance with the student, asking for the reasons. Then respectfully explain what you would like to see the next time.

⚠ Avoid giving the message of "no pain, no gain." Teach children the difference between initial fatigue or discomfort and pain, which could lead to injury. Teach that pain is the body's signal to slow down or stop.

Finding Time for Physical Activity

Even if you are able to teach physical education five days a week, you probably will not have enough time to give students the intensity and duration of physical activity they need to become truly fit, which indeed, should not be your goal. Therefore, the time to begin practicing physical activity as a way of life is now. So encourage your students to participate in physical activity during recess (instead of sitting or standing around) and outside of school through sport and recreation opportunities. Such activity is a major way to promote personal responsibility for participating in fitness activities as a way of life. Help students see how their personal free-time choices can have a significant impact on their health (Hinson 1995).

Basic Concepts of Fitness Education

Simply providing opportunities for physical activity and encouraging such activity outside of school are not enough; children must understand why physical activity is so important. Fitness education includes five major areas (Ratliffe and Ratliffe 1994):

1. Introducing fitness concepts
2. Cardiorespiratory fitness

COMPONENT— *Fitness as Punishment*

Appropriate Practice

Fitness activities are used to help children increase personal physical fitness levels in a supportive, motivating, and progressive manner, thereby promoting positive lifetime fitness attitudes.

Inappropriate Practice

Physical fitness activities are used by teachers as punishment for children's misbehavior (e.g., students running laps or doing push-ups because they are off-task or slow to respond to teacher instruction).

Reprinted from COPEC/NASPE 1992.

Cross-Curricular Teaching Tips: Language Arts

Consider integrating language arts into health-related physical fitness education in the following ways:

- Have students record physical activity time in a physical education journal. They could log the date, duration, and intensity of and feelings about each activity.

- For low-key public speaking practice, allow students to elect to share their journal entries aloud with classmates.

(Be sure to offer support and encouragement and encourage classmates to do so as well.)

- Have students read about sports heroes and record in their physical education journals what these people do to become fit. Discuss how to scale down the hero's choices to everyday life. Discuss the differences between skill- and health-related fitness.

---

3. Muscular strength and endurance
4. Flexibility
5. Healthy habits (including those that affect body composition, which is percent body fat) and wellness

The overriding factor in health-related physical fitness education, no matter the particular topic, however, is to explain why each activity you have students do to enhance their physical fitness is important and how it relates to the real world.

Thus, students should leave elementary school understanding

- the components of health-related fitness,

- the idea that physical activity that leads to health-related fitness is a healthful choice,

- that if they choose physical activity as a way of life, they can choose from many activities, and

- they are personally responsible for maintaining or increasing their own health-related fitness levels.

In the rest of this section, we'll provide a brief overview of the basic content you should cover in each of the five areas of fitness education.

Introducing Fitness Concepts

Introduce fitness concepts by teaching your students what it means to be physically fit, which activities promote physical fitness and which don't and why, and how to maintain and improve fitness (Ratliffe and Ratliffe

COMPONENT— *Concepts of Fitness*

Appropriate Practice

Children participate in activities that are designed to help them understand and value the important concepts of physical fitness and the contribution they make to a healthy lifestyle.

Inappropriate Practice

Children are required to participate in fitness activities but are not helped to understand the reasons why.

Reprinted from COPEC/NASPE 1992.

1994). Areas to cover include the five components of health-related fitness, skill-related fitness components, benefits of fitness, how to maintain and improve physical fitness, and understanding fitness testing. In each of the following sections, we'll briefly outline these concepts. Of course, you must scale your presentation of material to the time you have and the age and cognitive abilities of your students. See also the sample lesson plans for physical fitness at the end of this chapter.

Components of Health-Related Fitness and Understanding Fitness Testing

In introducing basic health-related fitness concepts, teach children the definitions of each component so they can begin to understand the reasons for working on each component when you focus on them in greater detail:

- Cardiorespiratory fitness—the ability of the heart to pump blood and deliver oxygen throughout your body (ACSM 1992)
- Muscular strength—the power aspect of muscular fitness; that is, the ability to lift a heavy weight (Ratliffe and Ratliffe 1994)
- Muscular endurance—the ability of the muscles to work over a period of time (Ratliffe and Ratliffe 1994)
- Flexibility—the ability to move your joints freely and without pain through a wide range of motion (ACSM 1992)
- Body composition—the ratio of the fat part of your body weight to the lean part (ACSM 1992)

Once students know what you're talking about when you say "health-related fitness," explain that you will periodically be testing them in each component or having them test themselves. Emphasize, however, that the purpose of testing is to monitor improvement and provide feedback for your lesson planning, not to judge them personally or to rank them against their classmates. Later in this chapter, we'll describe the basic fitness tests and discuss how best to conduct them in the section titled "Assessing Health-Related Physical Fitness and Conducting Fitness Testing."

Components of Skill-Related Fitness

As we have already pointed out, skill-related fitness is not the same as health-related fitness—and your students need to recognize the differences. This skill-specific aspect of fitness is comprised of the following components (Ratliffe and Ratliffe 1994):

- Agility—the ability to quickly and accurately change direction of the entire body in space
- Balance—the ability to maintain equilibrium while moving or stationary
- Coordination—the ability to apply sensory information to perform motor tasks accurately and smoothly
- Power—the ability to quickly change energy into force
- Speed—the ability to perform a movement quickly

But a person strong in one or more of these components is not necessarily strong in health-related physical fitness—and may very well be fairly out of shape. In contrast, a person strong in health-related physical fitness may be quite weak in skill-related physical fitness—but still quite fit. Indeed, nearly everyone can achieve health-related fitness, and therefore the benefits of physical activity, (see chapter 1) whether or not they possess sport skill and aptitude. Ensure that your students understand these differences.

Benefits of Fitness

Students need to be familiar with the many benefits of health-related fitness so that when they are working on a concept or activity, its relevance is clear. In this way, students begin to see the connections between concepts and real-life activities, helping to reinforce the importance of physical activity.

Maintaining and Improving Fitness

The U.S. Department of Health and Human Services (1996) points out that people who are already physically active will benefit even more by increasing the amount (e.g., duration, frequency, or intensity) of physical activity. To retain and build upon the benefits of physical activity, then, students need to first learn the basic principles for maintaining and improving physical fitness:

- Overload—This simply refers to the fact that you need to get more exercise than usual to become more fit, gradually and safely building up your strength and endurance. The factors making up the acronym FITT tell you how:

  Frequency—how often you exercise; more means greater fitness.

  Intensity—how hard you exercise; harder means greater fitness.

  Time—how long you exercise; longer means greater fitness.

  Type (specificity)—To develop an aspect of physical fitness, do things that focus on that component. For example, jogging longer will take you to a higher level of cardiorespiratory endurance and tone your leg muscles, but it will not affect your flexibility or arm strength much.

- Progression—Increase frequency, intensity, and time slowly and gradually to prevent soreness and injury. You can't become more fit if you're sitting on the sidelines because of an injury or feelings of discouragement. Choose type carefully to target the component you're working on. Allow students to make choices when applying the FITT principle.

Keep these principles in mind to help you plan effective health-related fitness units.

Once you have introduced the basic fitness concepts, your students should be ready to learn more about the major concepts. And although we must present them one at a time, your teaching of them may very well overlap. For example, even if you're focusing on enhancing cardiorespiratory fitness, you should take the opportunity to point out that jogging enhances the muscular endurance of the legs as well (but not of the arms). Let's turn, now, to the other four components of a well-rounded fitness education program.

Cardiorespiratory Fitness

Cardiorespiratory fitness is probably the most important component of health-related fitness. Why? A healthy heart is the reason for most health benefits of physical activity. Fortunately, you can enhance your students' cardiorespiratory fitness no matter what physical education unit you are doing. For example, a games unit should include plenty of moderate to vigorous physical activity. You can then briefly point out what the activity does to the heart rate. Moreover, you can integrate science and math into the study of this component, teaching science and math lessons back in the classroom that you can refer to during physical education. In this way, you reinforce physical education, science, and math simultaneously (see related sidebars below and on pages 129 and 131). Specifically, cardiorespiratory fitness content should include studying the vascular system and the respiratory system and calculating target heart rate. Remember, however, to tailor the difficulty and detail of such content to your students' abilities.

Vascular System

The vascular system includes the veins, arteries, and capillaries. Students, taught according to age and abilities, should understand that this system allows the heart to circulate blood. The stronger the heart is, the

---

Cross-Curricular Teaching Tips: Science

Science concepts and content lend themselves readily to integration into fitness education. The following are only a few of the many possibilities (see chapter 12 for more information):

- Studying the cardiorespiratory system
- Studying the musculoskeletal system
- Learning about proper nutrition

less hard it has to work. In other words, each beat of a strong heart pushes the blood farther through the vascular system and so the heart pumps less often to do the same work. Use charts, videos, CD-ROMs, and books to teach about this system.

Respiratory System

The lungs, of course, are affected by cardiovascular fitness training because breathing increases during physical activity. Explain to students that their lungs are like two balloons that fill up with and lose air as they breathe in and out. Their lungs take the oxygen out of the air, and oxygen passes to the blood and then the heart pumps this oxygen-rich blood to the body. Next the blood picks up carbon dioxide and other waste products and returns them to the heart. Then the heart sends the "old" blood with the waste products back to the lungs. When they breathe out, they get rid of the waste products and are ready to take in fresh oxygen to repeat the process. Working on cardiorespiratory fitness helps the lungs work more efficiently.

This is a good time to explain that smoking inhibits the lungs' capacity to make this oxygen and waste exchange with the blood. Therefore, smoking harms cardiorespiratory fitness.

Target Heart Rate

You probably know that you must elevate your heart rate to improve cardiovascular fitness. But how high is high enough? Generally, exercising at 60 to 80 percent of what we call *maximum heart rate (MHR)* is a safe, effective way to enhance cardiovascular endurance (assuming that this occurs for at least 20 minutes at a time, at least three days per week). Some researchers estimate that MHR is 220 beats per minute minus the person's age. We call the 60- to 80-percent range the *target heart rate zone (THRZ)*. The following is a calculation of the THRZ for an 8-year-old.

220 – 8 = 212, the MHR
60% of MHR = .60 × 212 = 127
80% of MHR = .80 × 212 = 170
THRZ = 127-170

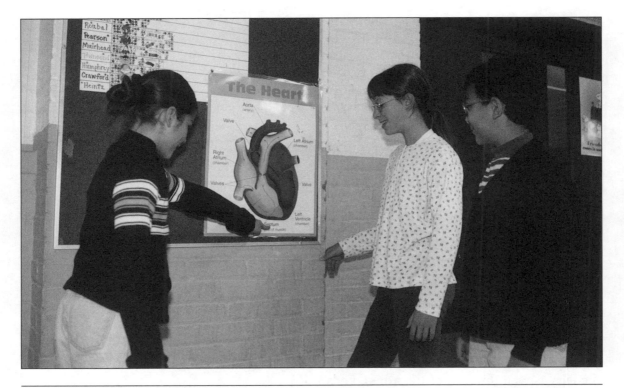

Figure 8.2 Explaining the vascular system to your students may help them understand what happens during physical activity.

Cross-Curricular Teaching Tips: Reading

Today's nonfiction books for children are both attractive and educational. Your school librarian should be able to help you find a multitude of books to enhance your teaching of health-related fitness. Some books include exciting science experiments and activities to try. Here are a few we recommend:

For primary-level students:

Cole, Joanna. 1989. *The Magic School Bus: Inside the Human Body.* New York: Scholastic. (Also available in video and CD-ROM forms.)

Showers, Paul. 1989. *A Drop of Blood.* New York: Thomas Y. Crowell.

Suhr, Mandy. 1992. *How I Breathe.* Minneapolis: Carolrhoda Books.

For intermediate-level students:

Ardley, Neil. 1990. *Muscles to Machines.* New York: Gloucester Press.

Burnie, D. 1995. *The Concise Encyclopedia of the Human Body.* London: Dorling Kindersley.

Parker, Steve. 1994. *How the Body Works.* Pleasantville, NY: The Reader's Digest Association.

VanCleave, Janice. 1995. *The Human Body for Every Kid.* New York: Wiley.

Children in fourth, fifth, and sixth grades should be able to find and count their heart rate (pulse) and may be able to calculate their own THRZ with guidance from you. Teach younger students to feel the heart rate by placing a hand on the chest and judging whether it is faster after physical activity.

Apply this knowledge by periodically having the students check their heart rates to see whether they are operating in the THRZ. They should know what the number of beats should be in six seconds (See math sidebar below). If their heart rate is too low, they should work harder; if it's above the THRZ, they should slow down until it drops back into the THRZ. This knowledge empowers students to exercise safely and effectively even when you're not around.

Muscular Strength and Endurance

Up to about the age of 12, girls and boys have similar potential to develop their muscular strength and endurance. Children need to understand that muscles are made of millions of tiny muscle fibers. These fibers operate in motor units upon signals from the brain. Regular exercise causes muscle fibers to

---

Cross-Curricular Teaching Tips: Math

When you're focusing on the concepts of health-related fitness, it is an especially good time to integrate math into physical education, and vice versa. The following lists only a few of the many ways (see also chapter 12):

- Counting the pulse for one minute or less than one minute and multiplying; for example, if the pulse is eight heartbeats in six seconds, the beats per minute (bpm) are

  $8 \times 10 = 80$ (just add a zero to the number of heartbeats)

- Counting number of sit-ups or curl-ups performed

- Calculating target heart rate zone

enlarge. Although children will not add muscle bulk, muscle strength and endurance helps an individual with many daily tasks and recreational pursuits.

You can help your students develop muscular strength and endurance by having them

- take their body weight on their hands, as in cartwheels or push-ups,
- suspend their bodies or climb on playground equipment,
- jump and land from playground equipment,
- do sit-ups and curl-ups, and
- lift milk jugs filled with sand.

As with all health-related fitness activities, remember the basic principles of progression and specificity. Have students gradually increase the number of repetitions of an exercise, beginning with a set of 8 to 12 (using a lighter weight, if necessary), adding sets as strength and endurance increase. Make sure they understand that if they want stronger arms they must do arm exercises; stronger legs require leg exercises; and so on.

Flexibility

Teach your students why flexibility is important, and teach them safe stretching techniques. Flexibility is important because being able to move the joints through a full range of motion reduces the likelihood of injury. The safe way to stretch is with *static* (slow and controlled), not *ballistic* (bouncing), movements. After they have completed a general body warm-up so that the muscles are warm enough to stretch safely, direct students to slowly stretch to the point of slight discomfort—not pain. Then ask them to hold this position for 10 to 30 seconds. Stretching that causes pain and bouncing can and do cause injury; ensure that your students know not to bounce when stretching and that stretching should not hurt. Teach students that they can safely increase their flexibility by gradually increasing throughout the course of the school year the distance they stretch, the length of time they hold each stretch, and the number of times they do each stretch.

Healthy Habits and Wellness

Concepts of body composition, nutrition, personal health habits, caloric balance, and self-management fit into this area of fitness education. Use physical fitness learning to reinforce your classroom health and wellness curriculum.

Body Composition and Nutrition

Body composition is the ratio of lean (muscle and bone) mass to fat mass. A child who is 80 pounds may be quite fit because of a high ratio of lean to fat mass, while another child the same height and weight may be out of shape because of a high percent body fat. Teach your students that a high level of physical activity leads to a healthier body composition but that any changes take time.

Students must understand that adequate and proper nutrition is vital to the growing body. Dieting, as in restricting calories, is not appropriate for elementary-age children. Rather, making good food choices (e.g., fresh fruit instead of donuts) along with plenty of physical activity in the THRZ is the best way to attain or maintain a healthy body composition. Note that obese children should exercise at the lower end of the THRZ until a basic level of cardiorespiratory fitness is achieved. This is a good time to study the Food Guide Pyramid and relate it to body composition.

Personal Responsibility

Finally, an individual cannot truly be considered "well" if she does do not have the tools and motivation to take personal responsibility for her own health and fitness. You can emphasize self-management by helping students understand how their choices affect their health, set fitness goals, and learn strategies that will help them reach their goals. Ratliffe and Ratliffe (1994) offer the following strategies children can learn:

- Listing reasons to be physically active
- Choosing activities they enjoy
- Setting realistic short-term goals
- Self-monitoring activities by writing in logs or making graphs

- Establishing their own self-rewards
- Asking family and friends to provide support
- Encouraging themselves to be more active, for example, by writing notes to themselves such as "Eat healthy snacks!" or "Be active!"
- Telling themselves they can succeed, and motivating themselves with statements such as "I can do this!"
- Making specific, written plans for accomplishing goals

An added bonus is that children can learn to apply these self-management strategies to all kinds of goals, not just fitness goals.

Teaching Strategies

We have already touched upon several specific tips for teaching health-related physical fitness in the chapter. Here we will focus on more general strategies to help you make learning about physical fitness more interesting, meaningful, and effective for your students. Specifically, we'll give you tips for delivering effective instruction, preventing injuries, and motivating students.

Delivering Effective Instruction

Ratliffe and Ratliffe (1994) offer eight basic strategies to use in teaching fitness concepts and activities:

Cross-Curricular Teaching Tips: Music

Integrate music into fitness education to, among other uses,

- engage cooperation and signal activity during warm-ups,
- provide motivation and infuse excitement during vigorous activity, and
- soothe and calm during cool-downs.

1. All activities in each fitness lesson should accommodate all students, no matter their ability levels or physical characteristics. Offer children choices, such as doing 5, 10, or 15 repetitions of an exercise, depending upon what they feel capable of. Timing activities is another good way to allow for individual abilities. For example, require students to do push-ups for 30 seconds instead of setting a number that may be too hard for some and too easy for others.

2. Ensure that your students know and understand the goals of each fitness lesson. No matter the topic, children learn better when they know why they are working on a particular aspect and how it fits into the curriculum. This is a good time to relate fitness education to real life as well, helping students apply these principles to other situations.

3. During the lesson, review key points. Choose a key word to use as a cue to reinforce the lesson, such as "Healthy hearts!" to remind students to work in their THRZ.

4. Encourage children to think and physically respond when you check for understanding. Have students answer, for example, a question about how to stretch safely by showing you they know how.

5. Incorporate visual aids whenever possible to reinforce fitness learning. Remember, related books, charts, and videos enhance all learning.

6. Repeat learning experiences throughout the year. Incorporate basic fitness concepts throughout your physical education curriculum by seizing teachable moments to reinforce them.

7. Create challenges to help students reach their goals. Start a fitness club or challenge students to set personal best goals for recess activities, such as using the monkey bars to increase arm and shoulder strength.

8. Offer students actual physical activity in school and encourage it out of school by offering challenges and incentives. You might call this a hands-on, *feet-on* curriculum.

Preventing Injuries

No instruction is effective if it encourages injury. Thus, you must understand basic ways to prevent injuries. First and foremost, never forget that children are not miniature adults. Their bodies respond differently to exercise and the environment. So take these factors into consideration to design appropriate lessons, including appropriate warm-ups and cool-downs, and educate yourself as to outmoded exercises and their safer alternatives.

Physiological Concerns

Ratliffe and Ratliffe offer the following information regarding physiological responses:

- Children's bodies do not get rid of heat as easily as adults' bodies do.
- Even though children produce more body heat than adults, during a given amount of physical activity, they can only sweat about 40 percent as much as adults.

In short, children cannot tolerate heat as well as adults, so you must take appropriate precautions during physical activity such as providing water to drink before, during, and after physical activity and completely avoiding exercising in extremely hot and humid conditions.

Warming up and cooling down with about five minutes of gentle whole-body exercise are important to preventing injury in all physical activity. Planning an effective, easily carried out warm-up is also a good way to offer instant activity, which can prevent behavior management problems (Graham 1992; see chapter 4). The following are some suggestions for appropriate warm-ups for health-related fitness lessons:

- Play 4 Corner (jog, skip, gallop, slide).
- Jump rope.
- Play tag with three or four taggers.

Safe Alternatives to Unsafe Exercises

Unfortunately, several harmful exercises are sometimes still used in physical education. Study figures 8.3 through 8.19 carefully to identify these harmful exercises and learn their safe alternatives.

Motivating Students

Naturally, the main way to motivate students to participate frequently in health-related fitness activities is to provide a fun and interesting fitness program that teaches principles and activities students can use on their own in a physically and psychologically safe

---

COMPONENT— *Calisthenics*

Appropriate Practice

Appropriate exercises are taught for the specific purpose of improving the skill, coordination, and/or fitness levels of children.

Children are taught exercises that keep the body in proper alignment, thereby allowing the muscles to lengthen without placing stress and strain on the surrounding joints, ligaments, and tendons (e.g., the sitting toe touch).

Inappropriate Practice

Children perform standardized calisthenics with no specific purpose in mind (e.g., jumping jacks, windmills, toe touches).

Exercises are taught that compromise body alignment and place unnecessary stress on the joints and muscles (e.g., deep-knee bends, ballistic [bouncing] stretches, and standing straight-legged toe touches).

Reprinted from COPEC/NASPE 1992.

Harmful Exercises   Safe Alternatives

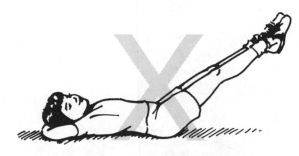

Figure 8.3 Double leg lift. Causes the back to arch and puts pressure on the spine.

Figure 8.4 Reverse curl. Helps strengthen lower abdominal muscles without excessive stretch on the lower back. Lift knees to chest, raising hips off the floor, but do not let knees go past the shoulders. Return to starting position, and repeat.

Figure 8.5 Straight leg sit-up with hands behind the head. Causes excessive stress on spine and lower back. Causes pulling and hyperflexion on the neck.

Figure 8.6 Bent knee sit-up. Helps strengthen abdominal muscles. Cross arms on chest with hands on shoulders; tighten up abdominal muscles and rise up to touch elbows to thighs. Then return to starting position.

Figure 8.7 Curl-ups. Helps strengthen abdominal muscles. Use fingers on side of head to support neck; tighten up abdominal muscles; lift shoulders and hold for six or more seconds; then relax to starting position.

All figures this page reprinted, by permission, from Ratliffe, T., Teaching Children Fitness, (Champaign, IL: Human Kinetics), 37-39.

Harmful Exercises

Safe Alternatives

Figure 8.8 Deep knee bend. Causes hyper-flexion, stretching, and stress to the knee joint.

Figure 8.9 Forward lunge. To stretch the quadricep, hip, and thigh muscles, take a step forward with the right foot, touching left knee to the floor. Knees should be bent no further than 90 degrees. Repeat with the other foot.

Figure 8.10 Standing toe touch with straight legs. Causes stretching of the ligaments and joint capsule of the knee.

Figure 8.11 Toe touch with slightly bent knees. This stretches the hamstring muscles and avoids straining the knee ligaments.

Figure 8.12 Neck circles. Tipping the head backward during any exercise can pinch arteries and nerves in the neck and put pressure on the discs.

Figure 8.13 Neck stretch. Instead of tipping the head back, stretch the neck muscles by dropping the head forward and slowly moving it in a half circle to the right and then left.

All figures this page reprinted, by permission, from Ratliffe, T., Teaching Children Fitness, (Champaign, IL: Human Kinetics), 37-39.

Harmful Exercises

Safe Alternatives

Figure 8.14 Donkey kick. Hyperextension and arching of lower back results when foot position is higher than the buttocks.

Figure 8.15 Knee-to-nose touch. To strengthen the buttocks muscles, keep the back straight with the leg in line with the back; keep head straight and in line with back; focus eyes at floor.

Figure 8.16 Ballistic bar stretch. Potentially harmful to the knee joint when extended leg is raised to 90 degrees or more and trunk is bent over leg.

Figure 8.17 Back-saver toe touch. To stretch the hamstrings, sit with one foot against the wall or extended out with one knee bent. Clasp hands behind the back and bend forward, keeping lower back as straight as possible.

Figure 8.18 Hurdler's stretch. Puts the knee in a rotated position which can cause excess stretching of the ligaments and damage to the cartilage.

Figure 8.19 Hamstring stretch. To stretch the hamstring and calf muscles, lie on the back with the knees bent. Raise one leg and grasp toes while pulling on back of thigh. Push heel toward ceiling and hold. Repeat with other leg.

All figures this page reprinted, by permission, from Ratliffe, T., Teaching Children Fitness, (Champaign, IL: Human Kinetics), 37-39.

learning environment. In addition, sometimes it is appropriate to provide small incentives to reinforce self-motivated fitness endeavors, such as allowing a student to choose the game the class will play or giving coupons for free frozen yogurt for every set number of minutes logged in physical activity (work with local businesses to supply incentives).

Assessing Health–Related Physical Fitness and Conducting Fitness Testing

You should be able to apply most, if not all, the ideas for assessment we discussed in chapter 3 to health-related physical fitness and physical activity learning. In general, be sure to

- assess not only the psychomotor but also the affective and cognitive domains,

- keep fitness test results private, and
- use assessment data to further shape your curriculum so that all students have a chance to reach their potentials.

Keep COPEC's guidelines (see sidebar) in mind as you study the appropriate assessments for each component of health-related physical fitness. You can make fitness testing a part of fitness learning by having students self- or peer-assess. Test more formally in the fall and spring.

Assessing Cardiorespiratory Fitness

Measure this component either by having all students run for nine minutes (six for younger students) and recording the distance they cover or by having all students run one mile (half mile for younger students) and recording their times. Timing the one-mile run is easier than tracking distance for nine minutes, but having everyone run the same length of time means no waiting for slower runners to finish and less chance of any chil-

---

COMPONENT— *Physical Fitness Tests*

Appropriate Practice	Inappropriate Practice
Ongoing fitness assessment is used as part of the ongoing process of helping children understand, enjoy, improve, and/or maintain their physical health and well-being. . . .	Health-related fitness tests are given once or twice a year solely for the purpose of qualifying children for awards or because they are required by a school district or state department.
Test results are shared privately with children and their parents as a tool for developing their health-related fitness knowledge, understanding, and competence.	Children are required to complete a physical fitness battery without understanding why they are performing the tests or the implications of their individual results as they apply to their future health and well-being.
As part of an ongoing program of physical education, children are physically prepared so they can safely complete each component of a physical test battery.	Children are required to take physical fitness tests without adequate conditioning (e.g., students are made to run a mile after "practicing" it only one day the week before).
	Reprinted from COPEC/NASPE 1992.

dren feeling embarrassed by their performances. This also is a good way to practice for a more formal test, such as the one-mile run.

Assessing Muscular Strength and Endurance

For the purposes of assessment, these two components cannot be separated. The following are two tests that measure the strength and endurance of various muscles:

- Flexed arm hang—This test measures shoulder strength and endurance. You need a chinning bar, mat, and stopwatch to administer this test (or use a bar on the playground with a safety surface underneath). Help the child get into the starting position (chin above bar, hands gripping as shown in figure 8.20). As soon as the child is in starting position, begin timing. End timing when the child can no longer hold the correct position. Do not allow swinging of the body or legs.

- Curl-ups—This test measures abdominal strength and endurance. Have students work in pairs on mats to count the number of curl-ups each can do correctly to a total of no more than 40 at a time. To

perform a curl-up correctly, begin with arms alongside the body, palms down, knees bent, and feet flat on the floor. Curl up, sliding the hands along the mat as shown (see figure 8.21). Lower the head completely back onto the mat. Do not emphasize speed because this discourages correct form.

Assessing Flexibility

The back-saver sit-and-reach test, which tests the flexibility of the lower back and hamstring muscles, is the most common method of measuring flexibility. This involves a sit-and-reach box (see figure 8.22) about 12 inches high with a measuring stick positioned on top of the box so that the 9-inch mark is on the near edge of the box and the zero point is hanging off the box (Safrit 1995). To measure hamstring flexibility, have each student follow these steps (Safrit 1995):

1. Remove shoes and sit with one leg straight out, foot flat against the front of

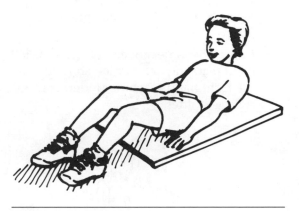

Figure 8.21 Curl up test.

Figure 8.20 Flexed arm hang.

Figure 8.22 Sit and reach test.

the box, and one leg bent with the foot flat on the floor about two to three inches from the inside of the opposite leg. Keep hips parallel to the box.

2. Place one hand on top of the other, palms down.

3. Reach as far as possible four times (slowly and safely—no bouncing), moving the hands across the top of the box. On the fourth try, hold the position for at least a second.

4. Do the same with the opposite leg.

5. Record the best score for each side to the nearest whole inch reached.

The shoulder stretch roughly measures arm and shoulder flexibility. Pair students so they can monitor whether their partners are doing the stretch correctly as follows (Safrit 1995):

1. Reach the right hand over the right shoulder and down the back.

2. Bring the left hand underneath the left shoulder and up the back, attempting to reach the fingertips of the right hand (see figure 8.23).

3. Repeat the same movements with the left hand reaching over the left shoulder and the right hand reaching underneath the right shoulder.

Figure 8.23 Shoulder stretch.

Assessing Body Composition

Percent body fat can be measured by taking skinfold measurement at key sites on the triceps and calf with special calipers (see figure 8.24), which measure skinfold thickness in millimeters. It is very difficult to learn to take and interpret these measurements accurately; therefore, you should not attempt to take these measurements unless you have been properly trained. Instead, ask a local certified health-fitness instructor or a nurse to volunteer to come to school to do this. Obtain permission from parents to test their children's body composition, allow each child to choose whether or not to undergo this testing, and ensure each child's privacy.

Planning Health–Related Fitness Unit and Lesson Plans

In chapter 6, we recommended integrating physical education content areas, teaching health-related fitness concepts in teachable moments. We stand by that recommendation, but there are times, however, when it is appropriate to dedicate an entire lesson to a fitness concept. Follow the outline of this chapter as you work to incorporate each of the five components of fitness education into your physical education curriculum. In addition, seize any and all opportunities to integrate other subject areas with fitness learning. Use the many "Cross-Curricular Teaching Tips" sidebars in this chapter as starting points for reinforcing these important concepts.

Summary

Remember, our goal is to educate children regarding health-related fitness concepts so that they are more likely to seek regular physical activity as a way of life—not to "whip" them into shape. Instead, it is more realistic to introduce and reinforce these concepts using the ideas in this chapter so that your students acquire basic knowledge of health-related fitness and the value of physi-

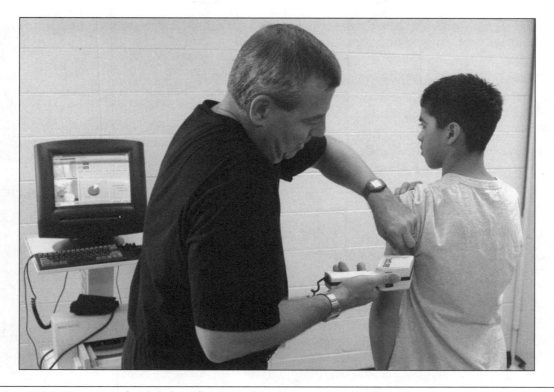

Figure 8.24 Have a professional perform skinfold tests to ensure accuracy.

cal activity they will need to lead healthful lives. Moreover, strive to encourage your students to be physically active outside of school as well.

Refer to the following checklist often.

Fitness Checklist

Philosophies differ regarding the incorporation of fitness into the physical education curriculum. However, there are certain things that most experts agree are important to establishing a developmentally appropriate fitness component in elementary physical education. Here are some key points.

✓ Fitness activities should never be used as punishment.

✓ Children should not be denied fitness or skill education because of poor performance in other subjects.

✓ Don't overemphasize fitness testing.

✓ Don't underemphasize the importance of self-esteem to lifelong fitness. Avoid negative comments about poor performance.

✓ Physical education specialists alone cannot make children fit. A cooperative effort is needed from parents, other teachers and school personnel, and the community.

✓ Fitness is for all children, not just athletically gifted ones. Design fitness activities to accommodate students of varying physical characteristics and levels of ability. Provide options for tasks to vary the level of difficulty.

✓ Fitness needs to be fun.

✓ Children need to understand fitness concepts.

✓ Fitness is temporary—fitness levels achieved during childhood will not last if students do not have the skills or motivation to continue to be active adults.

✓ Children are not miniature adults—fitness programming must be appropriate for their developmental levels.

✓ Involve students in learning experiences that help them apply fitness information.

✓ Teaching fitness should compliment the teaching of motor skills, movement concepts, dance, gymnastics, and games.

Teaching children to be skillful movers and to be physically fit are compatible goals.

✓ Children are naturally motivated to be active, but in today's society, they don't always have the opportunity to act on their motivation.

✓ How fitness is taught has a major impact on children's feeling about fitness and physical activity. You should inspire competence and confidence in your students.

✓ Clarify goals and key points of your fitness lesson—just because students do the activities doesn't mean they will realize why. Check for understanding.

✓ Use hands-on experience—children learn best by hearing, seeing, and doing. Avoid lecturing as your typical approach to teaching fitness. Provide students with challenges.

✓ Use a general body, large muscle warm-up before vigorous and extensive stretching.

✓ Relate fitness concepts to everyday experiences.

✓ Teach children the difference between initial fatigue and pain that may result in injury.

✓ Always make sure environmental conditions are safe for a fitness lesson.

✓ Be aware of harmful exercises. Some traditional exercises—ones you may have learned in high school—have been found to be hazardous. Read current literature to doublecheck the safety of all your exercises.

Reprinted from Wikgren 1993.

Sample Health-Related Physical Fitness Lessons

The following are sample lessons in health-related physical fitness. Note that although a grade level or range is given, you can adapt a lesson to use with older or younger students, according to their needs.

The first lesson, reprinted by permission from Ratliffe and Ratliffe's *Teaching Children Fitness* (1994), is most appropriate for preschoolers through second graders just learning about flexibility. The second lesson, also from Ratliffe and Ratliffe, targets third through sixth graders learning about cardiorespiratory fitness. Use the "How Can I Change This?" and "Teachable Moments" sections to help you extend these lessons into complete units. Use the "Look For" sections to help you assess student understanding.

Stretching Yourself

Objectives

As a result of participating in this learning experience, children will improve their ability to

- use slow and gentle movements when stretching,
- hold the stretched position for 10 counts without bouncing, and
- perform a series of stretches correctly

Suggested Grade Range

Primary (Pre-K–2nd)

Organization

Open area for each student to have a self-space; wall space or easel to display pictures of stretching exercises

Equipment Needed

Illustrations of stretching exercises shown in figure 8.25 (you can enlarge these pictures and laminate them); clamps, clothespins or tape to hang posters; 1 small mat or carpet square for each student or enough mat space so each child has a self-space

Description

Today we are going to learn how to stretch. We'll see who is most like the "rubber band

Figure 8.25 Stretching exercises.
Reprinted, by permission, from Ratliffe, T., *Teaching Children Fitness*, (Champaign, IL: Human Kinetics), 97.

man"—who stretches very easily. To start I want you to copy my actions. That's right, try to do exactly what I do. You are stretching your arms over your head and reaching for the sky—we'll call this the high-10 stretch. Now bend over and stretch between your legs. This is called hang time! This time sit on the floor and stretch your hands toward your toes. This is called the sit-and-reach. Relax. We should do stretching slowly. Let's try the sit-and-reach again and do it very slowly. Well done! Let's try the sit-and-reach again and hold it as we count to 10 together. Ready, stretch and hold, 1, 2, 3, 4, 5, 6, 7, 8, 9, 10, and relax. Let's do one more stretch together. Lie on your back, hug your knees, and point one foot toward the ceiling. Hold it while we count to 10. (Count.) That's great, you were stretching slowly and holding it for 10 counts.

Now when I give you the signal, I want you to go to the pictures on the wall, choose one and look at it, and then go back to your mat and copy it. Try as many of these as you want, but remember to stretch slowly and count silently to yourself to 10. Okay, go. (Watch children and provide feedback to help them do the stretches properly. After about 10 minutes, call the class together for closure.) You've worked on your stretching exercises very well! What makes a good stretch? Yes, (Carlos), we must do it slowly. That's right, (Michael), we hold it for 10 counts.

Before you go, show me how to do a stride stretch. (Have all children demonstrate.) Great, you've learned different ways to stretch! We'll practice these all year, so I'll be looking to see who remembers them!

Look For

- Do children stretch gently? If not, tell them to show you in slow motion.
- Do they hold the stretched position for at least 10 counts? Use the counting strategy to remind them.
- Can they look at the pictures and do the stretches properly? If not, pinpoint students using correct form to demonstrate the correct technique to the class.

How Can I Change This?

- Show each picture one at a time and have the whole class do the stretch together.
- Plan to give children some time in future classes to look at the pictures and practice the stretches.

Teachable Moment

Ask children when they could practice stretching besides in physical education class. Make sure they understand they can stretch at home or during recreational activities.

Reprinted from Ratliffe 1994.

Heart Pump Circuit

Objectives

As a result of participating in this learning experience, children will improve their ability to

- identify the different parts of the cardiovascular system and
- describe the flow of blood from the heart to the body (muscles), back to the heart and the lungs, and to the heart and the body again.

Suggested Grade Range

Intermediate (3rd-6th)

Organization

The heart pump circuit as shown in figure 8.26 must be set up before class in a space large enough for your whole class of children to move around in. The circuit represents major components of the circulatory system by boxes, hoops, and rope tunnels. Oxygen and carbon dioxide are represented by tennis balls and racquetball balls.

Equipment Needed

Two cardboard boxes (lungs), 8 long ropes (vessels), 2 hoops (heart pumps), 1 bicycle tire

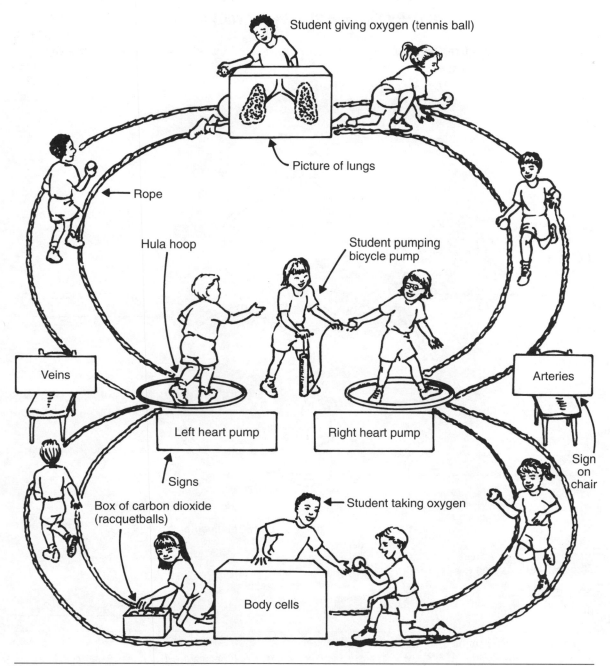

Student giving oxygen (tennis ball)

Picture of lungs

Rope

Hula hoop

Student pumping
bicycle pump

Veins

Arteries

Left heart pump

Right heart pump

Signs

Sign
on
chair

Box of carbon dioxide
(racquetballs)

Student taking oxygen

Body cells

Figure 8.26 Heart pump circuit.
Reprinted, by permission, from Ratliffe, T., *Teaching Children Fitness*, (Champaign, IL: Human Kinetics), 78.

pump (heart pumping action), 20 racquetball balls (carbon dioxide), 20 tennis balls (oxygen), poster of circulatory system from American Heart Association, 1 heart pump worksheet (see figure 8.27) for each student

Description

You know that the heart pumps blood, but do you know where the blood goes when it

leaves the heart? Today, you will actually travel the path of the blood through the body. We call this the circulatory system.

First look at the picture of the circulatory system (use a poster from the American Heart Association and point out the main components). We have a circuit set up on the floor today to symbolize these parts of the circulatory system. We'll call it the heart pump circuit because the heart has two pumps. One

Heart Pump and Blood Flow Worksheet

Label the parts of the heart pump circuit. Write the correct answer in the blank. Use the *Key Words* to help with spelling.

Key Words

capillaries   lungs   body   veins   arteries

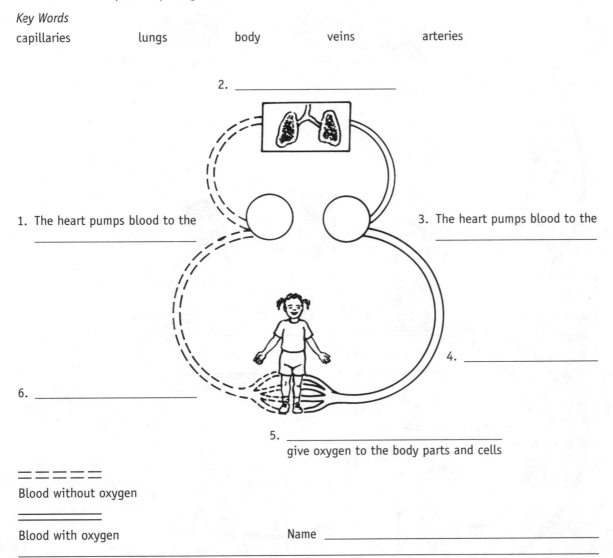

2. _____

1. The heart pumps blood to the
_____

3. The heart pumps blood to the
_____

4. _____

6. _____

5. _____
give oxygen to the body parts and cells

Blood without oxygen

Blood with oxygen   Name _____

Figure 8.27 Heart pump and blood flow worksheet.
Reprinted, by permission, from Ratliffe, T., *Teaching Children Fitness*, (Champaign, IL: Human Kinetics), 79.

side pumps blood to the lungs, and the other side pumps blood to the body.

The red blood vessels are called arteries. They carry oxygen to the muscles so that energy can be produced. The blue vessels are called veins. They carry carbon dioxide to the lungs, and it leaves your body when you breathe out. The heart makes all this possible by pumping the blood through both types of blood vessels.

We'll need some of you to help play the parts of the heart pump circuit. One person will use the tire pump and play the part of the heart. You will pretend to pump the blood just like the heart does. Then another person will play the part of the lungs by taking the carbon dioxide, these racquetballs, and giving oxygen, the tennis balls. Another person will stand at the body parts poster and take oxygen and give carbon dioxide as the blood passes through.

Now watch as (Jeremy and Joanne) go through the circuit. You'll start at the heart pump and get pumped to the lungs. There you will give up carbon dioxide—a racquetball—and pick up oxygen—a tennis ball. Then you'll come back to the left side of the heart and be pumped through the vessels to the area for the body parts and cells. Here you will give up oxygen and pick up carbon dioxide and carry it through the vessels back to the right side of the heart. From here the circuit repeats itself. You will start at the lung pump and keep moving through the circuit until I tell you to stop. As you travel through the heart pump circuit, I'll ask you to identify where you are in the circulatory system. At times I'll stop the whole class and check your knowledge by asking you to do things like, "Raise your hand if you are in the arteries," or "Jump up and down if you are blood carrying oxygen!" "Ready?" (Start a few children at a time and monitor their progress; gradually introduce students to the circuit until all students are participating. After they've gone through the circuit several times, have them go to another area to start filling out the heart pump worksheet [figure 8.27] to reinforce the lesson objectives.)

Look For

- Can children identify the part of the circulatory system they are traveling through?
- Can they correctly fill out the heart pump worksheet?

How Can I Change This?

- Focus only on the path of the blood by eliminating the oxygen and carbon dioxide and simplifying the worksheet.

- Follow up by helping children complete the worksheet back in the classroom. Use the worksheet as a homework assignment.
- In a subsequent lesson, change this experience to focus on the role of oxygen instead of on blood flow and call this the Oxygen Circuit. Add a hoop to travel through to represent the mouth and have children carry oxygen from the lungs to the heart and then to the muscles. You can use one, two, or three tennis balls to symbolize different amounts of oxygen. At the muscles, have children exchange oxygen for an equivalent amount of exercise, printed on a card. After doing the exercises the students pick up carbon dioxide (racquetball balls) and carry it back to the heart and then to the lungs to be removed from the body. Students will learn that as more oxygen is transported to the muscles, more energy is available to perform activities.

Teachable Moment

Ask questions to develop understanding of the circulatory system. For example, "Why does the blood flow to the lungs?" (to get rid of carbon dioxide and pick up fresh oxygen) and "What does the blood carry?" (oxygen and nutrients for the cells, carbon dioxide, and waste products). During other physical education activities, ask children to think about the heart pump circuit and ask questions to link exercise and the heart actions.

Reprinted from Ratliffe 1994.

Jason, 10

Chapter 9

Teaching Games

Danielle, 11

Mrs. Jenson's kindergarten class always plays a modified version of Simon Says. She first divides the students into two groups and has each group stand in its own line. When a child makes a mistake, he or she simply joins the other group instead of being eliminated. With so much practice time, the students' listening skills have greatly improved.

Play is the work of children, and what better way to learn than by playing games, right? That depends, when it comes to physical education. If the game (Morris and Stiehl 1998)

- enhances motor skill development,
- fosters feelings of self-worth,
- promotes physical fitness,
- cultivates enjoyment and satisfaction,
- encourages the use of cognitive skills, and
- nurtures social skills and a sense of community,

—it's an appropriate game for the elementary physical education curriculum. In this chapter, we will show you how to design effective games units by defining key issues related to the teaching of games, including developmental appropriateness, competition and cooperation, and integrating other physical education content into games. Then we'll outline appropriate games content, explain the basic methods for teaching games units, give you the specifics to help you develop your own units, and show you how to authentically assess games learning.

Key Issues

In this section, we'll look at developmental appropriateness and competition and cooperation as they pertain to games and at attaining physical education goals through games. We'll also offer safety guidelines. Keep NASPE's definition of a physically educated person (p. 5) in mind as you study these issues.

Developmental Appropriateness

The activities in a developmentally appropriate games unit are not the same as those appropriate for either athletic teams or recess. Specifically, a teacher planning a developmentally appropriate games unit takes into account student knowledge of and competency in movement concepts and skills and modifies rules, equipment, space, team sizes, and required skill levels so that all students are actively engaged in learning at their own ability levels a maximum amount of class time.

COPEC's guidelines to ensure that the content of games units is developmentally appropriate appear in the following three sidebars.

To be able to judge what may be appropriate for your particular class of children, it is

---

COMPONENT— *Rules Governing Game Play*

Appropriate Practice

Teachers and children modify official rules, regulations, equipment, and playing space of adult sports to match the varying abilities of the children.

Inappropriate Practice

Official adult rules of team sports govern the activities in physical education classes, resulting in low rates of success and lack of enjoyment for many children.

Reprinted from COPEC/NASPE 1992.

COMPONENT—
Number of Children on a Team

Appropriate Practice

Children participate in team games (e.g., two or three per team) that allow for numerous practice opportunities while also allowing time to learn about the various aspects of the game being taught.

Inappropriate Practice

Children participate in full-sided games (e.g., the class of 30 is split into two teams of 15 and these two teams play each other), thereby leading to few practice opportunities.

Reprinted from COPEC/NASPE 1992.

important to understand the levels of skill proficiency and how they relate to a games curriculum. Graham, Parker, and Holt-Hale (1993) outline four basic levels of skill proficiency:

1. Precontrol—A child at this skill level does not display a consistent motor pattern; every attempt at a skill is different. Success is random.

2. Control—A child at this skill level consistently uses a mature motor pattern but must concentrate to perform the skill successfully.

3. Utilization—A child at this skill level can combine skills effectively, perform well with others, deal with rules limitations, and play small-sided games under strictly set conditions.

4. Proficiency—A child at this skill level can successfully engage in team play under complex rules.

Note, however, that most children in elementary school do not progress beyond the utilization level. Therefore, you must design a games curriculum that not only allows students to succeed at the lower skill proficiency levels but also lays the foundation for eventual proficiency after elementary school.

Keep in mind, too, that different children in your class may display different proficiency levels for different skills. In these instances, designing units and lessons that build in chances for children to choose their own level of skill practice is vital. We will explore more about this later in the chapter.

Competition and Cooperation

Although we'll look at this issue in more detail in chapter 13, here we'll briefly explain our philosophy and list simple ways to

COMPONENT—
Equipment

Appropriate Practice

Equipment is matched to the size, confidence, and skill level of the children so that they are motivated to actively participate in physical education classes.

Inappropriate Practice

Regulation or "adult size" equipment is used, which may inhibit skill development or may injure or intimidate the children.

Reprinted from COPEC/NASPE 1992.

Physical Education Hall of Shame

According to Williams (1992), some of the most widely played and popular games in schools today are the least likely to help children meet physical education goals and, worse, are the most likely to turn kids off to the very idea of physical activity through excluding or otherwise embarrassing them. Following in this chapter and chapter 13 are some games that are charter members of the Physical Education Hall of Shame. They are denoted by this symbol ⊘. Use the Games Analysis Form in figure 9.1 to evaluate and improve traditional games.

Games Analysis Form

Name_____

Game   Equipment needed   Formation (draw)

_____ Maximum participation   _____ Nonelimination

_____ Enjoyable   _____ Safety concerns (Explain)

_____ Improves self-concept for everyone? (If so, how?)

_____ Reinforces motor skills? (Which skills and how?)

_____ Reinforces social skills? (Which skills and how?)

_____ Any cognitive operations involved? (Compare, contrast, problem solve, categorize, etc.—explain)

_____ Teaches or reinforces any concepts? (Which concepts and how?)

Explain any modification you will make to this game.

Figure 9.1 Games analysis form.
Reprinted, by permission, from Ashy, M., 1993, "The games students play," *Teaching Elementary Physical Education*, 4(5): 15.

modify traditional approaches to make a game cooperative.

We believe that children have much to gain from both cooperative and competitive experiences. As in other subject areas, cooperative learning groups help children develop vital social skills while helping one another learn content. Some children, however, enjoy friendly competition, and they should have the option of pursuing this approach. COPEC (1992) encourages teachers to allow competition to be a personal, child-directed choice, not a teacher mandate.

An easy way to make a competitive game cooperative is to simply play for what Grineski (1996) calls a "collective" score, which means the two teams in, for example, a net or invasion game, keep a total score from both sides, challenging themselves to achieve the highest possible collective total (see chapter 13).

You can select small-sided teams by having students who wish to play cooperative or competitive forms of the same game assemble in designated areas accordingly. Or you can have all teams play cooperatively, then "vote" among themselves to try a competitive version, as long as you allow those who do not wish to compete a cooperative alternative. Remember, though, that even competitive games should emphasize high levels of participation and self-improvement, not elitism and winning and losing.

DODGEBALL

⊘ The main goal of this game is to inflict harm, pain, injury, and embarrassment on opponents (Zakrajsek 1986). Although some motor elite students love this game, most students cower from the fear of pain and, of course, fail to develop any skills trying to protect themselves from grievous bodily harm. Indeed, Williams (1992) calls this game a "litigation action waiting to happen." Play Crows and Cranes instead: to begin, have teams form two lines close to the center of the playing area. Signal one team to chase the other to an end line. Have tagged players join the other team and continue playing, allowing each student to choose where to stand between center and end lines (Ashy 1993).

DUCK, DUCK, GOOSE

⊘ This game forces children to sit, not participate. When they do become the goose, they start chasing at a severe disadvantage; most children will likely not even get to participate as the goose. Play tag with three or four taggers instead. Change taggers often.

Attaining Physical Education Goals Through Games

In chapter 6, we recommended that you develop a curriculum that integrates all areas of physical education into each unit so that your students are becoming physically fit and practicing basic movement skills and concepts while learning more specific content. Making sure that your games content is developmentally appropriate goes a long way toward ensuring that your games units help students strive for appropriate overall physical education goals. In addition, when planning games units, keep in mind the following components of an effective physical education program: physical activity, cognitive and social development, and application of movement skills and concepts.

Physical Activity

Using small-sided teams, incorporating locomotor skills, and modifying traditional rules are three of the best ways to ensure that your students get adequate physical activity while learning and playing games. The following lists several simple ways to put these suggestions into effect:

- As mentioned earlier, limit teams to two or three players so that members have

⊘ Dodgeball—a game that demonstrates survival of the fittest.

KICKBALL

🚫 Children love this game and organize it for themselves, so why waste precious physical education time on it? Moreover, as popular as it is, the batter is on display for potential embarrassment, less than five percent of each child's time is spent actually performing any locomotor or manipulative skill, and one rule encourages players to hit and hurt others with the ball. Instead, play one-on-one kickball. To play, designate a pitcher and a kicker in each pair of students. Pitcher rolls soft ball to kicker, who kicks anywhere within cone-marked boundaries. Pitcher retrieves ball and tries to hit kicker below waist (or to tag with ball). Once pitcher hits or tags kicker, players switch roles. If inside, play only with students who know how to use general space safely (Hinson 1992).

MUSICAL CHAIRS

🚫 This game is sometimes played in the gym using hoops instead of chairs while children practice locomotor skills to music. The eliminated children, however, stop practicing—usually they are the children who need the most practice! Improve this game by playing a cooperative version. Make the goal finding a way for everyone to "fit" on any remaining chairs (or use hula hoops). If all players get even just a big toe on the last chair (or in the hoop), they're all winners!

STEAL THE BACON

🚫 With only a five percent participation rate, a great chance for embarrassment (two students perform at a time in front of everyone), and physical activity virtually absent, this game has no place in an effective physical education curriculum.

many opportunities to participate through movement, instead of standing around and waiting for the action to finally come to them. Indeed, members of small-sided teams are more motivated to participate because they feel more responsible for what's happening. This can also enhance social and cognitive development if they are allowed to work together to create rules and make other decisions as a group.

• Have students dribble a ball while moving through general space, changing directions, pathways, and speed.

• Have students throw and catch with a partner while on the move.

• Modify traditional rules to increase physical activity time, such as requiring every team member to touch the ball before shooting at the goal or basket.

Cognitive Development

Games offer ample opportunities to stretch your students' cognitive development. Simply having students design their own games brings the cognitive domain into play. Set up

game-designing challenges along set parameters such as those we'll describe later in the chapter. In addition, children can learn to compare and contrast different games, suggest acceptable modifications of teacher-directed games, and analyze whether their own or others' behavior is fair, ethical, or considerate.

Social Development

As students work together to play and design games cooperatively, they work on vital social skills. Beyond cooperation and fun social interaction, these social skills include communication, group problem solving, and peer support. When you have students analyze their own behavior in the physical education setting to aid cognitive development, you are, of course, also encouraging social development.

Movement Skills and Concepts

Games are conglomerations of basic movement skills and concepts. Design activities that incorporate the specific movement skills and concepts your students are competent in to both ensure success and reinforce the basics. Make sure students see the connections between the basics and game success. Finally, you can even design game-creating challenges in which you request that students apply particular skills or concepts as part of the parameters of the game. For example, you could require students to design a game that includes at least three different forms of locomotion.

Safety

Use the following as a checklist to ensure that your games units are safe (see also chapter 17).

- ✓ Survey the playing area. Make sure it is free of hazards such as broken glass, holes, and the like.
- ✓ Set and enforce rules for distributing, collecting, and retrieving balls and other objects so children do not get in the paths of flying objects.
- ✓ Make sure all equipment is of good quality and safe to use. Always inspect before using.

Games: Curriculum Content

Once you understand the term "developmentally appropriate" as it pertains to games and have thought about how to integrate other physical education learning into your games curriculum, you are ready to select specific types of games content. Before selecting a particular game, however, ensure that it scores well on the assessment form shown in figure 9.2.

The following lists the basic forms games may take and suggests ways to apply them in your curriculum (Belka 1994; Werner and Almond 1990):

- Tag games—These games involve moving, changing direction, and dodging. When we speak of tag games, however, we do not mean 30 students and 1 "it" or any type of elimination activity; instead, we are referring to games that involve everyone

Cross-Curricular Teaching Tips: Social Studies

When studying another country or culture, try playing a physically active game from that country or culture. Lorraine Barbarash's book *Multicultural Games* (1997) is an excellent resource. Just be sure to, if necessary, adapt the game you choose to your students' abilities and age.

most of the time in applying basic strategy. Advanced tag games may include an object to manipulate.

- Target games—Billiards, shuffleboard, golf, and bowling are examples of target games, but such games can be as simple as having a child toss a ball into a bin. These simply involve having students contact a target with a manipulative object. They are the easiest games to play and speak to a child's egocentric nature. One child with one ball and one target gains essential practice through continual play. You can bring cognitive abilities into play by having those children who are ready design their own target games. Although social interaction within a simple target game is limited, you can have students teach one another games they have designed. Integrate physical activity by requiring students to add a locomotor skill, such as running in Frisbee golf.

- Net or wall games—Opponents take turns in these games, usually on opposite sides of a net (e.g., volleyball, tennis) using a ball or other manipulative and, possibly, a racket. Net games allow more chances for social interaction, but an individual child may also use a wall as a partner. Be sure to modify rules or have children design a game within parameters you set so that all get adequate time to practice skills at their own proficiency levels. For example, allow more than one bounce of the ball in tennis or a bounce in volleyball.

Cross-Curricular Teaching Tips: Language Arts

When you have children design their own games in physical education, instruct them to write a description of it, including its rules, during a language arts lesson back in the classroom. During the next physical education class, have cooperative learning groups exchange descriptions and try to play one another's games. Allow time for groups to confer if something in the written directions is unclear. Back in the classroom again, have groups revise their written directions if necessary. This process will give your students valuable practice in writing accurate and understandable directions.

Assessment Criteria for Games

Use this chart to help select and assess games. For each criterion, circle the number that best describes the game. Select games that have many items rated as important or very important. Modify games with high-numbered scores. Discard games in which many items are rated as dubious or of no value. The following example assesses the game Hoop Toss.

Name and description of game: *Hoop Toss*

Do children possess the necessary prerequisites?   *Yes*

Scale

1 = Very important   3 = Some value   5 = No value
2 = Important   4 = Dubious value   6 = Not applicable

Criteria	Rating			Scale			
Allows maximum participation	1	①	2	3	4	5	6
Provides many quality turns	1	①	2	3	4	5	6
Is safe	2	1	②	3	4	5	6
Focuses on skills or strategy	1	①	2	3	4	5	6
Supports a developmental principle	6	1	2	3	4	5	⑥
Encourages efficient, effective movement	2	1	②	3	4	5	6
Builds on previous learning							
Skills	1	①	2	3	4	5	6
Concepts	1	①	2	3	4	5	6
Strategy	1	①	2	3	4	5	6
Helps children become better games players	1	①	2	3	4	5	6
Enhances social and emotional status	3	1	2	③	4	5	6
Promotes consideration of individual, differing abilities	2	1	②	3	4	5	6
Others _____		1	2	3	4	5	6
_____		1	2	3	4	5	6

What changes are needed to make this game acceptable?   *None*

Figure 9.2 Example of assessment criteria used to select games.
Reprinted, by permission, from Belka, D., 1994, *Teaching Children Games*, (Champaign, IL: Human Kinetics), 47.

Figure 9.3 Target games are one type of basic game that can be added to your curriculum when your students are ready. Ideally you would have enough equipment and children wouldn't have to wait in line. See chapter 18 for ideas on acquiring more equipment.

• Invasion games—In invasion games, the most socially complex game form, opponents score by getting an object (e.g., ball, puck) into a goal in opponent-defended territory within a common playing area. Most team games are invasion games (e.g., soccer, basketball, hockey). Ensure adequate physical activity by creating team sizes that allow for full participation of all students, and make sure that rules and equipment are modified to meet your students' needs. For example, create a three-on-three hockey game, each team with a goalie, forward, and halfback, playing a half-court game.

• Striking and fielding games—In these types of games, opposing teams take turns playing offense and defense on a playing field (e.g., baseball, softball). Again, ensure that team size, rules, and equipment are developmentally appropriate. For example, have the batting team players all run the bases in a line before fielders throw and catch to everyone.

For each type of game, you should emphasize its basic strategies as the main content (see table 9.1). Although each strategy for a particular type of game will be a factor in each game, emphasize only one at a time. Students will benefit from your narrowing their focus to one learnable piece per lesson.

Games: Instructional Strategies

As with any topic, with games you should introduce the lesson by briefly explaining its objective and the activity students will par-

Table 9.1   Basic Strategies for the Basic Types of Games

Game type	Basic strategies
Tag	Staying balanced at all times, ready to move in any direction
	Using fakes when tagging and avoiding being tagged
	Changing directions and speeds quickly to dodge
	Being aware of what is happening to your sides or behind you
Target	Staying as relaxed and confident as possible
	Taking your time; starting when you're ready
	Deciding whether to try to be very accurate or more safe, based on your skill level
	Concentrating, staying focused
Net or wall	Sending objects to the wall or over the net to the most open spaces
	Repositioning to the area that gives the best coverage after every return
	Varying play to make it difficult for opponents to anticipate what will happen
	Sharing coverage of the playing area with teammates
	Communicating with teammates effectively
Invasion	Creating open space and repositioning to gain an advantage
	Guarding space and repositioning to close or deny space
	Interfering with opponents' movements or object manipulation
	Moving an object to gain an advantage, reach a specified area, or score points
	Communicating with teammates and using their abilities effectively
Striking and fielding	Sending objects into open spaces
	Positioning to cover the playing area most effectively
	Repositioning to back up teammates

Reprinted, by permission, from Belka, D., 1994, *Teaching Children Games*, (Champaign, IL: Human Kinetics), 21-26.

ticipate in to reach the objective, then allow students to immediately begin practicing the day's game skill. Once students are actively involved, pinpoint a child or group performing correctly (focusing on form regardless of results), pointing out the specific target skill, then quickly return all to action. Avoid, however, always pointing out the highly skilled; even a low-skilled child can demonstrate, for example, how to communicate effectively with teammates. (See also chapter 5.)

Another teaching strategy is to allow students time to play, then stop them to offer helpful feedback, refining their play, and return them immediately to play. The advantage of this play-teach-play method is that students are more likely to understand and apply your comments effectively when those comments are vital to their success. In this way, they practice without feeling as if they're practicing: as far as they're concerned, they're *playing*.

In the following sections, we'll discuss how to organize the teaching-learning environ-

ment, how to adjust for individual needs, and how to encourage problem solving in the games setting.

Organizing the Teaching–Learning Environment

You can run lessons for which you carefully dictate each specific activity or you may choose to allow students to do the teaching or make more choices. Direct the action more closely when introducing a type of game or teaching a specific game you want the children to know how to play. In turn, concentrate on helping students learn and apply each basic strategy involved in the particular type of game or specific game. In addition, ensure that students possess the basic skills they need for the game. Finally, modify the specific game to better match the skill levels of your students before making the game more complicated or allowing students to modify the game.

Adjusting for Individual Needs

As mentioned, you should modify rules, equipment, space, team sizes, and required skill levels to meet all your students' needs in games units. Follow the COPEC (1992) guidelines, teach by invitation, and use intratask variations to make these adjustments. The following are some suggestions to help you get started.

- Teaching by invitation ideas for games:
  —Offer a choice of equipment (size of ball, and so on).
  —Allow students to play for points or not.
  —Give students a choice of target size.
- Intratask variation ideas for games:
  —Increase or decrease the number of defenders.
  —Increase or decrease the size of the target or goal.
  —Move service line closer or farther from net.

You may wish to have students suggest ways to modify games to meet their needs. For example, ask, "How can we increase the number of people participating actively for a greater amount of time?" Thus, teacher-directed games lessons should lay the foundation for child-directed games learning and the related problem solving.

Encouraging Problem Solving in Games

Games learning is a wonderful time to step back and allow children to both teach one another and solve problems. Pair up students who are having trouble applying a basic skill in a game with those who have mastered the skill to provide remedial practice in a supportive atmosphere (see chapter 15). Have students design games drawing on the games you have taught them and that they know from other situations. To ensure that valuable learning takes place, however, you must mandate what skills they will work on and other parameters as follows (Belka 1994, 32):

- Game's purpose
- Number of players
- Player organization
- Basic rules
- Skill types used
- Equipment used (kind and number)
- Playing area size

More experienced and older students may be able to handle more freedom to shape their games, but you must still ensure that the unit objectives are being met.

The following are sample game-designing challenges for primary and intermediate students:

- Primary—Place a circular target on the wall (e.g., a hoop). Mark off distances of 10, 20, and 25 feet from the wall. Have the student throw as many balls as she wishes at the target in 30 seconds. Score 5 for every hit from 10 feet, 7 for every hit from 20 feet, and 8 for every hit from 25 feet. Ask, "What is your strategy to score the most points?"
- Intermediate—Have groups of three make up a game using throwing, catching, and running.

Planning Games Units and Lessons

It is not enough to simply choose an appropriate game; you must organize your games curriculum to build progressively toward more complex skills and applications. In this section, we'll show you how to set priorities, create variety, and double-check your plans to ensure that you're on track.

Setting Priorities

Ensure that the skills and patterns you have students practice in simpler games will apply to more complex and, ultimately, standard-rules games. For example, having students perform jumping jacks after throwing a ball at a target will never apply in a real-world situation, but having them run to a "base" after each attempt more closely mirrors a traditional game.

Table 9.2 lists examples of complexity and factors that affect game play. The younger, less-experienced, or less-capable the players, the simpler every element of a game should be. Moreover, it is best to increase complexity in only one area at a time.

Note, especially, that most basic games do not require movement. Children need time to develop the ability to apply specific manipulative skills in game situations without worrying about where they are in space.

Finally, make sure that your expectations of strategy learning are age and ability appropriate. Younger or less-experienced players may only be able to learn one or two strategies for each type of game in the course of the school year. For example, second graders may be able to learn all the strategies for tag and target games, but only the first two strategies for net or wall games, none of the invasion game strategies, and only the first strategy for striking and fielding games. Your projection of the strategies your students may be able to learn should guide your choice of

Table 9.2   Examples of Factors and Complexity That Affect Game Play

Level of complexity	Players	Equipment	Area used	Rules	Movement	Strategies
Simple	1	Lightweight, soft/foam, short rackets	Specific to skill	Few, simple	None	None
	2		More to cover	More as needed	Move in personal space	One, simple
	3	Junior size, foam balls, light rackets	More crowded for offense			Few, simple
	4	Rubber baseballs	Teammates must communicate	More and intricate	One stationary, one moving	More, increased complexity
	5	Tennis rackets, baseballs, wooden bats	Nearer to regulation	Complex or regulation	Both moving, Both moving fast	Many
Complex	> 6				All moving, All moving fast	Many and more complex

Reprinted, by permission, from Belka, D., 1994, *Teaching Children Games,* (Champaign, IL: Human Kinetics), 33.

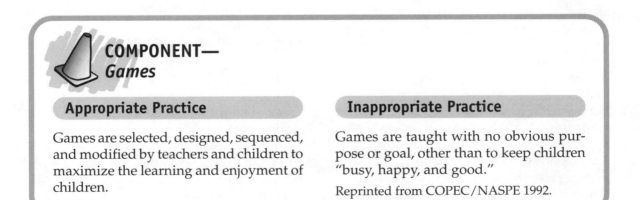

COMPONENT—
Games

Appropriate Practice

Games are selected, designed, sequenced, and modified by teachers and children to maximize the learning and enjoyment of children.

Inappropriate Practice

Games are taught with no obvious purpose or goal, other than to keep children "busy, happy, and good."

Reprinted from COPEC/NASPE 1992.

game types and shape your specific modifications.

Creating Variety

The following are ways to create variety in a games unit:

- Teaching by invitation
- Devising intratask variations
- Using less direct approaches

Use the suggestions in this chapter for each of these methods to help make each games unit both developmentally appropriate and fun.

Double-Checking Your Plans

Use the following checklists to determine whether your games unit is well-defined and developmentally appropriate.

Primary Checklist for Games Units

✓ Teach each motor skill in isolation.

✓ Teach individualized activities (one ball per child) or large group games of low organization (few rules).

✓ Address the whole class together for instruction.

✓ Use word cues but emphasize visual demonstrations.

✓ Modify equipment to size and strength of children.

✓ Emphasize one or two points per lesson; don't overload students with information.

✓ Provide for authentic assessment, that is, mastery of skills using process checklists.

Intermediate Checklist for Games Units

✓ Teach motor skills in combination: catch, then throw; dribble, then pass.

✓ Teach small-sided games, adding rules progressively from the "official" sport.

✓ Teach the whole class together, but allow for more small group work.

✓ Have students develop movement schemes for performance: what to do, when to execute it, how to use the skill in a game.

✓ Begin to use more "official" equipment.

✓ Teach chunks of information, relating similar ideas so students can begin to transfer knowledge from one situation to another.

✓ Provide for authentic assessment by having students use skills in game play.

Assessing Games Learning

Just as you should help students focus on one element of games at a time in each lesson, you should also assess only one element at a time. In the following sections, we'll suggest specific ways you can assess games learning in the psychomotor, cognitive, and affective domains.

Psychomotor Assessment

Teacher, self-, and peer assessment all work well in the games domain. The sample rubrics in figures 9.4 and 9.5 can be used by you, the student, or a partner. You can develop your own rubrics by using the strategy lists in table 9.1 or the learnable pieces of movement skills and concepts as applied to games (see tables 7.6 and 7.7).

Cognitive Assessment

You can assess student understanding of game strategy with simple written tests such as those described in chapter 3. You can also get an idea of student understanding of what makes a particular type of game by rating how well they follow directions for creating their own games. In addition, you can assess students by having them answer thought-provoking questions with physical responses. For example, you can ask them to show you an acceptable way to help a partner learn a new skill. This approach, of course, will also provide valuable data on the affective domain.

Affective Assessment

Frequently request that students share their thoughts and feelings regarding games

Game Performance Assessment Instrument

Date 4/16/96   **Class** 2C   **Game** Soccer (6 v 6)

Data sheet scoring key   5 = very effective performance
4 = effective performance
3 = moderately effective performance
2 = weak performance
1 = very weak performance

Criteria
Support—Player tries to be in a position to receive a pass
Marking—Player marks an opponent when ball comes into the defensive half of the field

Name	Base	Adjust	Decision making	Skill execution	Support	Cover	Guard or mark
Becky					4		5
David					3		3
Carolyn					5		4
Sheila					2		3
Susan					3		2
Larry					2		4

Figure 9.4 Game performance assessment instrument.
Reprinted, by permission, from Griffin, L., S. Mitchell, and J. Oslin, 1997, *Teaching Sports Concepts and Skills* (Champaign, IL: Human Kinetics), 223.

learning and its social aspects. You might ask simple questions such as the following:

- Did you like the game we played today? Why or why not?
- What was your level of play today— needs some work or ready for the pros?
- Did you feel you were able to help your partner enough? Why or why not?
- Do you feel you are learning what you need to know to play better?
- Evaluate your feelings about this game and yourself as a player of it.
- Were you a good teammate during the game? Provide examples.
- Did you encourage others and compliment them on their play? How?

Whole class or small group discussions may yield valuable information that will help you tailor your program to meet your students'

affective needs better. Or you might ask students to write about and explain the reasons for their thoughts and feelings in their physical education journals. Students can also analyze their social performances as shown in figure 9.6. (See also chapter 3.)

Summary

By striving to apply the principles we've outlined in this chapter, you'll be headed for the games hall of fame—not the hall of shame. Your students will enjoy applying basic movement skills and concepts in gamelike situations, thereby reinforcing their motor abilities, challenging their cognitive abilities, and providing adequate physical activity.

As you plan games units, build on your students' capabilities as you revisit games

Process Assessment of Skill

An important part of teaching is giving children specific feedback that is corrective, reinforcing, and congruent. This form can be used to assess a child's skill performance. The assessor observes the child for a period of time and marks the box that most accurately describes the performance.

Name ___Susie Learner___ Date ___April 3___

Skill ___Lead passes___	Almost always	Most of the time	Sometimes	Seldom
The passer				
Sends passes so that the receiver has to reach to catch				
To a stationary partner	X			
To a moving partner		X		
Sends catchable passes		X		
Sends passes to chest level				
To stationary partner	X			
To moving partner			X	
Adjusts lead to receiver's speed			X	
Leads well off a dribble				
To stationary partner	X			
To moving partner		X		
Leads well immediately after receiving a pass				
While stationary		X		
While moving			X	

Comments

Sue has consistent skills that have improved considerably in this past year. She has a tendency to avoid stopping to receive a pass or to dribble when she receives a pass while she is moving. In both cases, she doesn't look much for teammates who are open. We need to discuss this and have her set a goal for this skill.

Figure 9.5 Sample process assessment of skill in lead passes.
Reprinted, by permission, from Belka, D., 1994, *Teaching Children Games,* (Champaign, IL: Human Kinetics), 41.

learning at various times throughout the year. Finally, maximize your students' physical education time and reinforce learning by playing a mastered game just for fun sometime, perhaps during indoor recess or as a way to get blood flowing to the brain again (see also chapter 19).

The following provides a concise overview of how to ensure that a game, activity, or sport is appropriate.

Sample Games Lessons

The following are sample lessons in games education. Note that although a grade level or range is given, you can adapt a lesson to use with older or younger students, according to their needs.

The first lessons reprinted by permission here form a second grade games unit in *Physical Education Unit Plans for Grades 1-2* (Logsdon et al. 1997). As you will see, games units at this level should focus primarily on basic motor skills (in this case, throwing and catching) and basic movement concepts (in this case, speed as it relates to effort). These lessons create a fun, gamelike atmosphere by providing appropriate challenges such as rolling a ball in the early stages of working on these skills and working with a partner. Use the assessment tool provided to monitor student progress. The following list shows the context in which this unit takes place because this particular program strives

Feelings and Emotions

Like many activities, games cause people to feel certain things, say things, believe things, and behave in a number of ways. This form allows you to rate how you act when you play games, as well as some of your feelings when you play games. Use the following rating scale.

Evaluative scale
4 = I almost always am like this (9 out of 10 times).
3 = I am like this most of the time (6-8 out of 10 times).
2 = I am like this sometimes (4-5 out of 10 times).
1 = I am hardly ever like this (1-3 out of 10 times).
0 = I am never like this (0 out of 10 times).

1. I do my part to help the team do well and be successful.	4	3	2	1	0
2. I am considerate of others' ability levels. I never yell and get mad at them when they don't do something correctly.	4	3	2	1	0
3. I celebrate my own and my team's successes appropriately. I am a good winner.	4	3	2	1	0
4. I can lose without being angry and showing anger toward others. I am a good loser.	4	3	2	1	0
5. I play within the rules, even when no one else is watching.	4	3	2	1	0
6. I am fair to others.	4	3	2	1	0
7. I cooperate well with others.	4	3	2	1	0
8. I am willing to referee myself and tell others when I have broken a rule, such as traveling in basketball or using my hands in soccer.	4	3	2	1	0
9. I am considerate of the referee when there is one. I don't talk back and get angry at the referee.	4	3	2	1	0
10. I enjoy being a part of the team.	4	3	2	1	0

Figure 9.6 Sample self assessment of social and emotional behavior.
Reprinted, by permission, from Belka, D., 1994, *Teaching Children Games*, (Champaign, IL: Human Kinetics), 46.

to cover basic skills in a systematic and enjoyable way:

Sample Unit Sequence for Second Grade Games (Logsdon et al. 1997)

Unit 1
Passing With the Feet

Dribbling and passing the ball in different directions with the feet

Unit 2
Catching With One Foot Stationary

Reaching to catch while keeping one foot stationary

Unit 3
Dribbling With Either Hand

Dribbling a large ball with either hand while traveling in different directions

Unit 4
Tapping With Dominant Hand

Tapping a bouncing ball with the dominant hand

Unit 5
Throwing and Catching

Throwing and catching fly balls and grounders

Unit 6
Bouncing a Ball and Traveling at Different Levels

Bouncing a ball forcefully and traveling under or over it at different levels

Unit 7
Punting and Kicking

Punting and kicking a ball high and far

Unit 8
Batting From a Tee and Fielding

Batting a ball off a tee and fielding grounders

Unit 5:Throwing and Catching
4 to 5 lessons

Motor Content

Introduction to Basic Body and Manipulative Control; Introduction to Movement Quality (Effort)

Body

Manipulative activities—throwing and catching fly balls and grounders

Effort

Speed—returning the ball quickly after the catch

Objectives

In this unit, children will (or should be willing to try to) meet these objectives:

- Throw and catch fly balls and grounders and return the ball quickly with accuracy after they catch it, giving classmates as many turns as possible (reflects National Standard for Physical Education 1)
- Know that bringing the ball back in the line of flight at the moment the ball contacts their hands helps to spread the force of the ball over a longer period of time, helping to keep it from rebounding out of their hands (reflects National Standard for Physical Education 2)
- Learn that to throw the ball high in the air, the throwing hand needs to be traveling upward upon release and, to throw a grounder, the throwing hand needs to be pointing downward upon release (reflects National Standard for Physical Education 2)

Equipment and Materials

One small, soft ball for every one to two children (use sponge, yarn, or any other small, soft ball that will not intimidate catchers); optional: rope

Learning Experiences

1.0 Today, let's see if you can throw your ball to the wall so it comes back to you along the floor with very little bouncing. Get one ball, find a space away from others about 10 to 15 steps from the wall, and begin. (Make sure the children have enough space in between each other to throw the ball safely. You may also teach this unit outside or inside with the children working in pairs instead of against a wall.)

1.1 One of the first rules in catching a grounder (a rolling ball) is to move to get directly in front of the ball with your hands low to the ground, your palms facing the ball, and your little fingers close together. Work hard to travel and get in front of the ball. Do not let the ball get past you.

1.2 As you prepare to receive a rolling ball, get the foot on your nonthrowing side out in front of the other to help you return the throw quickly. Standing with your feet apart often lets the ball roll through your legs.

1.3 Bend your knees to help you get both hands close to the floor and your little fingers close to each other to catch the rolling ball.

1.4 Let's try to throw the ball overhand to make the ball come back faster. Release the ball when your throwing hand is pointed down. This will help you hit the wall close to the floor.

1.5 To throw harder, step forward on the foot opposite your throwing hand as you throw the ball.

1.6 Really have quick feet if the ball is not coming straight back to you, but be careful of others. Run and get in the path of the ball with your palms up and hands low.

1.7 Aim your release at a low spot on the wall. Make your hand follow through toward your target. (Putting pieces of masking tape on the wall near the floor may help some children aim their releases downward.)

1.8 Some of you may want to try "charging" the ball. Run up and collect the ball before it stops rolling, then return quickly to your throwing spot. If the ball is coming back very fast, you won't have time to run very far.

1.9 The moment you collect the ball, throw it quickly back to the wall. See how fast you can get rid of your ball.

2.0 Let's try rolling and collecting ground balls with a partner. Partners stand facing each other. Think a moment. Should we throw as hard to our partner as we did to the wall? No, we have to ease up a bit because our partner is going to try to collect the ball.

2.1 Roll the ball underhand, making your hand reach toward your partner so the ball rolls straight to your partner.

2.2 Catchers, be in the ready position as you wait for the ball. You need to be on the balls of your feet, knees bent, and hands low in front of you, ready to move to collect the ball.

2.3 Good partners try to roll exactly where they want the ball to go. Release the ball when your hand is straight out in line with your partner. This will make the ball roll straight to your partner.

2.4 Catchers, remember, the first thing you must think about when collecting a ground ball is to move to get your body and hands directly in front of the ball.

2.5 When collecting a grounder, keep your little fingers close together, palms facing the ball. Bend your knees to get lower to catch a ball coming low.

2.6 Let's see if you can throw the ball to the side of your partners so they will have to be ready to run in front of the ball to collect it.

2.7 When you catch, try to have one foot ahead of the other instead of side by side. Getting the foot forward opposite your throwing hand gets you ready to throw quickly.

2.8 Catchers, watch the ball carefully. Don't wait for the ball to come to you. Run up quickly to get it.

2.9 Keep your eyes focused on the ball. Let's count how many catches you can make without missing.

2.10 Go back to the ready position with your weight on the balls of your feet as soon as you throw the ball. The ready position prepares you to move quickly in any direction to catch a ball. Remember, your hands should be low to the ground with your knees bent and eyes focused on the ball.

3.0 Practice your overhand throw. Throw your ball up high on the wall and try to catch it with two hands. Select a ball you feel you can throw and catch, a place to work, and begin. (Pointing out an existing line high on the wall or some other easily identifiable mark helps to encourage children to aim high. Children can also throw to partners over a rope stretched 8 to 10 feet high between two standards.)

3.1 Because you want to throw the ball high, be sure when you release the ball to make your throwing hand point high in the air toward your target as you release the ball.

3.2 Remember to step forward on the foot opposite your throwing hand as you throw the ball high on the wall.

3.3 When you catch a ball above your waist, point your fingers upward, palms facing the ball, with your thumbs close together. (Have a child demonstrate. Caution the children to make sure they are not pointing their fingers directly at the ball so the ball can hit the ends of their fingers.)

3.4 Release the ball when your throwing hand is high above your head, pointing to your high spot on the wall. Pointing your hand will help send the ball to your target.

3.5 Good catchers always make their hands "give" in line with the ball as they catch the ball. Giving as you catch helps to keep the ball from bouncing out of your hands. (Demonstrate the "giving" action with the hands by bringing them toward you along the line of flight.)

3.6 After you throw, keep your eyes focused on the ball, moving quickly to get under the ball to catch it when it bounces off the wall.

3.7 Hit the wall as high as you can without making it difficult to catch. Then, the minute you catch it, throw it back again.

3.8 Count how many times you can throw the ball overhand up high against the wall and catch or collect it without it getting by you.

4.0 Let's show we are good, accurate throwers when we practice throwing high fly balls back and forth to a partner. Get a partner, one ball for the two of you, and begin.

4.1 It's great to see so many remembering to step forward on the opposite foot to throw the ball. Everyone try to finish your throw with most of your weight on the foot opposite your throwing arm (your front foot).

4.2 To throw the ball higher, lean back as you prepare to throw, aiming your release at a spot higher above the head of your receiver. Take care to judge how hard to throw the ball. See if you can send it high and make the ball come down right to your partner.

4.3 Catchers, watch the ball and move to about where it is going to drop. Catch the ball and return it quickly.

4.4 Still throwing the ball high, begin to aim your throw to make your catcher travel a step or two in different directions to catch the ball. Be caring as you throw. Don't make your catcher run into the space of other players.

4.5 To throw the ball higher into the air, release the ball as your hand is traveling upward. Throwing the ball higher gives the catcher more time to get to the spot where the ball will drop. Keep practicing your high overhand throw, remembering to keep your ball in your own working space.

4.6 Catch the ball when it is high. Focus your eyes on the ball from the time it leaves

Table 9.3   Assessing Overhand Throwing—Trunk Action

Name _____ **Rater** _____

Rating criteria: Steps 1-3 are based on a validated developmental sequence for "Trunk Action in Throwing and Striking for Force" with step 3 representing a more advanced pattern.

				Step 1 No trunk action or forward-backward movement (arm may pull trunk into a passive rotation, but there is no twist-up before throwing).	Step 2 Spinal or block rotation (spine and pelvis rotate away from intended flight, then begin forward rotation, acting as a unit or "block").	Step 3 Differentiated rotation (child twists away from intended flight, then begins forward rotation with pelvis while upper spine still twists away).
Date	Grade	Games unit	Task			
10/97	Pre-K	#5	3.0			
9/98	K	#5	2.0			
10/00	GR. 2	#5				

Reprinted, by permission, from Logsdon, B., 1997, *Physical Education Unit Plans for Grades 1-2*, (Champaign, IL: Human Kinetics), 98. Adapted from "Developing Children—Their Changing Movement" by M.A. Robertson and L.E. Halverson.

the hand of the thrower until it is in your hands.

5.0 Let's see if we can mix up our flies (explain term, if necessary) and grounders. Catchers be ready for either kind of throw.

5.1 Catchers, to help you get ready for either kind of throw, watch the arm and hand of the thrower. You can tell by the thrower's hand if the ball is going to be a fly or a grounder. If you see the throwing hand open up, pointing high in the air, you know the ball will be a high fly. If the hand is pointing down, you will be getting a grounder.

5.2 You might like to play a game where you score points for catching fly balls and grounders. Decide with your partner the points scored for catching a fly ball and for fielding (explain term, if necessary) a grounder.

5.3 (Some may be ready to work in groups of four or six. You may make this decision or let the children choose to enlarge their groups. If more than two are playing, however, emphasize giving everyone equal opportunities to practice throwing and catching.)

Reprinted from Logsdon 1997.

This final lesson, reprinted by permission from Belka's *Teaching Children Games* (1994), is most appropriate for fifth and sixth graders. Use the "How Can I Change This?" and "Teachable Moment" sections to help you extend this lesson into a complete unit. Use the "Look For" section to help you assess student understanding.

Defend the Shots

Prerequisites

- Experience in trying to block shots coming low or high to either side
- Acceptable balance and footwork for defending a goal
- Some successful practice at kicking balls toward targets

Objectives

As a result of participating in this learning experience, children will improve their ability to

- plan and execute a target kick toward a defended goal and
- defend a goal and anticipate attempts to score.

Suggested Grade Range

Intermediate (5th-6th)

Organization

One child sets a ball on the ground 15 feet from a 10-foot goal area defended by a second child. A third child is on the other side of the goal to retrieve balls (see figure 9.7).

Equipment Needed

One or two foam or soft #4 balls and 1 goal net (or other goal) for each group of three children (This could be done inside with taped goal areas on the walls.)

Description

Defending a free shot is different from defending during regular play. Our game today will help us defend a goal, or be a goalie. It's played in groups of three. One player stands still near the ball, which is on a place marked on the ground. The second player, the goalie, stands still near the middle of the goal in a good balanced position with hands ready. The goalie may not jump or let her or his feet leave the ground until the kicker touches the ball. When both players are ready, the third person says "Go" and waits to retrieve balls that get past the goalie. The kicker has about 15 seconds to plan and attempt a kick at the goal. Each kicker has three chances to score; then players change places. Be sure that everyone gets a chance to kick and defend the same number of times and that defenders get practice with both other players as

Figure 9.7 Defend the shots.
Reprinted, by permission, from Belka, D., 1994, *Teaching Children Games,* (Champaign, IL: Human Kinetics), 67.

kickers. On "Go," get with two other people, get equipment, set up, and begin. Go!

(Stop the class after a while.) Where do you think is the best part of the goal to kick to? Yes, (Brianna), the best target is in one of the corners of the goal. Why? (The corners are the most difficult areas to defend.) What can the goalie do to be a good defender? (Be balanced, with hands ready to catch; be prepared to move quickly in any direction; and watch intently to try to predict where the ball will be sent.)

Kickers need to use fakes—with their eyes, their body parts, and by changing the amount of time they use. They need to vary their attempts so that the goalie cannot predict their kicks. Keep these in mind as you play; we'll work on them other times, too. Go!

Look For

- Defenders who begin to read the kicker's probable target by watching where the ball is kicked to
- Good faking by the kicker to hold the goalie in place longer or conceal the direction of the shot

How Can I Change This?

- Increase the size of the goal to make it easier for the kicker. Reduce the size of the goal to make it easier for the goalie.
- Set up several balls for two kickers or one ball for three or more kickers. The goalie must prepare for another shot as soon as he or she plays the present shot.
- Allow the kicker to take several steps before kicking the ball (harder for the goalie).
- Goalie play can be changed to include a variety of methods to score (e.g., throwing as in team handball or striking as in field hockey).

Teachable Moment

There may be a need to discuss fairness— when to begin and whether a particular attempt was a goal or not. The third person assumes the referee's role; the others need to respect and accept the referee's decisions.

Reprinted from Belka 1994.

Chapter 10
Teaching Gymnastics

Christopher, 8

In my first elementary physical education teaching position, I had a gym but no equipment because the physical education program was new. So I held "open" gym programs for children and parents once a week for which parents contributed 50 cents to a dollar to participate in the featured activity. We also had a spaghetti supper to raise money. Within a year, I was able to pay for mats and every piece of brand-name gymnastics equipment I desired. Within two years, the skills the upper grade students had gained were amazing.

Since then, I have seen many teachers adapt to even more difficult situations, developing very effective gymnastics units. All it takes is a little imagination and persistence. No gym? Lay parachutes on the grass to protect children's clothing. No equipment? Make benches from 2-inch-by-12-inch lumber and stack newspapers in boxes so students can practice balancing and traveling over, along, onto, and off of. Hoops, wands, and jump ropes provide inexpensive small equipment to manipulate while traveling. It doesn't take state-of-the-art equipment for children to enjoy a wealth of gymnastics experiences based on the themes of traveling, balancing, and rotation.

—Peter Werner

By *gymnastics*, we mean *educational* gymnastics, an informal approach to basic body management skills. Educational gymnastics recognizes individual differences and uses an open-ended problem-solving approach, thereby allowing children to succeed at their own levels. With careful and thoughtful planning, even if you've never taken a gymnastics lesson, you can teach educational gymnastics effectively. In this chapter, we will explore the key issues related to teaching educational gymnastics, including developmental appropriateness, safety, obtaining enough equipment, and attaining physical education goals. Then we'll explore the specific content of an educational gymnastics curriculum, effective methods for teaching that content, helpful planning suggestions, and authentic assessment of gymnastics learning.

Key Issues

When planning and teaching educational gymnastics, you must answer four main questions:

1. Is this activity developmentally appropriate for my students?
2. Have I provided adequately for safety in regard to this particular activity?
3. Do I have the equipment and enough of it to carry out this activity effectively? If not, how can I obtain it?
4. How does this activity help my students meet our overall physical education goals?

Let's look closely, now, at each of these issues.

Developmental Appropriateness

As with all areas of physical education, you must ensure that you do not ask students to "run" before they learn to "crawl." Carefully preassess their abilities, ensuring that they have a foundation of basic movement concepts and skills before attempting to apply them in the gymnastics realm. Read in the sidebar what COPEC has to say about developmentally appropriate gymnastics.

Safety

To teach gymnastics safely, you must follow several basic guidelines. First, teach skills based on sound pedagogy and emphasize good body mechanics by teaching how to do

COMPONENT— Gymnastics

Appropriate Practice

Children are encouraged to sequentially develop skills appropriate to their ability and confidence levels in noncompetitive situations centering on the broad skill areas of balancing, rolling, jumping and landing, and weight transfer.

Children are able to practice on apparatus designed for their confidence and skill level and can design sequences that allow for success at their personal skill level.

Inappropriate Practice

All students are expected to perform the same predetermined stunts and routines on and off apparatus, regardless of their skill level, body composition, and level of confidence.

Routines are competitive, are the sole basis for a grade, and/or must be performed solo while the remainder of the class sits and watches.

Reprinted from COPEC/NASPE 1992.

---

skills properly. For example, for the forward roll, tuck chin to chest, bottom up, transfer weight from hands to shoulders (head never takes weight), tuck knees to chest (hands on shins), and return to feet. In addition, follow proper progressions from simple to complex elements. The following lists pointers for dealing effectively with specific safety issues (Werner 1994):

- Teach your students how to use each piece of equipment safely.
- Conduct gymnastics in a worklike atmosphere. Do not allow students to goof off or dare one another.
- Always have students practice and master a skill on the floor first, then allow them to try the skill at a low but elevated level on a wide base.
- Make sure children have enough room to move safely, without bumping into another child, a wall, or piece of equipment.
- Use a safe surface. Place mats under and beside equipment. Outside, check for glass and other sharp objects and provide a large parachute or mats to protect skin and clothing.
- Set up equipment on a nonskid surface (e.g., a rubber mat) to ensure that it does not move during use.

- Inspect equipment regularly. Make sure that children will not get splinters or scratch themselves on nuts and bolts using the equipment. Tighten nuts and bolts as well.
- Arrange equipment so that there is a natural flow of traffic from one piece to the next.

Obtaining Equipment

Although it would be nice, it is not necessary to have state-of-the-art equipment to teach basic educational gymnastics as long as what you do use is safe. See chapter 18 for information about improvised but safe equipment.

Attaining Physical Education Goals Through Gymnastics

It is possible to incorporate many aspects of physical education into gymnastics. You can plan for psychomotor, cognitive, and social development. In the following sections, we'll explore each area in more detail.

Psychomotor Development

Reinforcing and applying the movement concepts and skills in gymnastics enhances skill development. Working from the simple to the complex, your students will eventually be able to put skills together into sequences and routines in more complex relationships. Moreover, gymnastics provides opportunities to work on health-related fitness concepts, particularly muscle strength and flexibility.

Cognitive Development

Your gymnastics curriculum should enhance your students' knowledge of basic movement skill and concept terms. And, as in all areas of physical education, you can issue movement challenges as part of your gymnastics curriculum, thereby bringing problem-solving skills into play. Offer open-ended, process-oriented tasks as described later in this chapter. Remember, through cognitive development activities you teach your students how to learn.

Social Development

You can enhance student's social development by having them work together as partners or in small groups to explore simple to complex skills and work to solve movement problems. Classmates can give feedback to improve skills, offer encouragement, and help brainstorm possible solutions to movement challenges. Students can also work together to ensure safety in gymnastics by helping each other stay on task and follow the principles of good biomechanics.

Gymnastics: Curriculum Content

Werner (1994) describes one framework of educational gymnastics as consisting of movement skill elements in the form of traveling actions, static work, and rotational movements—all taking place within the context of the movement concepts of body, space, effort, and relationships. In this section, we'll define the content for the three components of the framework and show you how they relate to the basic movement skills and concepts (see chapter 7). Finally, we'll discuss linking various elements together.

Traveling

Many locomotor patterns have a place in educational gymnastics, whether used to move the body across the floor to a new position or over a piece of equipment. But traveling in gymnastics is not simply limited to steplike actions of the feet. Gymnasts can use their hands and other body parts to travel as well. Weight transfer also comes into play when gymnasts rock forward and backward or side to side or roll or slide to get from one place to another. Finally, flightlike actions involve takeoff, suspension, and landing elements. In time, gymnasts use flight actions to vault or hurdle, but novices should initially practice on the floor only. Table 10.1 lists the traveling actions of the body involved in educational gymnastics.

Statics

Werner (1994) defines static elements as "those activities in which the focus or intent is to achieve stillness or balance." Novices should initially learn to achieve stillness in a controlled manner. Actions as simple as running and then stopping and freezing can begin to develop this concept in children. In addition, a major part of static work is to learn to feel the tension in the muscles in relationship to moving and not moving. Once children can be still and balance on their feet, encourage them to explore balancing on other body parts, such as the knees or hands and feet. Although you should at first have students count to three or five to ensure that they're striving for control, deemphasize counting over time and focus on smooth flow from one element to the next. Table 10.2 lists the various static characteristics of the body in educational gymnastics.

Rotation

The following lists the three axes of the body and gymnastics actions that rotate around these axes (Werner 1994; see figure 10.1):

- Vertical (longitudinal)—Picture a rod placed vertically from head to toe; rotation around this rod is in the vertical

Table 10.1 Traveling Actions of the Body

Steplike— using feet	Steplike— using hands, feet, knees	Weight transfer	Flight
Walk	Crawl	Rocking, rolling	Takeoff
Run	Bear walk	Twisting, turning	Suspension
Hop	Crab walk	Sliding	Landing
Jump	Bunny hop		Trampette work
Skip	Mule kick		Vaulting
Gallop	Coffee grinder		
Slide	Walkover—front, back		
Leap	Wheeling (cartwheel, roundoff)		
	Springing (front and back handspring)		

Reprinted, by permission, from Werner, P., 1994, *Teaching Children Gymnastics*, (Champaign, IL: Human Kinetics), 22.

Table 10.2 Static Characteristics of the Body

Characteristics of balance	Principles of balance	Types of balance
Moments of stillness	Base of support	Upright or inverted
Tightness of body	Center of gravity	Symmetrical or asymmetrical
Control	Countertension/counterbalance	Hanging
	Linking actions	Supporting
	Movement into and out of balance	Relationship to equipment
		Individual or partner

Reprinted, by permission, from Werner, P., 1994, *Teaching Children Gymnastics*, (Champaign, IL: Human Kinetics), 23.

plane. Jumps with turns and logrolls are examples of vertical rotation.

- Horizontal—Picture a rod placed horizontally from hip to hip; rotation around this rod is in the horizontal plane. Somersaults and front and back handsprings are examples of horizontal rotation.

- Transverse (medial)—Picture a rod placed horizontally from front to back; rotation around this rod is in the transverse plane. The cartwheel and roundoff are examples of transverse rotation (see figure 10.1).

The distance from the axis of rotation around which the body parts twist, turn, or roll affects the speed of the rotation. The closer the body parts to the axis of rotation, the faster the body rotates. So staying tucked in a forward roll helps the gymnast spin more quickly. Table 10.3 lists the rotary actions of the body.

Cross-Curricular Teaching Tips: Science

Use gymnastic movements to explore the following science concepts:

- Momentum—Is it harder to achieve stillness and balance from a faster or slower speed of locomotion?

- Leverage—How do leverage principles affect balance?

- Rotation—How does the radius (distance from the axis) of the body parts affect the speed of rotation?

- Simple machines—Can you act out three of the simple machines, using gymnastics elements (screw, wheel and axle, inclined plane, lever, wedge)?

Figure 10.1 Gymnastic actions rotate around three axes of the body.

Table 10.3   Rotary Actions of the Body

Principles of rotation	Movement around three axes	Rotation of body
Radius of rotation	Vertical	In space
Eye focus	Spins	Around
	Turns	equipment
	Pencil or logrolls	
	Horizontal	
	Forward rolls	
	Backward rolls	
	Handsprings	
	Somersaults	
	Hip circles	
	Transverse	
	Cartwheels/wheeling	
	Roundoffs/springing	

Reprinted, by permission, from Werner, P., 1994, *Teaching Children Gymnastics*, (Champaign, IL: Human Kinetics), 26.

Movement Concepts

Traveling, statics, and rotation all occur within the movement concepts of body, space, effort, and relationships (see chapter 7). Indeed, as students work on these three types of gymnastics elements, they learn much about the actions of the body, where the body moves in space, how the body performs the movement, and relationships that occur in movement. This is why educational gymnastics could easily be called "body management" instead of gymnastics. Review table 7.1 (p. 85) to help you incorporate these movement "adverbs" into your students' gymnastics "Movement Language." Insist, too, that students take responsibility for their gymnastics language when it comes to safety issues. For example, when they're moving through space, they must do so with great body, space, effort, and relationship awareness so that they do not collide with others.

Linking Elements Together

Beyond enhancing student understanding of the basic movement concepts and applying movement skills, the goal of educational gymnastics should be to help students develop the ability to link the three types of elements together. The following are sample movement challenges that, once students have mastered the basic pieces, they might be able to link together:

- Jump, land on both feet, lower yourself to the floor, do a roll of your choice, and finish in a balance.
- Cartwheel over or off a bench into a balance of your choice.
- Perform a shoulder stand. Then use a rocking or rolling action out of your shoulder stand into a new balance position, either symmetrical or asymmetrical.
- Balance at a low level, roll, travel, jump, and turn; balance at a medium level.

Emphasize smooth flow from one element to the next.

Gymnastics: Instructional Strategies

Whether or not you're a gymnast yourself, in the following sections, we'll show you how to organize the teaching-learning environment, including giving effective gymnastics demonstrations and choosing the right teaching style at the right time, how to encourage problem-solving skills in gymnastics, and how to adjust for each individual's needs in gymnastics. Finally, we'll discuss how to spot and develop good body mechanics and aesthetics in your students' performances.

Organizing the Teaching-Learning Environment

To teach gymnastics effectively, expect children to take personal responsibility for their own safety and learning. Insist on a working, not playing, atmosphere and build in ample choices from which students can select to perform at their own ability level and time to practice. Finally, review the list of safety tips on page 171 often. Make sure that your students know and follow appropriate gymnastics safety rules.

Station learning for previously introduced skills and tasks is a good way to use limited equipment while keeping all students as active as possible. If you limit groups to about four students per piece of equipment or mat, each student will get several turns. Use the ideas for making equipment listed earlier in the chapter to keep lines short and time on-task high. For example, two pairs of two students can use one or two mats, with pairs taking turns rolling toward the opposite side of the mats (see figure 10.2). The waiting students can give the rolling students feedback.

Figure 10.2 Pairs of students can safely take turns using mats while waiting students offer encouragement and feedback.

To introduce new tasks, keep instructional time very short, allowing students to spend the majority of the physical education class practicing. You can briefly stop the action to offer a refining point, but then quickly restart the action.

Effective Gymnastics Demonstrations

We cannot stress enough that you do not need to be an elite athlete to provide effective demonstrations (see also chapter 5). Have students help demonstrate to show a new skill or examples of possible movement choices. Choose a group of several so that no one feels embarrassed. (Always allow a student the choice not to demonstrate.) Pinpoint students who are performing a component of the target skill correctly. By focusing on only one component at a time, you will help students do so as well. Moreover, you will not have to rely on the elite few for demonstrations. Remember, even a poorly skilled student can demonstrate one component of a skill. So watch students practice and catch them succeeding in great and small ways. Point out what they're doing right and save refining comments as to what they're doing wrong for private moments. In this way, all students will feel valued as contributors.

Another way to use demonstrations effectively that saves considerable class time is to have partners or small groups demonstrate for each other. This touches upon peer teaching, an effective tool in many situations (see chapter 15). As always, ensure that students know the specific component you're targeting for the lesson or activity and that they use caring words to encourage and teach each other.

Teaching Styles

A direct style of teaching presents the specific content you want the children to learn. An indirect style of teaching encourages exploration in search of the content. Werner (1994) recommends generally using a more indirect style of teaching in educational gymnastics, emphasizing discovery, questioning, and problem solving. Indirect methods automatically build in chances for students to adjust the lesson to fit their individual needs,

interests, and abilities. This is not to say, though, that you should have no input. You set the criteria students should meet and circulate the work area offering helpful suggestions to refine movement at each students' level.

Use a direct style of teaching, however, when teaching a specific gymnastics skill, good body mechanics principles, and new movement skills and concepts. You can still allow choices within the direct style of teaching to allow children to adjust the activity to their ability level. For example, when teaching the forward roll described earlier in this chapter (see section under heading "Safety"), have students who have mastered good body mechanics for this skill try to do the roll on a line on a mat for accuracy. Others who are more proficient can do the roll off a bench onto a mat on the floor or along a bench with protective mats on each side and a spotter.

Encouraging Problem Solving in Gymnastics

You can have students develop problem-solving skills by having them develop gymnastics sequences. As we've mentioned, teaching students to link various gymnastics elements together into a smooth and attractive performance should be one of your goals. Each sequence should have a beginning, middle, and end, creating a "movement sentence" from the basic skills and concepts. Here's how to teach a sequence (Werner 1994):

1. Offer an open-ended task—for example, "Travel, then perform a roll, then execute a balance on three body parts." (Three or fewer parts are best for younger students.)
2. Allow children time to explore the movement possibilities after you state the task.
3. Have the children choose the skills they like or can perform the best that meet your criteria.
4. Have the children practice their choices until they have memorized their sequence.

The following are sample problem-solving challenges for primary and intermediate students:

- Primary
  - Balance on points (smaller body parts) of your choice, roll, then balance on one or more patches (larger body parts) of your choice.
  - Starting five feet from the hoop, hop, jump, or step into the hoop, then create a balance.
  - Find different ways to bunny hop (e.g., feet, hands, feet, hands) along the rope on the floor. When you get to the end, create a balance.
  - Find three ways to move across the balance beam in a forward direction (at a low level, and so on).

- Balance on the bench. Use a traveling action (e.g., jump) or rolling action to dismount from the bench. Then create a balance on the floor.

- Intermediate
  - Travel to the bench, mirroring (matching) the actions of your partner. Balance against or on top of the bench using matching shapes.
  - Develop an individual routine using a mat and a bench. The routine must include two balances on the floor and two balances on the bench and use good weight transfer actions (i.e., smooth, logical) as you move from the floor to the bench and back.
  - With a partner, try different ways of balancing in inverted positions (head lower than hips); for example, do a

Figure 10.3 Gymnastics provides opportunities to work on muscle strength, endurance, and flexibility.

backbend, tripod, shoulder stand, headstand, or the like. Choose the one you like best and develop it into a sequence that includes an upright balance, transition, inverted balance, transition, and upright balance.

—Develop an individual or partner routine, and use music as a stimulus. Choose only instrumental music and record two or more short phrases lasting 10 to 30 seconds each. Contrast slow, smooth symphonic music (for slow, smooth rolling, and turning actions) with marching, more percussive music (for steplike actions, thrusts into a suddenly held balance). Contrast loud, more forceful music with softer, gentler sounds.

Adjusting for Individual Needs

Remember, when you offer an open-ended task you give children of all ability levels the opportunity to succeed while working toward your objectives. For example, in the open-ended task described in the previous section, a motor elite student may choose to hop on one foot, dive and roll, then balance on the head and both hands while a less capable student may jog, perform a somersault, then balance on both feet and one hand. Both students, however, gain confidence as they see they can meet your requirements while applying previous knowledge in a new situation.

Use or adapt the following ideas to help meet individual needs.

- Teaching by invitation ideas for gymnastics:

  —Perform a rolling action into a balance. You choose if you want to perform a seated, pencil (stretched out long, rolling sideways), forward, backward, or egg (tucked up with hands on shins, rolling sideways) roll.

  —When you feel good about doing your forward roll on the floor, you may choose to do it off a four-, six-, or eight-inch aerobics box onto the floor.

—Make up a short sequence of at least two balances. One must be symmetrical. The other must be asymmetrical. Use a smooth transition from one balance to the next.

—Balance three different ways on a combination of patches (large body parts) and points (small body parts).

—Choose whether you'd like to perform your balance beam routine on the floor or on a low or high beam.

- Intratask variation ideas for gymnastics:

  —If you are having trouble returning to your feet in your forward roll, try coming up to two knees, a knee and one foot, or just stopping the roll in a seated position.

  —As you take weight on your hands, you might try keeping your legs tucked up close to your chest. Try getting your shoulders and hips over your hands. Always return softly to your feet. When you can control this, you can kick up into handstand position.

  —Most children should be able to jump onto and off of a box or bench with an absorbent landing. Challenge the higher skilled to add a one-quarter or one-half turn in the air. Have the less skilled start on the box or bench and jump off only or use a lower box or bench.

  —Add more challenging moves to a previously practiced routine.

Good Body Mechanics and Aesthetics

Allowing children to make choices and operate at their own level of proficiency does not mean we as teachers have no say as to execution. Indeed, we must guide students to perform better. Thus, no matter the ability level, encourage good body mechanics and aesthetics in educational gymnastics.

You will find that you know instinctively what is aesthetically pleasing when you observe your students' movements. Specifically, encourage flowing transitions between movements within a skill and between skills in a sequence.

You can offer suggestions in the following areas to help students refine their body management skills through improving body mechanics:

- Avoiding crashing or falling—encourage self-responsibility; ban silliness.

- Performing soft, absorbent landings—teach bending at the hips, knees, and ankles to absorb impact.

- Using momentum effectively—for example, staying tucked in a roll.

- Maintaining muscle tension to create attractive lines with the body—discourage "saggy" bodies.

Of course, pinpointing students of all ability levels who are working hard to learn and apply good body mechanics and aesthetics is an effective way to reinforce these aspects. See the sidebar for an example of how a teacher uses a rubric to do so.

Planning Gymnastics Units and Lessons

In this section, we will outline how to plan gymnastics units and lessons that capture and maintain student interest, revolve around body management themes, meet individual needs, and provide ample practice.

Capturing and Maintaining Student Interest

Some of your students may be very interested in educational gymnastics, and some may not. Use the following suggestions to capture and maintain everyone's interest:

- Bring in pictures, videos, and books that feature Olympic gymnasts. Point out that although your program does not try to turn students into Olympic gymnasts, everyone can learn to move with more control, style, and grace.

- Point out connections between gymnastics moves and sport moves. For example, perfecting the ability to jump and land safely and with greater control can enhance basketball performance. And the ability to dive, strike, and return to the feet helps in volleyball.

- Call your gymnastics units "body management" units instead. This can help with nervous administrators as well.

- Invite a local group of serious gymnasts to put on a performance at your school or take a field trip to tour a fully equipped gymnastics center (try to arrange for a demonstration of basic skills as well).

Principles for Good Rolling Skills

Teacher: (Jose) has volunteered to help us with our rolls. Let's watch him do his roll now. We'll use our checklist to see how well he does.

1. Tight body _____
2. Rounded body surfaces (no "square tires") _____
3. Control from beginning to end _____
4. Definite beginning and end _____
5. Moves from one adjacent body part to the next _____

Teacher: Okay. That was an excellent pencil roll, (Jose). I think we all saw that you had a long, tight body like a pencil. Your whole body moved in unison from your back, to your side, to your front, to your side. You started and finished in a back-lying position and your body surfaces were round throughout. Who can show us a different kind of roll using the same good principles for rolling?

Developing Body Management Themes

As with all learning, focusing on a theme helps students put their learning into a memorable framework. The following lists sample educational gymnastics themes and their content:

- Balancing—upright and inverted; symmetrical and asymmetrical; bases of support
- Weight transfer—moving short distances from here to there to change base of support or balance position
- Jumping and landing—traveling
- Rolling—rotating
- Combining themes—for example, balancing, then using a weight transfer to move into a new balance

Ensure that you work on each skill within a theme in isolation before combining it with another.

Meeting Individual Needs

You can meet individual needs in gymnastics through planning carefully, ensuring that equipment is child-sized, offering open-ended tasks, and teaching basics first. If you have mainstreamed students with physical challenges, you can modify tasks so that such a child can feel successful alongside his or her classmates. For example, a child in a wheelchair can use her arms and spin the chair in place of locomotor tasks. Allow a low-skilled or obese child to take weight on hands in simple ways instead of doing a cartwheel. If you speak to such a child privately, you can affirm his abilities instead of calling attention to his inabilities. As always, strive to build in success for all students so they feel encouraged to attempt more difficult tasks in the future.

Providing Ample Practice

This is the heart of adequate and creative planning. In fact, Werner (1994) asserts that a "given lesson should provide 10 to 20 appropriate practice tries for each specific task." Thus, you must use the equipment and physical education time you have to the fullest in order to maximize learning (see the section under the heading "Organizing the Teaching-Learning Environment" earlier in this chapter). Moreover, focus on only a few different tasks per lesson so that students can practice each adequately.

Assessing Gymnastics Learning

In this section, we will show you how to authentically assess specifically in gymnastics (see also chapter 3). We'll look at the psychomotor, cognitive, and affective domains.

Assessing Psychomotor Development

As always, you can use self-, peer, and teacher assessment to monitor each student's progress in the psychomotor domain. Assess individual skills and sequences of skills and the competence of their linking. A checklist such as that shown in figure 10.4 helps you focus on the critical components of a skill. You can rewrite it for students to use it to check themselves and others.

If you use a checklist such as the one shown in figure 10.5, you can tell at a glance whether your students are creating varied routines. Moreover, if adapted for use as a peer or self-assessment, such a checklist will call students' attention to the need to provide variety in routines. The simple coding speeds and streamlines the assessment process, making it more realistic.

Assessing Cognitive Development

You can use quick written tests, poker chip surveys, and student demonstrations to check for understanding (see chapter 3). Remember, if you keep the test short and to the point, you will not lose too much physical activity or teacher time. You can give such tests at a station in the gym or back in the classroom.

Directions:
Check all the children for one critical component at a time. Use the coding system at the bottom of this chart for indicating your judgments.

Name	Arms and legs stretched	Hand, hand-foot, foot	Start/finish facing same direction	Smooth motion
1. *Devon B.*	Y	S	Y	Y
2. *Kevin H.*	Y	S	Y	Y
3. *Amy M.*	N	N	N	N
4. *Liz W.*	P	N	Y	N
5.				

Key:

Arms and legs stretched	Y = yes, like spoke in wheel;
	P = partial, slightly bent;
	N = no, legs bent at knee by 90° or more
Hand, hand-foot, foot	S = sequential, one at a time in order;
	N = nonsequential, 2 hands, then 2 feet
Start/finish	Y = face same direction;
	N = one-quarter turn or twist
Smooth motion	Y = rhythmical (1, 2, 3, 4);
	N = nonrhythmical (quick or slow in hand and foot placement)

Figure 10.4 Sample checklist of critical components for cartwheels.
Reprinted, by permission, from Werner, P., 1994, *Teaching Children Gymnastics*, (Champaign, IL: Human Kinetics), 40.

Assessing Affective Development

You can use smiley-face exit polls, written or oral surveys, and journal entries to monitor feelings about gymnastics learning. Be alert, too, to how well your students work together. Remember, peer assessment and cooperative learning groups should be supportive situations. You may have to role-play and talk your students through this important aspect in regard to gymnastics. Teach your students to point out what their partners are doing right and, when correcting performance, to offer specific, helpful suggestions in a kind and supportive way. For example, teach your students to say, "Smooth ending. Now, tuck tighter," instead of, "That was terrible!"

Summary

Encourage children to take responsibility for their own safety and learning in gymnastics.

Provide opportunities for them to work within their ability levels, developing movement skills based on sound mechanical principles. Don't be discouraged by lack of equipment. Make it! Or simply use the floor to explore basic gymnastics skills and concepts. Ensure that, whatever you cover in gymnastics, you provide ample practice time in a supportive and safe learning environment. And don't forget to challenge your students' minds by offering movement problems to solve. Finally, use self-, peer-, and teacher assessment to monitor psychomotor, cognitive, and affective progress.

Sample Gymnastics Lessons

The following are sample lessons in gymnastics education. Note that although a grade level or range is given, you can adapt a lesson to use with older or younger students, according to their needs.

Directions:

When you judge your partner's sequence, use the coding system at the bottom of the page.

Name	Balance—stillness (3 counts)	Balance—base of support (1, 2, 3, 4)	Balance—level (high/medium/low)	Balance—inverted/upright	Balance—shape (stretch/curl/twist)	Balance—symmetrical/asymmetrical	Roll—type	Roll—direction	Transitions—smooth	Contrasts—time(fast/slow)
1. *Lauren A.*	Y	3,2	L,M	I,U	S,T	A,S	B	B	Y	S
2. *Amy L.*	Y	1,4	L,L	U,U	S,S	S,A	P	S	Y	F
3.										
4.										
5.										

Key

Balance—hold for 3 seconds	Y = yes; N = no
Balance—base of support	Number of body parts supporting weight = 1, 2, 3, 4
Balance—level	H = high; M = medium; L = low
Balance—type	I = inverted; U = upright
Balance—shape	S = stretch; C = curl; T = twist
Balance—type	S = symmetrical; A = asymmetrical
Roll—type	F = forward; B = backward; S = seated; P = pencil; E = egg
Roll—direction	F = forward; B = backward; S = sideways
Transition—smooth	Y = yes; N = no
Contrasts—time	F = fast; S = slow

Figure 10.5 Sample checklist for floor sequence.
Reprinted, by permission, from Werner, P., 1994, *Teaching Children Gymnastics*, (Champaign, IL: Human Kinetics), 39.

The first lessons reprinted by permission here form a kindergarten gymnastics unit in *Physical Education Unit Plans for Preschool-Kindergarten* (Logsdon et al. 1997). As you will see, gymnastics units at this level should focus primarily on basic movement concepts and skills (in this case, transferring weight onto a variety of body parts to create locomotion). The following list shows the context in which this unit takes place because this particular program strives to cover basic skills in a systematic and enjoyable way:

Sample Unit Sequence for Kindergarten Gymnastics Units (Logsdon et al. 1997)

Unit 1
Traveling on Different Body Parts

Traveling on different body parts, responding to a signal, staying on own space, and moving independently

Unit 2
Forward Roll

Developing the forward roll

Unit 3
Changing Base of Support While Traveling

Traveling on different body parts, emphasizing changing the supporting body part

Unit 4
Safely Mounting and Dismounting Apparatus

Mounting and dismounting apparatus, landing softly on the feet, and rolling

Unit 5
Introduction to Weight on Hands

Placing weight on hands by lifting feet high in the air, then carefully placing feet back on the floor

Unit 6
Changing Levels and Directions on Balance Beam

Changing directions and levels by traveling on and back and forth over a balance beam and rolling on a mat

Reprinted from Logsdon 1997.

Unit 1: Traveling on Different Body Parts

2 to 4 lessons

Focus: Traveling on different body parts, responding to a signal, staying in own space, and moving independently

---

Motor Content

Introduction to the Body

Body

Locomotor activities—traveling on different body parts

Objectives

In this unit, children will (or should be willing to try to) meet these objectives:

- Seek empty spaces while traveling and move into them independently, avoiding others

- Create many different solutions to traveling on different body parts (reflects National Standards in Physical Education 1, 3, 4, 5, 6, 7)

- Listen while they move and respond to the stopping signal by holding their positions still when the teacher gives the signal (reflects National Standards in Physical Education 3, 4, 5, 6, 7)

- Learn that one beat or sound means "go," two means "stop and hold your position" (reflects National Standards in Physical Education 2, 3, 4, 6, 7)

Equipment and Materials

Small drum or tambourine for the stop signal for the teacher; one 6- to 8-foot long rope, hoop, or paper wand for each child. (You can make a wand by following three easy steps: (1) layer two to three pages of newspaper; (2) start in one corner and tightly roll diagonally to the opposite corner; (3) place a piece of tape around the middle of the wand.)

Learning Experiences

Signals Tell Us Things Too!

1.0 Sometimes we don't use words to tell people things. Sometimes we use signals. Can anyone think of a signal we make without talking. (Watch for responses.) Good, raising your hand is a signal. That signal said to me, "I want to share; I have an answer." See, you said all that by just raising one hand. Did anyone see a signal as you came to school? Did you see a traffic light? Have you ever seen a boy or a girl on a bicycle stick out their hand, signaling that they wanted to turn? (Continue to discuss other nonverbal signals.) We are going to use a drum (or what you will use for the signal) and I bet it can tell you when to stop and when to start without saying a word. If one sound means "go!" then what do you think two sounds mean? Right! Two sounds means "stop!" Carefully, without touching anyone, travel about the room and see if you can stop quickly when you hear two sounds. (Strike one sound) Go! (After the children have traveled just a moment or two, tap two sounds.) I am so impressed with how many of you stopped right away! You must have good ears! (Start and stop several times.)

1.1 (Give this task as soon as you see the speed of the children increasing to the point that some are endangering others.) This time travel any way except running. Be ready to choose a different way to travel when you hear the drum. Remember—don't run.

1.2 Let's have our ears listening for the drum. Everyone stop very quickly when the drum sends the message. (Start and stop the children frequently and comment on improvement in stopping. Stop the children before they develop speed that creates an uncontrolled situation, endangering the children and threatening your confidence in remaining in control of the situation.)

1.3 You are doing a nice job of traveling but, my, oh my, you're making so much noise with your mouths some people may not be able to hear the drum tell them to stop. Let's travel this time without making any talking noises. (The children need to learn to work in the physical education class without talking so they can hear your coaching comments as they work and don't develop the habit of distracting others who are working. This quiet working atmosphere needs to be instilled early and it will take continued work to accomplish it. In some classes, focusing on this need exists for long periods of time: weeks, months, even years—if the class tends to be very vocal.)

1.4 Oh! As we stop, let's make sure we don't fall down. It is easy to fall, but to be really good movers today, we have to stay on our feet. Listen for the drum: Here we go! (Keep stopping them soon after the have started traveling.)

1.5 This time, see if you can "freeze" every muscle and be very strong when the drum tells you to stop. (While the children are traveling, alert them that the stop signal is coming. This will help the children learn to listen and "freeze" on the signal. Try saying, "I bet everyone can stop quickly and freeze when you hear the drum.")

1.6 I can't believe how strong some of you are when you stop. I am going to be looking for someone who is really frozen solid. When you hear the go signal, be ready to travel and keep listening for the stop signal. (After the stop signal, look for a child who has really tight muscles and go over and try to move one of her arms and legs.) Wow! (Tricia) is really frozen hard. (Move quickly to other children.) Look, (Matthew) is as strong as an iron statue. I can't budge (Alexander's) arm. Now let's see if everyone can stop as soon as the second beat of the drum sounds. Off you go!

Travel in Big Spaces

2.0 As you travel, see if you can keep a great big bubble space all around you. Try very hard not to touch your bubble space to someone else's bubble. Remember to let the drum be the boss and tell you exactly when to start and stop.

2.1 When you hear the drum tell you to go, really look for big empty spaces so you have places to move where you won't get your bubble popped by bumping into another bubble or into someone else. (Keep reminding them to keep a big space around them as they travel. Point out the empty spaces.) Oh! Look over here, no one is in this corner. Wow! The space over there is really lonely.

2.2 This time when we stop, let's see if we can have our own bubble space away from everyone else. (Give the signal to go and, before you stop them, be sure you cue them to have a big space away from everyone else. Once they have stopped, comment on those who are spaced in their own big bubble spaces and point out this who are clustered like a "bunch of grapes or bananas.")

2.3 Try very hard not to follow anyone else. Choose your own places on the floor to visit. Be ready to stop quickly when you hear the drum talk. (You may need to step in to alter the path of a child or two who persist in following others. Obviously, overlook a child who is following if he is very shy because he may need the comfort that comes from following rather than venturing out alone.)

2.4 Now see if you can make your feet do different things as you travel and look for the empty spaces to fill. (Each time you stop the children, continue to comment on the "bunches of grapes" that exist or the beautiful way the children have found their own spaces.)

2.5 Let's pretend we have finger paint on our feet and see if we can paint footprints all over the floor (ground). Try to make every part of the space feel wanted. Remember your footprints shouldn't be following someone else's.

2.6 (Do several different things to bring about greater versatility in their modes of traveling. For example, ask one child to demonstrate what she did.) Some of you might like to try to make your feet travel the way (Martha) made her feet move. (Name the different forms of locomotion individuals are doing or not doing.) I saw (Felix) (sliding), but I didn't see anyone jumping (hopping, galloping, skipping).

Travel on Different Body Parts

3.0 Now you see how you can travel on other body parts besides just your feet.

3.1 Keep your big bubble space with you as you travel on different body parts.

3.2 You are doing a nice job of letting some other body parts touch the floor to do your traveling, but you are bunched up like a bunch of grapes again. When I stop you after you travel this time, see if you can be way away from everyone else. Find big open spaces.

3.3 Every time I say "change," see if you can change the body parts touching the floor as you travel looking for the empty spaces.

3.4 (Replace "change" in 3.3 with names of specific body parts to touch to the floor,

such as two hands and one foot, and so on.)

3.5 Some of you are scooting on your backs. This position makes it very hard to watch for empty spaces. No scooting on your backs. Keep changing the body part you feel touching the floor. (Even though this is an introductory unit in gymnastics, try to eliminate actions that are nothing more than aimless movements that children love to do but are lacking in any real challenge.)

Can You Walk on Different Body Parts?

4.0 Let's see how you can travel on different body parts by letting other parts do the walking on the floor beside your feet.

4.1 As you take steps with different body parts, be sure you care about how your body part feels when it touches the floor; place each body part gently on the floor. (While the children are traveling, name the body parts and actions various children select.)

4.2 (Recall the body parts and actions the children selected.) I saw (Mary) stepping with her hands and feet, (Irene) was jumping, skipping, and twirling, (Idella) softly jumped on two feet and hopped on one, and (Butch) constantly traveled in different ways changing his body parts touching the floor. (Allow the children to try their classmates' ideas.)

4.3 Let's travel a short time on one set of body parts. When you hear me say "change," see if you can travel on different body parts. (Say "change" frequently at first. After awhile say, "On your own, keep changing the body parts touching the floor.")

Traveling In, Out, and Over

5.0 Let's see how softly you can travel in and out over your own hoop (paper roll, rope). Remember those great big bubble spaces. Walk and get a hoop (paper roll, rope), place it down on the floor, and begin.

5.1 Think about your feet and make them do different things as they go in, out, or over the equipment. Try not to touch the hoop (paper roll, rope). (Some of the children will tend to play with their equipment rather than doing productive work.) Let's all find ways to go in and out and over.

5.2 Some of you might like to place your hands in the center of the hoop (on one side if the rope or newspaper wand) and see how you can take your feet in and out of the hoop (back and forth over the rope or paper roll).

5.3 Sit away from your equipment and let's share (demonstrate) some of your good ideas. You have been having lots of fun traveling over your equipment. (Have groups of children share, one half of the class at a time, or individual children. Space the moments of sharing throughout the lesson, keeping each time of sharing short to maximize active learning time and to satisfy each child's preference for being the performer.)

Reprinted from Logsdon 1997.

This final lesson, reprinted by permission from Werner's *Teaching Children Gymnastics* (1994), is a learning experience for teaching about rotation most appropriate for third and fourth graders. Use the "How Can I Change This?" and "Teachable Moments" sections to help you extend this lesson into a complete unit. Use the "Look For" section to help you assess student understanding.

A Roll by Any Other Name

Objectives

As a result of participating in this learning experience, children will improve their ability to

- demonstrate control in rolling actions used to move onto, along, or off equipment and
- develop an action sequence that includes the use of a roll onto, along, or off equipment.

Suggested Grade Range

Intermediate (3rd-4th)

Organization

A large open space is needed. Children should be in scatter formation with 1 or 2 to each piece of equipment.

Equipment Needed

At least 1 box, bench, low beam, or table is needed for every 2 students. Folded mats 4 inches to 6 inches high can substitute. Mats and carpet squares should also be placed beneath or beside the equipment.

Description

You already are very good at rolling in different ways and in different directions. Today we'll use rolls to move onto, along, or off the equipment. It will be challenging for you! First, let's warm up by jogging on the floor in open spaces. Light, up on the balls of your feet with springy, quick feet. Change your speed, faster and slower. Change directions. Jog and, as you come close to a mat, transfer smoothly into jumps. As you get to the mat, go into a roll and return to your feet. Keep moving to another mat. Jog, jump, jump, jump, land, roll. Good! Stop!

We'll start today by rolling *off* our equipment. Everyone, move to a piece of equipment you'd like begin at and sit down beside it. First we will get on our equipment in a squat or kneeling position. Watch as I do it first (or have a student demonstrate). From this position place your hands down on the floor. Stay tucked, chin and knees to the chest. Rock forward a little and transfer your weight to your hands and arms. Make your arms strong. Your bottom goes up; roll over to your feet. Think you can try it? Go ahead, everyone try it a few times. Stop.

What about rolling off sideways from a pencil position? Place one arm and leg down on the floor and roll. See if you can lie on your back or be in a shoulder stand and roll off backward. Use your hands to control your body position by holding onto the equipment. Go ahead and practice rolling off.

(Signal stop.) Well, I see we can roll off. Now let's try rolling onto the equipment. Stand facing your piece of equipment, just like (Danny and Meghan) here. Put your hands on the equipment. Tuck your chin to your chest. Begin to lower your body and take your weight on your hands and arms. Jump, bottom up, tuck, and roll. Your weight should go from the feet to the hands to the shoulders, back, hips, and feet. Stay tucked (demonstrate). Everyone try this. If you need to change to a different piece of equipment, you may—but ask the person who is there already. Good. Practice this several times. Stop.

Next, you'll turn around with your back to the equipment. Sit on the equipment and rock back. Feel for the equipment with both hands beside your head. Stay tucked and push with your hands. Roll over to your feet (demonstrate). This is a hard skill. Everyone may not want to do it. Some of you may want to do it with a spotter. See if you can find a way to roll onto the equipment in a sideways direction. (After a few minutes) Stop.

In order to roll along a piece of equipment, it must be fairly long. We can use the tables, benches, and folded mats for that. (Surfaces should be wide and low to build confidence. Only accomplished children will want to use a 4-inch balance beam.) Remember to try to do your rolls just as if you are on the floor. I will be looking for these pinpoints to make sure you are doing the skill correctly:

- Forward roll—tuck chin to the chest, bottom up, transfer weight to the hands, shoulders, back, hips, and feet.
- Backward roll—tuck, weight goes from the feet to the hips, back, shoulders; push with the hands and back to feet.
- Sideways roll—tight body, roll like a pencil or log.

Try not to get nervous just because you are on an elevated surface. If you can do your roll on the floor on a line, with practice you will develop the precision and control on the equipment. We have started on low, wide surfaces on purpose for your safety. You can also ask for someone to help spot for you.

(Mats can be stacked on both sides of a low bench or beam to reduce falling.) Practice each skill several times. Stop.

Now let's put these rolls into a sequence. You may choose the type of sequence you want.

- Start with steplike travel to equipment, then a roll of your choice onto the equipment, finish in a balance on the equipment.
- Start in a balance of your choice on the equipment, roll off the equipment, finish in a balance of your choice.
- Start in a balance on the equipment, go to a roll of your choice along the equipment, finish in a balance of your choice on the equipment.

Stop. Wow! I'm impressed, seeing the great variety as you perform your rolls onto, off of, and along the equipment. Let's show off your work. Everyone whose sequence involves a roll onto the equipment will perform their routine first. Everyone else, watch. Great ideas! Nice transitions! Now, everyone whose sequence involves a roll along the equipment, perform your routines. Yes, those were good quality rolls, and you maintained control. Finally, everyone whose sequence involves a roll off the equipment, perform your routines. I'm just as impressed with your work. Good weight transfers in your rolls off the equipment. They were smooth: I didn't see clunking or crashing. Thanks for your hard work.

Look For

- Children should execute these rolls on and off equipment as if they were on the floor (figures 10.6 and 10.7). Good form and smooth weight transfer are keys.
- Some children may be very apprehensive about trying one or more of these rolls. Don't force the issue. Find their comfort level; simplify a given roll by stacking extra mats. Provide spotting for those who want it. Allow children to choose a roll they are comfortable with. First master the roll on a line on the floor.
- When sequence work starts, look for smooth transitions into and out of rolls,

Figure 10.6 Rolling off the equipment.
Reprinted, by permission, from Werner, P., 1994, *Teaching Children Gymnastics*, (Champaign, IL: Human Kinetics), 123.

Figure 10.7 Rolling onto the equipment.
Reprinted, by permission, from Werner, P., 1994, *Teaching Children Gymnastics*, (Champaign, IL: Human Kinetics), 123.

onto and off of the equipment, without extra steps, indecision, or glitches; with good control.

How Can I Change This?

• Make the sequence more complex by combining rolls. For example, steplike travel to equipment, roll onto equipment, balance on equipment, roll off equipment, finishing it in a balance.

• Make up a partner-rolling sequence in which partners mirror or match each other. For example, use a cartwheel to arrive, jump onto equipment, lower into a balance of choice, roll off equipment, and finish in a balance of choice.

Teachable Moment

Rolling onto and off of equipment requires a certain amount of risk-taking and courage.

Make the situation safe and build for success. Start on the floor on a line with the rolls. Go to a low wide surface, such as a folded mat, where the risk is low. After students experience some success, use a narrower and higher surface. Spot when necessary. Building on a planned progression helps enormously in developing self-esteem. Teach for transfer. Make the conditions for rolling similar to those on the floor, using the same cues.

Reprinted from Werner 1994.

Danielle, 11

Merry, 6

Anthony, 8

Melissa, 8

Chapter 11

Teaching Dance

Macey, 5

I never danced a day in my life until I got to college. As I began my teaching career, I tried teaching dance a few times to my students. When I looked beyond the superficial comments of getting "cooties" and not wanting to hold hands with someone into real smiles, excitement, and anticipation, I was hooked. It was obvious both boys and girls enjoyed the experience. Now I teach dance as often as I can.

—Peter Werner

Why teach dance? Dance is the only form of movement that fulfills a child's innate need to express feelings, thoughts, and ideas through movement. All the other types of movement in the physical education curriculum focus on function—how to do a specific skill (Purcell 1994). But both functional and expressive movements are important to a well-balanced physical education curriculum. And, contrary to what many believe, dance is more than learning steps to music: "It is a way of moving that uses the body as the instrument for expression and communication. The child as a dancer can be compared to the paintbrush of a visual artist" (Purcell 1994). Music can also enhance movement and enjoyment in nondance areas of the physical education curriculum.

So you can't dance? Consider yourself a beginning dancer and learn alongside your students. Take risks and they'll take risks, too.

This chapter will show you how to motivate students to participate, teach dance without relying on teacher demonstrations, and authentically assess dance learning—all within the context of developmentally appropriate physical education that helps your students reach your overall physical education goals.

Key Issues

Key dance issues are similar to those found in gymnastics. How do you motivate students to participate fully and willingly? How do you make sure your dance curriculum is developmentally appropriate? Safe? How do you attain physical education goals through teaching dance? Let's look at each of these issues up close.

Motivating Students

Many people fear learning to dance. Why? They're afraid of looking foolish. You must ensure, then, that the same supportive atmosphere you have developed in other physical education content areas continues to prevail throughout your dance units. Thus, insist that students show respect for one another at all times. The following is a list of other suggestions for increasing enthusiasm for dance (Purcell 1994; Hopple 1993):

1. Don't use the "D" word right off the bat. Simply say something like, "This lesson is about exploring moving to the rhythm of the music." Label the unit's activities as dance once the children have had enough positive experiences to change their opinions.

Cross-Curriculuar Teaching Tips: Art

After having students dance to a piece of music (either creating a dance or performing a created dance), have them listen to the music again in the classroom. Ask them to draw or paint what the music makes them think of or the movements they used in their dancing. For example, if Rimsky-Korsakov's "Flight of the Bumblebee" (which you didn't tell them the name of) reminds them of cars on a busy road, they may draw cars. Or if the dance they created to the music included many zigzagging lines, they may draw these lines.

2. Acknowledge students' feelings about dance. When you hear, "I can't" or "I don't want to," say something to the effect of "I hear you. I'm learning this too, but all the movements in today's lessons are movements we already know; we're just combining them differently." When you debrief the lesson, discuss feelings again, allowing students to have a voice.

3. Allow students to help you shape the unit for future students by actively seeking their feedback, either in writing or orally. Make it safe for them to tell you how to make the unit better.

4. Teach by invitation (Graham 1992). Offer plenty of movement choices through open-ended tasks.

5. Actually participate with your students when possible.

6. Accept student interpretations of tasks as long as they are trying hard.

7. Do not require students to perform in front of the whole class; showing a dance to a partner or small group is sufficient and less likely to cause self-consciousness or embarrassment.

To this list we add the suggestion that you try disguising dance by incorporating equipment. For example, use balls with line dancing or dance with a parachute.

Developmental Appropriateness

Remember, as with all other areas of physical education, if you design a dance curriculum that allows children to respond and progress at their own levels and rates, you will be designing a developmentally appropriate dance curriculum. See the box for what COPEC (1992) has to say about developmentally appropriate dance learning.

In this chapter, we will show you how to design and teach a developmentally appropriate dance curriculum.

Safety

Follow these guidelines to keep dance lessons safe:

✓ Make sure that the work space is clean and free of hazards.

✓ Ensure that students have adequate space in which to move without colliding with walls, equipment, or other students.

✓ Make sure that props such as scarves, hoops, drums, and so on are in working order and that students know how to use them properly.

✓ Insist that students respect one another's space (no collisions!).

✓ Do not allow stockinged feet! Even on carpeting, sock feet can be too slippery.

Attaining Physical Education Goals Through Dance

You can design dance units to enhance your students' physical education learning in all the same ways games do. In this section, we'll look at the specific ways dance can help your

---

Cross-Curriculuar Teaching Tips: Science

Use the following and other movement tasks in dance learning to explore science concepts:

• Reflect the movement of a machine part (Purcell 1994); make the entire machine with your group.

• After studying a unit on the weather, have students create dances to show one or several elements of the weather—clouds, rain, storms, snow, heat, cold, and so on.

• After studying electrical circuits, use dance to demonstrate a circuit itself and the actions of the electrons through the electrical wires.

students progress in the areas of movement skills and concepts and cognitive and social development. We'll also show you how to incorporate adequate physical activity through dance.

Movement Skills and Concepts

Dance is an excellent way to enhance your students' understanding of movement skills and concepts. Combining skills in new and unique ways reinforces learning that will carry over into other physical education content areas. Exploring the movement concepts of body awareness, space awareness, effort, and relationships is at the very heart of what makes dance the expressive form of movement that it is. This, too, will carry over to learning in other physical education content areas. Moreover, through the movement exploration that dance can afford, children begin to "own" the movements for themselves in more deep and meaningful ways.

Cognitive Development

Studying dance increases your students' knowledge not only of dance but also of movement itself. The mental images you may mention to encourage movement (e.g., mimicking animals—"fly like a bird"—or interpreting more abstract language such as "wither away" or "move in slow motion") stretch language development into the bodily-kinesthetic realm. Creative dance allows students to make many decisions as to how they will interpret music, solve problems to answer an open-ended task, or include everyone. Creating dances to teach to other students challenges students' problem-solving and decision-making abilities as well.

Social Development

Cooperative learning belongs in dance, too. As students work together to learn a prescribed dance, create new dances, and teach one another their creations, they develop better communication and other social skills. Moreover, when you insist on a caring, inclusive, and supportive dance learning atmosphere, you reinforce the vital social skills of respect for and nurturing of individual needs and abilities.

Adequate Physical Activity

The degree of physical activity in a dance unit lesson will vary with the task and the individual's interpretation. For example, if you ask children to create a dance by pretending they are drops in a rainstorm, they will most likely incorporate more physical activity than if you ask them to create a dance in which they float to the ground like leaves. But even with the storm, you may have a student who decides to be a drop in a puddle.

COMPONENT—
Dance/Rhythmical Experiences

Appropriate Practice	Inappropriate Practice
The physical education curriculum includes a variety of rhythmical, expressive, and dance experiences designed with the physical, cultural, emotional, and social abilities of the children in mind.	The physical education curriculum includes no rhythmical, expressive, or cultural dance experiences for children.
	Folk and square dances (designed for adults) are taught too early or to the exclusion of other dance forms in the curriculum or are not modified to meet the developmental needs of the children.

Reprinted from COPEC/NASPE 1992.

Figure 11.1 Mental imagery can encourage creativity in movement.

At any rate, offer a variety of movement challenges across your dance curriculum to allow for physical activity. Perhaps use "calmer" ideas for warm-ups and cool-downs and "stormier" ideas for the main part of the lesson. Just make sure each dance lesson includes adequate physical activity by choosing words, dances, and music that require large muscle movement, excitement, and energy.

Dance: Curriculum Content

Dances can be created by the dancers or by others—whether tap, jazz, creative ballet, aerobic, basic rhythms, or folk and square dance. The three types that are appropriate for the elementary physical education curriculum are basic rhythms, creative dance, and folk and square dance. Each type can be created by the students for themselves or created by students, teachers, or cultures for students to learn. Let's examine each of the three types of dances more closely. Then we'll look at what aspects of the four main movement concepts you should focus upon.

Basic Rhythms

To help children learn basic rhythms, use 4/4 time music with a definitive beat (e.g., march music). Enhance these experiences with simple musical instruments such as drums, maracas, sandpaper blocks, and cymbals. Have students snap, clap, tap, bend, stretch, step, or jump to the first beat of a measure, starting with simple actions that use one body part, then two, then three, and so on.

In her record series *Rhythmically Moving* (1989), Phyllis Weikart outlines three ways to move to the beat of the music. Use these to develop beat and body awareness that may carry over to language development, reading readiness, and other academic areas:

- Unilateral movements—performed on one side of the body; for example, tapping the right knee to the beat

- Bilateral movements—performed on both sides of the body in unison (symmetrically); for example, tapping both knees at the same time

- Cross-lateral movements—alternating sides of the body; for example, tapping the right knee, then the left knee, then the right knee, and so on

In addition, children need opportunities to move to music throughout the physical education curriculum. They should move to music with equipment (e.g., balls, sticks, jump ropes, steps, etc.) They should move to the beat as they work to increase their heart rates (aerobics). In these ways, children can further develop timing and rhythm.

Creative Dance

This term describes dance movements created by the students themselves. This is where problem solving and decision making through dance learning really take center stage. Work especially on body awareness, space awareness, effort, and relationship concepts.

A word of caution is necessary for teaching creative dance: Unlike dances created by others, there's no hiding behind someone else's ideas in creative dance. One is truly exposed emotionally as well as physically. Although younger children may buy into the idea of creating and performing their own dances more readily than older children, you will be able to elicit quality work from older students by ensuring a caring, supportive atmosphere in which respect for all contributions is highly valued and encouraged. Moreover, when everyone is on-task at the same time, individuals may feel less self-conscious and more creative. Thus, never demand that students or groups perform solo in front of the class.

Folk and Social Dance

Folk and social dances are usually cultural dances that reflect a particular time period or a particular country or ethnic population. Such dances give you prime opportunities to integrate physical education across your academic curriculum. They are generally preset sequences of steps and range from the cha-cha to the line dances of the 1990s. You can borrow or buy recordings that help you teach these sequences or invite parents or other community members to share their interests.

Choose folk and social dances that are appropriate to your students' physical and cognitive abilities. If you must alter the dance to enable your students to learn it, you will lose some of its cultural and historical flavor (Purcell 1994). So when selecting folk and social dances created by others, stay within the parameters of your students' skills and needs. Finally, when teaching a dance of another culture, be aware how your own cultural background may influence your interpretation of the dance (Purcell 1994). Seek to present dances in an unbiased manner. For example, when teaching African dances, beware that no one perpetuates the common prejudices regarding African Americans as being only capable of singing, dancing, and playing sports. Instead, teach each ethnic dance in its native context, including the traditions from which it arises, what people wear while dancing it, and why the dance is performed. This will help students interpret the dances as they were intended to be interpreted—without individual cultural backgrounds (especially the teacher's) interfering. Finally, balance your dance choices, resisting the temptation to overemphasize folk and social dance to the exclusion of other forms.

Movement Concepts

Dance units provide excellent opportunities to teach, reinforce, and expand your students' knowledge of movement concepts—body awareness, space awareness, effort, and relationships. Table 11.1 lists the various elements of each of these four components.

Remember, movement concept elements are the "adverbs" in the "Movement Language." Just as we teach children basic sentence structure, then more descriptive language, to enable them to master written language, we can teach them to move more "descriptively" through dance. Figures 11.2 through 11.5 show several examples of the various elements of the four basic movement concepts.

When you work to extend your students' movement knowledge and vocabulary through dance, you will find that you can better show students how to apply these to other physical education and academic areas.

Table 11.1 The Movement Alphabet

Movement concepts—adverbs			
Body awareness	**Space awareness**	**Effort**	**Relationships**
Body parts	General space	Speed	Objects
Shapes	Self-space	Force	Partner
Curved	Directions	Flow	
Twisted	Levels		
Narrow	Pathways		
Wide	Extensions		
Symmetrical			
Asymmetrical			
Nonlocomotor			
Swing and sway			
Twist and turn			
Bend and curl			
Stretch			
Sink			
Push and pull			
Shake			
Base of support			

Reprinted, by permission, from Buschner, C., 1994, *Teaching Children Movement Concepts and Skills*, (Champaign, IL: Human Kinetics), 10.

For example, the ability to move through space helps in team sports, and a bodily-kinesthetic understanding of symmetrical and asymmetrical can be applied in math learning (see sidebar on page 200).

Dance: Instructional Strategies

Most, if not all, of the principles and tactics you use to teach in other physical education areas apply to the realm of dance. In this section, we'll show you how to organize dance learning, adjust for individual needs, encourage problem solving, and modify dances.

Organizing the Teaching–Learning Environment

As with any area, the organizational decisions you make when teaching dance have a significant impact as to what and how your students learn. In this section, we'll discuss teaching styles, forming learning groups, demonstrating and performing, and observing dance.

Teaching Styles

You can use both direct and indirect teaching styles in dance. A direct approach is appropriate when introducing a new task, particularly in folk, social, and other dances for which is it important to follow a prescribed sequence of steps (Purcell 1994). An indirect style helps students explore creative dance possibilities.

Forming Learning Groups

Have students work alone or in pairs or small groups. Be aware, however, that not all children will be ready to work with others. You may wish to offer the choice of working on a group, partner, or personal dance that meets the same open-ended task. By working alone, students can discover for themselves what movements they do and do not enjoy performing, which movements they do and do not feel comfortable doing, and which they

Figure 11.2 Body awareness.

can do well or would like to be able to do better (Purcell 1994). Then they may be ready to work with a partner or small group.

You can teach a small group of volunteers a dance during another time period (e.g., recess, before or after school), learning alongside them, so they can teach their classmates the dance as group leaders during physical education time. An opportunity to peer teach that comes with a private lesson may be an excellent way to help the reluctant dancer feel more comfortable and confident.

Demonstrating and Performing

Demonstrating is, of course, a key part of the direct style of teaching. If you feel comfortable, you can demonstrate a step or movement yourself. If not, talk a small group of student volunteers through the movements for the class to observe or, as mentioned, train a group of peer tutors to help demonstrate. It is best for observing students to see the movement from the backs of the demonstrators so that they do not have to reverse what they observe in their minds. If you are helping an individual student, stand side by side so that you can see each other.

When using an indirect teaching style, have students demonstrate their dances to one another. In fact, Pica (1993) recommends the indirect style of teaching for just this

Figure 11.3 Space awareness.

reason—students can discover, create, and do all the demonstrating, regardless of their teacher's dance skill level. This approach also enhances problem-solving skills because students learn more than simply how to imitate. You can have partners or small groups show each other a personal dance or have half the class observe while the other half performs, then switch. Or you can observe one group at a time performing while the other groups continue practicing. Remember, always respect feelings: *never* require or pressure students to demonstrate or perform solo.

Observing Dance

Students can learn a great deal from observing a professional dance troupe or advanced dance class perform whether in person or on videotape. Guide student observations by asking them to look for specific components of each dance. For example, students can look for (Purcell 1994)

- how the dance begins and ends,
- various feelings expressed by the dancers, and
- the different ways the dancers use curved and straight pathways.

Adjusting for Individual Needs

We cannot stress enough that a developmentally appropriate physical education curriculum allows for individual differences so that all may feel successful as they grow and learn in a physical education area. Use the following ideas to help you adjust your dance units for individual needs.

- Teaching by invitation ideas for dance:
  —Invite students to choose whether they'll work alone, with a partner, or in a small group.

Figure 11.4 Effort.

Figure 11.5 Relationships.

Cross-Curriculuar Teaching Tips: Math

You can use dance to reinforce mathematical concepts and skills, as shown in these examples for primary and intermediate students:

- Primary
  - Draw numbers in the air with one body part, then two. Draw numbers by traveling along pathways across the floor.
  - Move in diagonal, vertical, and horizontal lines across the floor.
  - Reinforce geometric concepts by having students create body shape dances.
  - Count dance steps and emphasize sequencing concepts.
  - Demonstrate quantitative ideas with the body: big, small, high, low, wide, narrow, fast, slow, heavy, light.

- Intermediate
  - Model the concepts of symmetrical and asymmetrical, then draw examples of this concept on graph paper.
  - In three concentric circles, create a dance demonstrating the three levels in space: low, medium, and high.
  - Have small groups demonstrate complex geometric concepts such as concave, convex, and lesser known shapes such as rhomboids, trapezoids, parallelograms. Create a sequence that uses a floor pattern in a geometric shape.
  - Act out the concept of sets.
  - Act out math operations.

- Allow students to choose the moves they'll use to interpret a theme you choose.
- Allow students to choose their own themes for creative dances.
- Give students the choice of performing with or without equipment.
- Intratask variation ideas for dance:
  - Suggest simpler steps (e.g., locomotor movements) in place of more challenging dance steps.
  - Challenge students who have mastered the basic dance steps to do more complex steps or to create their own variations of basic steps.

Encouraging Problem Solving in Dance

Problem solving challenges work in dance, too. As in other areas, an open-ended task allows individuals to adjust the level of difficulty to match their abilities. When using an indirect, problem-solving approach, however, be sure to set definite parameters. For example, for each creative dance lesson, clearly define what you expect but make the task open-ended enough to encourage creativity. The more inexperienced your students are in dancing, the more specific your instructions should be. For example, ask students to move at a low level for one minute, then a high level for one minute, allowing them to choose the force, direction, and shapes they'll use to do so. In addition, you can use the many cross-curricular suggestions for dances to perform in this chapter to help you develop tasks that suit your students' needs, interests, and abilities.

Modifying Dances

Of course, you must strive to meet your students' needs, interests, and abilities through dance learning, just as you do in other areas. In this section, we'll look closely at how to select and use music, props, and poems and stories to create relevant and effective learning experiences.

Music

According to Purcell (1994), you can use music in dance for one of the following four reasons:

1. To stimulate ideas for a dance
2. To support the tempo and rhythm of the movement
3. To create a mood for a dance
4. To provide structure for a dance

Your voice, too, is an instrument, and you can use it to define the mood and tone of student action. For example, if you say "Fall" gently and softly, students will respond differently than if you say "Fall!" in a loud and commanding voice. Using percussion instruments is another way to guide student dancing. And try the recordings available commercially that come with ideas for dance lessons. Finally, start with music your students are familiar with and like, then expand their music and dance knowledge by branching out to unfamiliar music forms. (See also chapter 18.)

Props

Props add interest and understanding to dance learning. You can use props to demonstrate an unfamiliar word or concept to students. Such a prop may be as simple as a drawing on the chalkboard of a zigzagged line or as familiar as a ball to represent round body shapes. Another way to use props is to allow students to manipulate them as extensions of their bodies to accentuate or define their movements. For example, partners can move through space together while holding on to opposite ends of a scarf or use scarves to highlight arm movements. Finally, props can help create the appropriate environment for a dance. For example, if students are creating a dance to illustrate their science lesson about weather, they might use blue scarves to represent rain or lightning. Or students can use props to create a scene or setting or the general atmosphere of the theme.

Poems and Stories

Poems and stories are excellent ways to inspire or accompany dancing while integrating language arts into your physical education curriculum. Perhaps your students especially like a story or poem you've used in the classroom, or perhaps you come across one you think will enhance a science or social studies unit. Have your students dance the story or poem as well, reinforcing learning across the curriculum (see the sidebar on page 203). Purcell (1994) offers the following additional advice for using poems and stories in dance:

- Initially read the poem or story straight through, then discuss it. If necessary, reread to help students become familiar with it.
- Read in your normal voice; avoid being overly dramatic.
- When using a poem or story for inspiration, list events, feelings, and actions that occur and discuss how these may be expressed through movement.

Cross-Curricular Teaching Tips: Music and Social Studies

Although this is a fairly obvious way to integrate dance across your academic curriculum, if possible, work with a music teacher, parents, and other community leaders to ensure that your music choices reflect the cultural diversity of your school population. Perhaps coordinate your choices with your social studies curriculum to speak to multicultural needs. Folk dances are an excellent way to explore the world through meaningful movement. But creative dances can also enhance multicultural learning, for example, when students develop and perform a dance to retell a story, event, or holiday from another culture.

Figure 11.6 Adding props to dance is another way to inspire creativity.

- Feel free to use only one line or section from a poem or story or the qualities of a particular character or setting as the basis for the learning experience.

Planning Dance Units and Lessons

Now that you've selected the content you wish to teach in dance and thought about the appropriate methods, you're ready to plan your dance units and lessons. A dance learning experience has three parts that you must plan for: how you will introduce the dance experience, how you will develop the content, and what the culminating event should be. Purcell (1994) recommends that you plan these three components in the reverse; after all, it always helps to know where you're going before you map out how to get there. Each journey may take one or several lessons. Let's see how to plan your dance trip.

Cross-Curricular Teaching Tips: Language Arts

Use a poem or story to inspire a dance lesson. Introduce the poem or story in the classroom before physical education class. Ask students to think about ways they will use movement to retell the poem or story or to express their feelings about the literature. Choose pieces that provide and evoke strong images and actions.

When teaching intermediate students, be especially careful to select topics that will be of interest to them; consider involving them in the selection process. *Wilma Unlimited* by Kathleen Krull (Harcourt Brace, 1996) is an example of literature that lends itself to dance interpretation by intermediate students.

Planning a Culminating Dance

As in other curricular areas, a culminating event helps students apply the knowledge and experience they have gained through the developmental stages. It should be designed to bring out the best in each student. To do so, ensure that your choice of culminating dance is relevant to students, within their physical capabilities, and otherwise developmentally appropriate and interesting. Whether student-created or created by others, a culminating dance has a beginning, middle, and end. For example, when dancing a story or poem, students might begin by entering the space, then perform the story line, and end by leaving the space. When using student-created dance, you will at the very least need to decide what movement elements students must incorporate; mandate more aspects if necessary or desired. When using dances created by others, you must identify their elements yourself before attempting to teach them to your students. Figure 11.7 shows an analysis chart that helps you outline the elements of a dance.

Developing the Elements of a Culminating Dance

Here you take the elements you have identified as being part of the culminating dance and introduce them to your students in sequence. This may be as straightforward as simply teaching each part of a dance in sequence or as complex as helping students

Spaghetti Dance

Body awareness	*Actions of the body:* Walk, run, leap, jump, hop
	Shapes: Curved and straight with whole body and body parts
Space awareness	*Levels:* High, medium, low
	Direction for travel: Forward
	Range: Big movements
	Pathways: Straight, curved
Effort	*Space:* Direct on straight paths Indirect on curved paths
	Time: Slow, fast
	Force: Strong, light
	Flow: Bound for all straight shapes Free on run and leap in curved shape
Relationships	Students move individually throughout dance
	Students can choose to connect
	Students move close together when in curved shapes

Figure 11.7 Sample analysis chart.
Reprinted, by permission, from Purcell, T., 1994, *Teaching Children Dance*, (Champaign, IL: Human Kinetics), 42.

incorporate open-ended parameters into their own creative dances.

Assessing Dance Learning

In this section, we'll show you how to authentically assess dance learning (see also chapter 3). We'll describe assessment tools in the psychomotor, cognitive, and affective domains specific for dance. Use the data you collect through assessment to help you better tailor your dance program to your students' needs, abilities, and interests.

Psychomotor Assessment

As in other physical education areas, you can use teacher, self-, and peer assessment to gauge psychomotor progress in dance. Figure 11.8 shows a sample psychomotor assessment form used to monitor an entire class. You can rewrite this using the same criteria for use in self- or peer assessment.

Cognitive Assessment

You can assess student understanding in dance with simple and short written tests, such as that shown in figure 11.9. You can also request physical responses to thought-provoking questions. Finally, a poker chip survey (Graham 1992) may be helpful as well (see chapter 3).

Affective Assessment

Once again, journal entries, smiley-face exit polls (Graham 1992), and class discussions can be very helpful in assessing affective

Type of Dance: Folk Dance

Level of performance	Evidence of student behavior	Student	Teacher comments
Basic	Cannot accurately reproduce all movements Loses rhythm Has steps but not arm or head movement Body parts not coordinated Moves out of formation Not focused during the dance Loses control	Sue	Needs to stay focused on the lesson, demonstrated difficulty staying on rhythm.
Proficient	Accurately reproduces movements Loses rhythm, but can regain Remembers the dance sequence Stays focused on dance Moves out of formation, but can regain Loses coordination on a movement Loses control on a movement	Steve Mary	Remembered the sequence of the dance and recalled the names of the steps. Stayed focused on lesson, demonstrated initial difficulty with coordination on the slide step; after continued practice successful.
Advanced	Performs all movements accurately in sequence and rhythm Includes movement details and arm and head movements Demonstrates good balance and strength Stays focused Stays in formation the entire dance Coordinates movements with others	Mark	Was very helpful to other students and took time to show them slides to the right and left and how to count the steps in rhythm to the music.

Figure 11.8 Recording sheet for psychomotor assessment.
Reprinted, by permission, from Purcell, T., 1994, *Teaching Children Dance,* (Champaign, IL: Human Kinetics), 49.

development. An affective questionnaire, such as that shown in figure 11.10, may also reveal important data to help you overcome student reluctance to dance.

Summary

Don't be afraid to add dance to your physical education curriculum. Start with a type of dance in which you are interested and get your dancing feet wet! Maybe a folk dance will enhance a social studies unit this semester, and you can try creative dance to enhance your poetry-writing unit next semester.

Can't dance? Call yourself a beginning dancer and kick up your heels alongside your students. You'll all have a lot of fun applying the basic movement skills and concepts in a new and exciting way. Use the content,

---

Sample Dance Knowledge Test Appropriate for Intermediate Level Students

1. Which of the following words is an example of moving in a specific direction in dance?
   a. straight
   b. sideways
   c. low
   d. wide

2. Which of the following descriptions best defines the word "jump"?
   a. weight transfer two feet to two feet
   b. weight transfer one foot to the same foot
   c. weight transfer one foot to the opposite foot
   d. weight transfer with a step and a hop

3. You hear soft, classical string music being played. It sounds like you might feel floating on a cloud. How would you most likely respond through movement?
   a. direct, firm
   b. fast, strong
   c. indirect, light
   d. straight, powerful

4. Choose one of the following words to indicate a relationship you may have while working with a partner.
   a. fast, slow
   b. light, strong
   c. general, personal
   d. lead, follow

5. Draw a picture of a dancer making a symmetrical shape at a low level:

[Answers: 1. b; 2. a; 3. c; 4. d; 5. Check drawing for symmetrical shape and low level.]

Figure 11.9 Sample dance knowledge test.

1. What parts of the learning experience did you like most? _____
   _____

   Why? _____
   _____

2. Would you like to perform this dance again? _____ Why? _____
   _____

3. What do you like most or least about dancing? _____
   _____

4. How do you feel when you are dancing? _____
   _____

5. Do you feel you can be creative in dance? _____ When? _____
   _____

6. Do you enjoy dancing with others as part of a small group? _____
   _____

7. Do you feel uncomfortable in any part of the dance learning experience? _____
   What part? _____
   _____

   Why? _____
   _____
   _____

Figure 11.10 Sample questionnaire to assess children's feelings toward dance.
Reprinted, by permission, from Purcell, T., 1994, *Teaching Children Dance,* (Champaign, IL: Human Kinetics), 52.

methods, and assessment tools outlined in this chapter to create a successful learning experience. Use the feedback you receive from students to help you do even better next time.

Sample Dance Lessons

The following are sample lessons in dance education. Note that although a grade level or range is given, you can adapt a lesson to use with older or younger students, according to their needs.

This first lesson, reprinted by permission from Purcell's *Teaching Children Dance* (1994), is a learning experience for teaching about effort most appropriate for preschool through second graders. Use the "How Can I Change This?" and "Teachable Moment" sections to help you extend this lesson into a complete

unit. Use the "Look For" section to help you assess student understanding.

The Cat

Objectives

As a result of participating in this learning experience, children will improve their ability to

- create different ways to move that are fast and slow, sustained and sudden,

- focus on moving isolated body parts, and

- perform a sequence of movements that emphasizes using fast and slow, sudden and sustained movements

Suggested Grade Range

Pre-K–2nd

Organization

Students will dance individually throughout the entire lesson.

Equipment Needed

Percussion instruments: a drum and triangle

Description

Today we are going to find different ways to move fast and slow. When I say go, I'd like you to find a self-space and run in place as fast as you can. Go! Now run in place as slow as you can. Now find a different way to travel through general space as fast as you can. Go all over . . . find another way. Stop. Now move through space as slow as you can, taking a long time for each step. Find another slow way to move. Stop.

Think of some things that you do to get ready for school in the morning—brushing your teeth, getting dressed, eating cereal. We are going to try each one slow and fast. Ready? Let's all do the movement of brushing our teeth as fast as we can . . . now as slow as you can. Now try slowly putting on your clothes . . . now get dressed as fast as you can. The third movement is about eating a bowl of cereal very slowly—put the cereal in the bowl slowly, pour the milk slowly, take your spoon and scoop up cereal slowly, and put it in your mouth slowly. Now eat the cereal as fast as you can. Feel the difference in your muscles when you move fast and slow.

Today I am going to play a triangle for all of our slow movements. Listen to how long the sound lasts after I hit the triangle. Now begin to move your arms when I hit the triangle and continue to keep them moving until you do not hear the triangle (tap triangle). Keep your movement smooth and slow. Feel your arm moving for a long time. Can you keep the movement going? Now try this with another body part. I want to see if you can listen to the sound and move one

body part slowly until the sound of the triangle stops. I see that some of you are moving your arms forward and backward, moving them together and apart, or moving one arm and then the other. Some are moving your shoulders, legs, whole body. You are taking a long time for each movement when you move slowly.

I will also use the drum today for our fast movement and one loud drumbeat as the signal to stop. Listen to the drum and hear the difference between the fast beat for running and the loud beat for the stop (give one regular series, one loud beat). Now show me you hear the difference by running in place when you hear the fast beats and stopping when you hear the single loud beat (play regular, fast beats and one loud beat to stop).

I am now going to play the drum very fast; see if you can move your arms as fast as you can until you hear the drum stop. Ready, go (play regular beats). Arms moving high and low, forward and backward, together and apart, and stop (loud beat). This time point with your arm to a different corner of the room as fast as you can when you hear the drum (tap drum). Point . . . point . . . point . . . point. Try the pointing again with the other arm. Point . . . point . . . point . . . point.

This time, run as fast as you can and stop when you hear me hit the drum (begin regular drumbeat; end with loud beat). This time take the run up in the air using a leap or jump when you hear the beats; stop on the loud sound of the drum (repeat regular drumbeats, one loud beat). This time after the run and the stop, begin to move your arms slowly. Let me repeat those movements again. You'll run as fast as you can, sometimes going up in the air, stop, then move your arms slowly. I will call out the movements to help you as you do them. No drums this time. Ready? Run . . . stop . . . arms slow. This time practice the movements again, and I will play the drum fast for running, hit it once loud to stop, and then play the triangle for the slow arm movements. Let the sounds of the instruments give you the directions instead of my words. Here we go! (Give eight regular drumbeats, one loud beat, triangle taps.)

In our dance today you are going to dance the movements of a cat who moves slow and fast. Each person find your own personal space on the floor. We are going to do many different cat movements, then put them together into a dance. The first cat movement shows a cat sleeping. What are the different shapes a cat uses for sleeping? Yes, curved, perhaps stretched. Find another sleeping cat shape, and another. I see many of you in round curled shapes, some of you are on your back, others are sleeping on the sides of their bodies, some are curled up while sitting. Slowly change from one sleeping shape to another each time you hear the triangle sound. I will tap the triangle four times. Ready? (Tap triangle.) Make your first sleeping shape . . . now slowly change to your second shape . . . the third different shape . . . now slowly into the last shape. That was great! You used four different sleeping shapes and moved very slowly into each shape.

Now the cat begins to wake up and slowly stretches. I will tap the triangle when I tell you which body part to stretch. The cat stretches one arm, then the other, then one leg, and then the other. Slowly the cat begins to move the head, then the back, and the shoulders. Now it slowly rises up from the floor standing on two feet. Make sure you slowly stretch each part of your body as you wake up (see figure 11.11).

Now the cat will move fast when it suddenly sees a mouse. Move your arm quickly to point like you did in the beginning of the class—to a corner of the room, then to another corner as if to point to another mouse, then another corner, and to another corner. I will hit the drum once for each pointing move-

ment. Ready? Point (tap drum) one, two, three, four.

Then the cat begins to chase the imaginary mouse around the room. I will beat the drum very fast for this chasing part; you'll run as fast as you can and sometimes take your run up in the air. Ready? Run one, two, three, four, five, six, seven, eight.

Finally the cat stops (give one loud drum beat) and catches the mouse. Slowly bend over to pick up the mouse and slowly pretend to drop the mouse into your mouth to eat. You are so tired after chasing and eating the mouse that you slowly go back to sleep. Move slowly down to the floor into a sleeping shape as I play the triangle for the slow movements.

Now let's put all the movements together. I will play the instruments and tell you what movements to do. (Repeat sequence with no stops.) (With triangle) Sleeping shape one two three . . . four. Stretch one arm . . . other arm . . . one leg . . . other leg head back . . . shoulders . . . stretch up. (Drum taps) Point one, two, another corner, another. (Fast drumbeat) Run one, two, three, four, five, six, seven, eight. (One loud drumbeat) Catch the mouse, pick it up and eat it (triangle taps). Go to sleep one . . . two . . . three . . . four. Nice job! Let's see if all you people who were cats can nicely line up ready to go.

Look For

- How children change from fast to slow movement. They will need to learn to slow down the fast movement, espe-

Figure 11.11 The cat.

cially after running, before they begin to perform the slow movements.

- The ability of children to isolate movement in one body part. This learning experience isolates movements in two ways: the arm moving fast for pointing at the corners and separate movements of the arms, legs, head, back, and shoulders during the slow part of the dance.

How Can I Change This?

- Develop more short phrases that combine fast and slow movements. For example, "Choose one movement with your arm and try it using this phrase: Slow-fast-slow." Students can decide how long the slow and fast movements will last. Try different combinations with stationary and traveling movements.

- Another idea pairs students as partners. One partner does a movement fast or slow and the other partner responds doing the same movement in the opposite tempo. For example, partner one touches the head with the hands, turns around, and makes a stretched shape using a fast tempo. Partner two responds by doing the three movements using a slow tempo.

Teachable Moment

Take time to have children listen to the sound of the triangle and drum in the way you will use them in the learning experience.

Reprinted from Purcell 1994.

The last lessons reprinted by permission here form a sixth grade dance unit in *Physical Education Unit Plans for Grades 5-6* (Logsdon et al. 1997). As you will see, dance units at this level focus on more complex concepts than at the primary level but still consciously apply basic movement concepts and skills. The following list shows the context in which this unit takes place as this particular program strives to cover basic skills in a systematic and enjoyable way:

Sample Unit Sequence for Sixth Grade Dance (Logsdon et al. 1997)

Unit 1
Altering Body Shape Using Partners

Altering the body shape using a partner to add dimension to the shape

Unit 2
Introducing Theme and Variation

Introducing theme and variation, deliberately alternating movement by changing the body, space, and effort elements

Unit 3
Designing a Repeatable Dance Sequence

Combining traveling with changes of pathways in small groups to design a repeatable folk dance sequence

Unit 4
Strict Canon, Free Canon, and Moving in Unison

Contrasting the choreographic forms of strict and free canon with moving in unison to design small group dances

Unit 5
Designing a Partner Sequence Around Interpersonal Relationships

Combining and contrasting simple interpersonal relationships while designing a folk dance sequence with a partner

Reprinted from Logsdon 1997.

Unit 1: Altering Body Shape Using Partners

Motor Content

Introduction to Relationships; Awareness of Shape in Movement

Body

- Shapes of the body—curved (round), straight (narrow, angular), wide (spread), twisted

- Nonlocomotor—counterbalance, counter-tension

Relationships

Interpersonal—individual to individual: apart, together; above, below; in front of, behind, at the side of; over, under

Objectives

In this unit, students will (or should be willing to try to) meet these objectives:

- Make a variety of different body shapes with a partner for the purpose of changing the dimension and pattern of mutually formed shapes, demonstrate their most interesting shapes, and discuss the reasons for their choices
- Understand and demonstrate underlying principles of alignment, balance, and weight shift
- Use countertension and counterbalance to invent sequences with a partner, clearly demonstrating the principle of transition
- Explain and demonstrate examples of concepts used in dance and disciplines outside the arts
- Work safely and cooperatively with a partner by forming shapes and balances that are challenging, visually interesting, and controlled

Equipment and Materials

One drum; musical selections that are quiet and not identified by a strong beat, such as New Age music, e.g., Kitaro's "Silk Road"; Nakai's "Desert Dance"; or Winston's "Forest"; or classical music set to sounds in nature.

Learning Experiences

Note: Text in quotation marks indicates where teacher should chant the instructions to the beat of the music.

1.0 (Accompany work with quiet music.) Start with an opening body shape in which you and your partner are joined or connected by your hands (or hands to wrists). Keep changing your shape by making it wider, narrower, more angular, or more curved. Find a partner and begin.

1.1 Quietly share ideas with your partner and work cooperatively. Make each shape a joint effort rather than a performance of two soloists.

1.2 What other body parts could you link or join together to create a mutual shape? As you connect to your partner with a variety of body parts, change your level to achieve new, interesting shapes.

1.3 Make up a sequence with your partner, beginning with a straight, narrow shape, changing to a wide, spread shape, and ending with an angular body shape you both can hold. Work to make the transition from one shape into the next very smooth.

1.4 (Tap a slow, steady beat on the drum.) Gradually change your shape on taps one, two, and three, then freeze on the fourth tap. Think of some gelatinous or amoebalike substance that changes slowly as you change the mutual shape. Take a beginning pose. "(Tap:) Change, (tap) change, (tap) change, and (tap) hold; and change, 2, 3, and freeze (4)." (Repeat.)

1.5 Improvise some new body shapes with your partner. As I tap the drum (slow, steady pace), quickly make a shape on the first tap and hold it during the next three taps. Then both make a sudden change and hold that shape. "Shape number 1, hold 2, hold 3, hold 4; now a different shape, hold 2, hold 3, hold 4." (Repeat several times.)

1.6 Remember to change your level and the body parts you join together. Make each shape look new and different. Challenge yourselves, but make sure you can hold each shape. (Practice without the drum to give students time to explore multiple solutions and select and order new shapes. Then have students perform partner sequences with the drum.)

1.7 Anticipate each change and make your transitions sudden, clear, and purposeful.

2.0 In dance, one individual can relate to another individual by positioning themselves above, below, in front of, behind, over, under, or alongside. With a partner, demonstrate a variety of different spatial relationships as you create combined shapes. Rather than being face to face all the time, change your relationship to your partner, still maintaining a physical connection. (Provide time to experiment.)

2.1 Show a variety of shapes where you are back to back with your partner. Try to mutually lean your bodies against each other while your feet form a wide base to achieve counterbalance.

2.2 Remember to work safely with your partner by selecting shapes or balances that both of you can hold. What body parts can lean toward each other and connect to hold firm, strong shapes?

2.3 (Tap a drum at a slow, steady pace.) Change your spatial relationship to your partner every four counts and name aloud the relationship you are making with your partner. "Take your first position (above or below), 2, 3, 4; now change (behind), 2, 3, 4." (Repeat many times.)

2.4 (Accompany work with a quiet selection of music.) This time, design a short sequence that changes your spatial relationship to a partner. Take an opening shape with your partner and gradually alter the shape four different ways by changing your positioning. As you plan and perform your shapes, make the entire dance flow from one shape into the next with smooth transitions.

2.5 This half of the class, quickly take a seat and watch the other half perform their sequences. Observe one set of partners. Do they clearly demonstrate four different spatial relationships? (After several tries, have groups reverse roles.)

3.0 Let's review what we have learned about spatial relationships. Carefully lean or push against your partner and try to maintain your balance by creating counterbalance. (Have two students demonstrate.) Find a partner, an open space, and begin.

3.1 As you lean or push gently against your partner, change your levels and bases of support. Exactly how much muscle tension do you need to move into and hold each shape? To move smoothly out of each shape?

3.2 Remember to maintain wide bases of support in each position of counterbalance. Work with the weight of your partner to feel the balance.

3.3 To feel the difference between counterbalance and countertension, let's experiment with positions of countertension. Stand very close and hold on to your partner, then gradually lean away. Remember, the only way to achieve countertension is by mutually pulling away so both partners are responsible for each other's balance.

3.4 Select positions of counterbalance and countertension and alternate them. Work hard to make the transitions between these positions smooth—no unnecessary movements (see figure 11.12).

3.5 Experiment with a variety of spatial relationships as you demonstrate counterbalance and countertension. Side by side? In front of, behind? Close together? Far apart? Above, below? Over, under, on? Pull away from your partner or lean against him or her to achieve different relationships.

3.6 Design a short sequence of counterbalances and/or positions of countertension that clearly demonstrates changes in spatial relationships.

3.7 (Play quiet music to accompany work time.) As you design your sequence, allow the musical phrasing to sometimes determine when you alter your shape. The music will serve as the impetus for making the changes.

4.0 Beginning in several different places away from your partner, travel toward and connect momentarily in passing with your partner. (Use the term "con-

Figure 11.12 Try to lean toward your partner to create a shape that you can both hold. This is counterbalance.

nect" interchangeably with "join," "link," and "bond.")

4.1 Each time you join with your partner, make a slightly different shape. At first, you are creating only brief, momentary connections with your partner.

4.2 Consider changing your connecting body parts, your spatial relationships, and your bases of support each time you meet your partner.

4.3 With each contact, stay awhile longer, so each relationship with your partner lingers a little longer. A temporal relationship means the time spent with a partner.

4.4 Don't be in such a hurry to rush off; stay with your partner. Take longer to form your new shapes but don't lose your performance attitude. Keep alert and focused on creating shapes but ready to move on.

4.5 (Provide music for work time.) Design a sequence where you travel together (in unison), separate to travel alone, then meet and stay for a longer relationship as you change your shape with your partner on the spot.

4.6 In your dances, be prepared to say how your relationships with your partner are changing. Combine at least two spatial and two temporal relationship changes. Remember, a temporal relationship involves the amount of time you spend with your partner.

4.7 Show a clear change in the amount of time you spend with your partner. Stay with the partner a long time, then the next time linger just a moment.

4.8 (Provide music to accompany dances.) Let's see your dances in groups of four or five partners. Hold your opening position until you hear the music, then begin. Remember to travel into the empty spaces during your traveling parts and be aware of those dancers changing their shapes on the spot. Hold very still at the end of your dance until the music is turned off.

Reprinted from Logsdon 1997.

Chapter 12

Integrating Physical Education Across the Curriculum

Alex, 8

Because children are concrete learners, we need to be able to take conceptual information that is often abstract and present it in a practical, hands-on manner. Because children learn by doing, we need to provide a learning environment in which we actively engage children in learning experiences.

—Cone, et al. 1998

As we outlined in chapter 2, teaching across the curriculum is an important part of the elementary school mission of enhancing the growth of the whole child. We have offered many tips for integrating other subject areas into physical education and vice versa. In this chapter, we'll go beyond outlines and quick tips and offer you a more in-depth look at what cross-curricular, or *interdisciplinary*, learning is. Then we'll offer lesson plans for primary and intermediate physical education that incorporate math, language arts, science, and social studies. We have adapted this material with permission from *Interdisciplinary Teaching Through Physical Education* (1998) by Theresa Purcell Cone, Peter Werner, Stephen L. Cone, and Amelia Mays Woods.

What Is Interdisciplinary Learning?

In interdisciplinary learning, several subject areas are integrated with the goal of enhancing learning in each subject. This approach to learning emerged as educators realized that children's interest in their environment is not subject specific. Tarnowski (quoted by Wilcox 1994) says that the "interdisciplinary nature" of children's own play should be a model for planning and teaching. Integration of the curriculum is not new; teachers often integrate subjects such as the language arts with mathematics, the visual arts with social

studies, mathematics with science, or music with physical education.

There is no one model that describes all the ways interdisciplinary learning can be delivered. Elliot Eisner (College Board 1996) says that the curriculum can be structured using an idea as a focal point; a central theme can be the focus of several disciplines that each examine that theme. He also suggests that another approach is to develop problems that need more than one disciplinary frame of reference to be solved. You may find that implementing an interdisciplinary learning experience requires rearranging the order of your teaching to coincide with a concept being taught in another subject area.

Advantages of Interdisciplinary Learning

Interdisciplinary learning enhances and enriches what students learn. One of the strongest arguments for interdisciplinary learning is that by breaking through disciplinary boundaries, teachers can make the curriculum more relevant because they can embed knowledge and skills in real-life contexts (Wasley 1994). Also supporting this concept of learning is Gardner's Theory of Multiple Intelligences (chapter 2). When multiple intelligences are used to teach a skill or concept, it naturally becomes an interdisciplinary learning experience. Children make sense of the world through expressing their thinking in a variety of ways. "For the young child, movement is the first and foremost vehicle through which a child is able to communicate their feelings about themselves and their world to others" (Fraser 1991). Movement as a language is a natural and powerful way to express ideas and demonstrate understanding. The physical education program, as part of an interdisciplinary approach to learning, helps students gain the essential kinesthetic learning experiences that will enhance their ability to learn both movement and other subject areas through movement.

Additional support (Bucek 1992; Gilbert 1992; Friedlander 1992; Gallahue 1993; Connor-Kuntz and Dummer 1996) for interdisciplinary programs emphasizing a movement orientation includes the following:

1. Using movement promotes active involvement in learning (versus passive learning) that leads to increased understanding.

2. For young children, movement is a natural medium for learning. As children learn fundamental concepts such as height, distance, time, weight, size, position, and shape, movement gives meaning to an abstract system of language symbols.

3 . Movement stimulates development of the motor and neurological systems.

4. Movement can be experienced as a means of expression and communication.

5. Movement activities motivate children and capture their interest.

Despite the interest in interdisciplinary education, some concerns have been raised that moving away from a discipline-based curriculum will cause important content to fall by the wayside. Also, teachers, especially at the upper level grades, fear that the "purity" of their subjects and the logical scope and sequence will be lost in integrated units. But as a precaution, Jacobs (1989) emphasizes that teachers should integrate disciplines only when doing so allows them to teach important content more effectively.

Cross–Curricular Learning Experiences

The Rumpus Dance

Suggested Grade Level

Primary (K-3rd)

Interdisciplinary Connections

Children listen to a reading of Maurice Sendak's *Where the Wild Things Are* as part of

Figure 12.1 Playing and moving can help children understand how skills and knowledge are connected.

an author-of-the-month program and create a dance expressing the feeling of being at the wild rumpus.

Language Arts

Listening and responding to a story through movement; demonstrating comprehension of word meaning

Physical Education

Performing traveling movements using change of direction, level, and tempo that express the meaning of a word; creating a dance that has three movements; observing and responding to a dance performed by another student

Objectives

As a result of participating in this learning experience, children will

- verbally discuss and create a written list of words to define the word "rumpus" from Sendak's *Where the Wild Things Are,*
- explore different movements that express the list of descriptive words for rumpus, and
- create a rumpus dance using changes of level, direction, and tempo.

Equipment

Where the Wild Things Are, fast-tempo music, chalkboard or chart paper, chalk, or markers

Organization

Students create and perform movements individually and then work with partners to observe each other's dances.

Description

"You have just heard the story *Where the Wild Things Are.* This is an exciting story about the adventure of Max as he visits a strange land where the Wild Things live. Now you are going to create a dance about the wild rumpus that happened in the story."

Write the word "rumpus" on the top or in the center of the chalkboard or chart.

"Do you remember when the rumpus happened in the story? Let's look at the pages in the book and see how the Wild Things and Max are moving during the rumpus."

Show students the pages in the book.

"What kinds of movements are they doing at the rumpus?" Students respond, for example, with "hopping, jumping, skipping, turning, hanging, swinging, stretching, marching." (See figure 12.2.)

Write the words on the chalkboard or chart paper.

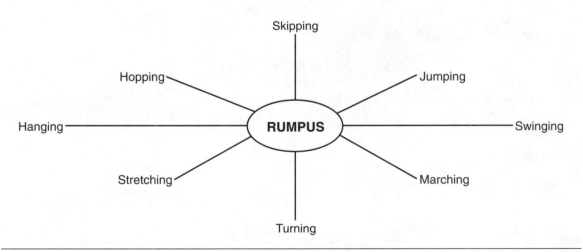

Figure 12.2 Rumpus movements.
Adapted, by permission, from Cone, T., P. Werner, S. Cone, A. Woods, 1998, *Interdisciplinary Teaching Through Physical Education*, (Champaign, IL: Human Kinetics), 37.

Tell the students that they will try these movements as part of their warm-up today.

First, have each student find his or her own space and begin hopping forward, backward, and sideways. Remind students to give each foot a turn. Ask them if they can hop four times on one foot in one direction and four times on the other foot in another direction.

Next, encourage them to try big skips that lift them up off the floor. Ask them to find a way to add a turn while they are skipping.

Now have them combine jumping and stretching together. Jump and stretch to the right, then jump and stretch to the left. Repeat the movement to the right and left several times.

Tell them that they will not be using swinging today, but they will use swinging the next time they use the gymnastic apparatus.

"Now we are going to create our own rumpus movements. Tell me some words that describe a rumpus." Students answer, "Wild party, going crazy, being very excited." "What movements can you do to express the meaning of the word rumpus that we did not do

in the warm-up?" Students answer, "Roll on the floor, spin around fast, shake your body, kick your legs up."

Add these words to the rumpus words on the chalkboard or chart paper.

"Each person, choose one movement from the list of words on the chalkboard. Now find a space and practice your movement using a forward, backward, and sideways direction. I will play the music while you are practicing." (See figure 12.3.)

Move through the class and ask students to identify their movement and demonstrate it in the three directions.

"Everyone stop and return to the chalkboard. Now choose a second movement from the list, find a space, and practice doing this movement changing from low to high and high to low. Again, I will play the music while you practice."

After a brief practice time, have the students stop, then ask them to put the two movements together in a sequence.

"Be sure to move smoothly from one movement to the other. See if you can find a

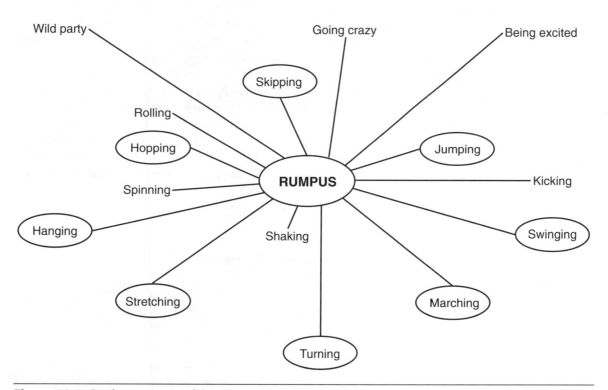

Figure 12.3 Student-suggested rumpus movements.
Adapted, by permission, from Cone, T., P. Werner, S. Cone, A. Woods, 1998, *Interdisciplinary Teaching Through Physical Education*, (Champaign, IL: Human Kinetics), 38.

way to blend the end of one movement into the beginning of the second movement.

The teacher moves through the class and observes how children are moving from the first movement to the second.

"Now stop, return to the chalkboard, and choose a third different movement from the list. Practice the movement using strong and fast energy that becomes slower and slower until you stop in a still shape. Can someone demonstrate how they can make a movement start strong and fast and let it become slower and slower until the movement stops in a still shape? I see Meredith would like to demonstrate. What movement are you going to use?" Meredith responds, "I'm going to spin around and wave my arms up and down to show how I go crazy and then get tired at my rumpus." "That sound great. Let's watch Meredith to see how the tempo of her spinning movement becomes slower and slower until she stops in a still shape." (Meredith demonstrates for the class.) "Thank you Meredith."

Write the sequence on the chalkboard or chart paper.

"Now practice putting all three movements you have chosen from the chalkboard in a sequence. Remember, the first one uses three different directions, the second one changes levels, and the third one starts fast and strong and ends in a still shape. The music will be playing while you practice." (See figure 12.4.)

While all the students are practicing, approach individual students and ask them to explain their sequence and to demonstrate the movements.

"Now let's show each other the rumpus dance you have created. I would like half the class to sit and observe while the other half demonstrates their rumpus dance. Perform your dance once, then hold your still shape until everyone in the group has finished. I will play the music while you are performing."

Each group performs its rumpus dance while the music is playing. Lower the music volume as the students begin to stop in their still shapes.

"The second time you perform, I will assign a person to observe your rumpus dance. When you are finished, your observer will tell you what movements he or she observed. Then you will switch places."

Assessment Suggestion

- Use the partner conversation at the end of the learning experience as one type of peer assessment.

- The form in figure 12.4 can be completed as a self-assessment. The student writes the first, second, and third movements of his or her rumpus dance on each line. Children can also add a drawing or comments about their feelings as they performed the dance.

- The teacher can videotape small groups of students performing their rumpus dance and have the students observe their performance and match the words they have written describing the dance to the movements they perform in their dance.

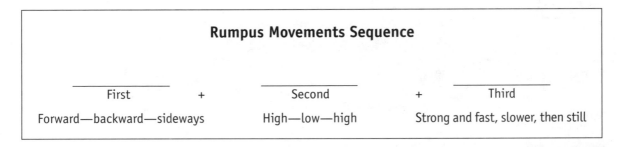

Figure 12.4 Sequence of rumpus movements.
Adapted, by permission, from Cone, T., P. Werner, S. Cone, A. Woods, 1998, *Interdisciplinary Teaching Through Physical Education*, (Champaign, IL: Human Kinetics), 40.

Look For

- Clear changes of direction, level, and tempo and ending the dance in a still shape.
- Smooth transitions from one movement to another. Do the children blend the end of one movement with the beginning of the next?

How Can I Change This?

- Emphasize other elements of movement such as size (big or small) or pathways, or develop a specific rhythm for each movement.
- Perform three movements using a pattern, such as first movement, fast and strong; second movement, slow and strong; third movement, fast and strong.
- Use other words or phrases from the story.
- Have students work in pairs or groups of three to select the words and develop the three movements of the dance. They can practice and perform in unison.

Teachable Moments

- Emphasize proper technique for performing movements, such as safe landings from a jump, using balance and strength to make smooth transitions from one movement to another, or using the correct rhythm for a skip.
- Encourage experimentation with the sequence of movements in the dance.

Reprinted from Cone 1998.

Measuring Sticks

Suggested Grade Level

Intermediate (3rd-5th)

Interdisciplinary Connections

As children learn how to measure using different units in mathematics, they can use this learning experience for practical application in physical education by measuring and graphing the distances of their traveling actions.

Mathematics

Measuring and graphing

Physical Education

Locomotor patterns (hop, jump, leap)

Objectives

As a result of participating in this learning experience, children will improve their abilities to

- use good body mechanics to hop, jump, and leap;
- combine basic locomotor actions into a sequence (e.g., hop, step, jump);
- measure and record their performances on scoring sheets; and
- diagram their performances on charts and make decisions about which efforts produce the best results.

Equipment

A ruler, yardstick, newspaper wand, bat, or stick with which to measure; a score sheet or histogram chart and pencil to record results; markers to mark jump length (Popsicle sticks, tape, pencil line, etc.)

Organization

Students will work in pairs in an indoor or outdoor space.

Description

"Good morning, boys and girls! Are you ready to do some exciting jumping today? What I have in mind for us is to do different styles of jumping and to see which ones allow us to jump the farthest. In addition to jumping today, the most important thing we are going to learn is how to measure our jumps, record our scores, and graph our performances.

"First, get a partner and stand back to back. Go. . . . If you don't have a partner yet, raise your hand, and I'll help you find one. Good. Now let's warm up. Play Follow the Leader with your partner, trying to stay close to each other. Vary the way you travel: sometimes jogging, hopping, jumping, skipping, and so on. Remember to change directions, pathways, and speeds. Perhaps take long and short steps, heavy and light steps. Stop. . . . Change leaders. Repeat. . . . Stop. Now let's do a few stretching exercises especially for our legs because we are going to use them a lot today."

Perform exercises of your choice, but remember to stretch hamstring, quadriceps, and calf muscles.

"Stop. Quickly come here in front of me. Sit down. I'm going to hand out some score sheets, graphs, measuring sticks, and pencils to each of you. (Distribute materials.) When I say "Go," you and your partner will find or make a (chalk) line within our space. This will be your jumping line. Each time you jump, you will start with your toes on, but not over, the line. (Demonstrate.) That is important because you will use that line for measuring every jump. After placing your toes on the line, you will make your jump. Your partner will mark your jump by putting a marker where your heels land or, if you fall backward, the part of your body that touches nearest the takeoff line." (Demonstrate.)

Note that children's abilities to measure accurately differ. Depending on the level of the child, crude measurements may be used, such as the number of lengths of a shoe, folded newspaper, book, or forearm. Children who have more advanced measuring abilities may use more accurate measures, such as the nearest yard, foot, inch, or centimeter. Work in the classroom on measurement skills.

"Each time you make a jump, measure it with your partner and record it on your score sheet. (Demonstrate.) Spread out and find a good jumping space with your partner. Go. . . . Stop. For your first jump, I want you to place your toes on the line and jump. Use a two-footed takeoff. Don't swing your arms much or bend your legs. Just an easy jump.

(Demonstrate.) Measure and record it on your score sheet. (See figure 12.5.) Take turns with your partner. On your next jump, try swinging your arms back and then forward and up (reach for the sky). (Demonstrate.)

"Make three jumps, and record your best jump. Go. . . . Remember to measure accurately, then record the score on your sheet. Stop. Now, let's try crouching and exploding in addition to the arm swing. (Demonstrate.) Swing, crouch, explode. Try three more jumps each, and record your best score. Remember to take turns, and help each other mark the jump and measure. Go. . . . Does anyone need any help with the score sheets or with their measuring? Stop. . . . Do you think it makes any difference if we lean forward (45 degrees) as we jump? (Demonstrate.) Swing, crouch, lean, explode! Try three more jumps, and record your best score. Go. . . . Stop.

"Let's graph what we have so far. (On the horizontal graph line (X axis), indicate the type of jump. On the vertical line (Y axis), mark the distance of your jump. (Demonstrate.)

"Everyone, graph each of your best jumps. Use the scores from your score sheets. Work with your partner, and help each other. Make sure you get each jump recorded correctly. Okay, look at your graph. What type of jump gave you the best results? Yes. As you added body parts (arm swing, leg explosion, trunk lean), you were able to jump farther. In sci-

Figure 12.5 Measure your jumps with a bat, book or other object.
Adapted, by permission, from Cone, T., P. Werner, S. Cone, A. Woods, 1998, *Interdisciplinary Teaching Through Physical Education*, (Champaign, IL: Human Kinetics), 86.

ence this is called using a summation of forces to get better results. Can you think of any other type of physical activity where you use a summation of forces to get better results? Yes, when we throw or kick, we use our whole body in our effort to throw or kick a far distance.

"Now let's try some other types of loco-motor skills and see how for we travel through the air. What about a hop (one-footed takeoff, same-foot landing)? Try three hops and record your best score. Go. . . . Stop. Now try a leap (one foot to the other). Try three leaps, and record your best score. Now graph those performances and compare them with your jumping performances. Were you able to travel farther with a jump, hop, or leap? (See figure 12.6.)

"What I want you to do now is to take several steps before you jump so that you have forward momentum as you go into your jump. It will be important to plant your take-off foot or feet on, but not over, your measuring line. (Demonstrate.) As in the rules for track and field, any takeoffs that go over the line do not count. Make several tries at jumping with a walking approach. Work out your steps to get them just right. Try a one-footed takeoff (hurdle step) and a two-footed take-off. (Demonstrate.) Always land on two feet. Remember to still swing your arms and ex-plode with your legs at takeoff. As you land,

rock forward from heels to balls of your feet and lean forward. Go. . . . Stop. Now that you have your steps down, choose your best way of jumping and make three tries. Measure each attempt. Record your best score. Place the score for your moving jump on the graph. Measure from the takeoff line to the point of impact nearest the line each time. Each score is to the nearest inch (or foot, book, stick). Go. . . . Your graphs are giving you an accurate picture of your results. Stop. Everyone come in here and sit down. Let's talk about jumping and what your scores and graphs are telling you. Were you able to jump as far or far-ther using a moving jump? What does this tell us about momentum and the sum of forces? You are learning a lot, not only about how to jump better, but also about how mathematics and science can help us under-stand how our bodies move."

Assessment Suggestion

- In addition to the graph in figure 12.6, have the children graph the distances of other traveling actions, such as a hop, leap, and moving long jump. Also give them an oral or written test on their understanding of the concepts of mo-mentum and summation of forces.

Look For

- Children need to use good mechanics to get optimal results. A good arm swing, explosive leg action, and leaning at a 45-degree angle are the key to success-ful results. Timing is also a key. Some children will swing their arms, then stop and jump. Others will crouch, then stand up straight and jump up. Placing a bar-rier (a towel or small hurdle to jump over) sometimes helps.
- Children are often confused about measuring. Be clear about the unit of measurement. Start with crude measure-ments. It is easier to understand "five books" or "five sticks" than inches as a fraction of a foot or yard. Also be clear about where to start the measurement and how far to measure.

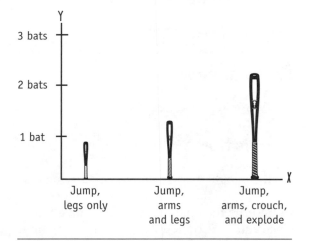

Figure 12.6 Graph the distance of your jumps. Adapted, by permission, from Cone, T., P. Werner, S. Cone, A. Woods, 1998, *Interdisciplinary Teaching Through Physical Education*, (Champaign, IL: Human Kinetics), 87.

- Converting scores to graphs is not an easy task. Work on helping the children understand the meaning of the results. Analysis and interpretation require higher-level thinking skills.

How Can I Change This?

- Combine locomotor skills into a sequence. How far can children jump using a step or leap (from one foot to the other), then a hop (from one foot to the some foot)? Three jumps in a row (two feet to two feet)? A hop, then jump? A hop, step, jump?
- Measure and graph high-jumping skills.
- Measure and graph throwing or kicking efforts.
- Measure and graph heart rate after different types of exercise of different durations and levels of intensity.

Teachable Moments

Although this lesson is about learning to jump better, it is also about learning in a very practical way how to use mathematics and science. Rather than measuring lines in a book to the nearest fraction of an inch or centimeter, the children are actually doing an experiment in human performance. They are learning to measure and graph real attempts and can see which attempts produce better results. They can also readily see that by using certain scientific principles, such as summing body forces and using momentum, their performances will improve.

Reprinted from Cone 1998.

The following are abbreviated lesson ideas from *Interdisciplinary Teaching Through Physical Education* (Cone, Werner, Cone, and Woods 1998).

Spaced Out

Suggested Grade Level

Intermediate (3rd-5th)

Science

Space: the new frontier

Physical Education

Inventing a game, designing a movement experience

- Create a movement sequence by going on an exploratory space mission. Begin with a rocket takeoff. Include a tethered space walk, moon walk, a work experiment, a computer glitch and technical engineering resolution, return flight, and reentry to earth.
- Invent a new game that has never been played before. Play the game as if it were being played in weightless conditions. Write out the rules to the game. Describe how to play the game to some aliens that you meet in outer space. Play the game with the aliens.

Watch Me Change

Suggested Grade Level

K-6th

Social Studies

People grow and change

Physical Education

Creating and performing movement sequences

Description

All the people that we know are growing and changing. Make a movement sequence that represents the changes that you have made since you were born until today. You can think about drinking from a bottle, learning to sit up, learning to roll over, learning to stand, learning to walk, learning to drink from a cup, learning to throw and kick a ball, learning to ride a tricycle or bicycle.

Sports News

Suggested Grade Level

Intermediate (4th-6th)

Language Arts

Increasing vocabulary; word meaning and use

Physical Education

Identifying sport movements and skills

Description

The teacher and students clip movement phrases used by sportswriters from articles on the sports pages. Discuss the phrases and demonstrate their meaning through movement.

It's Getting Loud in Here

Suggested Grade Level

Primary (1st-3rd)

Mathematics

Volume, pitch, tempo

Physical Education

Responding to music qualities

Description

Volume, pitch, and tempo are quantitative mathematical concepts. Experiment with volume, pitch, and tempo concepts using music and dance. Focus on concepts such as loud or soft, high or low, and fast or slow.

• Make loud sounds on a drum, triangle, or another percussion instrument, and have the children respond with big, powerful movements. Make soft sounds, and have the children respond with small, light movements. Develop patterns of loud and soft sounds.

• Can the children move against the music? Have them move with big, powerful actions when the sound is soft and with small, light actions when the sound is loud.

• Change the tempo of the music being played. Have the children move quickly when it is fast and move slowly when the tempo slows. Create patterns of fast and slow tempos.

• Find several short pieces of music that contrast the concepts of volume, pitch, and tempo. Use pieces with high pitch, fast tempo, and loud volume; low pitch and slow tempo; fast tempo and soft volume; and so on. Have the children respond accordingly.

Reprinted from Cone 1998.

Rachel, 5

Refining Physical Education Teaching Strategies

Congratulations! You've studied the basics in parts 1 and 2. And we hope you've had a chance to teach at least a few physical education lessons. Now, you're ready to refine your physical education instruction techniques.

What questions arose as you studied parts 1 and 2 and taught during part 2? The material we'll cover in part 3 should answer most, if not all, of them. For example, did your students have trouble working well together? Then chapter 13 may have the answers as we delve into cooperation, competition, and responsibility in the physical education setting. Did you apply the strategies of teaching by invitation and intratask variation (chapter 5) but find that one or two students' needs still were not met? Chapter 14 covers inclusion strategies for special situations. Did you find you simply needed more help running an effective physical education class? We'll discuss peer tutoring and collaboration strategies in chapters 15 and 16, respectively.

Chapter 13

Cooperation, Competition, and Responsibility

Suzanne, 7

Classroom management and rhetoric about building character through sport and exercise are not enough to effectively address the social problems and needs of kids today. Teaching personal and social responsibility is one of several approaches that holds promise for doing more to help youngsters grow socially.

—Hellison 1996

Cooperative learning isn't only for the regular classroom; students can obtain the same benefits from this approach in the gym and on the playing field. Indeed, cooperative learning is a good way to teach social skills and personal responsibility through physical education. But what about competition? Don't we need to help kids cope with a dog-eat-dog world? We believe that neither competition nor cooperation is good or bad by definition; it's how you as the teacher approach these concepts. In this chapter, we'll explore how you can apply cooperative learning principles in your physical education program, design appropriate competitive experiences, and teach social and personal responsibility through physical education.

Overview

But first, what exactly are cooperation, competition, and responsibility? In this section, we'll define these three terms in relation to physical education.

Cooperation

Cooperation in physical education is the same as cooperation in science, social studies, or any other subject area. Grineski (1996) describes a cooperative program as one in which "students work together to achieve a goal. All students must make a contribution to goal achievement and are held accountable for their contributions. Goal achievement is mu-

tually inclusive." Weinberg and Gould (1995) assert that "through cooperation, children learn to share, empathize, and to work to get along better. The players in the game must help one another by working together as a unit, leaving no one out of the action, waiting for a turn. They have freedom to learn from mistakes rather than trying to hide them." Thus, cooperative learning enhances social skills and feelings of empowerment and responsibility, outcomes that may carry over into the rest of the school day. But to be effective, your use of cooperation must be systemic and consistent over time (Orlick, McNally, and O'Hara 1978).

Cooperation in physical education may involve anything from giving helpful feedback to a partner to solving a movement challenge in a small group to experiencing a team building activity in which students must function at the highest levels of critical thinking and problem solving. It may also involve working well as a team in a competitive situation. Later in the chapter, we'll describe several simple ways to create cooperative physical education experiences or turn traditional activities into cooperative ones.

Competition

Competition and physical education seem inseparable in many people's minds—and in many school physical education programs. And many people consider competition either as essential to good performance or as an evil to be eradicated. Weinberg and Gould (1995), however, define competition as "inherently neither good nor bad. It is neither a productive nor a destructive strategy—it is simply a process." They go on to say, "It's not that competition itself produces negative consequences—it is the overemphasis on winning that is counterproductive." But by emphasizing skill acquisition, teamwork, and good sportsmanship, you can include competition in appropriate ways, which we'll discuss later in the chapter.

Responsibility

Students can learn and practice responsibility in physical education. Stiehl (1993) defines

Figure 13.1 Cooperation learning can enhance students' social skills.

responsibility in physical education as "taking care of ourselves, others, and our surroundings. This includes fulfilling our obligations, keeping our commitments, striving to do and be our personal and moral best, and nurturing and supporting one another." Of course, these are principles we want children to uphold the rest of the school day as well.

Teaching Cooperation Through Physical Education

Cooperative learning involves teaching social interaction as a skill, rather than punishing students for not possessing these skills (Mercier 1993). Some believe that physical education is a primary, rather than a secondary, venue for teaching these important skills. In this section, we'll look at how you can create, choose, and plan cooperative learning activities.

Creating a Cooperative Learning Experience in Physical Education

Grineski (1996) outlines seven cooperative learning structures he has adapted from other researchers' work. These structures are "content free and serve as building blocks for lessons." They provide ways to create a new activity, no matter the physical education content area, or adapt an existing one to make it cooperative in nature. These structures will help you teach a holistic, cooperative physical education curriculum that targets essential social skills that are, indeed, life skills—while working on physical education content.

Think-Share-Perform (Based on Think-Pair-Share; Kagan 1992)

This involves thinking, sharing, negotiating, and performing. It helps with games, creative dance, obstacle courses, and problem-solving skills when practicing game and sport strategies. To use, (1) provide a challenge, (2) let individuals think of possible solutions, (3) allow students to share their ideas with a partner, and (4) have students perform at least one idea from each partner and negotiate which solution to apply in the activity.

Wand Grabbing is an example of the Think-Share-Perform structure appropriate for both primary and intermediate students. Note that it can be adapted to fit the Collective Score structure described in the next section.

WAND GRABBING

Activity challenge: To trade places with your partner without either wand falling on the ground

Description: Students in pairs stand five feet apart and each vertically holds a three-foot wand on the floor. On an agreed signal, all students let go of their wands and run to grab the wands of their partners. Teachers should remind students to keep their heads up and eyes fixed on their partners' wands when changing places with their partners.

Equipment: One three-foot wand for each student

Psychomotor goals: Enhance effort awareness

Cognitive goals: Promote negotiating behaviors; stimulate problem solving skills

Affective goal: Use positive interactions to grab partner's wand before it touches the ground

Variations: After pairs of students develop skill in releasing and grabbing, increase the distance between the students. Also, students may work in groups larger than pairs. It is challenging to work toward an entire class of students releasing and grabbing simultaneously. Once students experience success with the activity, introduce the cooperative learning structure Collective Score. To use Collective Score in the Wand Grabbing activity, students increase the distance from their partners by one foot when they can successfully grab their partners' wands three times in a row. The "score" would be how far apart partners are at the end of a specified time. The distance could be added for a class total.

Cooperative learning structure: Think-Share-Perform (Collective Score can also be used as noted in "Variations.")

Reprinted from Grineski 1996.

Collective Score (Orlick 1982)

This involves adding together to find a total group score. It helps with anything that can be counted, from goals to push-ups. To use, you can (1) add scores of individuals within each group to find a group score (don't compare with other groups, though) or (2) add all individual or group scores for a total class score. Challenge your students to best their collective score over time, but, remember, this takes time and not every attempt will or should produce a better score. Set reasonable goals and work together as a class to reach them.

Bump Over is an example of the Collective Score structure appropriate for intermediate students.

BUMP OVER

Activity challenge: To score a maximum number of points by bumping a ball over a net so it can be returned and bumped back

Descriptions: Two small groups of players stand on either side of a net and bump, or pass with the forearm, a volleyball over the net so it can be bumped back to the other group. A point is scored every time a ball is successfully bumped over the net.

Equipment: A soft volleyball, net of appropriate height, and playing space for two small groups

Psychomotor goals: Refine effort awareness; refine spatial awareness; improve manipulative skills

Cognitive goals: Understand biomechanical (i.e., how the body moves while performing a skill) principles of flexion, extension, and force production and absorption associated with bumping a volleyball

Affective goal: Use positive interactions to encourage all players' efforts of bumping

Variations: This "game concept" can be used to practice and apply learning in various skill games, such as basketball passing and throwing and softball catching

Cooperative learning structure: Collective Score

Reprinted from Grineski 1996.

Jigsaw Perform
(Based on Jigsaw; Aronson 1978)

This involves very strong positive interdependence in which students divide the labor and share the work by learning and performing one part and teaching it to the others in the group. It helps with teaching rules of group games and dances that have several parts. To use, (1) assign a task with several components, (2) make each group member individually responsible for learning and practicing one part, and (3) have each group member teach his or her groupmates his or her assigned part.

Routines: "Let's Do It Together" is an example of the Jigsaw Perform structure appropriate for both primary and intermediate students.

ROUTINES: "LET'S DO IT TOGETHER"

Activity challenge: To cooperatively create and perform floor routines

Descriptions: Following instruction on basic tumbling skills and stunts, small groups of three students make skill/movement cards for creating routines to perform for the rest of the class. Each 3- by 5-inch card should have symbols representing a skill or movement for use in a routine. For example, "—"could represent straight-line rolling while "***" could represent a curled body shape. The teacher should check that the skills and movements include all of the tumbling and balancing skills the students have learned, in addition to including all movement concepts. Divide the routine cards equally among pairs of students, making each pair responsible for creating a portion of the routine. Once you create each portion of the routine, teach each pair and combine into a whole routine to be performed by the class.

Equipment: Ten 3- by 5-inch cards for each group, marking pencils, mats, and any appropriate equipment for each pair of students

Psychomotor goals: Develop and refine tumbling skills

Cognitive goals: Enhance problem solving

Affective goal: Use positive interactions to teach other students routines

Cooperative learning structure: Jigsaw Perform

Reprinted from Grineski 1996.

Pairs-Check-Perform
(Based on Pairs Check; Kagan 1992)

This involves encouraging individuals to stay on-task and help others learn. It helps with learning gymnastic stunts and locomotor, manipulative, sport, and dance skills. The directions for this structure are as follows: (1) explain, demonstrate, and check for understanding of the target skill; (2) create groups of four, divided into two pairs; (3) have student #1 practice the skill while student #2 acts as an encourager or helper;

(4) have partners switch roles when student #1 has performed the skill correctly; (5) when all four group members think they are ready, they watch each other to confirm mastery; (6) if students disagree, then they must continue to practice until they can agree before moving on to a new skill or component.

Sportball Juggle is an example of the Pairs-Check-Perform structure appropriate for intermediate students. Note that it can be adapted to many other cooperative learning structures.

SPORTBALL JUGGLE

Activity challenge: To successfully move a maximum number of different sportballs in sequence within a team of five players

Descriptions: Five students approximately 12 feet apart in a star pattern attempt to move sportballs simultaneously around the star pattern. Students decide on the types of skills and balls and different levels for each ball. For example, bounce a basketball at a medium height, kick a soccer ball low, set a volleyball high, pass a football straight, roll a bowling ball low, and underhand toss a softball low. The group begins with one ball and adds a ball after the group can successfully move the preceding ball or balls three times around the star.

Equipment: One basketball, volleyball, football, softball, bowling ball, and soccer ball for each group of five

Psychomotor goals: Refine manipulative skills; extend effort awareness

Cognitive goals: Improve concentration skills

Affective goal: Use positive interactions to verbally and physically help and support teammates

Variations: To vary Sportball Juggle, reduce or increase the distance between players, use balls of varying size and texture, or determine how many times a specified number of balls are passed around the star pattern.

Cooperative learning structure: Jigsaw Perform

Reprinted from Grineski 1996.

*Learning Teams
(Based on STAD [Slavin 1980]
and Learning Together
[Johnson and Johnson 1975])*

This involves sharing responsibility and leadership, collaborating to reach group goals. It helps with skill acquisition in any physical education content area. The directions for this structure are as follows: (1) explain, demonstrate, and check for understanding of the target skill; (2) inform students of the performance outcome and the necessary social skills to accomplish it; (3) create groups of four; (4) assign roles (performer, observer-checker [should also give feedback], feedback giver, equipment retriever); (5) have

---

TINIKLING

Activity challenge: To perform tinikling skills as a result of belonging to a Learning Team

Background: The actions of the dance represent a long-legged bird walking in tall grass. Tinikling is popular in Southeast Asia.

Descriptions: Students are placed in groups of four, with the following roles: one performer or dancer, one helper, and two strikers or pole movers. The dancer practices the tinikling dance steps while the helper provides visual and/or verbal feedback regarding performance. The strikers manipulate the poles, enabling the dancer to perform the tinikling dance steps. Students rotate through all roles.

To perform the basic tinikling dance step, each group needs two 8-foot bamboo poles. The strikers kneel at each end and hold the poles about 12 inches apart on the floor. The striking pattern is two vertical taps to the floor and one sliding movement of the poles together (i.e., tap, tap, together). With the dancer standing next to one of the poles, the basic dance step is as follows:

1. Step over pole with right foot and stand *in* between poles while the left foot remains *outside* the poles on the first vertical tap of pole.

2. Step over pole with left foot and stand *in* between poles on second vertical tap of pole.

3. Step *outside* of poles with right foot and stand on right foot, lifting left foot straight *up* into the air as poles move together.

The following cue words are used: *in, in, out/up* for the dancer and *tap, tap, together* for the striker.

Equipment: Two 8-foot tinikling poles for four students

Psychomotor goals: Improve locomotor (dance) skills

Cognitive goals: Refine concentration

Affective goal: Use positive interactions to teach and encourage group members

Variations: Once students master the basic tinikling step (i.e., *in, in, out/up*), they will enjoy these variations:

1. Jump *in*, jump, jump *out*.

2. Starting by standing in between poles: Jump, jump, jump *out*.

3. Repeat #1 and #2 using hopping skills.

4. Require students to create new patterns.

Cooperative learning structure: Learning Teams

Reprinted from Grineski 1996.

students carry out their roles during practice time; (6) have group members assess one another's performances; and (7) score students on an individual, group, or classwide (collective) basis.

Tinikling is an example of the Learning Team structure appropriate for intermediate students.

Co-op Play (Based on Learning Together; Johnson et al. 1984 and Orlick 1978, 1982)

This involves accepting and including everyone to achieve a group goal. It helps with modifying or creating games, obstacle courses, skill development activities, and dances. The directions for this structure are as follows: (1) explain, demonstrate, and check for understanding the activity or ask problem-solving questions to guide students; (2) directly teach the collaborative skills necessary, emphasizing how vital they are for success; (3) reinforce how important each individual's efforts will be; (4) have students do the activity while you reinforce the necessary social skills; (5) debrief the activity, discussing why a group was successful or not; and (6) encourage students to think about how they could achieve the goals more efficiently.

Human Obstacle Course is an example of the Co-op Play structure appropriate for both primary and intermediate students.

HUMAN OBSTACLE COURSE

Activity challenge: To maintain and negotiate obstacles for a predetermined amount of time

Descriptions: Students in small groups make obstacles using their joined bodies. The obstacles should be spread throughout the play space. The remaining players, in groups and holding hands, attempt to negotiate the obstacles without touching any obstacles.

Equipment: None

Psychomotor goals: Enhance body and spatial awareness

Cognitive goals: Encourage problem solving

Affective goal: Use positive interactions to maintain obstacles and move without touching obstacles

Variations: Begin with groups of two players and expand to larger groups of up to five players when students can successfully maintain and negotiate larger obstacles. Use a variety of movement concepts in building obstacles. For example, wide-narrow, tall-short, high-medium-low, and curvy-straight. Different body parts could also be used to form obstacles (i.e., hand, feet, elbows). Teachers can instruct students who are negotiating obstacles to move in forward, sideways, or backward directions and at different speeds.

Cooperative learning structure: Co-op Play (Collective Score could also be used with the number of obstacles negotiated in a certain time counted.)

Reprinted from Grineski 1996.

Figure 13.2 Having students navigate obstacles develops problem-solving skills.

Co-op Co-op Perform
(Based on Co-op Co-op; Kagan 1992)

This involves having small groups create a project to share with the rest of the class. It helps with creative dance and games. To use, (1) discuss the theme of the activity; (2) divide the theme into parts; (3) assign each group a part; (4) have each group discuss how to break its part into smaller components and decide how to perform each component; (5) have each group perform its part for the class; (6) help groups link the parts together to create a class performance; and (7) combine all parts and have students give the class performance.

Thunderstorm Dance is an example of Co-op Co-op Perform appropriate for primary students.

THUNDERSTORM DANCE

Activity challenge: To create and perform a creative dance based on a thunderstorm theme

Descriptions: Follow these steps to create the Thunderstorm Dance:

1. Conduct a class discussion about the elements of a thunderstorm, such as wind, rain, clouds, lightning, thunder, and hail.

2. Assign small groups of students to each element.

3. Each group discusses its element and thinks about what movements might communicate its characteristics to an audience (e.g., running through many pathways at different levels with differing amounts of force to represent wind) and what props would be appropriate (e.g., throwing Frisbees for the wind).

4. Each group practices its portion of the dance.

5. Each group performs its portion of the dance for the rest of the groups.

6. Appropriate groups (e.g., clouds with rain) are connected as practicing continues.

7. Combine all groups for a performance.

Equipment: Whatever props are needed to support each group's creation

Musical accompaniment: Tchaikovsky's *1812 Overture* or Holst's *The Planets*

Psychomotor goals: Promote body and spatial awareness

Cognitive goals: Encourage problem solving

Affective goal: Use positive interactions to work together through talking, planning, and supporting; use positive interactions to support the work of others

Variations: Themes can originate from student interest (e.g., space travel), the season (e.g., blizzard), or an upcoming event (e.g., sports tournament).

Cooperative learning structure: Co-op Co-op Perform

Reprinted from Grineski 1996.

As you can see, you can create many cooperative activities using these structures. To get started, try one structure and allow yourself and your students to become familiar with it, then try another, and so on. Collective Score and Pairs-Check-Perform are two good starting places. Or you may be using jigsawing in another subject area, such as science or social studies, so Jigsaw Perform might be a good place for you to start.

Choosing Cooperative Activities

Now that you've created or adapted an activity to make it cooperative, you should double-check to ensure that it truly is a cooperative experience. Mercier (1993) lists the following criteria for determining whether an activity is cooperative:

- Positive interdependence—students must help one another and work together to succeed.

- Individual accountability—there is a mechanism for checking for full participation and acceptable individual effort (task sheets or scoring rubrics can help here).

- Positive social context (team building)—the activity develops and enhances team spirit.

- Social skills instruction—there is obvious input into what social skill is being targeted and how to perform it properly (role-playing a new focus is a must).
- Structure—the teacher has set parameters for the activity (set goals and guidelines when you offer a challenge).

To plan effective physical education cooperative learning experiences, you should also attend to issues of team formation (see chapter 9) and class management (see chapter 4).

Planning Cooperative Activities

The cooperative learning lesson has the same components as any other physical education lesson: set induction, core activities, and closure (see chapter 6). The difference is that the cooperative learning lesson has certain relevant affective goals, such as giving appropriate feedback to a partner. And the cooperative learning lesson strives for these goals by offering ample opportunity to practice the social skill. Finally, the cooperative learning lesson closure activity should review the so-cial skill, discuss ways it can be applied elsewhere in life, and provide opportunities to sincerely compliment classmates (see sidebar "Social Skills Are the Foundation").

Teaching Appropriate Competition Through Physical Education

Even very young children can become conditioned to society's emphasis on the importance of winning, and in so doing, they become unable to play simply for the fun of it. But although competition has the potential to do great harm in physical education, and cooperation can enhance many vital social skills, this is not to say that competition has no place in your physical education program. You must, however, play a prominent role in teaching teammates and even opponents to help one another, be sensitive to others' feelings, and compete in a fun-filled, friendly way (Weinberg and Gould 1995).

Social Skills Are the Foundation

Michelle Rusnak, physical educator at Brykerwoods Elementary in Austin, Texas, believes so strongly in teaching social skills through physical education that she has made them the foundation of her program. Rusnak bans laughing at others and encourages students to compliment and help one another. She posts rules of good sportsmanship in the gym and teaches principles of encouragement, communication, compromise, teamwork, sharing, honesty, and compassion. Rusnak has students spell out the principle of the day while doing warm-ups instead of counting. At the end of the lesson, she holds "Nice Time," in which the students discuss what they learned and compliment one another. At first students were embarrassed, but Rusnak reports, "Now they won't shut up."

Students go through three levels until they can function as "teachers" because they know all the rules, can perform physical skills well, and possess the necessary social skills. These students help those at lower levels do better—without making fun of them. "Improving yourself is a big thing with me, and they know that," says Rusnak.

As a classroom teacher, you can apply this approach throughout your curriculum—not only in the gym. In fact, it may be easier for you than for a specialist because you can ensure consistent application of a social skills learning program throughout the school day.

Summarized from Lipowitz, "Social Skills Are the Foundation," *Teaching Elementary Physical Education* 7(4): 22 (1996).

Fifth and sixth graders may benefit especially from being introduced to competition in a supportive learning environment. Some children, usually the motor elite, truly enjoy competition and can therefore benefit from it. One way to include competition is to vary a task by offering a small group of students the chance to play a competitive game away from the rest of the class. Many of the less-skilled students may be relieved to focus on basic skills without the more skilled students watching them (Graham 1992).

Creating Appropriate Competitive Activities

You can, indeed, incorporate opportunities to compete into your physical education program without harming self-esteem or creating bad memories for tomorrow's adults by following some simple dos and don'ts:

Competition Dos and Don'ts

Do

✓ make competition a choice;

✓ choose teams in sensitive ways (see chapter 9);

✓ keep teams small to enhance participation;

✓ insist on good sportsmanship;

✓ emphasize and facilitate self-improvement and enjoyment, not who wins;

✓ compliment and reward high rates of participation and good sportsmanship;

✓ experiment with keeping score differently (counting number of encouraging remarks, number of people who touch the ball before scoring, and the like) or have one game going in which score is not kept at all;

✓ change the rules to enhance participation (e.g., require a minimum of players to touch the ball before attempting to score, rotate positions or tasks of players frequently);

✓ give positive feedback and encourage all students, regardless of competitive outcome; and

✓ offer opportunities to develop and practice psychomotor skills in competition.

Don't

✓ force students to compete;

✓ allow overaggressiveness;

✓ create large teams and therefore long waits for turns or other participation;

✓ have team captains choose sides (see chapter 9);

✓ allow humiliating comments, teasing ("Aaaayy-batter, aaaayy-batter . . . ; Easy out! Easy out!"), or other unkind attitudes and actions; and

✓ make a big deal of who wins (e.g., don't praise only winners, don't post winners on bulletin board).

Keep in mind, too, that competition doesn't have to be devoid of cooperation. In fact, Weinberg and Gould (1995) recommend a blend of competitive and cooperative elements in an activity (e.g., working as teammates while competing against another team). With your encouragement, students can help one another succeed, enjoy, and learn while competing by choice (see sidebar titled "Teaching Good Sportsmanship").

A Different View of Competition

A great performance by one competitor spurs the other to greater heights. This is how basketball great Magic Johnson viewed Larry Bird. Indeed, in his retirement speech, Johnson told how much his rivalry with Bird meant to him. Magic felt he had to play better to compete with Larry. Their competition was positive motivation to continually improve and refine their skills.

Adapted from Weinberg and Gould 1995.

Choosing Appropriate Competitive Activities

If you follow the dos and don'ts we've listed, you'll be well on your way to choosing appropriate competitive activities. As a final check, COPEC (1992) offers guidelines for competition in physical education:

Remember, physical education is not the same as athletics. Children and their parents can seek athletic experiences elsewhere; your goal should be to ensure maximum time on-task to help children acquire the basic move-

---

Teaching Good Sportsmanship

Clifford and Feezell (1997) believe that kids can be taught to show respect for opponents and teammates, but they must be *taught*; they will not learn it by osmosis. In their book *Coaching for Character*, they offer the following suggestions for encouraging respect:

Respect for Opponents

Give your best effort.

Avoid displays of disrespect.

Celebrate victory respectfully—no rubbing it in. Remember, if you're opponent hadn't tried hard, you'd have nothing to be proud of.

Follow the "Silver Rule": Don't do to others what you don't want them to do to you.

Practice rituals of respect, such as shaking hands after a game and saying "Good game."

Respect for Teammates

Be truthful about your strengths and weaknesses instead of trying to dominate or withdraw.

Play your role in the game as assigned by teammates or teacher; make sure your teammates can count on you.

Make individual sacrifices for the good of the team. For example, don't hog the ball; pass it to an open player.

Praise one another for little achievements, not just scoring.

COMPONENT— *Competition*

Appropriate Practice

Activities emphasize self-improvement, participation, and cooperation instead of winning and losing.

Teachers are aware of the nature of competition and do not *require* higher levels of competition from children before they are ready. For example, children are allowed to choose between a game in which the score is kept and one that is just for practice.

Inappropriate Practice

Children are *required* to participate in activities that label children as "winners" and "losers."

Children are *required* to participate in activities that compare one child's or team's performance against others (e.g., a race in which the winning child or team is clearly identified).

Reprinted from COPEC/NASPE 1992.

ment skills and conceptual understanding they'll need to be successful in physical activity—in ways that encourage them to enjoy physical activity and seek it independently. It all comes down to maintaining a supportive learning environment.

Physical Education Hall of Shame

Remember the Physical Education Hall of Shame we described in chapter 9? This page shows two more inductees (Williams 1992, 1994).

Planning an Appropriate Competitive Activity

You can plan an appropriate competitive activity by building in choices and emphasiz-

ing good sportsmanship and physical skill acquisition rather than winning and losing. As part of your efforts to keep team sizes small, you should have several games or activities going on at once. In this context, it is easy to simply say, "Your two teams may choose to play a cooperative game (define scoring) or a competitive game." Or, "Your two teams may choose to keep score or not."

In the lesson's set induction, you can have students role-play a particular aspect of showing respect for opponents in a competitive game, such as giving your best effort, and discuss why this is part of good sportsmanship. Then tell students if they choose to play a cooperative game, you will still be asking them how they showed one another respect. During closure, you can reinforce this principle by asking students to share how they showed respect for their opponents. Then ask

RELAY RACES

⊘ Too much time standing around and too little time spent on physical activity or skill development. Winning and losing are the center, and the child who runs last usually gets blamed for the loss even though all participants contribute to the final result. Students standing around waiting for their turns tend to waste a lot of energy screaming

ELIMINATION GAMES

⊘ In addition to Musical Chairs (see chapter 9), unmodified versions of tag, Simon Says, Dodgeball, and the like eliminate the children who need the practice the most, allowing them no opportunity to improve.

⊘ *Relay races—a way to prepare children for standing in line.*

students who chose to play a cooperative game how they showed respect for one another. Brainstorming ways to display good sportsmanship outside of physical education (e.g., recess, extracurricular sports, and so on) can encourage students to practice applying the principles of good sportsmanship as a life skill. Work on a different aspect of good sportsmanship each lesson, week, or unit, depending on your students' needs and abilities. Finally, ensure that each lesson that includes competition follows the dos and don'ts listed earlier in this chapter.

Teaching Responsibility Through Physical Education

As we stated in chapter 2, a physical education program can and should support the elementary school mission of enhancing the growth of the whole (cognitive, affective, and psychomotor) child through education. Teaching social and personal responsibility is an essential part of this process. But how do children learn to be responsible? Greenberg (1992) offers the following three sources of responsible behavior:

1. People are motivated to be responsible by an urge to contribute something to someone—another person or one's own best "self."

2. Responsibility grows out of self-esteem, which, in turn, has grown out of independence, initiative, and competence. "To decide to be responsible is to make a choice—a choice that can be made only by children . . . who feel personally significant and capable."

3. Responsibility also grows out of an ability to see others' points of view and empathize with them.

Let's look more closely, now, at each of these points as well as ways to help develop these sources of responsibility through your physical education curriculum. Then we'll discuss a formal model for teaching personal and social responsibility.

The Desire to Contribute

Young children naturally have a desire to contribute to family, friends, and classmates, from insisting on "helping" with the dishes at home to eagerly volunteering to serve as a guide for the new kid in school. You can build on this in your physical education program. Pica (1993a) suggests that incorporating cooperative activities into physical education is a good place to start. When each child in a cooperative learning group knows she plays an essential role in reaching a common goal, she accepts responsibility for this role and the group's success. Moreover, children can learn to account for their performance and behavior through child-directed activities in which they must make their own choices (Morris 1980). So strive for a balance of child-directed and teacher-directed activities (Pica 1993a).

Competitive activities can also elicit responsible behavior when you teach and insist upon good sportsmanship.

Self-Esteem

It's hard to take responsibility for yourself or others if you don't feel good about yourself. The cornerstone of students' feeling good about themselves in physical education is the supportive and caring atmosphere you create as the teacher. Greenberg (1992) reminds us, too, that self-esteem grows out of independence, initiative, and competence. When you create a physical education program and learning atmosphere that encourages these three areas, you enhance student self-esteem. Specifically, open-ended problem-solving activities allow students to function independently on the cognitive, psychomotor, and affective levels (Mosston and Ashworth 1990). Students have to take initiative to work toward solutions, and feelings of competence and therefore self-esteem are a natural outcome when they experience success working at their own developmental rates and levels (Pica 1993b). Greenberg (1992) states, "Frequently having a choice and often having a voice are important building blocks in establishing a feeling of responsibility." Ultimately, if a child develops confidence in his ability to learn, solve problems, find out, practice, act, and so on, he has a good chance of growing into a responsible adult (Klein 1990).

Empathy

How do we get children to put themselves into other people's gym shoes? First, we model empathy by planning and teaching lessons that follow both the Golden and Silver Rules—do and don't do to your students as you would want your physical education teacher to do and not do to you. You can also model empathy by acknowledging feelings in the physical education setting. Have students explore their own feelings about physical activity and education through journals to help them identify not only their own feelings but also those of others. Second, when children must work together to meet a challenge or solve a problem, they learn tolerance of others' ideas (Pica 1993a). Moreover, they learn to accept diversity among other children as people. Thus, multicultural activities, such as learning dances from other countries, can help develop feelings of empathy in children.

Insisting upon good sportsmanship can also elicit empathy. Pica (1993a) asserts that to feel empathy, you have to be able to imagine what it's like to be someone else, so the elementary physical education curriculum should include opportunities to imagine. This could include anything from creating a dance in which children move like a spider to role-playing respect for opponents.

Hellison's (1996) Model of Teaching Personal and Social Responsibility

Now that we've examined several facets of the idea of teaching responsibility through physical education, we'd like to describe a particular model for teaching responsibility that is being used successfully in physical education and other settings. As described by Graham (1992), Hellison's Model of Teaching Personal and Social Responsibility (TPSR) describes responsibility in terms of five levels,

0 to 4, to help children understand and practice responsible behavior:

- Level 0—Irresponsibility. At this level, a child does not take responsibility for her own actions and tends to interfere with others' learning.
- Level 1—Self-control. A child at this level performs at a minimal level with teacher prompting and without interfering with others' learning.
- Level 2—Involvement. A child at this level is actively involved in learning. He tries hard, does not bother others, and is genuinely interested in self-improvement.
- Level 3—Self-responsibility. Under direct supervision of the teacher, a child at this level makes independent decisions about what she needs to learn and how she might go about learning it. This often involves child-created games, dances, and sequences. This level also includes taking the initiative to engage in physical activity or learn a new skill outside of physical education. If working in a cooperative learning group in school, problems may arise if one or more children is not able to function at this level.
- Level 4—Caring. At this level, a child goes beyond simply working with others to provide genuine support and help for others.

As you can see, understanding and applying these levels could help children function better throughout the school setting and beyond—not only in physical education. Figure 13.3 shows Masser's (1990) depiction of Hellison's model in multiple settings.

Summary

Physical education is an ideal arena in which to teach cooperation, appropriate competition, and personal and social responsibility. From keeping a collective score in a cooperative game to insisting on good sportsmanship in a competitive game (and throughout your physical education program), you

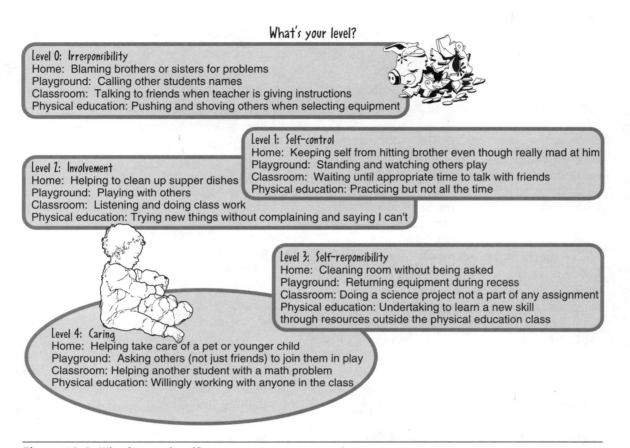

What's your level?

Level 0: Irresponsibility
Home: Blaming brothers or sisters for problems
Playground: Calling other students names
Classroom: Talking to friends when teacher is giving instructions
Physical education: Pushing and shoving others when selecting equipment

Level 1: Self-control
Home: Keeping self from hitting brother even though really mad at him
Playground: Standing and watching others play
Classroom: Waiting until appropriate time to talk with friends
Physical education: Practicing but not all the time

Level 2: Involvement
Home: Helping to clean up supper dishes
Playground: Playing with others
Classroom: Listening and doing class work
Physical education: Trying new things without complaining and saying I can't

Level 3: Self-responsibility
Home: Cleaning room without being asked
Playground: Returning equipment during recess
Classroom: Doing a science project not a part of any assignment
Physical education: Undertaking to learn a new skill through resources outside the physical education class

Level 4: Caring
Home: Helping take care of a pet or younger child
Playground: Asking others (not just friends) to join them in play
Classroom: Helping another student with a math problem
Physical education: Willingly working with anyone in the class

Figure 13.3 What's your level?
This figure is reprinted with permission from the *Journal of Physical Education, Recreation & Dance*, vol. 61, p. 19. *JOPERD* is a publication of the American Alliance for Health, Physical Education, Recreation and Dance, 1900 Association Drive, Reston, VA 20191.

can encourage personal and social responsibility. Consider adapting Hellison's model to fit your situation. Teaching your students to identify the level at which they are functioning and consistently discussing ways students can move to a higher level will create an awareness of responsibility. This, in turn, will encourage students to be more responsible—in and out of physical education.

Remember, neither cooperation nor competition is inherently good or bad. Rather, it's how you as the instructor structure various situations to maximize time on-task, positive interactions, skill acquisition, and personal improvement and enjoyment.

Chapter 14

Including Everyone in Physical Education

Kirsten, 9

Mrs. McLarney has taught third grade physical education for 12 years. She feels very comfortable doing so and has a set curriculum, which is mainly motor skills and movement education. This year she has Jason and Sara in her class. Jason has spina bifida and uses a wheelchair, and Sara has Down Syndrome, causing her trouble with some of the basic locomotor skills as well as with understanding and following directions. Mrs. McLarney does not know how to change her curriculum, which has worked so well for so long.

When you teach by invitation and use intra-task variation to meet the individual needs of your students (see chapter 5), you go a long way toward including everyone. Yet there will be times when a student's needs will require you to look more closely at your physical education program to ensure that you are practicing true inclusion. In this chapter, we'll examine the major inclusion issues, including gender, multicultural considerations, special needs, and ability issues. Then we'll offer sample awareness activities to help you teach empathy to children without disabilities.

First, however, what exactly is *inclusion*? Although many authors have offered definitions, Davis and Davis (1994) offer the following summary:

> Inclusion describes a philosophy of educating children with disabilities alongside their nondisabled peers.

In this chapter, we'll expand the definition of inclusion to include gender equity, multiculturalism, and helping students considered physically awkward. For each group, we'll follow the organization of Vogler and Block's (1994) work regarding adapting curriculum for children who are physically challenged and show you how to adapt to individual needs. Adapt

- what you teach,
- how you teach, and
- who teaches.

Next, we'll outline our basic philosophy of inclusion.

Our Philosophy

Inclusion is not mandated by law; only educating a child in the least restrictive environment (LRE) is. LRE means that children should be educated with peers without disabilities to the greatest extent possible with the necessary support (see figure 14.1). To this end, we believe a child should experience physical education alongside his peers if at all possible—no matter the level of support services necessary. Thus, our philosophy is based on both legal parameters and our basic belief that physical activity is for everyone and that all children should be able to progress in and enjoy physical activity at their own developmental level and rate, empowering them to make physical activity a lifestyle choice.

Children With Special Needs

The Education for All Handicapped Children Act and the Individuals With Disabilities Education Act require that qualified physical education personnel teach the students with physical or mental challenges. The law also states the child must be provided with an Individualized Educational Plan (IEP). Thus, you should advocate for such a student to ensure that his IEP is appropriately written and carried out. Beyond this, you can and should work with the specialists involved to include such a student in your

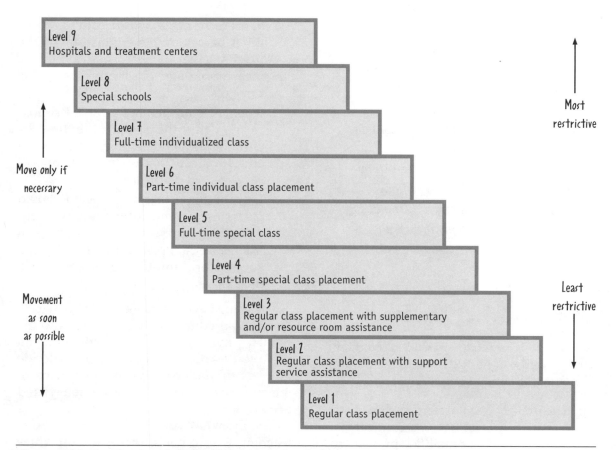

Figure 14.1 Continuum of alternative instructional placements in physical education.
Reprinted, by permission, from Winnick, J., 1995, *Adapted Physical Education and Sport, 2nd ed.*, (Champaign, IL: Human Kinetics), 21.

Individuals With Disabilities Education Act and Education for All Handicapped Children Act

These laws include physical education in the definition of special education as well as mandates to develop physical and motor fitness, fundamental motor skills and patterns, and aquatic, dance, and individual and group sports and games skills. Therefore, physical education is a *direct* service that must be provided by qualified personnel in the least restrictive environment.

All children should be able to progress in and enjoy physical activity.

general physical education program whenever possible. In this section, we'll describe the IEP process regarding physical education, and outline ways you might be able to include such a child in your regular physical education program.

Mrs. McLarney decides she wants her curriculum to include all children, so she creates a physical education setting in which all activities are accessible to all. First, she conducts awareness activities so the other students understand what it is like to travel using a wheelchair or crutches. She also ties 10-pound weights to the students' ankles so they understand what restricted movement feels like.

When the lesson involves practicing locomotor skills, she includes walking, logrolls, and crawling for the kids who cannot gallop or hop. She assigns peer tutors to assist with socialization, demonstrations, and chasing stray balls. In addition, she breaks down her instructions so all children understand the rules and directions. When any student does not understand, she does not ridicule the student; rather, she patiently repeats and demonstrates.

Changing What You Teach

You should base what you teach a child with special needs on her IEP. The IEP should include the following components:

1. The present level of performance as determined by at least two assessment tools administered by a qualified professional and given in the child's native language. This process should glean information regarding the three "p's": the *process* by which the child executes a skill, the *product* she produces with a skill, and the *parameters* surrounding a skill, such as the environment and the amount and type of assistance.

2. Short-term goals and objectives. These must be attainable extensions of the present level of performance and be measurable and observable using the three p's.

3. Extent of mainstreaming. The IEP should clearly define the percentage of time the child will spend in regular physical education class and with what support services.

4. Level of support services. The IEP should clearly state the intent, length, and amount of support services, such as a teacher assistant as needed for physical support or a full-time interpreter for a deaf student.

Once you have examined the IEP in regard to physical education, determine how the regular physical education curriculum can improve the child's weaknesses. Then decide how best to adapt your curriculum and teaching methods to meet the child's interests and needs.

Finally, what you teach should include teaching your other students to empathize with and include the child. To this end, we have included three awareness activities at the end of this chapter.

Changing How You Teach

The same basic strategies you use with children without disabilities can also be effec-

Teaching Inclusive Behavior

Craft (1994) suggests the following for teaching children without disabilities appropriate inclusive behavior:

- Challenge any disrespectful behavior students show toward one another (whether they have disabilities or not).

- Establish a learning environment in which it's okay for everyone (including you) to make mistakes.

- Discuss with students why people tease or make cutting remarks. Help students

understand that such behavior often reflects insecurity.

- Encourage students to ask questions and discuss differences in positive ways because combating ignorance is vital.

- Invite positive role models to speak to your class about how they enjoy physical activity and sport activity despite a physical challenge.

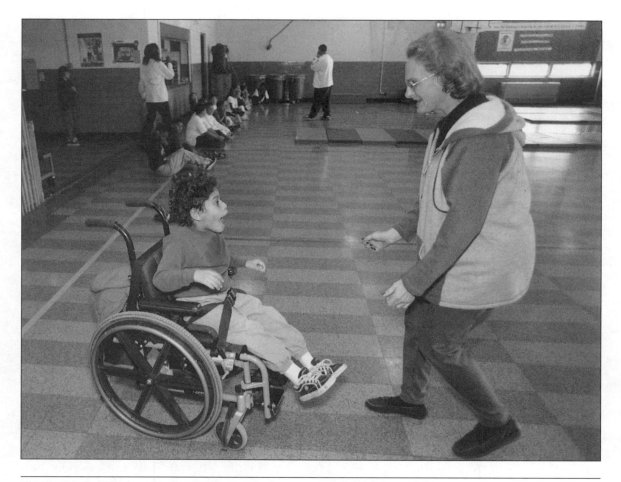

Figure 14.2 Offering alternatives ensures that everyone gets to participate.

Did You Know?

- Individuals with disabilities generally display the same physiological responses to exercise found in non-disabled persons.
- Although specific disabilities may affect the intensity, duration, and frequency of exercise, individuals with disabilities can benefit from training, including improving their performances.
- Wheelchairs can be adjusted or modified to improve physical activity performance.
- Athletes in wheelchairs have completed the Boston Marathon.

Adapted from Depauw 1996.

tive with students with disabilities (Depauw 1996; Mawdsley 1977; Taylor and Loovis 1978). Offering choices to the *individual* rather than to the *disability* is the key. So focus on how you can help the individual increase time on-task, give positive specific feedback, challenge the individual's intellect, and stimulate positive growth in physical activity.

Moreover, you can modify an existing game or activity or use an entirely different approach to teaching (Vogler and Block 1994). Experts offer the following examples for the four main areas in which you might modify a game:

- Rules—allowing two bounces in tennis or, in volleyball, allowing the ball to bounce, allowing more than one hit, or allowing a player to catch, throw, and walk with the ball
- Equipment—using a beach ball, balloon, or volleyball trainer in volleyball (Lieberman and Cowart 1996)
- Environment—marking highly visible boundaries, decreasing stimulation (e.g., noise), creating a rest area, or using a smaller or larger court
- Instruction—using trained peer tutors (Houston-Wilson, Lieberman, Horton, and Kasser 1997), different teaching styles, or teacher's aides, providing one-on-one instruction whenever possible

One of the main ways you can change your teaching approach is to be sure you're using cooperative activities rather than competitive ones (Slavin and Stevens 1991). When students of all abilities work together to reach a common goal, they learn to be creative and include the child with physical or mental challenges in not only the physical education activity but also in other school activities. Moreover, as we discussed in chapter 13, you can teach children empathy through teaching personal and social responsibility.

The following list offers several other specific ways you can adapt your teaching to better meet the needs of a special needs child. See also the suggestions listed in tables 14.1 and 14.2.

- Explain what you want the child to do in simple terms, and repeat explanations as often as necessary.
- Demonstrate what you want the child to do. Use a peer without disabilities as often as possible for demonstrations.
- Physically assist or guide the child through the target skill or movement.
- Use Brailling with children who are blind. For this technique, you let the child feel a peer or instructor execute a skill or movement that the child has not been able to learn otherwise (Lieberman and Cowart 1996).

- Especially when including children with behavioral (e.g., attention deficit disorder), cognitive (e.g., mental retardation, learning disabilities), and autistic challenges, keep your classes as structured as possible (Tucci 1994).
- Use cooperative games (Tucci 1994).
- When possible, change the size and texture of equipment when necessary to maximize success (Tucci 1994).
- Ask the child with a disability for ideas about activities, modifications, and interests (Tucci 1994).
- When the entire class is warming up and stretching, it may be beneficial to take the child out of the wheelchair for the warm-up *only*.
- A child in a wheelchair can play almost any game, but occasionally you may need to modify things a bit. For example, allow the student to use modified or no equipment, such as attaching a hockey stick to his hand with an Ace bandage or having him throw a ball instead of batting.
- A child who can walk but has poor balance or speed may benefit from using a scooter or other riding toy, changing from running to another locomotor activity, or sitting so that the child and classmates are safe (Tucci 1994). This child may also benefit if you slow down the entire activity.
- Finally, be sure to frequently assess progress of the child with a disability. Use a form such as the one in table 14.3 to help you discern the child's progress

Changing Who Teaches

You should not be alone in your quest to include the child with special needs. Craft (1994) offers several suggestions for garnering the support you need. First and foremost, you should be working closely with the child's special education teacher and adapted physical education specialist (if available). They can share technical suggestions and personal insights that will help you assist the student. Then, tap into the knowledge

Table 14.1 Helpful Hints for Adapting Physical Education Activities for Children With Special Needs

These activities are enjoyable ways for individuals with disabilities to attain a healthy lifestyle.

Bicycling	Jogging	Motor skills	Dance
Ride a tandem bicycle or a surrey or duo bike with a friend or aide. Ride a stationary bicycle independently. Use a bicycle stand.	Hold on to a guide's elbow, shoulder, or hand. Both the runner and a guide hold on to a tether (short string, towel, or shoelace). A guide rings a bell or shakes a noisemaker while running side-by-side with the child. Hold on to a guidewire or wall to run independently. Run toward a sound source such as a clap or bell. Run on a controlled and safe treadmill. For partial vision, run along white lines on a track that is relatively empty.	Motor activities should be planned to provide the student with an opportunity to learn self- or body awareness and explore the environment (McGinnis and Treffry 1993). They should involve <ul><li>initiating movement in different planes and places,</li><li>initiating movement on different surfaces, and</li><li>promoting movement as a medium for the activity (Smith 1994), using scooterboards, roller-skating, swings, or locomotor skills.</li></ul>	Dancing allows free movement and encourages exercise as well as a chance to socialize (Smith 1994). Adaptations include <ul><li>playing music very loud or turning up the bass,</li><li>using footprints on the floor to guide,</li><li>using strobe lights that reflect the beat of the music to help the student note the rhythm,</li><li>dancing on a wooden floor to increase auditory and tactile cues,</li><li>having participants hold a balloon, which can pick up and reflect the vibrations of the music (Smith 1994), and</li><li>using peer tutors to model and physically assist (Lieberman and Cowart 1996).</li></ul>

Table 14.2 Helpful Hints for Adapting Games and Sports for Children With Special Needs

There are many variables when teaching games, activities, and sports. The following are some variables that need to be considered to ensure increased success when working with individuals with disabilities.

Participant	Equipment	Playing area	Rules	Role of the players	Other players
Know the abilities of the student (mental, visual, auditory, ambulatory)	Make the playing object bigger or smaller	Make the area larger or smaller	Change the rules of the game (e.g., player who has a disability has no defense or must get the ball before a score is attempted)	Change the role of the players (e.g., offense to defense, outfield to infield)	Simulate the disability
Know their previous experiences	Make it softer or harder	Mark off visible boundaries (i.e., rope with tape on top, large cones, or mats on the floor at the edge of the playing area)		Limit or add responsibility (e.g., just run or just bat or only offense or defense)	Be a peer tutor
Know their age and choose age-appropriate activities	Make it audible or bright		Change the objective of the game (e.g., from competitive to cooperative)	Limit commands on the student to one or two parts	Develop adaptations themselves
Know likes and dislikes	Change the texture of the object	Orient individual to the activity area	Increase tactile cues (e.g., partial participation, hand-over-hand)	Decrease competition	Take turns being captain or leader (Lieberman 1996)
	Make it heavier or lighter	Lower height of the goals	Add guidance, a leader, or peer tutor		
	Increase the size of the target		Change the number of players (i.e., more or less)		
			Increase chances (e.g., four strikes or more time before the defense can defend)		
			Decrease time of activity or add rest periods		
			Reduce repetition, or slow the pace		

What Is Best for the Students Involved?

Cathy Bryan, adapted physical education specialist at the Fairhill Elementary School in Fairfax, Virginia, offers the following advice for including special needs students in regular physical education classes (Hopple 1994): "You always have to think first about what is best for the students involved—their health and safety. At the same time, it's important to realize that every child does not have to be included 100 percent of the time in 100 percent of the activity. For example, if a child kicked his or her respirator instead of a ball, this could be . . . fatal. . . . But the child could work on the sideline on a similar manipulative skill, or be involved in the activity in another way." (Remember, however, that by law it is your responsibility to provide the least restrictive environment.)

Table 14.3　Basic Locomotor and Object Control Skills and the Five Basic Questions That Guide Assessment

Locomotor skills	Object control skills
1. Walk or use wheelchair	Roll/bowl
2. Run	Throw
3. Ascend/descend	Catch
4. Jump	Bounce/dribble
5. Hop	Strike
6. Leap	Kick
7. Gallop	Stop/trap
8. Skip	
9. Slide	

Basic assessment questions

1. Performance—Does student perform skill?
2. Functional competence—Does student use skill in activities for fun and/or fitness?
3. Performance standards—Does student meet form, distance, accuracy, speed, and function standards for age group?
4. Constraints—Does student have muscle tone, bone, or joint abnormalities that limit success and/or contraindications to be remembered?
5. Developmental level or form—Is form immature, mature, or adapted to accommodate pathology?

Reprinted, by permission, from Sherrill, C., 1998, *Adapted Physical Activities, Recreation and Sport, 5th ed.*, (New York, NY, McGraw Hill Companies).

Title IX

Your program must offer reasonable opportunities for physical activity to students of both genders. Title IX does *not* require equal *results*, only reasonably equal *opportunity*. This issue is far less volatile in noncompetitive environments such as the physical education classroom. However, if you separate genders for activities, ensure that the activities are reasonably equivalent. For example, it would be improper to allow the boys to play flag football while requiring the girls to do basic ballroom dance because those activities are not reasonably equivalent (not to mention stereotyped). We recommend that you do *not* separate genders at all at the elementary level.

parents and caregivers have about a child's likes, dislikes, experiences, and aspirations. If the student has the assistance of a paraprofessional, this person should come to physical education with the child. Be sure, however, to clearly define the type of help you want from this assistant. If the child does not have a paraprofessional, request one through the IEP committee, at least for the physical education time.

Finally, use other students and volunteers to assist the student. Just ensure that you train them as to how to provide appropriate guidance to the student (see peer tutoring suggestions in chapter 15). You can also use students and volunteers to help with the rest of the class while you focus on the special needs student for a while. Use the following suggestions for selecting and training volunteers. After training, they should

- still want to be a volunteer,
- demonstrate that they understand correct instruction and feedback techniques,
- have knowledge of correct skill analysis (Vogler and Block 1994),
- be positive,
- know how to maximize time on-task for the individual student (Vogler and Block 1994), and
- recognize which social behaviors they should reinforce and which they should discourage (Vogler and Block 1994).

Volunteers should also understand appropriate feedback techniques and know how to record improvements. The adapted physical education specialist and the special education teacher should be able to help with all these aspects of training volunteers and peer tutors (see also chapter 15).

Gender Issues

Despite legislation to the contrary (e.g., Title IX), society still socializes young girls and boys to believe that they are inherently different on the playing field and in the gymnasium. Cohen (1993) lists the following influences society has over each gender's participation in physical activity:

- From a very young age, society encourages boys to like sports and girls to wear dresses and be passive observers.
- Society labels some sports as "girls'" sports and some as "boys'" sports. Boys and girls tend to adhere to these prejudices.

- Society "punishes" those who do not stick to the gender lines drawn in sports, labeling girls who play "boys" sports as "tomboys" and boys who participate in "girls" sports as "sissies."
- On the playground, girls tend to play noncontact and less active sports, such as 4-Square or jump rope, while boys play tag, soccer, or kickball.

Mr. White has been teaching for over 20 years, and his students adore him. He tries to keep up with the times in his curriculum and approach in all areas, including physical education. One day, one of his fifth graders, a girl named Clara, approached him with trepidation. She said, "Mr. White, we play basketball all the time in physical education, but I never get better. You help the boys, but you don't help the girls. I love basketball and want to play better." Mr. White could not imagine how this could have happened. He prided himself on being gender fair. He asked his student teacher to count the frequency of corrective, positive specific and positive general feedback he gave to boys and to girls for one week. To his surprise, he gave boys 70 percent more positive specific and corrective feedback than girls. For example, he told boys practicing shooting to "follow through toward the target" while he told girls "try again." He and the student teacher developed different ways to eliminate this negative teaching behavior. He apologized to Clara, and she is now captain of her middle school team.

The research is in: boys get more of the kind of feedback that leads to improvements in movement skills while girls receive general—and unhelpful—feedback. Thus, boys improve while girls merely participate. Furthermore, teachers tend to use boys more often to demonstrate and lead. Finally, teachers tend to push boys to finish a physical challenge, such as running a mile, while permitting girls to walk or even skip the last lap or two (Cohen 1993; Hutchinson 1995; Sadker and Sadker 1995).

But the research also shows that girls who fully participate in sport and physical education are less likely to become pregnant as teens, more likely to leave abusive men, less likely to drop out of school, and less likely to become involved with drugs (Sadker and Sadker 1995). In this section, we'll outline ways to create gender equity in physical education so that young girls can grow into a lifetime of satisfying, successful, and healthful physical activity.

Changing What You Teach

Given society's persistence in maintaining gender bias in physical activity, it is imperative that you strive to send a more positive message to both girls and boys. Primarily, you must simply assert that it's okay for both girls and boys to be actively involved in *all* sports—no matter what they have been previously led to believe. And that, indeed, in your program, you expect everyone to be fully involved.

Nilges (1996) offers the following checklist to help you ensure that the content of your program is gender equitable:

Equity Checklist for Physical Education

✓ Is your curriculum gender inclusive? Include a variety of experiences because a predominantly games curriculum tends to be gender biased (Hall 1996).

✓ Do students participate in gender-integrated classes? If you segregate students by gender, you send a powerful message of "separate and different" that can affect children for life.

✓ Are teaching styles varied to accommodate different learning styles and preferences? Boys and girls often develop different learning styles as a result of the broader socialization process (Vandell and Fishbein 1989).

✓ Is gender inclusive language used? Use, for example, "person to person" and "player to player" instead of "man to man" defense.

COMPONENT— Gender-Directed Activities

Appropriate Practice	Inappropriate Practice
Girls and boys have equal access to individual, partner, small group, and team activities. Both girls and boys are equally encouraged, supported, and socialized toward successful achievement in all realms of physical activities.	Girls are encouraged to participate in activities that stress traditionally feminine roles, whereas boys are encouraged to participate in more aggressive activities.
Statements by physical education teachers support leadership opportunities and provide positive reinforcement in a variety of activities that may be considered gender-neutral.	Boys are more often provided with leadership roles in physical education class. Statements by physical education teachers reinforce traditional socialization patterns that provide for greater and more aggressive participation by boys and lesser and more passive participation by girls.
	Reprinted from COPEC/NASPE 1992.

✓ Do instructional materials portray both genders as active participants in a variety of activities? Give both genders ample opportunities to see both males and females enjoying and succeeding in a variety of physical activity pursuits, making a concerted effort to dispel myths. Use posters, bulletin boards, and role models.

✓ Do you give equal attention to boys and girls during classroom practices such as questioning, demonstration, and feedback? Abolish a hidden curriculum that favors one gender over the other.

✓ Are local community resources used to help erode gender barriers to sport participation? Invite guest speakers who have challenged and overcome gender barriers in sport. The local YMCA and city and religious leagues are good places to start.

✓ Is time consistently reserved for gender dialogue? Open the lines of communication on this topic. Work as a group to dispel myths. For example, have each student write what he or she likes about being a boy or girl in physical education and what he or she would like to change. Post anonymously on a bulletin board.

✓ Do you hold high expectations for both boys and girls? Rid yourself of any bias.

✓ Is gender equity a pervasive schoolwide goal? Work with colleagues and administrators to promote and coordinate gender equity across the curriculum.

Adapted from Lynda Nilges, "Ingredients for a Gender Equitable Physical Education Program," *Teaching Elementary Physical Education*, October 1996, 28-30.

Changing How You Teach

Ms. Anderson is a student teacher in an urban elementary school under the supervision of Mr. Nunn. When she chooses a girl to demonstrate in physical education, the students protest because Mr. Nunn has told them, "Girls can't demonstrate!" Because this went against everything she was taught, she approached Mr. Nunn after class. He stated he felt boys were better athletes so they should always be used to demonstrate because "girls can't do it right."

You can and should do better than Mr. Nunn. First, give equal feedback to both boys and girls (see chapter 5). Second, use both boys and girls for demonstrations. Finally, teach all sports to all children. Then double-check that you can answer "yes" to the points listed in the "Equity Checklist for Physical Education."

Oops!

Immediately after spending two hours reading some of the research for this chapter, I ran to teach my son's first grade class physical education lesson. I proceeded to call on boys almost exclusively to answer questions and had only boys help lead the activity. Was I ever embarrassed when I recognized what I'd done! My intention was to "neutralize" and develop a positive relationship with the children who spent less time on-task, but there were girls in this category, too. At least I was multicultural in my choices of students, and I did give specific feedback to both girls and boys . . . but I sure gravitated toward the boys. I'll have to work on this!

Changing Who Teaches

Here again, you don't have to overcome gender inequity alone. Inviting role models who have crossed gender barriers successfully in various sports to speak to your class can work wonders in dispelling myths. These do not have to be big or even local stars; a mom who plays hockey, a dad who can demonstrate dance steps or gymnastics stunts, a male teacher who ice skates, or a female teacher who has a black belt in karate is a down-to-earth, close-to-home way to make the point. You may be able to tap into these sources on a regular basis to augment the teaching of various units (a real boon for your entire program), then point out to students how rewarding it is that these people have challenged tradition.

Students as teachers is another way to cross gender lines. Select peer tutors equally from both genders. And mix genders in both cooperative and competitive groups. If you notice that one gender or individual tends to dominate leadership roles in learning groups and on teams, discuss this phenomenon openly, challenging it. Beyond this, you may need to coach individuals privately about taking a more assertive role. Practice gender equity across your curriculum as well.

Multicultural Issues

Sadia is a student in a suburban elementary school. She and her family moved to the United States from Egypt after her mother accepted a job at the local university. Her dress is much different from that of the other children, and her parents forbid her from participating in some of the everyday activities the other kids enjoy. The other kids make fun of her. When she sits out of physical education activities, her teacher gives her no alternative activity and does not attempt to modify the planned activity so she can participate.

Physical education programs tend to be very American-tradition based, sport oriented, competition based, and devoid of cultural diversity (Banks 1988). But every student needs to learn to be comfortable with himself yet still able to function in society. Approaching education through multicultural and multiethnic avenues gives children the information they need to form their own opinions and practices. Knowledge breaks down barriers and discrimination. Indeed, wider cultural awareness can result from better racial and ethnic understanding (Barbarash 1997). Even more important is a teacher's ability to infuse the content knowledge naturally in both the cognitive and affective domains within the discipline (Sparks and Verner 1995). How? Restructure the curriculum content and use pedagogical strategies that complement a diverse student population (Sutliff 1996).

Changing What You Teach

A culturally sensitive physical education curriculum takes into account what all students want to learn, respecting their differences. Figure 14.3 shows a survey developed to help you determine what students are interested in. Incorporate written or oral responses into your physical education plans. Lowy (1995) asserts that "if your students believe that their opinions and perspectives are valued and used, then you have taken the first step in setting up a culturally sensitive environment." The first step is for you to want to interact and communicate effectively with people from different cultures.

For example, if you come from a European cultural background, but teach in a school where most of the students come from a Hispanic cultural background, you should try to learn as much as you can about Hispanic cultures. Or if you come from an Asian cultural background, but teach in a school where many of the students come from an African cultural background, you should try to learn as much as possible about those cultures, and so on. Avoid buying into stereotypes, however. Allow students and their families to tell you what they want to explore. Finally, even if you come from the same cultural

Student Opinions

Finish the sentences using your own opinions. I will use your answers to plan your physical education program for the school year.

1. I like to _____ play with my friends at home.

2. I like to _____ with my family.

3. I would like to get better at or learn how to _____
_____

4. My favorite PE activities are: _____
_____

5. In PE I don't like: _____
_____

6. I like to play with _____
_____

7. I don't like to play with _____
_____

8. I would like PE better if _____
_____

Figure 14.3 Student opinions.

Adapted, by permission, from Lowy, S., 1995, "A multicultural perspective on planning," *Teaching Elementary Physical Education*, 6(3): 14.

Figure 14.4 Celebrate cultural difference in your class as an opportunity to learn new customs.

Teaching the Limited English or Non-English-Speaking Student in Physical Education

A student who doesn't speak English as his first language can still succeed in and enjoy physical education. Here, he can see what the teacher is talking about through teacher and student demonstrations and from keeping an eye on peers. The following will also help such a student:

- Assign an English-speaking buddy to help the student in physical education class. If possible, choose someone who speaks the same language as the non-English speaking student (Mohnsen 1997).

- Physically move a student through a skill to help her comprehend what you want.

- Use gestures and other visual aids, such as toy people and small balls (Mohnsen 1997).

- Use facial expressions and voice inflections to emphasize your points.

- Remember to speak slowly and enunciate clearly as you would in the regular classroom (Mohnsen 1997).

- Emphasize the target skill's key word or phrase as you work with the student and have the student's buddy do so as well.

- Encourage the student to repeat the words or phrases as she executes the skill so she will learn the language that goes with the actions.

- Learn some of the important words and phrases from the child's native language.

background as all of your students, don't assume that they and their parents will automatically share all your values, interests, and beliefs. Instead no matter your situation, above all, strive to get to know individuals and their families.

The following lists specific ways you can make your physical education curriculum more culturally inclusive. Note how many of these suggestions facilitate cross-curricular learning:

- Include activities from other cultures.
- Teach games from other cultures.
- Celebrate holidays and other special traditions from other cultures.
- Teach dances from other cultures.
- Use music from other cultures.
- Have students research other traditions, values, customs, and activities from other cultures through the Internet and other resources.
- Have students try foods from other cultures.

- Have students cultivate pen pal relationships with peers in other countries through the Internet.
- Put on a physical education show including activities, games, and sports and have students dress to represent other cultures.

Changing How You Teach

Banks (1988) outlines three dimensions you should be sure to address when planning physical education lessons:

1. Content integration—tapping into the cultures of your students for physical education content

2. Prejudice reduction strategies—planning activities that facilitate understanding among cultures

3. Culturally responsive pedagogy—respecting cultural differences and exploring the history and meaning of different traditions and values

You can help further sensitize yourself by studying the philosophies and sociology that may affect physical education learning. A child and her parents will probably be more than happy to share their beliefs and wishes with you. Finally, understand that gender equity is not valued in all cultures, so you must respect the different expectations for girls and boys within each culture.

Use this information to help you build in choices that allow for cultural diversity. For example, Hispanic girls in one class would not do any type of straddle stretch, so their teacher allowed all students to choose one stretch from each group of stretch pictures

Alaska's Native Youth Olympics
By Barbara Cadden and Kathy Harris

Many people have heard about Alaska's wealth of natural resources, but the story of the state's rich multicultural heritage has finally reached beyond the Alaskan boundaries. The Native Youth Olympics is one of the events that has helped to foster respect for the forefathers of the people of Alaska.

The first recorded Native Youth Olympics (NYO) was held in Anchorage, AL in 1971. The original NYO organizers hoped that by sharing these challenging games, the people of Alaska could proudly pass on their cultural history. NYO is currently sponsored by the Cook Inlet Tribal Council and the Johnson O'Malley Program.

The Injut games that comprise the NYO are said to have originated from the barren coastal region of the far north. The Alaskan people living along the coast went out on treacherous ice flows to hunt—a task that demanded great mental and physical fortitude. The elders used games to teach young hunters the skills needed to become good providers, and these games were passed onto succeeding generations. The games demanded excellent jumping skills and strength. Some of the kicking, running, and jumping games evolved from the reactions of the men after the hunt, while other games were developed from imitating the movements of animals. Each game demands the total coordination of physical and mental fortitude.

By incorporating the games into their programs, teachers nationwide have a wonderful opportunity to develop a multicultural and interdisciplinary unit for focusing on the people of Alaska. Through NYO, their students can gain an understanding of the physical strength and endurance needed to live a subsistence lifestyle as portrayed through these games. As educators, we have a clear mandate to address the serious divisions currently existing in our American society. Through the inclusion of multiculturalism within our curriculum, we each can actively begin bridging the gaps created by existing social and racial injustices and inequities (Singer 1994).

Although the age group for participation in the official Native Youth Olympics is limited to students in grades 7 through 12, most of the games are introduced at the elementary level. For example the "Seal Hop" can be performed by kindergartners with average arm strength. The other games are more physically challenging but capture the interest of children from second grade and above.

You can find the description and history of these games in *The Native Youth Olympics Handbook*, prepared and printed by the Cook Inlet Tribal Council & Johnson O'Malley Program (1995).

Adapted, by permission, from Cadden, B., and K. Harris. "Alaska's Native Youth Olympics," *Teaching Elementary Physical Education*, (6)3: 1 and 6.

(Lowy 1995). This met both the girls' and the program's needs—without singling the girls out.

Sadia obviously does not like her new school. It is hard for her to make friends because she is so different. At recess, she plays games from Egypt with her brother. Her teacher notices her sadness and asks Sadia to teach him her games. He also reads up on some of the other traditions of the Egyptian culture. Then he works with Sadia to teach a new game from Egypt each week to her classmates. He also modifies his physical education lessons so Sadia can participate the majority of the time. Sadia brings in traditional garb for the other kids to try on and even some traditional middle eastern food. Finally, the teacher gives an assignment in which students research several games, holidays, and histories from around the world on the Internet. Soon, the other kids are fighting over who will be Sadia's partner—in and out of physical education.

Changing Who Teaches

Once again, you don't have to be alone. As you see in the vignette, Sadia helped her teacher teach the rest of the class her games and traditions. What a powerful statement regarding cultural inclusiveness! You can also invite parents from other cultures or international students at a local university to share their physical activity and other traditions.

Ability Inclusion

When you teach by invitation, use intratask variation appropriately (see chapter 5), adapt for students with special needs, and encourage gender equity and cultural diversity, you will meet most of your students' needs—no matter their basic motor skill levels. But there will still be a few students who are extremely talented or extremely challenged (but not classified as having a disability). In this section, we'll look at how to help the student who is motor elite and the student who is physically awkward.

The Motor Elite Child

Not worried about Johnny who can do every gymnastic stunt in the book or Susie who can hit a home run with her eyes closed? Maybe you don't need to be, but don't neglect these students either. Although you should use students of all abilities to demonstrate skills and lead activities, you may find the motor elite make excellent peer tutors. Not only will this give them something interesting and challenging to do, it also may build social skills that may be lacking. In addition, take an interest in these students' extracurricular sport activities and perhaps have them share their activities with the rest of the class, emphasizing that it's the extra time on physical activity that can really help an individual succeed in sport—not merely natural talent. Finally, don't hesitate to apply the teaching method of intratask variation (see chapter 5) to create the type of challenge the motor elite student needs in physical education. You can also use rubrics, extending them to meet everyone's needs.

The Physically Awkward Child

At times you will come across a student who seems to lag behind his peers in physical development. Such a student never seems to develop smooth coordinated movements, despite your attempts to modify activities. Wall (1982) defines the physically awkward child as one "without known neuromuscular problems who [fails] to perform . . . motor skills with proficiency." Many children who are physically awkward go undetected or receive little or no help overcoming their problems. Many parents and educators assume that these children will simply outgrow the problem; the truth is many do not

(Schincariol 1994). Thus, they tend to drop out of physical activity, thereby compounding the problem.

The physically awkward child needs extra practice time, instruction, and encouragement (Schincariol 1994)—just as a child having trouble learning to read needs remediation. Indeed, although a child may be able to cover the fact that he can't read well, everyone can easily see physical awkwardness. So work hard to create situations in which the child who is physically awkward can succeed and have fun. This will help instill the value of physical activity despite the child's problems.

If you are worried that a student has motor skill delays, see that she is given a test of motor proficiency by a trained professional (Schincariol 1994). For example, the Test of Gross Motor Development (Ulrich 1985) may yield valuable information. Then work in consultation with an adapted physical education specialist and the parents to develop an individualized physical education program (Schincariol 1994). This student may need one-on-one help in the same way as a student with special needs, so seek a volunteer, paraprofessional, or trained peer tutor if necessary. These helpers or parents can work with the child who is physically awkward using skill rubrics.

Keep in mind that physical awkwardness is a serious problem, and failing to provide adequate remediation may cheat the student out of a lifetime of physical activity and its benefits (Schincariol 1994).

Summary

Sound like a lot to juggle? Certainly. But no more than you manage the rest of the school

ALL THUMBS

Innovator: Lauren Lieberman, PhD

Grade level: K-5th

Disabilities: muscular dystrophy, cerebral palsy, learning disability, juvenile rheumatoid arthritis

Materials needed: gloves, mittens, Velcro, tape enough for half of the class

Time allotted: 20-25 minutes

Space needed: classroom or small gymnasium

Description of activity: Describe a disability where the child will have fine motor difficulties (e.g., muscular dystrophy, cerebral palsy, learning disability, juvenile rheumatoid arthritis). This simulation will help them understand how those kids feel every day. All the kids try to tie their shoes, button their shirts, zip their flies, or braid shoelaces or hair with gloves, mittens, or something obstructing their hands.

Safety considerations: common sense

Variations: Have kids try to type on the computer, open a door with a key, brush their hair, button buttons, open their lunch bags, open their milk, and so on (anything fine motor).

Questions you can ask include the following:

1. What was hard about this exercise?

2. What was easy?

3. How did you feel?

4. How could you help a child with a fine motor problem?

5. What would you do if you had to go through your entire life with this disability?

day. We're simply saying that inclusion should not stop at the gym door. In fact, inclusion in the physical education setting can enhance your students' social skills and knowledge across the curriculum. But we cannot stress enough: you don't have to be in this alone! Any number of resource people are available to help you help everyone get off to a good start for a lifetime of enjoyable physical activity. From paraprofessionals to parents to local heroes and heroines to the students themselves, you only have to ask, and help will be on the way toward a more inclusive learning environment—in and out of physical education.

MARSHMALLOW MADNESS

Innovator: Dr. Georgia Frey, Texas A & M University

Grade level: K-6th

Disabilities: cerebral palsy, Down Syndrome, speech disorder

Materials needed: 6 marshmallows per child. Three-inch-by-five-inch cards listing short sentences the child has to say when mouth is stuffed with marshmallows.

Time allotted: 20-30 minutes

Space needed: classroom, or small gymnasium

Description of activity: Describes when and why some children have speech problems. Go over characteristics and common problems. Then have students find a partner, and one person at a time puts four to six marshmallows in his mouth and tries to say a phrase or sentence on a card given by the teacher. The other student tries to understand what he is saying for two or three tries, then switch. Use discussion questions to help keep this activity from becoming silly and disrespectful to the child with the speech problem. Use your judgment to decide whether or not the child with the disability should be present for this activity.

Safety considerations: Make sure they don't eat too many marshmallows. Don't continue if they are laughing too hard.

Variations: Allow them to make up phrases or sentences. Switch partners. Don't allow them to look at the student simulating the activity.

Questions you can ask include the following:

1. What did you feel like when you were trying to talk and it was hard?

2. What did you feel like when you were trying to listen and it was hard to understand?

3. Were you clear on the phrase or sentence?

4. What would it feel like to talk like this every day?

5. What could you do to help a student with this problem?

6. Could you think of other effective ways of communicating?

SHOW ME THE SIGN

Innovator: Lauren Lieberman, PhD

Grade level: K-12th

Disabilities: hard of hearing or deaf

Materials needed: sign book or a teacher who knows sign

Time allotted: 10-15 minutes

Space needed: classroom or small gymnasium

Description of activity: First describe the "culture" of people who are deaf or hard of hearing. Then talk about common characteristics. Then sign one to five sentences and see whether any of the kids understand what you are talking about. This is very similar to a situation in which a deaf child is sitting in a classroom, the teacher is talking, and there is no interpreter or clear communication.

Safety considerations: none

Variations: Turn on a TV with no volume and try to guess what is happening. Tell some of the kids and not all the kids what is being said and the others will know what it is like to feel left out of the conversation. Tell a joke in sign and tell some of the kids what you are saying but not all. It will be frustrating for the others just as it is for children who are deaf or hard of hearing.

Questions you can ask include the following:

1. How did you feel when you did not know what I was saying?

2. What would you do if you were in this situation?

3. What would you do if you were in this situation all the time?

4. How can you make a child who is deaf feel better in your classroom?

5. What would it feel like if all the kids in your school spoke sign, and you were the only person who could speak and hear?

Chapter 15

Peer Tutoring Strategies

Melissa, 8

Ms. Carron is very familiar with her fourth graders' abilities and is always trying to help them master new physical education skills. She went to a conference and learned some really exciting balancing and tumbling activities called "Kidnastics." But with 30 students, she didn't quite know how she was going to teach these more complex skills—only that she would have to be very creative.

She decided to pair her students and give each pair task-criteria sheets with the preliminary skills broken down into distinct steps. After demonstrating each skill, she allowed students in each pair to teach and evaluate each other, according to the task sheets. The students checked off each other's sheets and gave each other feedback. At the end of each class, Ms. Carron collected the task sheets so that she could plan the next lesson, based on her students' strengths and weaknesses. The students enjoyed the whole process and were very proud of their new social and physical skills.

It can be hard to meet the needs of all students in your quest to include everyone. Some students, such as those with mental retardation, must have one-on-one help to learn in physical education (Sherrill 1998). Other students with less severe or no particular problems can also benefit from more attention. One way to fill the gap is to have peers tutor fellow students. Even students as young as third grade are capable of observing and correcting one another's movement errors (Mosston and Ashworth 1986).

Peer tutoring can be informal or formal. In informal situations, students help one another, perhaps in a cooperative learning group or on a competitive team with little or no training as to how to do so effectively. In formal situations, however, trained students teach one another to help facilitate the learning process. Both tutors and the tutored benefit from peer tutoring programs. In this chapter, we will list the benefits of formal peer tutoring, describe how to select and train peer tutors, and explain how to assess a formal peer tutoring program. We'll also explain the various types of peer relationships: unidirectional (one-way), bidirectional (reciprocal), and classwide (everyone using the reciprocal approach at once).

Overview of Peer Tutoring

Peer tutoring is instruction by a peer to help provide individualized instruction, improve skills, increase student understanding, provide more opportunities to practice targeted skills with feedback, and facilitate an ongoing way to monitor and assess progress. These benefits, in turn, promote high levels of success (Delquadri et al. 1986; Greenwood, Carta, and Kamps 1990; Houston-Wilson, Lieberman, et al. 1997).

In addition, several researchers have noticed specific benefits of peer tutoring:

- Increased academic learning time (DePaepe 1985; Lieberman, Newcomer, McCubbin, and Dalrymple 1998; Webster 1987)
- Increased appropriate motor behaviors (Houston-Wilson, Dunn, et al. 1997)
- Increased physical activity (Lieberman, Dunn, et al. 1996)
- Improved attitudes toward physical education (Long et al. 1980)
- Improved socialization (Lieberman, Dunn, et al. 1996)

As you can see, peer tutoring can provide many benefits to your students.

Training Peer Tutors

To reap the greatest benefits of peer tutoring, however, students—both tutors and the tutored—must understand their roles and your academic and social expectations. In this section, we'll offer you a training program developed by Cathy Houston-Wilson, PhD, an assistant professor at the State University of New York, College at Brockport.

The peer tutoring training program is composed of four components: choosing peer tutors, teaching peer tutors appropriate instructional methods, teaching tutors how to give appropriate feedback through simulating the peer tutoring setting (using awareness activities and focusing on developing effective communication skills), and assessing your program. This peer tutor training program will take one to three hours to complete, depending on the age group, the content of the unit, and the disability of the student to be tutored. You can hold the training before or after school, during recesses or lunchtimes, or on a teacher inservice day. Let's look, now, at each component of the training program.

Choosing Peer Tutors

Initially at least, some children will make better peer tutors than others. You might wish to train only a few most likely candidates to kick off peer tutoring in your physical education program, then train others when you feel they're ready. Look for students who are willing to learn how to be a peer tutor and choose those who are motivated to try hard in physical education. Although the motor elite child may be helpful, a child does not have to be above average in motor skills to help another child learn. In addition, make sure peer tutor trainees are sensitive and empathetic toward the needs of others. Children with younger siblings often possess these qualities. Finally, select cooperative students, those who are willing to work closely with you and able to accept and benefit from constructive criticism.

Teaching Peer Tutors Instructional Methods

Activities in which students simulate the disability of the student to be tutored help students learn how to be effective teachers. The game on page 268 is a sample awareness activity.

As we all know, effective communication skills are vital to effective teaching. Thus, peer tutor trainees also need to learn how to explain, demonstrate, and provide physical assistance to teach skills. Each lesson, make sure that each peer tutor knows and can correctly use the specific vocabulary pertinent to the skill being taught and specific procedures for demonstrating and physically assisting each student being tutored. The following is a sample handout to use in your training program. Use it as is with older students, and use it as a guide with younger students. As you can see, it also provides further ideas for role-playing peer tutoring situations.

Giving Verbal Signs and Cues

Explanation: Verbal signs and cues tell someone what to do with words.

Examples

"John, run around the cones."

"Jane, it is your turn for pull-ups."

"Let's stand on the black circle."

"Sara, show me the crab walk."

Modeling

Modeling is a way of demonstrating how to do the activity. After you give a verbal cue, if the student does not do the activity or does the activity wrong, you should repeat the cue and demonstrate what you want him or her to do.

Examples

"Mary, hop like this."

"Continue to perform sit-ups like this."

"When we get to station 3, do push-ups like this."

Physical Assistance

Physical assistance is used to help the student if he or she is unable to do the activity after you have given a verbal cue and modeled the activity. You should only physically assist the student by directing his or her body part with your hands. But ask permission to touch, first. (Note that you should always document

TUNNEL VISION TOSS AND CATCH

Grade level: K-6th

Disabilities: retinitis pigmentosa or any visual impairment that results in tunnel vision

Materials needed: safety goggles, masking tape, balls, paper, pens, bats

Time allotted: 30-40 minutes

Space needed: gymnasium or large classroom

Description of activity: First discuss what tunnel vision is and why people have it (it results from retinitis pigmentosa—a hereditary progressive degenerative disease of the eye that limits the field of vision). Next have students wear goggles with peripheral vision blocked out with the tape, and then have students form pairs. (You can have both students or one at a time simulate in this activity.) They need to toss and catch, kick, or bat a ball while simulating tunnel vision.

If you have limited space, you could also have students write sentences on paper while simulating activity, so they can see how hard it is to write when you have tunnel vision.

Safety considerations: Place students in stations, and/or in static position to prevent collisions. Have students complete skills in same direction. Have a few students act as teachers or peer tutors.

Variations: Vary the size of the holes to look through (e.g., 1/4 inch, hole punch size, pinhole, and so on. Add another disability, such as a person in a wheelchair or with cerebral palsy.)

Questions you might ask include the following:

1. Can you see the sides?

2. Is it easy to see the target?

3. What would it be like to see like that all the time?

4. Is it easier to throw or catch the ball?

5. Which skills were harder?

6. How could you help a peer with tunnel vision?

7. What other skills may be hard?

Created by Rodney Allen and Tim Eustice, students at SUNY, Brockport.

---

physical assistance for teaching purposes and to cover you and your peer tutors legally.)

Examples

Stand behind the student and physically assist with a sit-up.

Stand sideways in front of a student holding hands, then bend knees and jump over the rope.

Tap the student on the shoulder when it is his or her turn.

Developed by Cathy Houston-Wilson, PhD.

Teaching Peers to Give Appropriate Feedback

When you give positive specific feedback to students on a regular basis, you will model the type of feedback peer tutors should give. In addition, create opportunities for students to role-play giving helpful feedback to give them the practice they need. The following is a sample handout you can use to teach children the differences between positive general, positive specific, and corrective feedback.

Discuss the value of each: general keeps a person trying; specific helps reinforce the skill.

Learning to Give Feedback

Positive General Feedback

Positive general feedback is a supportive statement about the student's motor skill performance that encourages the student to keep trying.

Examples

"Good skipping!"

"Nice crab walk!"

"Great!"

"Wow!"

"Good job!"

Positive Specific Feedback

This is a supportive statement that includes exact information about what was good about the motor skill performance. If you can't find anything good to say, praise the person's effort and use corrective feedback in a supportive manner.

Examples

"Great high knees while skipping."

"I like the way you use your arms when you run."

"That's the way to keep your feet moving in that station."

Figure 15.1 Having students work as peer tutors encourages clear communication.

Corrective Feedback

This is a statement, made after an attempt at a skill, that gives information about what component of the skill may be missing.

Examples

"Good try, Tim. Don't forget the follow-through."

"Keep your elbow up, Sarah."

"Excellent effort, Jamie! Now try stepping with the opposite foot."

Simulations

Use the following scenarios to help you practice being a peer tutor.

Scenario 1

Tutor: Give the cue. ("Mary, jump over the rope.")

Student: (Acceptable response.)

Tutor: Give positive specific reinforcement. ("Good job jumping over the rope so many times.")

Scenario 2

Tutor: Give the cue. ("John, do five push-ups.")

Student: (Unacceptable response.)

Tutor: Give positive general feedback. ("Good try!")

Tutor: Repeat cue and model the activity. ("John, do the push-ups like this.")

Student: (Acceptable response.)

Tutor: Give positive specific reinforcement. ("Nice job, I like the way you bent your elbows all the way.")

Scenario 3

Tutor: Give the cue. ("Sue, do the crab walk.")

Student: (Unacceptable response.)

Tutor: Repeat the cue and model the activity. ("Sue, do the crab walk like this.")

Student: (Unacceptable response.)

Tutor: Question the student. ("Can I help you?")

Tutor: Provide physical assistance. (Help student lift her hips up for a correct crab walk.)

Student: (Acceptable response.)

Tutor: Give positive specific reinforcement. ("That's the way to lift your hips. Now try to do it yourself.")

Developed by Cathy Houston-Wilson, PhD.

When you think your peer tutor trainees are ready, give them an oral or written test, such as the quiz on the next page (edit vocabulary to be age-appropriate).

Assessing Your Peer Tutoring Program

As with any teaching method, it is important to periodically monitor and assess whether your peer tutoring program is effective. Beyond ensuring that the tutors are actually tutoring, you must determine whether the children being tutored are

- attempting the skills,
- becoming more involved in activities,
- receiving appropriate feedback, and
- learning the targeted skills.

How can you monitor and assess these factors? First, keep in mind that peer tutoring does not excuse you from teaching. You should circulate around the gym or playing field, offering helpful suggestions to encourage effective peer tutoring, giving feedback to both the tutors and tutored. As you observe, you will be able to easily determine whether your students' peer tutoring is generally proceeding in an appropriate and effective manner. To gather specific data on peer tutoring effectiveness, you can have peers fill out assessment rubrics (Block, Lieberman, and Conner-Kuntz 1998) these also provide guidance as to what to work on. Periodically, you should assess targeted skills yourself to monitor progress. You can also monitor and record the time students spend on-task or keep a frequency chart, which simply tracks the number of times a student attempts or performs a particular skill or level of skill (Houston-Wilson, Lieberman, et al. 1997) each day (peer tutors can report this to you). Finally, you should assess student understanding and feelings about peer tutoring. Journaling and class discussion are good options

Name _____   Date _____

Peer Tutor Quiz

Choose the correct answer:

    positive specific feedback
    physical assistance
    verbal cue
    positive general feedback
    model

1. A sign or signal to tell someone what to do is a _____ _____.

2. If the student does not understand how to do the skill, or is doing it wrong, you should _____.

3. You should give _____ _____ to the student only if the verbal cue and modeling do not work.

4. A statement that is supportive and gives exact information about what was good about a skill is called _____.

5. A statement that is supportive but does not give exact information about what was good about a skill is called _____.

6. An example of a positive specific feedback statement is:
    a. "Good job!"
    b. "Good sliding sideways. I like the way you used your arms."
    c. "Good try."
    d. "Slide like this."

7. The student you are working with is unable to gallop. A verbal cue you may give to help the student gallop might be:
    a. "Slide your back foot to your front foot, then step with your front foot again."
    b. "Gallop!"
    c. "Try again."
    d. "You will get it this time."

8. After giving a verbal cue to jump with knees bent, the student is unable to do the skill correctly, so you say:
    a. "Almost, try again."
    b. "That was pretty good."
    c. "Watch me: bend your knees and jump."
    d. "Good jump."

9. After giving a verbal cue and model for the student, he or she is still unable to perform a hurdler's stretch (with knee bent and foot to inside of other knee) correctly, so you say:
    a. "Is it okay if I help you?" and if the student agrees, sit beside him and put hand on outstretched leg.
    b. "Do you want me to take your turn for you?"
    c. "Do you want to do something else?"
    d. "Try again, I know you will get it."

10. "Good job throwing" is an example of a
    a. positive specific statement
    b. corrective feedback statement
    c. verbal cue
    d. positive general feedback statement

Answer key: 1. Verbal cue, 2. Model, 3. Physical assistance, 4. Positive specific feedback, 5. Positive general feedback, 6. b, 7. a, 8. c, 9. a, 10. d

Created by Cathy Houston-Wilson, PhD.

Figure 15.2 Use this quiz to check students' readiness to be peer tutors.

here, as are quizzes such as the one shown on the previous page to conclude initial peer tutoring training.

Sample journal prompts might include the following:

- Are you an effective teacher? Why or why not?

- Are you enjoying the peer tutoring program? Why or why not?

- Are you a better performer because of your teaching and demonstrating? Why or why not?

Sample discussion questions might include the following:

- How would you improve this program? What would you change?

- Was the training effective?

- Were you a successful tutor or tutored student?

- Was performance enhanced as a result of this program?

Assess the overall progress of your program with the help of the checklist in figure 15.3.

If you note through conscientious assessment that peer tutoring is not proceeding smoothly, you must adjust your program to compensate for any deficits. Perhaps you need to scale down your use of this strategy for the time being. Or maybe you need to provide more inservice training. One simple way to alleviate problems is to meet with the tutor and the tutored five minutes before the start of each class to review and help the pair focus on the current lesson's objectives. You should also ask your students for suggestions for improving peer tutoring in your physical education program. They may know exactly what will help or at least provide some helpful clues. Moreover, involving them in your assessment process will help give them in-

Peer Tutor Progress Sheet for the Instructor

Use this progress sheet on an ongoing basis during tutoring programs to ensure accountability of both the peer tutor and the tutored student.

Check all that apply:

1. ☐ Tutoring is occurring
    ☐ unidirectional (one-way)
    ☐ bidirectional (reciprocal)
    ☐ appropriately delivered

2. ☐ Child(ren) is/are attempting skills and involved in activities

3. ☐ Child(ren) is/are receiving appropriate feedback
    ☐ positive specific
    ☐ positive general
    ☐ corrective
    ☐ nonverbal

4. ☐ Learning is occurring: documentation/accountability
    a. frequency charts for fitness or attempts at skills
    b. skill analysis forms
    c. time involved in activity

If any of these areas are not being addressed, retraining and monitoring of the tutor(s) will need to proceed. If this form continues to reveal problem areas, another tutor would be appropriate to ensure success of the child(ren).

Created by Lauren Lieberman, PhD.

Figure 15.3 Check program progress with this form.

creased ownership of the method; therefore, they may take more responsibility for making it work.

Peer Tutoring Situations and Strategies

Mr. Gomez, a fourth grade teacher, began a peer tutoring program by training three enthusiastic students to help Pat, a student who has diplegic spastic cerebral palsy. Pat can walk but has a scissor gait that greatly affects his speed and performance of locomotor skills. Pat sat in on the last training session so the tutors could discuss his needs, strengths, and weaknesses with him. Each class, the tutors took turns demonstrating, offering a shoulder for balance, and retrieving balls for Pat. They all progressed both in their individual and peer tutoring skills and became fast friends. Their relationship carried over into the classroom and onto the playground. Now Mr. Gomez has a waiting list of 14 students who want to be Pat's tutor!

There are many ways to organize and use your trained peer tutors. For each peer tutoring situation, modeling (the basis of tutoring) seems to be most effective when there is age and gender similarity (Sherrill 1998), although older tutors have been used successfully (Lieberman, Newcomer, McCubbin, and Dalrymple 1998). In this section, we'll outline several different situations and the related specific strategies.

Unidirectional (One-Way) Peer Tutoring

In unidirectional peer tutoring, one student teaches the other, with the instruction going only one way. Usually the tutor is a more skilled or older student. In this situation, the tutor is trained and the other child is not.

Unidirectional peer tutoring works best if the peer tutor is attentive and continually instructs and gives appropriate feedback. This peer tutoring method is a good choice to use with a student with more involved disabilities such as severe mental retardation or severe cerebral palsy.

Bidirectional (Reciprocal) Peer Tutoring

In bidirectional peer tutoring, two children take turns tutoring each other. Both children are trained to tutor a peer. Mosston and Ashworth (1986) call this type of peer tutoring situation *reciprocal* peer tutoring. You can use this with one or a few pairs of students or on a classwide basis (see next section).

Bidirectional peer tutoring works best if students are trained, take turns, have equal time tutoring, and are given specific criteria to teach and observe. This type of tutoring is a wonderful way to build leadership and communication skills, so give any child who is able bidirectional peer tutoring opportunities. Even children with behavior disorders, autism, mild mental retardation, or mild orthopedic impairments can participate in this form of peer tutoring.

Classwide Peer Tutoring

In classwide peer tutoring situations, the entire class is organized into pairs of students working together and taking turns as each other's tutors in reciprocal relationships. Every child is trained to be an effective peer tutor. One child instructs and gives feedback while the other practices the target skills (Block, Oberweiser, and Bain 1995). Then the two children switch roles after one has mastered the skill, when the allotted time has run out, or class period by class period. Both children in each pair document the progress of the other.

You may opt to include any or all of the following four components in classwide tutoring situations (Greenwood, Delquadri, and Hall 1984; Greenwood, Terry, Arreaga-Mayer, and Finney 1992):

1. Weekly competing teams—in which each pair is on one of two teams. Each component of each rubric is worth a point. Whichever team ends up with the most points at the end of the unit wins.

2. Highly structured teaching procedures—giving tutors specific guidance through the command style of teaching.

3. Daily point earning with public display of student performance—As students become more proficient in one skill and earn more points on the related rubric, they can show the entire class their progress (if they choose).

4. Direct practice of motor skills—in which students practice specific components of skills on a rubric or similar task analysis sheet.

Students With Special Needs

As we saw in the second vignette, Mr. Gomez was able to find the help his student Pat needed by training other students to be peer tutors. You can work with a special needs student's teaching team (special education teacher, adapted physical education specialist, occupational therapist) to train peer tutors. Practice is especially important when training peer tutors to work with students with special needs. Use disability simulation activities such as those at the end of chapter 14 and the one on page 268 as well as the scenarios on page 270.

Summary

The benefits of peer tutoring go beyond improved motor skills. Students who tutor learn valuable life skills in communication, empathy, responsibility, and physical activity. Both they and students who are tutored have more opportunities to practice social interactions and make friends in the physical education setting. Through implementing peer tutoring as one of your many instructional methods, you will enhance the positive class atmosphere so important to success in physical education and the development of positive attitudes toward healthful physical activity as a way of life. Moreover, you will reinforce peer tutoring strategies you're using and get benefits you're seeing in your regular classroom, and vice versa.

Chapter 16

Collaboration Strategies

Timmy, 11

*It's amazing what gets done
when no one worries about
who gets the credit.*

—Author Unknown

Collaboration can occur in many forms: volunteers (see chapter 14), peer tutors (see chapter 15), community businesses and agencies, and physical education specialists. In this chapter, we'll focus on working with physical education specialists and community resources. First we'll outline how to help a specialist who already works with your students extend physical education learning. Then we'll discuss how to find a specialist to collaborate with even if your school does not have the services of one. Finally, we'll describe how to tap into community businesses, such as fitness clubs and sporting goods stores, and agencies, such as the park district.

Working With a Physical Education Specialist

Having a physical education specialist to work and consult with should prove to be an invaluable resource. In this section, we'll examine how to work closely to support a physical education specialist assigned to your school. Then we'll outline how to coordinate with a physical education specialist if your school does not have one on staff.

Extending an Existing Program

If you find yourself teaching in a school that has a part- or full-time physical education specialist, consider yourself fortunate. You will have a fully trained expert on hand to guide your students toward becoming physically educated individuals. Chances are, however, that this specialist will not be able to meet with your class five days a week. Indeed, he or she may only have your students as infrequently as once a week. But you can and should work to extend the existing physical education program by teaching physical education to your students on the days they do not meet with the specialist.

Collaborating with a physical education specialist can be a formal or informal process. A formal process should include the following steps on a staffwide basis:

1. Reviewing the importance of physical education
2. Designing a schedule and implementing a rotation through units to avoid equipment shortages
3. Giving classroom teachers a chance to discuss questions, concerns, and problems with the specialist
4. Allowing time for everyone to think about and discuss her feelings about the collaborative physical education program

Ask the physical education specialist to share his or her yearly plan, goals, and objectives with you, so you can work together to provide a well-rounded physical education program to your students. Specifically, you can then design lessons to reinforce what the specialist is teaching. In addition, to help you plan effective lessons, ask the specialist to recommend other written resources and refer to the many resource books listed in this book (see pages 325 to 326).

A specialist can also help with scheduling the physical education facilities and equipment. Scheduling different grades to use different equipment at different times can increase the time you can spend on physical education by reducing waiting time for the things you need. With or without a specialist's help, another way scheduling can help make your physical education program run more productively is to have a set of skill and theme units for your grade level to rotate through. This way, for example, if your school has three fourth grade classes, you can teach the dance unit three times, once to each class. Meanwhile, your fellow fourth grade teachers can teach two other units, rotating through all three fourth grade classes as well. This gives each teacher a chance to focus completely on one theme, enabling him or her to perfect his or her strategies and troubleshoot problems.

You can also work closely with a physical education specialist to design and implement

Good Morning, Fitness!

Fourth, fifth, and sixth grade students at Jefferson Elementary School in Sacramento, California, begin each Monday, Wednesday, and Friday morning with 30 minutes of "Morning Fitness" station activities supervised by classroom teachers. The purpose of this program is to give students the opportunity to increase their physical fitness levels through a variety of fun and innovative fitness stations and activities. Sixth grade "Morning Fitness Helpers" are in charge of setting up the equipment, and fifth graders return equipment to storage after the sessions because they are the last to use the stations.

After jogging a quarter-mile lap to warm up, students report to the designated stretching area where they perform safe stretches that do not require them to sit on the blacktop or grass. Next they begin at one station and rotate until "Morning Fitness" ends. Three stations—one per grade—are sufficient. Teachers issue awards for appropriate participation and behavior slips for inappropriate behavior.

Debbie Vigil, physical educator at Jefferson Elementary, plans the stations, troubleshoots problems with classroom teachers, and changes activities frequently to maintain interest and enthusiasm. And what do teachers and students think? Here are a few of their comments:

Teachers say
As a teacher, I found the morning fitness program to be a real energizer for my class. Starting the day with fresh, oxygenated blood supplied to the body was essential to the success of the day. Now as the principal, I find that the fitness program is even more crucial. [It] is good for the body, good for team building, and good as a stamina builder for the individual.

—John Paris Salb, Principal

[Morning Fitness] energizes the kids and gets them ready to learn. The students look forward to our fitness days because they have fun with it. But I also believe it has helped them learn the value of being physically fit for a lifetime, and that is the true benefit of morning fitness.

—Julie Baggett, fifth grade teacher

[Morning Fitness] not only helps shape up my students physically but also mentally they are energized and ready for a day of learning. A healthy mind and body go hand in hand.

—Julie Hanson, sixth grade teacher

Students say
Morning Fitness is a good way to wake up in the morning. It keeps you fit for sports and it even helps you to run for longer periods of time.

—Michael, student

I know I'll do good in any sports because I'm well-trained and healthy.

—Arthur, student

I think Morning Fitness teaches kids that being fit isn't just to please others, it is about feeling good and staying healthy.

—Whitney, student

Fitness helps me to get going in the morning. This will help me in the future so I will not get out of shape.

—Mallory, student

---

cross-curricular units (see chapters 2 and 12). Remember, this approach helps

1. those weak in bodily-kinesthetic intelligence develop this area,

2. everyone enhance memory,

3. those strong in bodily-kinesthetic intelligence succeed in the classroom setting, and

4. children learn the "whys" and "hows" of their physical education activities.

See the dos and don'ts below for a summary of ways to support your physical education specialist.

Supporting Your Physical Education Specialist

Do

The following lists suggestions for helping your physical education specialist, providing he or she desires your help:

- ✓ Ask for physical education lessons or resource suggestions to teach on non-physical education days.
- ✓ Provide class time for students to finish written or art assignments introduced in physical education.
- ✓ Collect physical education homework assignments.
- ✓ Help design cross-curricular units.
- ✓ Store physical education portfolios.
- ✓ Project to students how important physical education, wellness, and physical activity are.
- ✓ Set a good example for students by eating right and exercising regularly.
- ✓ Assist enthusiastically with special projects (field days, family fitness nights, and the like).
- ✓ Act as a liaison between parents and the physical education program and specialist.
- ✓ Befriend the specialist, who may feel very isolated, especially if he or she serves more than one building as an itinerant teacher.

Don't

Follow these suggestions to avoid undermining your physical educator's program:

- ✓ Keep students out of physical education class or other physical activity times for punishment; the students who need to move the most are the most likely to lose the chance! Design alternative consequences or remediation for misbehavior or unacceptable academic performance.
- ✓ Use physical activity as punishment (e.g., "Do 10 push-ups for talking out of turn!").
- ✓ Treat physical education as a frill that you can only tolerate because it gives you a planning period.

Finding a Physical Education Consultant

What if your school does not have a physical education specialist on staff? There are some fairly simple ways to find a specialist with whom you can consult on physical education issues. Start by contacting your school district's curriculum director. Ask whether a specialist certified to teach at the elementary level is available to act as a consultant to classroom teachers. Perhaps a local middle or high school physical education teacher has assumed this role. If the school district has not designated such a person, request that it do so. In the meantime, contact likely individuals yourself. Be sure, however, that any person you use as a resource is qualified to help with the unique needs of the elementary-aged child.

A local university's Health and Physical Education Department might yield a willing and qualified individual to suit your needs. Such a specialist may also be able to help you tap into other community resources as well.

Can't find help? Don't give up. Meanwhile, use the community resources listed next to help broaden and improve your program.

Using Community Resources

The resources you'll find in your community will be limited only by your imagination. Ask community businesses and agencies to volunteer their services in exchange for free publicity. For example, your school could print an advertisement for a local health club in the PTA newsletter in exchange for a lesson on strength training. Here's a quick list of other resources and activity ideas:

Local restaurant—Sample heart healthy foods and discuss how to prepare them.

Health club—Visit for equipment demonstrations.

Dance studio—Take a jazz dancing lesson.

Nurse—Request blood pressure screening.

Nutritionist—Discuss healthful snacking habits.

University Health and Physical Education Department—Have an expert perform body composition testing.

Sports apparel store—Learn how to select the correct athletic shoe.

Exercise physiologist—Dispel myths about exercise.

Grocery store—Take a tour and allow students to "purchase" foods with play money. If you can get the store to ring the purchases up, students can take the receipts back to school to analyze their choices according to the Food Guide Pyramid.

Park district—Conduct a "Fun Run" with awards for all participants in each age division.

Food bank—Organize a canned foods drive, emphasizing foods low in fat, salt, and sugar. Teach students how to read the labels accurately. Perform arm curls holding a can in each hand.

Senior citizen center—Pair students and seniors to walk, exercise, and visit together once or twice a month. Encourage participants to share their feelings and experiences regarding exercise. These same partners can be pen pals, enhancing language arts and social studies learning.

Adapted from Virgilio 1997, 75-77.

These are only a few of the many ways your physical education program can benefit from the resources in your community. We're sure you can think of many more!

A Developmentally Appropriate Field Day

Finally, a field day can be a fun, interesting, and worthwhile way to collaborate with parents, community members, and physical

Figure 16.1 Community resources can supplement your curriculum with knowledge from people in different careers or stages of life.

education and health specialists. The box below gives COPEC's views about this area of physical education.

To this end, we'd like to offer an alternative to the traditional overcompetitive field day as adapted from Virgilio's book *Fitness Education for Children* (1997).

Fitness Field Day

This schoolwide activity is ideal for the spring or early fall. Promote the fitness field day with the central theme of physical activity for health and fun. It helps to identify the event with a special title, for example, "The Fun, Food, and Fitness Field Day!" Unlike traditional field days that focus on competition in various events, your field day should emphasize participation, physical development, and social interaction.

Form a field day committee to help organize this event. Include a few classroom teachers, special area teachers, and at least two parents. Contact the local university for student volunteers. Health, physical education, and elementary education majors at a nearby university make ideal personnel to help manage this event. Of course, parents, grandparents, and members of the community can also assist. In addition, ask the local school site committee from the American Heart Association to help develop a display.

Ensure that each class has an opportunity to participate in each activity by using a station approach. Set up at least 10 stations throughout the outdoor physical education area (see figure 16.2).

Organize the field day into two phases: kindergarten through third grade and fourth through sixth grades. Consider this sample schedule:

8:30 to 9:00 a.m.	set up
9:00 to 11:00	kindergarten through third grade
12:30 to 2:30	fourth through sixth grades
2:30	clean up

Assign each class a station number to begin the field day. Then have classes move through the stations in sequence. Use a loud horn to signal a change of station every 11 to 12 minutes. At the end of your fitness field day, give each participant a special "Fun, Food, and Fitness" certificate, pin, ribbon, headband, or button. Ask local businesses to donate incentives such as water bottles, key chains, or T-shirts with a health message to distribute to everyone.

The following are sample stations you might develop.

Station 1: Step Aerobics

Ask a local health club if a qualified instructor would lead this station. Be sure you have

---

COMPONENT—
Field Days

Appropriate Practice	**Inappropriate Practice**
The field day, if offered, is designed so that every child is a full participant and derives a feeling of satisfaction and joy from a festival of physical activity.	Field days, if offered, are designed so that there is intense team, group, or individual competition with winners and losers clearly identified.
Opportunities are provided for children to voluntarily choose from a variety of activities that are intended purely for enjoyment.	One or two children are picked to represent an entire class, thereby reducing others to the role of spectator.
	Reprinted from COPEC/NASPE 1992.

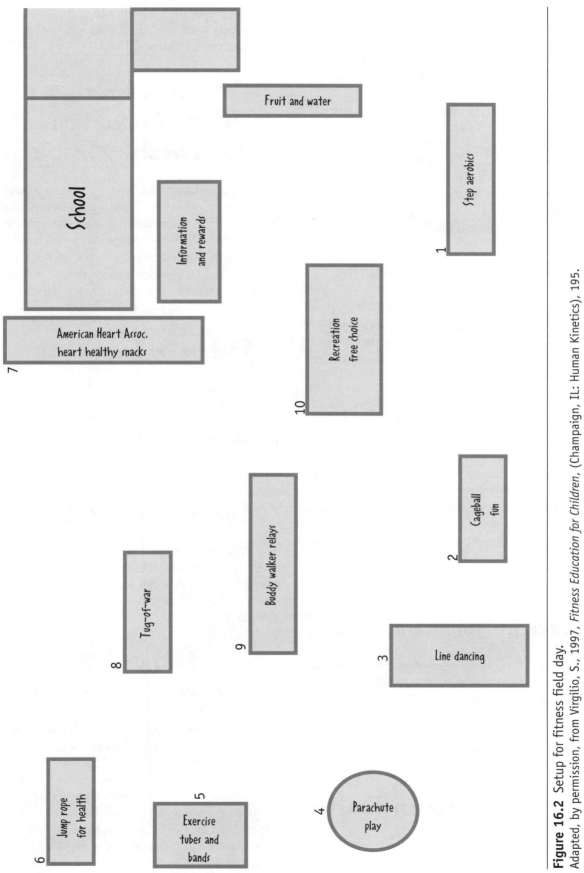

Figure 16.2 Setup for fitness field day.
Adapted, by permission, from Virgilio, S., 1997, *Fitness Education for Children*, (Champaign, IL: Human Kinetics), 195.

observed a few of the specialist's classes before extending the invitation to your school.

Station 2: Cageball Fun

Set two cageballs in automobile tires approximately 30 yards from a starting line. Divide the class in half and at the signal each team runs to their tire and rolls the cageball out of the tire and to the finish line before rolling it back to the tire. The first team to place the cageball back in the tire is the winner. Change teams for the second round.

Station 3: Line Dancing

Line dancing is an ideal physical education activity because it requires no partners, the steps are easy, the music is popular, and everyone is moving together, which makes students feel more secure.

Station 4: Parachute Play

Take a group jog with everyone grasping a large parachute then play Pop Out. Divide the class into two teams. Place one or two playballs in the center of the parachute then have the teams try to pop the balls over the opposing teams' heads to score a point. Three points wins the game.

Station 5: Exercise Tubes and Bands

Design a large task card describing and, if possible, demonstrating the specific exercise you selected for this station. Be certain to provide a large number of different exercises and a variety of tension levels for the tubes and bands so everyone will be able to participate and feel successful.

Station 6: Jump for Health

Allow students to jump rope at their own pace or participate in groups. Provide enough types of ropes so students can choose a variety of physical activities that will enhance arm muscle endurance.

Station 7: American Heart Association Heart Healthy Snacks

Ask a volunteer from the American Heart Association to set a display and provide a brief explanation about heart healthy foods two to three minutes long. You might want to distribute healthy snacks such as yogurt, low-fat cookies, or rice cakes, as well as a handout with recipes for healthy snacks.

Station 8: Tug of War

This is a great way to encourage teamwork and cooperation. If possible, use the lightweight synthetic fiber webbing ropes to help prevent cuts and burns.

Station 9: Buddy Walker Relays

A walker is 2 seven-foot wooden runners with 12 nylon stretch cord handles (2 per player, 1 per side). Six students step on the runners, hold a strap in each hand, and move in unison.

Station 10: Recreation Free Choice

Provide a number of recreation options: hopscotch, jump bands, balance sticks, horseshoes, paddleball, individual balance boards, etc.

In addition to the 10 basic stations you may wish to organize a fruit and water station supervised by the PTA, perhaps setting it up as a chance for a break in the field day circuit, in addition to the healthful snacks at station 7. Use the information and incentives station as a central organizing and equipment area.

Reprinted from Virgilio 1997.

Summary

Remember, you're not alone! You can find many ways to help improve and enrich your physical education program. Collaborative relationships, however, take time and effort to develop. In many cases, it may take a couple of years to smooth out the rough edges. But with a little perseverance and dedication, a quality physical education program can emerge, one that you and your colleagues will be proud of *and* one your students will love and thank you for.

Brody, 4

Austin, 7

Timmy, 11

Emily, 7

Creating a Safe Physical Education Environment

Although we have touched upon safety issues at times thus far in this book, we now must turn to look at this issue more closely. As your students' physical education instructor, you are, of course, responsible for their safety in the physical education setting. Although laws that address your accountability vary from state to state, they do contain many common threads. Many points we'll cover in part 4 are simply common sense; however, some points we'll make are less obvious but still vital. Read and study this part of the book carefully, remembering the adage that helps you manage student behavior: "An ounce of prevention's worth a pound of cure!" Indeed, managing student behavior effectively is a cornerstone of safety management.

In chapter 17, we'll discuss the basic safety and liability issues. In chapter 18, we'll show you how these issues apply to the equipment, space, and facilities you use as well as how to get the most out of these factors. Finally, in chapter 19, we'll describe how to manage playgrounds and free play safely as well as how to help your students get the most out of these chances for physical activity.

Chapter 17

Physical Education Safety and Liability Issues

Rachel, 5

One lawyer in a small town will starve to death. Two, however, can each make a pretty good living.

As in your regular classroom, you have a legal and moral responsibility to provide the safest possible physical education learning environment for all students. The best way to avoid getting sued is to prevent the problem. But things may sometimes go wrong, despite your best efforts. Yet, this does not have to mean you will lose an ensuing lawsuit. Although we cannot possibly tell you whether you (or your school) are liable in a particular set of circumstances, we will help you prevent problems. This chapter can help make you an informed legal consumer so you can protect your own rights because you know *how* a lawyer can help you as well as *what* the lawyer needs to know to help you. Specifically, we'll describe ways to prevent safety and liability problems and the basic legal concepts behind these issues

Preventing Safety and Liability Problems

The physical education settings of the gym and playing field present special safety and liability problems. Although no one expects your physical education program to be injury free, you must strive to limit injuries. Indeed, those who entrust their children to your care expect you to teach students in a safe learning environment. Thus, it's important to recognize and understand the specific responsibilities involved in being your students' physical education instructor. Your duties fall into five categories: to provide proper instruction, to provide proper supervision, to properly classify students, to provide a safe learning environment, and to promptly respond to injuries. In this section, we'll discuss each duty in detail.

Duty to Provide Proper Instruction

The duty to provide proper instruction is especially important in a physical activity situation because failure to do so can result in injuries. Let's look closely at what and how you should teach.

What to Teach

As your students' physical education instructor, you must properly instruct students in several areas:

- Movement skills and concepts
- Sport-related skills
- Social development skills
- Outdoor adventure experiences (e.g., rope courses, rock climbing)
- Skills that will equip students to engage in life-oriented experiences (e.g., using health-fitness equipment, jogging)

School administrators, parents, school board members, and society as a whole expect you to teach these skills safely.

Instruction Action Plan

What exactly does it mean to provide proper instruction? Courts have defined proper instruction as the explanation of basic rules and procedures, suggestions for proper performance, and identification of the risks associated with the activity (Van der Smissen 1990). Specifically, you should (Sutliff 1996)

- make sure that the sequencing of information is developmentally and age appropriate by planning and organizing your entire teaching series or unit to ensure a logical progression;
- ensure that the demonstrations are clear and check to see if all students understand;
- warn of any dangers associated with the activity (based on what is reasonable);
- never assume students have prior knowledge or experience in skills;
- use the most appropriate teaching strategy;
- pinpoint inappropriate executions of a skill and help the student make adjustments;
- make sure students understand and follow all rules and regulations and provide appropriate consequences for those who

don't, possibly including removal from the experience when repeated failure to obey creates a risk of injury (see also inclusion issues later in chapter);

- keep abreast of new instructional methods and techniques; and
- consider the state, school district, and institutional guidelines and frameworks as standards when developing a sequence of learning experiences.

Duty to Provide Proper Supervision

The typical physical education lesson involves students propelling objects, moving in confined spaces, exploring new skills while active with others, or using potentially dangerous equipment. Thus, you must properly supervise your students to help limit the potential for injuries. This duty stems from the legal "duty of care" (tort law), which we will introduce later in the chapter.

Teacher Presence

Surprisingly, many teachers openly invite claims of negligence related to improper supervision because they directly or indirectly remove themselves from the class. These removals may involve, for example, leaving the class site completely or ignoring some activity, such as allowing play to continue while dealing with a serious discipline problem or injury incident or talking to an administrator during an activity ("indirect removal").

If an incident involves complete absence of the teacher ("direct removal"), lawyers consider the following issues when investigating cases involving supervision, and, in turn, courts consider these factors in determining liability:

- Reasons for the absence
- Length of the absence
- The age and maturity level of those left unsupervised
- Location of the injured student when left unsupervised
- The activity students were engaged in immediately prior to the teacher's absence

- The teacher's ability to foresee the potential dangers compared with a reasonably prudent person

Types of Supervision

Supervision is the qualitative and quantitative control exerted by teachers over their students for whom they are responsible (Dougherty et al. 1995). Courts have defined three types of supervision: general, specific, and transitional.

1. General supervision—This refers to the teacher being physically present while the physical education class is in session. If the teacher is called out of the class, an alternative supervision plan must be followed; the teacher should never leave the class unattended.

2. Specific supervision—This reflects the need for the teacher to be present and assisting during certain executions of high-risk-oriented skills, such as tumbling or gymnastics.

3. Transitional supervision—This occurs when the teacher makes a major modification or change in the activity. This also could occur when the class is arriving at or leaving the gym or playing field.

Make sure that you understand and take responsibility for these three types of supervision to limit needless student injuries.

Supervision Action Plan

Consider the following points when planning for the duty to provide proper supervision:

- Establish, communicate, and practice emergency plans and protocols for physical education class.
- Remember the management principle of "back to the wall" (see chapter 4) to maximize your ability to observe all students at all times during each lesson.
- Never allow even a reliable group of students to go unsupervised.
- Never use an activity that appears dangerous or you are not certain is safe.
- Survey the playing area and confirm that all potential hazards are either removed or communicated to students.

- Don't ask another teacher to cover two classes.
- Don't ask an aide, older student, or volunteer to completely supervise your class, but do use these resource people to assist you in supervising more effectively.

Duty to Properly Classify Students

Physical education teachers have a legal duty to properly classify students for competitive and noncompetitive movement experiences. When a teacher makes students responsible for forming their own groups, selecting teams, or numbering off, he or she gives the students the duty to properly classify students that rightfully belongs with the teacher. This type of classification calls for extreme caution because then you have limited control over who competes against whom, and the result can lead to liability problems. Use a methodical, organized system to match students equally based on height, weight, maturity, experience, and mental readiness for situations with a lot of physical contact. Thus, if you allow students to form teams or choose partners, reserve the right to make changes to provide for even matching (see chapter 9 regarding team formation).

Consider, too, the activity itself in relation to the participants. Can you foresee potential problems with certain student groupings? Avoid these!

In addition, don't ever force students to participate if they express fear, uncertainty, or strong hesitation. Moreover, if you participate in an activity, do so with caution. It is important to be a good role model, and children enjoy having teachers participate, but you must be very careful that your participation does not leave some students unsupervised or that your skill level is too high, thereby placing students at risk through mismatches in skill.

Inclusion of Students With Special Needs

Ensure that both you and all aides have thoroughly reviewed the IEP for relevant issues.

Don't assume anything! For example, a student with ADD (attention deficit disorder) "completely controlled" by medication may only be "completely controlled" in a relatively sedate classroom. Another student barely controllable in the classroom may be "in her element" with physical activity. *Plan for inclusion.* You'll reduce the stress for yourself and your students if you know ahead of time how you'll deal with anticipated problems (see chapter 14).

Inclusion means inclusion. Just as you cannot expel a student whose misbehavior is caused by his or her disability *(Doe v. Koger; S-1 v. Turlington)*, you cannot exclude a student from an activity if it is possible to include her without creating a safety hazard, however inconvenient (see also *School Board v. Malone* and Osborne 1997).

Cooperative Learning

Employ cooperative learning techniques (see chapter 13) to reduce the risks of mismatches. Noncompetitive games and situations are especially valuable when your class has many mismatches. Cooperative learning techniques may also reduce the risk of injuries caused by student aggression.

Duty to Provide a Safe Environment

Does your gymnasium have exposed electrical outlets? Does your playground? What about other hazards, like splintering wood, sharp edges, and unpadded corners? Inspect everything—facilities, equipment, clothing—for obvious hazards (see also chapters 18 and 19).

Inspections

Determine who is responsible for inspection and maintenance of your school's playing fields and gymnasium. This person needs to understand the duties involved in this responsibility and should follow a systematic plan to ensure the safety of everyone who uses the facilities. Legally, these inspections must be conducted routinely before anyone uses the facilities. This is what lawyers call the "last clear chance" doctrine. Under this doctrine, a teacher who notices an unsafe condition—such as loose floorboards under the basket before a basketball game—and takes no steps to correct or avoid the condition (i.e., allows the activity to continue without correction) may be liable, even if a resulting injury was "really" caused by the unsafe condition. This liability is similar to your being at least partially at fault if you see a car run a red light and don't make an attempt to avoid an accident.

Inspections should cover the following areas (if available):

Activity rooms

Bathrooms

Meeting rooms

Gymnasiums

Tennis and racquetball courts

Multipurpose fields

Football and soccer fields

Baseball diamonds

Bleachers

Sandboxes

Playgrounds and their equipment (see also chapter 19)

Any other areas used by students, spectators, or members of the public

In addition, the inspector should pay particular attention to floor surfaces, wall and ceiling areas, air flow and ventilation, temperature, humidity, and other environmental factors (Herbert 1995).

Ensure that facilities and equipment have been properly maintained, cleaned, and inspected for hidden as well as obvious hazards and debris. Inspections are best done through documented periodic inspection by physical education or facilities specialists. The inspection document should include a list of inspected areas, inspection times and dates, and names and signatures of the people who inspected.

Dealing With Hazards Effectively

An area or equipment problem that presents an unreasonable risk should be repaired, removed, or labeled unsafe with a clear warning sign appropriate to the age and maturity of the students using the facility. Then, the hazard should be corrected as soon as possible. Some possible dangerous conditions include the following:

Unstable bleachers

Slippery floors

Water fountains in unlighted areas

Debris or unused equipment lying around a field or gym

Ungroomed fields hiding debris

Holes on fields, cracked blacktop surfaces, and dangerously loose gym floorboards

High flood areas and deep water on playing fields

Sports fields too close to playgrounds

Unsafe traffic conditions, such as classes walking through the instructional area because it is the only route available

> *Warning*: Holes on auxiliary fields used by physical education students, cracked blacktop surfaces, and dangerously loose gymnasium floorboards are lawsuits waiting to happen. Administrators must take decisive action to repair facilities or they will face a lawsuit as a result of student injury.

A request for a repair, correction, or alteration should be responded to with an estimate of how long it will take to remedy the problem.

If the learning environment simply cannot be made safe through warning signs or removal of the hazard until a repair can be made, then do not proceed with the planned activity. Instead—without hesitation—cancel class or employ a backup plan.

If *you* notice any problem between regular inspections, notify the correct authorities in writing and ensure that no one uses the problem area until the situation has been resolved. Even though you are not a physical education specialist, you have a duty to foresee potentially dangerous situations in the physical education setting and take immediate and proper action to prevent injuries.

Last, but not least, enforce all safety and equipment rules. Students who do not use safety equipment (e.g., batting helmets in softball) do not play. And don't neglect your own safety equipment—set the example.

Duty to Promptly Respond to Injuries

Sometimes, despite our best efforts, an injury or illness does occur. In such cases, you must be properly prepared to act effectively and calmly. Moreover, your school is responsible for developing, practicing, and implementing a systematic plan to deal with emergencies. Finally, you must be able to deal with special circumstances that may arise.

Planning for Student Injuries

Situations in which students are injured or otherwise require some type of medical aid occur daily in physical education classes across the country. You have an obligation to recognize and respond to such situations. You have two main duties in case of an emergency. First, you must know and successfully implement the proper first aid as required until trained medical personnel arrives. Specifically, you should know how to treat heat-related illness, shock, impaired-breathing, cuts and bruises, and sudden illness, such as seizures, diabetic emergencies, and fainting. Obtain a list from the school nurse regarding those students who have preexisting health conditions (e.g., bee sting allergies, diabetes, and so on) so that you know what to be prepared for. Second, you must exercise reasonable care in procuring medical treatment for the injured or ill student. A life-threatening emergency is always time dependent. You must, therefore, remain calm enough to exercise your first aid duties.

Having said all this, it should come as no surprise that all teachers and administrative staff should have up-to-date certifications in Community First Aid and Safety as well as in CPR—whether you teach physical education or not. You must also have some basic medical equipment and supplies readily available. Ensure that first aid kits are strategically located throughout the school and gymnasium. You can carry a fanny pack outside. Figure 17.1 lists the basic items that should be in each first aid kit.

Finally, you should not be acting in a vacuum. Your school should develop, practice, and implement an Emergency Action Plan so that staff members and teachers are well aware of their responsibilities in an emergency. Figure 17.2 lists the components of such a plan. Ensure that your school has one.

Special Circumstances

Sometimes a link in a school's emergency plan breaks down, and you may find yourself acting alone for a longer-than-planned

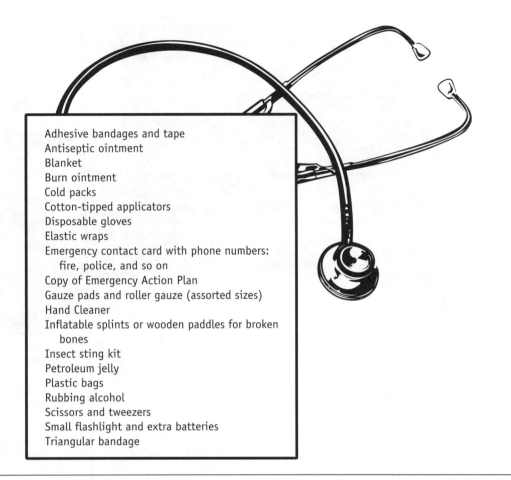

Adhesive bandages and tape
Antiseptic ointment
Blanket
Burn ointment
Cold packs
Cotton-tipped applicators
Disposable gloves
Elastic wraps
Emergency contact card with phone numbers:
    fire, police, and so on
Copy of Emergency Action Plan
Gauze pads and roller gauze (assorted sizes)
Hand Cleaner
Inflatable splints or wooden paddles for broken
    bones
Insect sting kit
Petroleum jelly
Plastic bags
Rubbing alcohol
Scissors and tweezers
Small flashlight and extra batteries
Triangular bandage

Figure 17.1 Medical kit contents.

time. At other times, the special needs of a student with a disability will make an emergency especially trying to deal with. Let's look closely at each of these special circumstances.

No Help Available   If you must deal with an injury without help from another adult (which, if your planning has been adequate, should really not happen), *stop the physical activity and have the students wait quietly*. If you allow the students to continue without your active supervision, another student may be injured and you could be liable for failure to supervise (Baley and Matthews 1989).

Students With Disabilities   The key to effective first aid is to stabilize the victim—that's why it's only *first* aid. This is especially important with students with disabilities. For example, a scratch to most people is a serious wound to a hemophiliac. Tailor your aid efforts to your knowledge of the student's disability.

Basic Legal Concepts

A lawsuit arises when someone (the plaintiff) alleges that someone else (the defendant[s]) breached one or more duties owed to the plaintiff. For the purposes of this book, there are three relevant kinds of duties: contractual (promises), statutory (laws and regulations), and tort (duty of care). If a lawsuit goes to trial—and less than 5 percent of all lawsuits ever do—the "trier of fact" (judge or jury) will find the defendant either liable or not liable to the plaintiff for the breach. A finding of liability may result in compensatory damages, punitive (sometimes called exemplary) damages, equitable relief (such as injunctions), or a combination.

Contractual Duties

You should seldom encounter contract problems in a physical education classroom. One

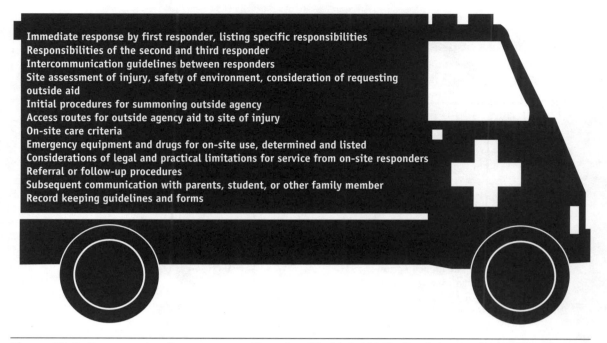

Immediate response by first responder, listing specific responsibilities
Responsibilities of the second and third responder
Intercommunication guidelines between responders
Site assessment of injury, safety of environment, consideration of requesting outside aid
Initial procedures for summoning outside agency
Access routes for outside agency aid to site of injury
On-site care criteria
Emergency equipment and drugs for on-site use, determined and listed
Considerations of legal and practical limitations for service from on-site responders
Referral or follow-up procedures
Subsequent communication with parents, student, or other family member
Record keeping guidelines and forms

Figure 17.2 Components of emergency action plan (Herbert 1995). *Special note: Part of the plan should always include a way to get another responsible adult on the scene pronto. That person need not be a teacher—a secretary to keep an eye on the other kids until treatment is complete or medical aid arrives is probably enough.*

example is painting over the Acme Athletic Equipment logo on equipment donated by Acme under the condition that it be used "as is." Detailed consideration is outside the scope of this book.

Statutory Duties

Some of your duties are established by the elected government, not the courts. These range from the length of the school day to who may be assigned bus duty. Two statutory duties will have an increasing impact on those teaching physical education: inclusion of students with disabilities and gender discrimination.

Disabilities and Inclusion

The Americans with Disabilities Act (ADA) essentially outlaws discrimination—difference in treatment—on the basis of a recognized disability. The ADA recognizes disabilities that significantly affect one or more "major life activities." Education is certainly a "major life activity"! The ADA does make an exception for safety purposes, but the

courts have been very skeptical of most efforts by employers to use safety as an excuse to discriminate *(Barber)*. Very few decisions in an education context have interpreted these seemingly contradictory provisions. This area of education law will undoubtedly develop substantially during your career.

The key to avoiding problems under the ADA (and similar state statutes, particularly those in California and New York) is treating individuals with disabilities as individuals, not as inconveniences. You should discuss any potential restrictions based on your safety concerns with the student, and his or her parents (if possible), *before* the activity unit begins. You should agree on appropriate safeguards for the student with disabilities and for those around him or her. This may include alternate activities, additional supervision or equipment (such as a helmet), or other provisions.

On occasion, prior planning will not enable you to satisfy safety requirements, the student, and his or her parents. This is the time to consult a physical educator with experience dealing with the same kind of disability, an administrator, and possibly the school's lawyer.

Gender Discrimination and Title IX

Title IX should not trouble you much, except if your program does not offer reasonable opportunities for physical activity to students of both genders, for which you could be sued. Title IX does *not* require complete equality of *result*, only reasonable equality of *opportunity*. It is far less relevant in noncompetitive environments such as the physical education classroom. However, if you separate genders for activities, ensure that the activities are reasonably equivalent *(Roberts)*. For example, it would be improper to allow the boys to play flag football while requiring the girls to do basic ballroom dance because those activities are not reasonably equivalent (not to mention stereotyped). We recommend that you do not separate genders.

Tort Duties ("Duty of Care")

Most of the current ill will toward lawyers results from seemingly outrageous awards in tort suits, usually involving a personal injury, such as the infamous "I was scalded by hot coffee" case in 1996. With very few exceptions, a lawsuit filed after someone gets hurt is a tort case.

What's a Tort?

A tort is a civil (which may include criminal) wrong that caused harm to a person or property for which the courts will provide a remedy (usually damages; Statsky 1994). Put another way, a tort is a breach of the duty of care owed to the plaintiff (injured party) by the defendant(s) that caused the harm to the plaintiff or her property. Generally, this includes every civil lawsuit that does not involve a contract (White 1985; see also Rabin 1990).

A tort always includes the following elements (compare Statsky 1994):

- The defendant owed a duty of care to the plaintiff.
- The defendant breached that duty of care.
- The breach was the proximate (legal) and foreseeable cause of the plaintiff's injury.
- The nature of the injury allows the court to fashion a remedy (usually damages).

What's a Duty of Care?

A tort can only result from a breach of the relevant duty of care. There are four levels of the duty of care that you might encounter while teaching physical education:

- Intent: Everyone has a duty to avoid an intentional act or omission (failure to act) that would harm another with intent to cause that harm. For example, you have a duty to avoid slugging another person in

To think I always thought a tort was a very rich Viennese cake!

the stomach (a "battery"). It is hoped that you'll never have to deal with this. You may have a privilege to use force to prevent students from intentionally harming one another; check state/local law concerning your rights to use physical force against a student.

• Knowledge: Everyone also has a duty to avoid an omission (or sometimes act) that he knows would harm another. For example, if three students in a row trip over a loose floorboard in the gym while you're watching, you commit a knowing omission by failing to stop the fourth student from running over the same floorboard. Even if you don't *intend* to harm anyone, a reasonable adult knows that this kind of activity leads to people getting hurt.

• Recklessness (related to "gross negligence"): Everyone has a duty to avoid reckless acts or omissions that could harm another. For example, throwing baseball bats across the room into the closet is a reckless act because it substantially increases the risk of harm to others without regard for their safety.

• Negligence: An individual with a specific duty of care must act as a reasonably prudent person to avoid acts or omissions that harm another. For example, as an instructor you have a duty to provide proper instruction and supervision to students involved in physical activity.

The vast majority of all tort lawsuits involve allegations of negligence (Rabin 1990; White 1985). Negligence is different from the other three duties of care in a very significant way: the other three duties of care apply to everyone, but negligence arises from specific relationships. The significant relationship for the purposes of this book is *instructor-student*. Your students have been placed in your care, with the expectation that you will enhance their physical, mental, emotional, and social development while keeping them safe.

As a teacher, your duty of care for children is higher than that of, say, a baby-sitter because you have professional credentials. This leads to two questions:

1. "But I wasn't trained as a physical education teacher. Why should I be held to a higher standard in an area for which I haven't been trained?" This is a case-by-case determination. Because so many injuries (and the resulting lawsuits) involve failures of supervision, your training in supervising children does justify a somewhat higher standard—perhaps not as high as the certified physical education teacher, but higher than an untrained adult. Different states have different laws, and these continue to evolve.

2. "What about children with disabilities?" If you *are* certified to work with such children, that certification will certainly result in a higher standard of care. If you are *not* so certified, your status as a teaching professional may nonetheless result, again, in a somewhat higher standard—not as high as a certified special education instructor, but higher than an untrained adult. This question is largely untested; courts take awhile to react to changes such as the inclusion movement.

What's a Breach?

A breach, very simply, is a failure to satisfy the relevant duty of care. This works in a hierarchical fashion—if the relevant duty of care is knowledge for a particular situation, negligent acts or omissions are not a breach of the duty of care.

One additional twist is the breach *per se*, also known as *res ipsa loquitur* ("the thing speaks for itself"). When something causes an injury (we'll talk about cause in a moment) without fault of the injured person, the thing is under exclusive control of the defendant, and the injury is one that would not occur in the course of normal events absent a breach of the defendant's duty of care, the defendant will be held liable for that breach without any other evidence to help her case unless she has an exceptionally good explanation (*Lux Art Van Service; Hillen*)

What's Proximate Cause?

You can understand proximate cause by asking two questions:

1. Absent the alleged breach of duty (act or omission), would the injury have occurred with the same severity? For example, assume that Reynaldo trips on the playground, falls on his face, and knocks out a tooth while engaging in a race in your class. If Reynaldo was tripped on purpose by another student, your actions are probably not a proximate cause of his injuries. If, however, Reynaldo tripped over loose blacktop in a "three-legged race" when his partner is a foot taller than he is, the severity or fact of his injury was probably worsened by your actions.

2. Was the alleged breach the last negligent (reckless, knowing, intentional) act that preceded and contributed to the injury? Consider the *Ward* case (the adjacent playing fields case discussed earlier). In that case, there were certainly other actions after the breach (failure to ensure that the fields had adequate clearance for normal use), but the last action that constituted a breach of a duty that contributed to the injury was the mis-siting of the fields.

Different states have different laws about particular situations that may (or may not) be proximate causes. Some states, for example, are very strict about intervening causes (other factors that contributed, whether breaches of duty or not); some states are very strict about the victim's own role in the injury. This area of the law is also constantly evolving. You should obtain specific advice only from a lawyer who practices in your state.

What Does "Fashion a Remedy" Mean?

Money damages are just one kind of remedy that courts can impose. They are by far the most common in suits involving injuries. The injury, however, must justify the damages. The injury must be identifiable, to the victim or her property. One example is medical expenses; another is the cost of replacing a broken pair of glasses. Your lawyer can help you understand just what damages are at issue in a given case. The standards are rapidly changing, through both the "tort reform" movement and changes in the legal conception of a teacher's duties.

So, Am I Liable?

No textbook can possibly tell you in advance if you are liable under a specific set of facts. Even if you are "objectively" liable, the other side may not pursue the issue properly (resulting in a win for you). Your attorney is in the best position to advise you. Take legal advice from nonlawyers with a teaspoon or so of salt—sometimes it's good, but you don't want to be the one who finds out otherwise!

Summary

Remember, the best way to avoid getting sued is to prevent a problem before it can occur. Yet, despite your best efforts, something may go wrong. If this happens, refer to this chapter to help you understand the legal process. Keep in mind, however, that we cannot presume to tell you everything you need to know. You must advocate for yourself should an incident lead to a threat of a lawsuit; find a lawyer who can help you wade through the pertinent legal issues in relation to your state's laws.

A word of encouragement: Don't let these cautions prevent you from teaching physical education. A developmentally appropriate curriculum taught in a sensitive, caring environment such as that presented in this book will prevent most, if not all, problems and give your students a good start on a lifetime of healthful and safe physical activity.

References—Cases

This is just a sampling of cases. They point out areas for concern. They may *not* represent the state of the law now or in your area.

Barber v. Nabors Drilling U.S.A., Inc., No. 97-20102 (5th Cir. Nov. 12, 1997).

Cohen v. Brown University, 991 F.2d 888 (1st Cir. 1993), *cert. denied.*

Doe v. Koger, 480 F.Supp. 225 (N.D. Ind. 1979).

Greider v. Shawnee Mission Unified School District, 710 F.Supp. 296 (D. Kan. 1989).

Hillen v. Hooker Constr. Co., 484 S.W.2d 113 (Tex. Civ. App. 1972).

Lux Art Van Service, Inc. v. Pollard, 344 F.2d 883 (9th Cir. 1965).

Roberts v. Colorado State Board of Education, 998 F.2d 824 (10th Cir. 1993).

S-1 v. Turlington, 635 F.2d 342 (5th Cir. 1981).

School Board of the County of Prince William v. Malone ("Malone"), 762 F.2d 1210 (4th Cir. 1985).

Sheppard v. Midway R-1 School District, 904 S.W.2d 257 (Mo. Ct. App. 1995).

Skinner v. Vacaulle Unified School District, 43 Cal. Rptr.2d 384 (Ct. App. 1995).

Ward v. Community Unit School District 220, 614 N.E.2d 102 (Ill. Ct. App. 1993).

Zalkin v. American Learning Systems, Inc., 639 So.2d 1020 (Fla. Ct. App. 1994).

Chapter 18

Equipment, Space, and Facilities

Rebecca, 11

Mrs. Chen's second grade class carried the instructions and additional equipment for their physical education learning stations down to the gym. Each group set up in an area designated by a sign Mrs. Chen had posted on the wall during lunchtime. At each station, students in groups of four or five practiced a ballhandling skill. Each student had her own ball, and the students worked continuously until Mrs. Chen momentarily stopped the music tape to signal them to move to the next station. Although the stations were all similar in goal, student time on-task remained high because Mrs. Chen had carefully selected balls that facilitated success because of their size and weight and had thoughtfully varied the type of ball and other equipment to create and maintain interest.

Can you imagine having 10, or even 2, students sharing a pencil to practice basic math skills? Would you want even one student with her own pencil to have to throw and retrieve the pencil after each math problem? Would you place 15 students in a science cooperative learning group because you only had one microscope per 15 students and expect them to get much out of the lesson—let alone behave themselves while waiting? Maximizing time on-task in physical education is enough of a challenge without expecting students to share too little or improperly sized or weighted equipment. Indeed, effective class management, maximal time on-task, and therefore maximal learning all depend on ample and developmentally appropriate equipment in any subject area, and, of course, this includes physical education.

COPEC (1992) offers guidelines regarding physical education equipment in the sidebar below.

Acquiring Equipment

Keeping an open mind, you can tap into many traditional and unique ways to obtain the equipment you need. It is important to get help in this endeavor, however. Work to generate enthusiasm among administrators, fellow teachers, parents, and students to buy, make, borrow, or otherwise find the equipment that a developmentally appropriate physical education program requires.

COMPONENT— *Equipment*

Appropriate Practice	Inappropriate Practice
Enough equipment is available so that each child benefits from maximum participation. For example, every child in a class (has) a ball.	An insufficient amount of equipment is available for the number of children in a class (e.g., one ball for every four children).
Equipment is matched to the size, confidence and skill level of the children so that they are motivated to actively participate in physical education classes.	Regulation or "adult size" equipment is used, which may inhibit skill development and injure or intimidate the children.
	Reprinted from COPEC/NASPE 1992.

Buying Equipment

Although few, if any, schools are endowed with generous equipment funds for any subject area, you can and should make an effort to buy suitable physical education equipment. Work with your administrators, colleagues, and parent-teacher association to choose and obtain small and large items (see "Selecting Equipment" later in this chapter). If you purchase a few items each year, over time the equipment available in your school will slowly increase—definitely a move in the right direction. Your school's PTA or PTSO may be willing to hold a fund-raiser to add to the physical education program. Or you may be able to institute a small annual fee for purchasing new equipment, just as many schools do for textbooks or other school supplies.

Schiemer (1996) suggests that teachers seeking funding for physical education equipment prepare an "Equipping Students for Success" educational packet informing administrators and parents of the need for adequate and appropriate equipment. Perhaps you can convince your administrator that forming a committee (including teachers and parents) to create this packet would be helpful. Such a committee should explain why you need the equipment, espousing the value of teaching developmentally appropri-ate physical education, advocating COPEC's appropriate practices regarding equipment, and outlining a long-term plan for obtaining equipment. This is also a good time to ask parents to donate supplies to make certain equipment (see tables 18.1 through 18.3) or to let you know of a good source for borrowed or donated equipment. This shows you're working to create an economical yet ample and developmentally appropriate supply of equipment.

Making Equipment

You can make safe and useful equipment from common household items and school supplies. Tables 18.1, 18.2, and 18.3 list ideas for games, gymnastics, and dance equipment and suggested uses to help you create appropriate and safe physical education equipment. Send a list of needed supplies as part of your "Equipping Students for Success" packet (see previous section).

Borrowing Equipment

The same people and businesses you collaborate with to help you teach physical education (see chapter 16) may also be willing to loan or donate equipment. Just be sure each item is safe for young children. For example,

Table 18.1   Making and Improvising Games Equipment

Item	Suggested uses
Garbage bags	Toss and catch a lightweight ball while holding bag corners with a partner; fill with inflated balloons or wadded-up newspaper and tie shut to play toss and catch; strike a hanging, filled bag
Tires	Targets (also good for gymnastics stunts or obstacle courses)
Sock and yarn balls	Soft to catch and don't rebound and have to be chased
Milk jugs	Fill with sand and use as cones; duct tape on cylinder of sturdy cardboard to use as tee
Aluminum pie pans	Paddles
Wire hangers covered with panty hose	Paddles
Cut-up bath mat	Define nonskid personal spots for working on skills; make islands to travel to and from while practicing locomotor skills
Carpet squares	Define personal spots for working on skills; make islands to travel to and from while practicing locomotor skills (also good for padding in some gymnastics activities)

Table 18.2   Alternative Equipment for Gymnastics

Piece	Specifications	Suggested uses
Boxes—from school cafeteria, empty cases of school paper	12"-18" high 18"-24" long and wide Filled with newspaper Ends sealed with masking tape	Jump onto, off of, over Balance on completely or partially Roll onto, off of Cartwheel over
Benches	12"-18" high 10'-12' long 10"-12" wide Base wide, stable to prevent tipping	Travel along Balance on Jump onto, off of, over Roll along, onto, off of Cartwheel over, off of
Tables	2'-3' high 24"-36" wide 6'-8' long Stable, sturdy nonfolding	Balance on completely or partially Roll off of Jump off of
Chairs	Stable, sturdy Four legs, back	Balance on Vault over Jump onto, off of
Plastic crates—milk, soft drink	6"-18" high 18"-24" long and wide Place upside down on mats or nonskid surfaces	Balance on Jump over, onto, off of Roll onto, off of Cartwheel over

Reprinted, by permission, from Werner, P., 1994, *Teaching Children Gymnastics*, (Champaign, IL: Human Kinetics), 15.

castoff secondary equipment may be too large (balls, gymnastics pieces) to be safe or useful for elementary children (Schiemer 1996). Keep in mind, too, that worn or damaged equipment is best discarded for safety reasons.

Developing a Music Collection

Music makes the world go round—and physical education, too! Dance is the obvious place to use music, but you can also incorporate it to teach the movement concepts of light and strong, slow and fast, and free and bound flow (Pica 1991) that will help students learn body control to succeed in other physical education areas, such as games and gymnastics. In addition, music stimulates language and listening skills, and some have said it motivates children to communicate better (Pica 1991). Furthermore, music can give you movement activity ideas as well as add enjoyment and excitement to your physical education program. Used either as the focus of a lesson or as a pleasant background, music is essential to a well-rounded physical education pro-

gram. In this section, we'll discuss how to select music for your collection. Then have your school or city librarian and school music teacher help you find what you want.

Important Features

Purcell (1994) makes the following suggestions for choosing appropriate music for dance experiences. Include music that

- has a definite even beat;
- varies tempo;
- varies rhythms;
- varies the moods it evokes (e.g., peaceful, powerful);

Table 18.3   Making and Improvising Dance Equipment

Item	Suggested uses
Feathers, streamers, scarves	Imitate or enhance movement
Hats	Props

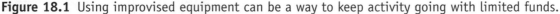

Figure 18.1 Using improvised equipment can be a way to keep activity going with limited funds.

- evokes feelings and images (e.g., "Sounds like giants dancing"); and
- represents a specific time period or culture.

Choose music that is familiar to and popular with students as well as new types to expand their music knowledge and movement ideas.

Creating Variety

Variety is essential because each type of music will evoke a different movement response. Pica (1991) offers the following guidelines to help you create variety in your collection and therefore your lessons. Choose music of varying

- styles—rock and roll, opera, jazz, country and western, folk, disco, swing, blues, and so on;

- periods—Renaissance (e.g., "Greensleeves" played at Christmastime as "What Child Is This?"), baroque (e.g., Bach), classical (e.g., Mozart, Haydn), romantic (e.g., Prokofiev's *Peter and the Wolf*), and so on;
- ethnicities—German and Austrian waltzes, Irish jigs, Polish and Mexican polkas, African chant and drum music, Jamaican reggae, Latin, and so on; and
- textures—orchestral, percussion, violin sonatas, solo piano, voice alone (*a cappella*), acoustic guitar, and so on.

Choosing Equipment

Collect percussion instruments because these make an easy resource to accompany dance (Purcell 1994). They have at least two advantages: they're easy to carry, and you can evoke a different mood, depending on your choice of instrument. For example, the strong beat of a drum, the quick vibratory sound of maracas, and the light, lingering sound of a triangle will each elicit a different movement response (Purcell 1994). Find percussion instruments at music stores (including second-hand), yard sales, toy stores, and school catalogs. If necessary, borrow them from your school's music teacher (this resource can also teach you a few simple rhythms to help you get started; Purcell 1994).

Although you can make do with a cassette or CD player for playing prerecorded music, better equipment can make for a better learning experience. You can improve upon the equipment you have, for example, by adding a speaker or two to help carry the sound farther. If you have the opportunity to purchase a new sound system for use in physical education, Purcell (1994) recommends the following wish list:

- Variable speed recorder
- Cassette player with dual speakers that will project the sound into space
- A dual tape player with a remote control (which gives you flexibility)
- Compact disk player with dual speakers that will project into the space and remote control
- Portable microphone and speaker, allowing you to speak over the music as you move anywhere in the space
- Blank cassette tapes with 15 minutes a side for an easily accessible library of music
- Cleaning kits for players
- Storage cases for CDs or audiotapes

Maximize Use of the Equipment You Do Have

Whether equipment is scarce or abundant, store-bought or homemade, take care of it! In this section, we'll look at ways to store equipment and use it fully.

Storing Equipment

It doesn't matter if you have three dozen Koosh balls if you can't find them! The fol-lowing lists ways to store physical education equipment so that whatever you need will be at your fingertips when you need it.

- When storing equipment you own,
  —use see-through bins, baskets, and bags whenever possible, particularly for small equipment;
  —hang bags of equipment on walls or clotheslines in the classroom;
  —use a large trash can on wheels for storing and transporting larger items such as larger balls, rackets, and carpet squares;
  —store it by unit at home if item is highly specialized and storage space is limited, then bring it to school when teaching that unit; and
  —neatly and clearly label each storage container you use.
- When storing school-owned equipment, enlist the help of other teachers to
  —obtain bags, bins, and baskets for sorted items;
  —neatly and clearly label each storage container and its place on the shelf or wall;
  —develop and use a sign-out–sign-in procedure for taking equipment out of the storage room (especially when using during times that aren't your "gym time"); and
  —inspect items on a regular basis and repair or replace items as needed.

Learning Stations

Remember the cooperative science lesson I mentioned with groups of 15 students and one microscope? Of course, it would be expensive to purchase enough microscopes to keep group sizes adequately small, and it may be impossible to borrow enough. Thus, most teachers would handle such an equipment problem by circulating smaller groups through a microscope station to minimize time waiting for turns. This could be done while other groups worked on another part of the science lesson or through setting up a learning center for this phase of science studies. Learning stations and centers pro-

Figure 18.2 Keeping equipment organized will save time and keep equipment in better shape between uses.

vide the same boost for limited equipment in physical education as well. In fact, it may be an advantage to only have five of each kind of small ball because practicing with a variety of balls can help make an otherwise monotonous activity more exciting, such as throwing at a target (you can vary the targets, too). See also chapter 19.

Selecting Equipment

Once you've begun fund-raising and have organized the equipment you do have, it's important to follow some guidelines for selecting new equipment and deciding whether to keep existing equipment. You should share your wish list through the "Equipping Students for Success" packet based on the guidelines we'll discuss here.

Because of the myriad of equipment available these days, you will have to sift through catalogs and already obtained equipment and determine which items are developmentally appropriate for your students. Here, we'll look at some guidelines for selecting the most common types of equipment (Schiemer 1996):

• Jump ropes—cloth cord, beaded, or speed ropes (vinyl ropes with plastic handles that are very light and fast), which are best? Beginners fare better with cloth ropes because these hurt less if they come in contact with the user. The slower travel and the sound made against the floor of both cloth and beaded ropes also help beginners. Colorful ropes provide helpful visual cues. Vinyl, or speed, ropes are very motivating for intermediate jumpers. A rope is the right size if a student can stand on it and have the ends reach his or her armpits. If jumping with a partner, the rope should reach to the shoulders of the taller student. Color code ropes for easy size recognition.

Table 18.4 Recommended Minimum Equipment List for Elementary Physical Education

Equipment name	Size	Number
Beanbags	Hand size	One per student
Yarnballs	3"	One per student
Dense/foam balls (variety of sizes & colors)	6"-8"	10-20
Footballs	Foam and/or rubber—Jr. size	10-20
Playground balls	3"	One per student
Playground balls	6"-8"	10-20
Basketballs Grades K-3	Mini	One per student
Basketballs Grades 4-6	Jr. size	One per student
Volleyballs	Soft bladder type	10-20
Whiffle balls	Softball size	One per student
Beach balls		One per student
Softballs	Soft rubber	10-20
Tennis balls	Used	One per student
Soccer balls	Size #4 and #5	10 each
Paddles—short handle	10"-12"	One per student
Paddles—long handle	14"-16"	One per student
Hula hoops		45-60
Jump ropes	Individual	45-60
Jump ropes—long	16'-20'	10
Wands	3"	One per student
Thick plastic bats (K-3)		10
Plastic hockey sticks	Short and long	One per student
Gymnastic mats	5' by 10'	10-20
Boxes	12" × 12" × 12" and 14" × 16" × 18"	10-20
Benches	10' long × 12" high × 6" wide	8-10
Cones	12" high	One per student
Poly spots/carpet squares/markers	6" × 6" to 12" × 12"	One per student
Skin fold calipers		1-3
Sit-n-reach box		1-2
Tape measure		One
Stop watches		1-3
Pull-up bars	6', 7', 8'	3-5
Portable tape recorder/tapes		
Record player/records		One
Air pump		One
Chalk board		
Bulletin boards		1-3

From the South Carolina Physical Education Guidelines, Vol. I (K-6). SC State Dept. of Educ. 1989. Columbia, SC.

• Balls—This is another area for which the choices seem limitless. Balls made from soft materials that cannot fly or bounce far are the best for young children, beginners, and students with special needs because they travel slower and are less scary to catch. Generally, these are very appropriate for indoor or other restricted movement areas. Moreover, providing a choice of balls for the same activity enables you to teach by invitation (see chapter 5), allowing students to adjust the difficulty of the activity to fit their ability levels.

• Mitts and paddles—no-miss mitts, Velcro-covered paddle mitts, and the like help young children, beginners, and special needs students succeed in catching. Their larger surface areas help students learn to track an object moving toward them better. Generally, these are very appropriate for indoor or other restricted movement areas.

• Bats, rackets, and hockey sticks—going bat-y making choices? Wide body, flat-sided, foam—each feature offers advantages to the beginner. You can even find plastic rackets with tacky grips that fit and stay better in small hands. A larger surface area with which to strike increases success rates, building up student confidence. A shorter handle can help, too. These choices are also safer than what you may have grown up with. Look for items that combine several features to enhance success and safety.

• Basketball and soccer equipment—Basketballs and soccer balls come in a wide variety of sizes and weights. Nerf and foam balls can be especially useful. Choose sizes and weights that enhance student success and safety.

No matter the type of equipment, ensure that your choices foster success and increase safety.

Using Space and Facilities Efficiently

Few schools are blessed with facilities exclusively used for physical education. Most have to use the gym or multipurpose room as a cafeteria, auditorium, or even music or art room. But these demands on a facility's time are no excuse not to teach physical education. In this section, we'll examine how to find, create, and use various spaces to the advantage of your physical education program.

The Gymnasium or Multipurpose Room

It's important that your school administration set up a schedule for using your gymna-
sium or multipurpose room. This way, you will be able to count on set times for your physical education lessons. In addition, an outside area should be clearly marked as an instructional area only. Scheduling for this outside area should not overlap with recess times.

Outdoor Spaces

Many activities are easier, more practical, and safer to conduct outside in wide-open spaces. Indeed, a grassy playing field and certain playground equipment can be a real asset to your physical education program—if the weather cooperates.

Grass can slow down the path and response of equipment, especially balls, providing more control when, for example, dribbling with the feet (Pica 1995). Make sure grassy areas are flat and free of "potholes," broken glass, and other trash.

Playgrounds aren't only for recess! Monkey bars and other similar playground equipment are great ways to develop upper body strength—in and out of physical education class. Benches, if the ground around them is properly padded, provide makeshift but sturdy gymnastics equipment. Even the edge of a sandbox may be wide enough for primary students to practice balancing. Many playground items offer chances for students to practice going over and under and soft, safe landings when jumping off (Pica 1995; see also chapter 19). If using playground equipment for formal physical education instruction, however, choose a time when other classes are not out for recess and explain to your students that this is physical education—not recess. Then insist on businesslike behavior. If space is available, consider setting up a permanent health-related fitness circuit outside.

The Classroom

Perhaps you'd like to spend more time on physical education than your gym schedule allows. Or maybe you don't have a gym at all, and it's too cold, wet, or hot to hold class outside. Here are some effective ways to use your classroom as a physical education facility. Use and adapt them to maximize physical activity time and learning.

✓ Introduce activities and concepts in the classroom so that when you arrive on the playing field or in the gym, students already know what they'll be working on and can get right down to business. Reinforce concepts back in the classroom as well.

✓ If doing a physical activity in the classroom, teach your students the proper protocol for moving and replacing furniture quickly, quietly, and safely, offering a reward consistent with your discipline program for doing so appropriately.

✓ Choose activities in which you can ensure that students do not collide with one another, furniture, or walls.

✓ Use equipment-free activities whenever possible, such as working on a health-related fitness component (see chapter 8).

✓ Emphasize the cognitive aspects of physical education.

✓ If you use equipment, make sure it is very soft and cannot travel far. For example, a yarn ball (big pompon) will not rebound off or hurt anything, but a Nerf ball might.

✓ Be especially cautious regarding electrical wiring and lighting.

✓ Set up a physical education learning station in the back of the room. Train students to work at the station quietly, staying in the designated space. Introduce the station, then have small groups, partners, or individuals visit the station throughout the school day (however, don't use this as a punishment or reward; remember, all students need physical activity and motor skills practice).

✓ Expand to the hallway if safe and permissible (stand in the classroom doorway to keep an eye on both areas).

Finally, although a gym or playing field may not be available, is there an empty classroom you could use? See whether you can borrow one temporarily or set one up for all teachers to use for physical education on an ongoing basis. Ensure, however, that if it is a temporary situation, no damage occurs to another teacher's equipment and supplies. If setting up an extra room permanently, design a usage schedule and equipment storage procedures to prevent misunderstandings.

> *A final word of caution*: Review the "Duty to Provide a Safe Environment" section in chapter 17 before using any nonstandard area for physical education.

Using Technology in Physical Education

Technology can enhance your physical education program. Look for CD-ROMs that teach about the human body and fitness. Obtain and use heart rate monitors from which students can download and print out results (see *Lessons From the Heart* by Beth Kirkpatrick and Burton H. Birnbaum, Champaign, IL: Human Kinetics, 1997).

Summary

Adequate equipment and facilities are essential to an effective physical education program, but this is not to say everything must be state-of-the-art. Use the ideas in this chapter to find creative and effective solutions to your needs. Remember, a student cannot learn if he is waiting for a turn. Thus, you must find ways to keep time on-task at a maximum with purchased, improvised, borrowed, and donated equipment. Ensure, however, that everything you use is developmentally appropriate and in good working order and therefore safe. And store equipment properly to prevent loss or damage. Finally, don't forget technology when it comes to physical education.

Chapter 19

Managing Playgrounds and Free Play

Aaron, 6

I have fond memories of my childhood playground experiences: hanging upside-down on the monkey bars like the circus man on the flying trapeze; walking down railroad tracks balancing like the person on the high wire; playing in the sand, creating imaginary worlds; sliding endlessly down the slide; playing in a tree house with special friends . . . you get the picture.

Boy, were those days fun, but they were so much more. As I look back, I appreciate how directly and indirectly each of these experiences contributed to my development—to both my large and small muscle development, my sense of spatial awareness, my social interaction skills, and my ability to imagine, create, and solve problems. I wouldn't trade these memories and their legacy for anything.

—Peter Werner

Many physical educators cringe at the idea of "free play" because they associate it with recess. In turn, recess is associated with idleness, lack of activity, socializing while standing around, wasting time, and so on. In contrast, however, many early childhood educators view free play as a vital time for imaginative and creative play, role-playing, socialization, and the like. We believe that free play is just as important to developing motor skills, movement concepts, and health-related fitness as formal physical education. But you have to know how to organize it to obtain the maximum benefits. In this chapter, we'll look at ways to supplement your physical education program and your students' cumulative physical activity time by using the playground to its fullest. Specifically, we'll define two main types of play, tell you how to maximize physical activity time, and explain how to enhance several areas of learning on the playground. Finally, we'll explain how to supervise, design, and equip playgrounds so that all children can participate safely and fully.

Child Development and Play

As you probably know, play is the work of a child. Indeed, play is essential to well-rounded and maximal child development. In this section, we'll examine the different types of play environments and how to maximize play involving physical activity.

Play Environments

There are two main types of play environments: structured and free. They differ mainly in how much teacher direction is involved. Both are necessary to create a developmentally appropriate approach to physical activity. Neither should substitute for the other. Let's look closely at each.

Structured Play Environments

A structured play environment is teacher-directed and seeks to attain specific learning goals. The teacher consciously plans the activities that will help the children reach physical education program goals. We call this *instructional physical education* because it is more than merely a series of games and activities. All children work toward learning the same skills, whether affective, psychomotor, or cognitive. To do so, they may play a game or learn a manipulative skill, dance, or gymnastics stunt. Although a teacher may use less direct methods in a structured play environment, such as posing a movement challenge, and should plan for individual skill levels and rates of development, he or she still controls the content of the play to a large extent.

Free-Play Environments

Most children would agree that "real" play is less structured than the structured instructional physical education environment. Play environments in which children may choose their activities as on a playground during recess at the elementary level or in learning

COMPONENT—
Physical Education and Recess

Appropriate Practice	Inappropriate Practice
Physical education classes are planned and organized to provide children with opportunities to acquire the physical, emotional, cognitive, and social benefits of physical education.	"Free-play," or recess, is used as a substitute for daily, organized physical education lessons. Free-play, in this case, is characterized by a lack of goals, organization, planning and instruction. Reprinted from COPEC/NASPE 1992.

centers in the preschool classroom evoke free play. Free play involves three concepts (Neuman 1971):

1. Internal reality—the player suspends reality from the real world to establish rules, procedures, and content of the play, according to his wishes.

2. Intrinsic motivation—the player is self-motivated, not by adults or other outside forces.

3. Locus of control—the objective of the play is self-determined.

In short, free play is child-directed rather than teacher-directed.

Maximizing Physical Activity

Your role during both structured and free play is to ensure that children spend an optimal time on physical activity. Remember,

Figure 19.1 Physical activity enhances learning the rest of the day.

physical activity enhances learning the rest of the school day (see chapter 1). Children should have at least 20 to 30 minutes per day of total quality physical activity time of moderate to vigorous intensity (heart rate elevated to 140 to 160 beats per minutes for sustained periods), plus rest and recovery time. Keep in mind, too, that children who are sedentary only have a 2 percent chance of becoming physically active adults (Werner, Timms, and Almond 1996). Finally, many children in urban areas do not have a safe place to play actively outside of school, so the school must make every attempt to fill this gap.

You can supplement your students' physical activity time in three main ways: by encouraging active play during recess, taking health-related fitness breaks during the school day, and extending the physical education time students have. Let's turn, now, to each method of increasing total physical activity time.

Encouraging Active Play During Free Play

Don't assume that simply because children have the opportunity to run and jump, throw and kick they will. Some may sit off to the side watching others or talking to friends. And these choices have their place in the world of a child. But there are many ways you can encourage active play during free play. Indeed, free play can actually be organized, planned, and instructive—given a well-designed playground and appropriate teacher intervention. Teacher intervention might include, for example, making sure that children have a choice of equipment to use, helping a child find an appropriate partner to play with, helping a child find an activity he likes to do, suggesting a few activities the child might be successful at, and so on.

Talking about the benefits of physical activity is one of the most obvious—but often ignored—ways to encourage it. Explain that even five minutes of physical activity that makes them "huff and puff" is beneficial, if such bouts of activity add up to at least 30 minutes a day. Encourage students to monitor themselves to see whether they accumulate at least 30 minutes total of huff-

and-puff activity per day. They can record this time in their physical education journals. You could also use a form such as that shown in figure 19.2 to track a student's activity. Another way to teach young children to check if they're playing hard enough is to have them ask themselves if they are getting warm from the activity; older children can learn to check their heart rates to see if they stay at 140 to 160 beats per minute for a sustained time.

Play actively with your children. Let them see you enjoy physical activity. Remember, however, to keep an eye on those who are not participating but who are still under your care. Don't dominate the action; stay on the perimeter of the play area and simply model involvement for short times while still performing your supervisory role. If you see a child who is consistently sedentary during free-play times, encourage her to be more active by offering to play an active game of her choice. Or pair this child with a more active friend.

Teach children games they can and might choose to organize for themselves during free play, such as variations of tag that involve at least three taggers.

Finally, ensure a variety of play choices based on the large and small equipment available. Provide plenty of balls, cones, ropes, and hoops and encourage children to use their free-play time to explore this equip-

Being Active on the Playground

Name *Jessica*

Skill or activity	Time
Riding tricycle	_____
Playing on large equipment	_____
Running or playing tag	*7 min*
Jumping rope	*3 min*
Engaging in ball activities (e.g., bouncing, throwing)	_____
Playing a ball game (e.g., soccer, basketball)	_____
Other (e.g., hula hoop)	*5 min*
Total	*15 min*

Figure 19.2 Playground activity checklist.

ment; suggest that perhaps they design a huff-and-puff game to teach others. Provide the equipment your students are currently using in physical education so, if they choose, they can explore it further. Large playground structures should encourage imaginative and active play—but more on this later in the chapter.

Taking Health-Related Fitness Breaks

We mentioned in chapter 1 that movement facilitates the development of increased blood vessels that carry learning-essential water, oxygen, and nutrients to the brain (Hannaford 1995). So when your students' brains are sluggish, hold a fitness break to stimulate blood flow to the brain. Just 5 to 10 minutes of stretching (flexibility component), selected calisthenics (muscular strength and endurance), line dancing (cardiorespiratory endurance), or walking or jogging on a fitness course (cardiorespiratory endurance) can get students back on the academic track without taking too much time out of the school day. You can conduct most fitness break activities right in the classroom. Students will return to academic work refreshed and ready to concentrate—until the next fitness break.

Extending Physical Education Time

This book is all about extending your students' instructional physical education time, whether you are supplementing the work of a specialist or "flying solo." Use the ideas in this book to create a physical education program that systematically develops psychomotor skills in a progressive, developmentally appropriate manner. If you do have a specialist to rely on, ask for suggestions as to how you can reinforce the physical education unit your students are currently working on (see chapter 16).

Your role in guiding this structured form of play is multifaceted. For children to get the most out of the instructional physical education you teach, you must set objectives, plan, teach, assess, keep children on-task, give feedback, and manage the overall learning environment. Use this book as a resource to assist you in developing and leading a quality physical education program.

Learning on the Playground

As we have mentioned, learning on the playground can take the form of structured and free play. Simply interacting positively with children can greatly enhance learning on the playground. Refrain, however, from talking constantly. The well-timed, appropriate question or remark is more valuable. The key is to facilitate rather than dominate or over-direct children's play environments (Frost 1992). Allow children privacy in their play when they show a desire for it. In this section, we'll point out the ways you can encourage child development on the playground through equipment and pedagogical choices and suggest sample open-ended questions for each area of learning.

Motor Development

To develop both small and large motor skills, children need not only instruction and maturation but also ample opportunities to practice. Practice can and should occur in both structured and free-play situations. A well-designed playground can provide excellent motor skill practice opportunities. Creative playgrounds nurture motor development by facilitating natural development through free play (Frost 1992). You can encourage this type of play by asking open-ended questions that encourage physical exploration of the play environment. Sample questions might include the following:

- When you climb to the top of the tower, what might you imagine you are doing?
- How many ways can you go over and under the playground equipment?
- While hanging from the monkey bars (or horizontal ladder) in an upright or upside-down position, what types of body shapes can you make? Wide or narrow, straight or bent, curved?

Remember, however, don't talk too much; you might be interfering with the natural learning processes taking place.

Figure 19.3 Creative playgrounds nurture motor development.

Body and Space Awareness

As we defined these terms in chapter 7, body awareness is an individual's ability to understand what the body does while moving, and space awareness is the ability to be aware of both general and self-space to dodge an object and otherwise move in a game, sport, or dance. Space awareness also involves understanding directions, levels, pathways, and extensions. (See tables 7.2 and 7.3 for lists of specific movement concepts.) A well-designed playground encourages both body and space awareness.

Children develop greater body awareness as they swing, sway, twist, stretch, and turn on larger play structures. Smaller equipment can encourage pushing, pulling, and so on. Creative play may call for any of these actions and more.

When studying shapes in physical education, reinforce the concepts by helping children discover ways to apply the concepts on the playground. Questions might include the following:

- Can you make an asymmetrical shape balancing on the climbing tower?
- Can you hang in an inverted symmetrical shape from the horizontal ladder?
- Can you make a matching shape with a partner? A contrasting shape? Try to hold your shapes for three seconds.

Children develop greater space awareness as they learn to deal with the available space in, under, around, and through play structures and the playground itself. A well-designed playground should encourage space awareness exploration.

You can further challenge students to extend their practice of space concepts by asking questions such as the following:

- Can you move at a low or middle level across the balance beam?

- Can you move in a curved or zigzag pathway to get across the playground safely?
- Can you change directions while moving about the playground—up, down; forward, backward; left, right?

Remember, don't talk too much! Let children explore. You may need to require older students to try these challenges, then record their activities in their physical education journals. Use your judgment as to their interests, needs, and maturity level, however.

Cognitive Skills

Children learn problem-solving skills through play, perhaps better than through formal training (Frost 1992). Pretend play especially promotes problem solving (Frost 1992). Divergent (no-right-answer) play leads to divergent problem-solving abilities. Closely related to this idea is the creativity children develop and display when they play in creative play environments. Through these opportunities, children develop a problem-solving attitude that can transfer to other situations (Dansky and Silverman 1973, 1975; Pepler and Ross 1981).

You can encourage problem solving and creative behavior during physically active play by providing a stimulating play environment and facilitating, rather than directing, play. Ask questions such as the following:

- Imagine taking a walk in space while out on the playground. What obstacles must you overcome? How can you solve these problems?
- Imagine the playground is in a rain forest. What animals and birds do you see? Can you move like them?
- Pretend the climbing tower is in *Jurassic Park*. What type of dinosaurs do you see? Can you develop an escape plan if they attack?

For a more formal approach, have students take their physical education journals out, and on a signal, stop playing and record their activities, then resume playing.

Social Skills

Young children's play is the central process of social and emotional development (Eriksen 1956; Freud 1971). Why? Play enhances language development as children

Helping Tammy

Tammy was a kindergartner who appeared to have poor self-confidence; her physical skill level was low, and her social skills were lacking. In addition, she was often not dressed well and often had a runny nose or drooled. Her peers seldom chose her as a playmate.

Tammy was afraid of the large play structures on the playground and would not, for example, go down a slide. Finally, after much coaxing, her teacher climbed the stairs with her. At the top of the slide, the teacher sat down and put Tammy in front of her. That first trip, the teacher eased down the slide inch by inch, Tammy

screaming all the way. The next time, she went a little faster. Then, she left Tammy alone to decide for herself about slides. About a week later, Tammy came running up to her teacher and said, "Come, I want to show you!" She led her teacher to the slide, proceeded to climb the stairs alone and go down the slide without prompting—this time with a smile and a laugh. This success led to increased self-confidence and greater willingness to try other new skills. Over time, Tammy was accepted by others as a friend and playmate.

attach language to their play, which, in turn, enhances both cognitive and social skill development (Frost 1992). Although many have tried to define what a socially competent individual is, for our purposes, we define such a person as "one who functions effectively in society, deals with issues appropriate to one's age or developmental group, and gains peer acceptance through quality social interaction" (Frost 1992). Play and playgrounds can facilitate an individual's developing social competence.

Many identifiable social skills can be developed on the playground. These include beginning a new friendship, practicing interpersonal strategies, solving problems, seeing others' perspectives, making moral judgments, and practicing communication skills (Eisenberg and Harris 1984). These can all develop through physically active play.

Again, the adult role in this process is best as a facilitator and mediator—not a director. Encourage children to talk to others, interact, share, cooperate, lead and follow, and role-play. Ensure that the design and layout of playground pieces do not isolate children. For example, wide slides encourage children to slide together. Tire swings can hold two or three children at a time. Sand areas and climbing towers also encourage children to play together and interact, enhancing their social development.

Self-Esteem and Emotional Growth

Developing competent physical and social skills naturally leads to increased self-esteem and emotional growth. As children learn to trust you and their environment, they are enabled to adopt an "I can do it!" attitude, which helps them take appropriate physical and social risks, leading to further emotional and physical development and enhanced self-esteem.

The playground atmosphere of having fun and "legally" letting off steam helps children see that being physically active is a healthy and satisfying way of life, which contributes not only to physical but also to emotional well-being.

Playground Logistics

Many components work together to provide a safe and educational play environment. In this section, we'll discuss supervising free play, types of playgrounds, specific types of equipment and their safety specifications, and common hazards and appropriate safety measures. Finally, we'll outline the features of a playground accessible to all children, including those with disabilities.

Supervising Free Play

Some estimates reveal that as many as 40 percent of injuries children sustain on America's playgrounds involve lack of supervision as a contributing factor (King 1991; Thompson, Hudson, and Mack 1997). Foresight, control, and the "Q" factors (quantity and quality) are the most important elements of adequate playground supervision. In this section, we'll discuss each, summarizing the work of Thompson, Hudson, and Mack (1997). Figure 19.4 provides a checklist to help you spot potential playground supervision and maintenance problems.

Foresight

To be a good playground supervisor, you have to be able to foresee potential problems. Keep an eye on the following factors:

- The size of the equipment should match the size and age of the children playing on it. Separate play areas for younger and older children should be maintained.
- The play areas should be free of broken glass, other sharp objects, and other trash.
- The loose materials (pea gravel, sand, or the like) under play structures should be at the proper depth in places where children are likely to fall.
- Children should not be wearing improper clothing; that is, pieces of clothing that could become entangled in equipment, such as strings on jackets

Suggested Public Playground Leader's Checklist

- Prepare written guidelines for playground operation, defining goals and procedures.
- Insist on first aid and accident training for playground leaders.
- Provide for constant supervision by establishing a written schedule.
- Instruct children and playground supervisors on how to use equipment. (Playground equipment safety should be taught in the classroom.)
- Conduct daily cleaning and check for broken glass and other litter.
- Do not permit children to use wet or damaged equipment.
- Do not permit too many children on the same piece of equipment at the same time; suggest that children take turns, or direct their attention toward other equipment or activities.
- Constantly observe play patterns to note possible hazards and suggest appropriate equipment or usage changes.
- Make periodic checkups, and request that worn or damaged pieces of equipment be replaced.
- Prepare written accident reports with special attention to surface conditions, type and extent of injury, age and sex of child, how the accident occurred, and the weather conditions.
- Make sure surfaces around playground equipment have at least 12 inches of wood chips, mulch, sand, or pea gravel, or are mats made of safety-tested rubber or rubber-like material.
- Check that protective surfacing extends at least six feet in all directions from play equipment. For swings, be sure surfacing extends, in back and front, twice the height of the suspending bar.
- Make sure play structures more than 30 inches high are spaced at least nine feet apart.
- Check for dangerous hardware, like open "S" hooks or protruding bolt ends.
- Make sure spaces that could trap children, such as openings in guardrails or between ladder rungs, measure less than 3.5 inches or more than 9 inches.
- Check for sharp points or edges in equipment.
- Look out for tripping hazards, like exposed concrete footings, tree stumps, and rocks.
- Make sure elevated surfaces, like platforms and ramps, have guardrails to prevent falls.
- Check playgrounds regularly to see that equipment and surfacing are in good condition.
- Carefully supervise children on playgrounds to make sure they're safe.

Figure 19.4 Suggested public playground leader's checklist.
Reprinted from U.S. Consumer Product Safety Commission (public domain).

(you may need to alert parents to this hazard to educate them to look for products without strings).

As a playground supervisor, it is your job to see that any hazards you spot are minimized or eliminated before allowing children to play in the area (see also chapter 17).

Control

As a playground supervisor, you must HELP children stay safe:

How children play

Eye control

Limiting the number of children on each piece of equipment

Proximity control

Developed by Mick Mack, project coordinator for the National Program for Playground Safety, each component HELPs prevent injuries.

How Children Play Most children like to jump, run, and climb. Young children tend to explore, use manipulative materials, and play by themselves. Older children tend to challenge their developing physical abilities and play with peers; they also like to use equipment in ways it was not intended to be used.

Falls from the top of tall equipment are more likely with older children. Thus, you must provide extra supervision near tall equipment.

Eye Control   Maintain eye contact with individual children to remind them you are alert to their tendency to break rules when no one is looking.

Limiting the Number of Children on Each Piece of Equipment   Prevent dangerous overcrowding by following the manufacturer's recommendations and using common sense. Simply put, if it seems likely that children will bump into one another, the piece of equipment is too crowded.

Proximity Control   Stay near children as you move continuously about the area. Your presence will often settle a potentially dangerous situation—before an injury occurs.

The "Q" Factors

Quantity of supervisors per number of children is an important safety factor. The size of the area, the ages and numbers of children, the number of pieces of equipment, and the *quality* of the supervision will all make a difference.

The quality of supervisors can and should be raised through training in how to inspect the playground, watch children, prevent misuse of equipment, and handle an emergency, should anyone be injured.

Types of Playgrounds

The three main types of playgrounds found at schools are developmental, fitness, and adventure. None is better than the other. Each school should seek to create the playground that suits its population's needs.

- Developmental playground—This type of playground encourages the development of basic readiness skills in locomotion, balance, and so on. It provides places to climb, balance, swing, slide, and move over, in, out, and through.
- Fitness playground—This type of playground is designed with primary exercise stations such as a fitness trail with health-related fitness stations.
- Adventure playground—This type of playground focuses primarily on encouraging cognitive and social play through interaction and opportunities to rearrange the environment.

Equipment and Safety Specifications

In general, equipment should be nontheme so as not to limit imagination. For example, the theme of a firefighter's pole is somewhat limiting, but a tire tree could be a tree house, crow's nest on a ship, or many other creative possibilities. Equipment should be arranged so that there is a natural flow from one area to another and so that children are encouraged to interact with one another. Movable parts help engage children with disabilities (Frost 1992) but discourage children without disabilities from participating in physical activity. Each school has to decide how to best address this conflict to meet the needs of all its students (see also the section titled "Accessibility" later in the chapter). Overall, there should be a variety of equipment that fosters a variety of motor skills. Figure 19.5 shows a "playground matrix," which lists the various psychomotor, cognitive, and affective skills that each of several types of equipment enhances.

Swings

Swings should be to the side or in a corner of the playground, out of the way of foot traffic. Clearance between regular swings should be at least 24 inches, and 30 inches should be between supports and swings. Tire swings require even more room. Swings should be made of flexible, soft materials or be padded to protect little bodies from impact injuries.

Slides

Slides should be wide enough for two children. Their incline should not exceed 30 degrees to prevent injuries from excessive momentum. In addition, slides (especially metal ones) should face north or be in shade whenever possible to prevent their overheating and burning children. Even so, use discretion based on your climate, "closing" slides if

Playground Matrix

	Swing—time	Slide—wide	Balance beam	Tire tree	Climbing apparatus	Firefighter's pole	Seesaw	Merry-go-round	Swinging bridge	Overhead ladder	Rings and hoops	Cargo net	Water	Sand
Physical														
Moving with/against gravity	•	•			•	•	•		•		•			
Inner ear stimulation	•	•					•	•						
Climbing		•		•	•	•					•	•		
Sliding		•				•								
Hanging	•			•	•	•					•	•		
Swinging	•										•			
Upper torso development				•	•	•					•	•		
Locomotor skill			•	•	•				•	•		•		
Balancing—vertigo	•		•		•				•	•		•		
Hiding					•									
Crawling			•	•	•							•		
Cognitive														
Problem solving			•	•	•	•			•		•	•	•	•
Space awareness			•		•			•	•		•	•		
Manipulation													•	•
Choosing/interpretation				•	•						•	•	•	•
Social														
Interacting	•	•		•	•		•	•					•	•
Role-playing		•		•	•	•			•		•		•	•
Cooperation	•				•			•	•		•	•	•	•
General														
Flexible					•						•	•	•	•
Linkages			•		•	•			•					
No movable parts		•	•	•	•	•					•	•	•	•
Nontheme	•	•	•	•	•		•	•	•	•	•	•	•	•

Figure 19.5 Playground matrix.
Reprinted, with permission, from *Dimensions of Early Childhood*, Southern Early Childhood Association, 7107 W. 12th St., Suite 102, Little Rock, AR 72204, 800-305-7322.

burns are possible. Table 19.1 lists other specifications for safe slides.

Climbing Equipment

A variety of interesting climbing equipment is available today. Keep in mind that children love hiding spaces, but these should be large enough for adults to gain access if necessary. In addition, follow these guidelines to ensure safety:

- Examine spacing of support pieces and climbing bars to ensure that they match the climbing and reaching capabilities of the children who use them.

Table 19.1   Safety Specifications for Slides

Feature	Specifications
Height over four feet	Sides at least 2.5" high for foot and hand guides
	Barriers at least 38" high with a platform at least 10" wide
Exit surface	At least 16" long, absorbent in nature
Exit height	9" to 15"
Steps and rungs	Evenly spaced, 7" to 11" between them, depending on the leg and arm reaches of the children
	At least 15" wide
	Within 2 degrees of horizontal
	Stairways should have an angle of 35 degrees
	Steps, 50-75 degrees
	Rungs, 75-90 degrees
	Continuous handrails
Average incline	30 degrees

Data compiled from CPSC 1981 and Frost 1992.

- Bars children must grip for support should be about 1 5/8 inches in diameter.
- If it's easy to climb, make sure it's also easy to descend.
- Bright or contrasting colors as well as slip-resistant materials on steps or rungs help children see and feel if they have adequate footing and handholds.

Seesaws

Using a seesaw (teeter-totter) is fairly complex because it requires two children to cooperate and combine their actions. Therefore, experts do not recommend these for preschool-age children unless they have a spring-centering device to prevent one end slamming to the ground should one child choose to dismount (CPSC 1981). Placing absorbent material such as a half-buried tire under the seats will prevent limbs from getting crushed and soften the impact with the ground (see figure 19.6).

Merry-Go-Rounds

Rotating parts of merry-go-rounds should be circular. Prevent falls with handrails attached to the base; however, these should not protrude beyond the edge of the base. Spaces in the rotating part of the base should be no larger than three-tenths of an inch in diameter.

Hazards and Safety Measures

Not surprisingly, a playground contains many potential hazards. In this section, we'll go over the most common ones. However, we urge you to also obtain and study a copy of the *Handbook for Public Playground Safety* (1994) from the U.S. Consumer Product Safety Commission (CPSC; see appendix). In addition, figure 19.7 shows a sample playground maintenance checklist. Make sure that your school has such a checklist, tailored to your facilities' particular special features and uses.

In general, the CPSC recommends the following:

- Label equipment intended for a specific age group as such.
- Playground equipment should be made of durable materials, be structurally

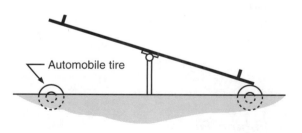

Figure 19.6 Typical fulcrum with see-saws.
Adapted from U.S. Consumer Product Safety Commission (public domain).

Maintenance Checklist

Date detected	Date repaired	
		Hard surface under and around equipment in fall zones
		Resilient surface material pitted or scattered
		Insufficient space between equipment
		Equipment not sized for age of children
		Entrapment areas
		Excessive or unprotected heights
		Shearing and crushing mechanisms
		Cracking, bending, warping, rusting, breaking, or missing components
		Pinching actions, open S hooks, deformed rings, links, etc.
		Loose or uncapped bolts, nuts, etc.
		Worn bearings or axles
		Worn swing hangers (swivels) or chains
		Metal slides in direct path of sun
		Slide beds loose, metal edges accessible to fingers
		Heavy swing seats or seats with protruding elements
		Exposed or damaged concrete footings
		Equipment improperly anchored
		Sharp edges and points
		Exposed or projecting elements, caps missing
		Railings of insufficient height
		Railings invite climbing (horizontal instead of vertical)
		Exposed metal in tires or swing seats
		Suspended elements (e.g., ropes, cables) in movement areas
		Deteriorated (splintered, cracked, rotting) wood
		Broken or missing railings, steps, swing seats, rungs, deck components, etc.
		Slippery footing areas on decks, steps, walkways
		Trash (broken glass, foreign objects, etc.) in area
		Vandalism (fire damage, broken or missing parts)
		Obstacles (rocks, roots, trash, badly placed equipment) in movement area
		Poor drainage (standing water)
		Accessible electrical apparatus (air conditioners, switch boxes), climbable poles, guy wires, ladders accessing electrical lines
		Fence not installed or in need of repair, gates not securable (younger children), extra protection for pools
		Signs illegible and in poor repair
		Moving parts not lubricated
		Toxic materials
		Foreign material or equipment parts in fall zone

Figure 19.7 Maintenance checklist.
Reproduced, by permission, from Frost, J.L., 1992, *Play and Playscapes*, (Albany, NY: Delmar Publishers).

Figure 19.8 Children's play methods change as they mature.

sound, and be constructed according to manufacturer's instructions.

• Check that equipment is stable.

• Ensure that equipment is assembled with connecting and covering devices (rings, bolts, and so on) that won't open.

In addition, a safe playground has separate areas for different age groups. Preschool, primary, and intermediate children have very different physical, emotional, and social needs.

Preschool children are egocentric. They need plenty of opportunities to play alone, parallel to other children. They need the smallest equipment, such as play centers with trucks, pails, blocks, small shovels, rakes, and the like and other chances to adventure play (sandbox, water play, and the like).

Primary grade children are more likely to engage in cooperative play because they tend to be more social in play. They need somewhat larger play equipment than preschoolers need.

Intermediate grade children need the largest equipment to provide the challenges they seek in play. They also need more wide open area to run and play in than younger children do.

Thus, the size and type of equipment provided for each age group should meet the developmental needs of the children. Keep areas intended for different age groups separate to prevent injuries caused by improperly sized equipment and larger children colliding with smaller children. Placing play areas near the school exits closest to each age group's classrooms is helpful.

Surfaces

Surfaces under and around climbing and moving equipment should be soft and absorbent. Experts recommend pea gravel, shredded tires, wood chips, sand, or a manufactured material that is smooth and firm enough for wheelchairs but resilient enough to cushion falls, such as AstroTurf. Critical heights range from 4 to 12 feet, depending on the piece of equipment.

The playground should also offer hard surfaces on which children can play a variety of games with balls, hoops, and ropes or ride tricycles. This is also the place to stimulate play and academic learning by painting on game grids. In addition to the traditional game of 4-Square, see figure 19.9 to learn about other creative grid games.

Zones

Fall zones are the areas onto which a child may fall from a piece of equipment. These should, of course, be cushioned appropriately as described in the previous section. No-encroachment zones are the areas just outside the fall zones that children may use when moving from one play piece to another. These areas should be free of obstacles.

Entrapment

Look for angles or openings in which a child's head or other body part could become trapped. Cover angles of less than 55 degrees where two pieces of wood or metal join.

Clothing Entanglement

Ensure that parts of a moving apparatus that a child can access and parts next to sliding surfaces such as ladders and handrails are designed to prevent a child's clothing from becoming entangled. Encourage parents to look for clothing without drawstrings, which is becoming more available for safety reasons.

Ouch! Places

"Ouch! places" include anything sharp (points, corners, and edges), anything that could pinch or crush, and anything that protrudes or projects. Ensure that your school's equipment has such features as countersunk bolts and (or) protective caps and self-locking nuts to protect children's skin and clothing from scratches, cuts, and punctures. Accessible pinch, crush, or scissorlike areas should be eliminated or covered; inspect gliders, seesaws, and merry-go-rounds closely.

Accessibility

Children with disabilities need quality places to play, too. In this section, we'll outline ways a playground and its equipment can be designed or adapted to meet the needs of children with disabilities so they can play alongside their nondisabled peers.

The adventure playground serves children with disabilities well. As discussed earlier, this type of playground includes sand and water play (raised tables in this case); structures that encourage exploration, gross motor, and fantasy play; carpentry; and gardening and digging (Frost 1992). An abundance of loose parts stimulates creative play.

To make these features accessible, however, even a child in a wheelchair must be

Regular Hopscotch   Snail Hopscotch   4-Square

Figure 19.9 Playground designs.
Reprinted from *Homemade Play Equipment for Children* (1990) with permission from the National Association for Sport and Physical Education (NASPE), 1900 Association Drive, Reston, VA 20191-1599.

able to reach the equipment. Imagine trying to push or propel a wheelchair through sand or wood chips! Thus, a firm enough surface must be used to create wide pathways interconnecting play areas and equipment. Ramps must connect the paths to elevated equipment. Table 19.2 lists other important features of an accessible playground. Finally, a play-ground used by children with disabilities requires extra attention to safety issues, including supervisors trained in the special emotional, psychomotor, and cognitive needs of these children.

Table 19.2　Additional Safety Guidelines

Feature	Specifications
Ramp width	4′ with a 4″ curb
Ramp angle	Maximum slope 8.33% or 1″ every 12″
Switchback or turning platform	5′ × 4′ minimum
Basketball hoop	7″ diameter minimum
Ramped bridge	10° maximum slope
Elevated sand table	24″ reach, 32″ maximum height

From *Play for All Guidelines: Planning, Design, and Management of Outdoor Play Settings for All Children*, Moore, Gottsman, Iacofana, 1987, Berkeley, CA: MIG Communications. © MIG Communications, Berkeley, CA.

Summary

Both free and structured play are vital to developing a healthy, well-rounded child. In structured play, your role is to design and control the learning experience to a great degree. In free play, your role is to provide a stimulating play environment and facilitate active play without interfering with the natural processes taking place.

Remember, it's important for students to accumulate a minimum of 30 minutes of huff-and-puff activity each day, and your focusing on this need will help students learn to do so as well. Use the information, tips, and guidelines in this chapter to supplement your students' physical activity time as well as to ensure that the quality of your students' playground experiences is optimal.

Chris, 6

Teddy, 6

Epilogue

We hope you have enjoyed learning about the latest in physical education and that you feel ready to employ the suggestions and techniques you've studied in this book. We encourage you to find what works for you and adapt this information as you see fit while adhering to the COPEC guidelines for developmentally appropriate physical education. We wish you all the best as you strive to create a well-rounded school and physical education curriculum that integrates physical activity in systematic and innovative ways.

Although we cannot answer you personally, we'd love to hear how things are going for you as you continue to apply what you've learned in this book. How did this book help you? What could we do better in a future edition? We invite you to share your stories with us so that together we can help other classroom teachers and their students grow and thrive in physical education. You can write us at

Human Kinetics
P.O. Box 5076
Champaign, IL 61825-5076

We would also like to recommend the following books and other resources to help you further as you teach physical education and integrate movement across the curriculum.

Recommended Reading

Multicultural Games: 75 Games From 43 Cultures by Lorraine Barbarash (Human Kinetics, 1997).

Teaching Children Games: Becoming a Master Teacher by David Belka. (Human Kinetics, 1994).

Rhythmic Activities and Dance by John P. Bennett and Pamela C. Riemer (Human Kinetics, 1995). Includes detailed descriptions of specific dances.

Teaching Children Movement Concepts and Skills: Becoming a Master Teacher by Craig Buschner (Human Kinetics, 1994)

Interdisciplinary Teaching Through Physical Education by Theresa Purcell Cone, Peter Werner, Stephen L. Cone, and Amelia Mays Woods (Human Kinetics, 1998).

Cooperative Learning in Physical Education by Steve Grineski (Human Kinetics, 1996).

Fitness for Children by Curt Hinson (Human Kinetics, 1995).

Positive Behavior Management Strategies for Physical Educators by Barry W. Lavay, Ron French, and Hester L. Henderson (Human Kinetics, 1997).

Physical Education Unit Plans by Bette J. Logsdon, L.M. Alleman, S.A. Straits, D.E. Belka, and D. Clark (Human Kinetics, 1997). Available for pre-K-K, Grades 1-2, Grades 3-4, and Grades 5-6.

Experiences in movement by Rae Pica, (Delmar, 1995).

Teaching Children Dance: Becoming a Master Teacher by Theresa M. Purcell (Human Kinetics, 1994).

Teaching Children Fitness: Becoming a Master Teacher by Thomas and Laraine Ratliffe (Human Kinetics, 1994).

Quality Daily Physical Education Lesson Plans for Classroom Teachers by Robin Reese (Kendall/Hunt, 1992).

Fitness Education for Children: A Team Approach by Stephen Virgilio (Human Kinetics, 1997).

Teaching Children Gymnastics: Becoming a Master Teacher by Peter Werner (Human Kinetics, 1994).

Journal Articles

"Culturally responsive teaching: Part I" by J.R. Chepyator-Thompson, feature editor, *Journal of Physical Education, Recreation and Dance* vol. 65 no. 9 (1994) pp. 31-32.

"Culturally responsive teaching: Part II" by Chepyator-Thompson in the same journal, vol. 66 no.1 (1995), pg. 41.

"Multicultural considerations in physical activity: An introduction" by Chepyator-Thompson, *Quest* vol. 47 no. 1 (1995), pp. 1-6.

"Curriculum and instruction in primary school physical education: A critique and a visionary perspective for reform in teacher education" by Chepyator-Thompson in C.A. Grant and M.L. Gomez (eds.) *Campus and Classroom: Making Schooling Multicultural*, (Merrill Palmer, 1996) pp. 389-90.

Record Series

Rhythmically moving, a nine-record series by Phyllis Weikart, available (CD, CS, and LP.) from Highscope, Educational Research Foundation, 600 N. River St., Ypsilanti, MI 48198. Telephone 800-407-7377.

Dillon, 5

Chris, 6

Macey, 5

Rachel, 5

References

Chapter 1

American Heart Association. 1992. AHA labels physical inactivity as fourth risk factor for coronary heart disease. A news release of the American Heart Association.

Council on Physical Education for Children (COPEC). 1992. *Developmentally appropriate physical education practices for children.* Reston, VA: National Association for Sport and Physical Education (NASPE).

Franck, M., G. Graham, H. Lawson, T. Loughrey, R. Ritson, M. Sanborn, and V. Seefeldt. 1991. *Physical education outcomes: A project of the National Association for Sport and Physical Education.* Reston, VA: NASPE.

Gallahue, D. 1996. *Developmental physical education for today's children.* Dubuque, IA: Brown and Benchmark.

Gilbert, A.G. 1977. *Teaching the three Rs through movement experiences.* Minneapolis: Burgess.

Graham, G. 1992. *Teaching children physical education: Becoming a master teacher.* Champaign, IL: Human Kinetics.

Hannaford, C. 1995. *Smart moves: Why learning is not all in your head.* Arlington, VA: Great Ocean Publishers.

Human Kinetics, 1998. *Active youth: Ideas for implementing CDC physical activity promotion guidelines.* Champaign, IL: Human Kinetics.

Logsdon, B., L.M. Alleman, S.A. Straits, D.E. Belka, and D. Clark. 1997. *Physical education unit plans for preschool-kindergarten: Learning experiences in games, gymnastics, and dance.* Champaign, IL: Human Kinetics.

Masser, L.S. 1990. Teaching for affective learning in elementary physical education. *Journal of Physical Education, Recreation and Dance* 67(2): 18-19.

Morford, L. 1997. Developmentally appropriate physical education. *Teaching Elementary Physical Education* (March): 3-5.

National Association for Sport and Physical Education (NASPE). 1992. Outcomes of quality physical education programs. Reston, VA: American Alliance for Health, Physical Education, Recreation and Dance (AAHPERD).

———. 1995. *Moving into the future: National physical education standards.* St. Louis: Mosby.

Pica, R. 1995. *Experiences in movement.* Albany, NY: Delmar.

U.S. Department of Health and Human Services (USDHHS). 1996. *Physical activity and health: A report of the Surgeon General executive summary.* Atlanta: USDHHS, CDC, National Center for Chronic Disease Prevention and Health Promotion.

———. 1997. Guidelines for school and community programs to promote lifelong physical activity among young people. *Morbidity and Mortality Weekly Report* 46(RR-6): 3.

Chapter 2

Armstrong, T. 1994. *Multiple intelligences in the classroom.* Alexandria, VA: Association for Supervision and Curriculum Development.

Corso, M. 1993. Is developmentally appropriate physical education the answer to children's school readiness? *Colorado Journal of Health, Physical Education, Recreation and Dance* 19(2): 6-7.

Fauth, B. 1990. Linking the visual arts with drama, movement, and dance for the young child. In *Moving and learning for the young child*, ed. W.J. Stinson, 159-87. Reston, VA: American Alliance for Health, Physical Education, Recreation and Dance (AAHPERD).

Gardner, H. 1983. *Frames of mind: The theory of multiple intelligences.* New York: Basic Books.

———. 1993. *Multiple intelligences: The theory in practice.* New York: Basic Books.

Hannaford, C. 1995. *Smart moves: Why learning is not all in your head.* Arlington, VA: Great Ocean Publishers.

IAHPERD. 1995. *Catch 22: Physical education public hearing kit.* IAHPERD.

Logsdon, B., L.M. Alleman, S.A. Straits, D.E. Belka, and D. Clark. 1997. *Physical education unit plans for preschool-kindergarten: Learning experiences in games, gymnastics, and dance.* Champaign, IL: Human Kinetics.

Pica, R. 1996. Moving and learning across the curriculum. *Early Childhood Connections* 2(2): 22-29.

Placek, J. 1996. Integration as a curriculum model. In *Student learning in physical education: Applying research to enhance instruction,* ed. S.J. Silverman and C.D. Ennis, 287-311. Champaign, IL: Human Kinetics.

Reiff, J.C. 1992. *Learning styles: What research says to the teacher series.* Washington, DC: National Education Association.

Ryan, K., and J.M. Cooper. 1992. *Those who can, teach.* 6th ed. Boston: Houghton Mifflin.

U.S. Department of Education. 1986. *First lesson.* Washington, DC: U.S. Department of Education.

Chapter 3

Carnes, L. 1997. Using models to direct curriculum: Incorporating benchmarks and standards. *Teaching Elementary Physical Education* 8(3): 45.

Clark, C., and S.W. Sanders. 1997. Visually reporting skill performance to parents. *Teaching Elementary Physical Education* 8(3): 6-7, 19.

Council on Physical Education for Children (COPEC). 1992. *Developmentally appropriate physical education practices for children.* Reston, VA: National Association for Sport and Physical Education (NASPE).

Freeland, K., and J.E. Moore. 1996. The six assumptions of assessment. *Teaching Elementary Physical Education* 7(2): 22-23, 26.

Graham, G. 1992. *Teaching children physical education: Becoming a master teacher.* Champaign, IL: Human Kinetics.

Hopple, C. 1995. *Teaching for outcomes in physical education: A guide for curriculum and assessment..* Champaign, IL: Human Kinetics.

Rink, J., and L. Hensley. 1996. Assessment in the school physical education program. In *Physical education sourcebook,* ed. B. Hennessy, 39-55. Champaign, IL: Human Kinetics.

Schiemer, S. 1996. A positive learning experience: Self-assessment sheets let students take an active role in learning. *Teaching Elementary Physical Education* 7(2): 4-6.

Strand, B., and R. Wilson. 1993. *Assessing sport skills.* Champaign, IL: Human Kinetics.

Wolf, D. 1994. *Physical education curriculum for Charleston, IL District #1 Schools, K-6.* Charleston, IL: District #1 Schools.

Chapter 4

Council on Physical Education for Children (COPEC). 1992. *Developmentally appropriate physical education practices for children.* Reston, VA: National Association for Sport and Physical Education (NASPE).

Faber, A., and E. Mazlish. 1995. *How to talk so kids can learn—At home and in school.* New York: Rowan Associates.

Graham, G. 1992. *Teaching children physical education: Becoming a master teacher.* Champaign, IL: Human Kinetics.

Grineski, S. 1996. Improving practices in elementary physical education: Obstacle courses and learning stations. *Teaching Elementary Physical Education* (September): 14-15.

Lambdin, D. 1989. Shuffling the deck: A flexible system of classroom organization. *Journal of Physical Education, Recreation and Dance* 60(3): 25-28.

Lavay, B., R. French, and H. Henderson. 1997. *Positive behavior management strategies for physical educators.* Champaign, IL: Human Kinetics.

Chapter 5

Council on Physical Education for Children (COPEC). 1992. *Developmentally appropriate physical education practices for children.* Reston, VA: National Association for Sport and Physical Education (NASPE).

Graham, G. 1992. *Teaching children physical education: Becoming a master teacher.* Champaign, IL: Human Kinetics.

Rink, J. 1996. Effective instruction in physical education. In *Student learning in physical education: Applying research to enhance instruction,* ed. S.J. Silverman and C.D. Ennis, 171-98. Champaign, IL: Human Kinetics.

Werner, P. 1995. Moving out of the comfort zone to address critical thinking. *Teaching Elementary Physical Education* 6(5): 6-7, 9.

Chapter 6

Buschner, C. 1994. *Teaching children movement concepts and skills: Becoming a master teacher.* Champaign, IL: Human Kinetics.

Carnes, L. 1997. Using models to direct curriculum: Incorporating benchmarks and standards. *Teaching Elementary Physical Education* (8)3: 4-5.

Gallahue, D. 1996. *Developmental physical education for children.* Madison, WI: Brown and Benchmark.

Graham, G. 1992. *Teaching children physical education: Becoming a master teacher.* Champaign, IL: Human Kinetics.

National Association for Sport and Physical Education. 1995. *Moving into the future: National standards for physical education.* Reston, VA: Mosby.

Rink, J. 1993. *Teaching physical education for learning.* St. Louis: Mosby.

Chapter 7

Buschner, C. 1994. *Teaching children movement concepts and skills: Becoming a master teacher.* Champaign, IL: Human Kinetics.

Council on Physical Education for Children (COPEC). 1992. *Developmentally appropriate physical education practices for children.* Reston, VA: National Association for Sport and Physical Education (NASPE).

Graham, G. 1992. *Teaching children physical education: Becoming a master teacher.* Champaign, IL: Human Kinetics.

Chapter 8

American College of Sports Medicine (ACSM). 1992. *ACSM fitness book.* Champaign, IL: Leisure Press.

Centers for Disease Control and Prevention. 1995. *Healthy eating and physical activity: Focus group research with contemplators and preparers.* Atlanta: Nutrition and Physical Activity Communications Team, National Center for Chronic Disease Prevention and Health Promotion, Centers for Disease Control and Prevention.

Council on Physical Education for Children (COPEC). 1992. *Developmentally appropriate physical education practices for children.* Reston, VA: National Association for Sport and Physical Education (NASPE).

Farquhar, J.W. 1987. *The American Way of Life Need Not Be Hazardous to Your Health.* New York: W.W. Norton & Co.

Fauth, B. 1990. Linking the visual arts with drama, movement, and dance for the young child. In *Moving and learning for the young child,* ed. W.J. Stinson, 159-87. Reston, VA: American Alliance for Health, Physical Education, Recreation and Dance (AAHPERD).

Graham, G. 1992. *Teaching children physical education: Becoming a master teacher.* Champaign, IL: Human Kinetics.

Hinson, C. 1995. *Fitness for children.* Champaign, IL: Human Kinetics.

International Life Sciences Institute (ILSI). 1997. *Improving children's health through physical activity: A new opportunity, A survey of parents and children about physical activity patterns.* Washington, DC: ILSI.

Ratliffe, T., and L. Ratliffe. 1994. *Teaching children fitness: Becoming a master teacher.* Champaign, IL: Human Kinetics.

Safrit, M. 1995. *Complete guide to youth fitness testing.* Champaign, IL: Human Kinetics.

U.S. Department of Health and Human Services, Public Health Service, Centers for Disease Control and Prevention, National Center for Chronic Disease Prevention and Health Promotion, Division of Nutrition and Physical Activity. *Promoting Physical Activity: A Guide for Community Action.* Champaign, IL: Human Kinetics, 1999.

U.S. Department of Health and Human Services. 1996. *Physical activity and health: A report to the U.S. Surgeon General.* Washington, DC: USDHHS, Public Health Service.

Chapter 9

Ashy, M. 1993. The games students play. *Teaching Elementary Physical Education* 4(5): 14-15.

Barbarash, L. 1997. *Multicultural games: 75 games from 43 cultures.* Champaign, IL: Human Kinetics. (also chapter 14)

Belka, D. 1994. *Teaching children games: Becoming a master teacher.* Champaign, IL: Human Kinetics.

Council on Physical Education for Children (COPEC). 1992. *Developmentally appropriate physical education practices for children.* Reston, VA: National Association for Sport and Physical Education (NASPE).

Graham, G., M. Parker, and S. Holt-Hale. 1993. *Children moving.* Mountainview, CA: Mayfield.

Griffin, L., S. Mitchell, and J. Oslin. 1997. *Teaching sports concepts and skills.* Champaign, IL: Human Kinetics

Hinson, C. 1992. Let's play kickball . . . Yes, kickball! *Teaching Elementary Physical Education* (3)4: 16.

Logsdon, B., L.M. Alleman, S.A. Straits, D.E. Belka, and D. Clark. 1997. *Physical education unit plans.* Champaign, IL: Human Kinetics.

Morris, D., and J. Stiehl. 1989. *Changing kids' games.* 2d ed. Champaign, IL: Human Kinetics.

Grineski, S. 1996. *Cooperative learning in physical education.* Champaign, IL: Human Kinetics. (also chapter 13)

Werner, P., and L. Almond. 1990. Models of games education. *Journal of Physical Education, Recreation and Dance* 61(4): 23-27.

Williams, N.F. 1992. The physical education hall of shame. *Journal of Physical Education, Recreation and Dance* (August): 57-60.

Zakrajsek, D. 1986. Premeditated murder: Let's bump off killerball. *Journal of Physical Education, Recreation and Dance* 57(10): 49-51.

Chapter 10

Council on Physical Education for Children (COPEC). 1992. *Developmentally appropriate physical education practices for children*. Reston, VA: National Association for Sport and Physical Education (NASPE).

Graham, G. 1992. *Teaching children physical education: Becoming a master teacher*. Champaign, IL: Human Kinetics.

Werner, P. 1994. *Teaching children gymnastics: Becoming a master teacher*. Champaign, IL: Human Kinetics.

Chapter 11

Council on Physical Education for Children (COPEC). 1992. *Developmentally appropriate physical education practices for children*. Reston, VA: National Association for Sport and Physical Education (NASPE).

Graham, G. 1992. *Teaching children physical education: Becoming a master teacher*. Champaign, IL: Human Kinetics.

Hopple, C. 1993. *Teaching for outcomes in elementary physical education: A guide for curriculum and assessment*. Champaign, IL: Human Kinetics.

Pica, R. 1993. Discovering dance: A nontraditional approach to a traditional subject. *Teaching Elementary Physical Education* 4(3): 6 and 9.

Purcell, T. 1994. *Teaching children dance: Becoming a master teacher*. Champaign, IL: Human Kinetics.

Weikart, P. 1989. *Rhythmically moving* record series. (CD, CS, and LP.) Available: High/Scope Press, 600 N. River St., Yipsilanti, MI 48198. Telephone: 313-485-2000.

Chapter 12

Bucek, L. 1992. Constructing a child centered dance curriculum. *Journal of Physical Education, Recreation and Dance* 63(9): 43-48.

College Board. 1996. The role of the arts in unifying the high school curriculum. *National Center for Cross-Disciplinary Teaching and Learning Newsletter* 2(2): 2.

Cone, T.P., P. Werner, S.L. Cone, and A.M. Woods. 1998. *Interdisciplinary teaching through physical education*. Champaign, IL: Human Kinetics.

Connor-Kuntz, F., and G. Dummer. 1996. Teaching across the curriculum: Language-enriched physical education for preschool children. *Adapted Physical Activity Quarterly* 13: 302-15.

Fraser, D. 1991. *Playdancing*. Pennington, NJ: Princeton Books.

Friedlander, J. 1992. Creating dances and dance instruction: An integrated arts approach. *Journal of Physical Education, Recreation and Dance* 63(9): 49-52.

Gallahue, D. 1993. *Developmental physical education for today's children*. Dubuque, IA: Brown & Benchmark.

Gilbert, A. 1992. A conceptual approach to studio dance, PreK-12. *Journal of Physical Education, Recreation and Dance* 63(9): 43-48.

Jacobs, H.H. 1989. *Interdisciplinary curriculum: Design and implementation*. Alexandria, VA: Association for Supervision and Curriculum Development.

Wasley, P. 1994. *Stirring the chalk dust: Tales of teachers changing classroom practice*. New York: Teachers College Press.

Wilcox, E. 1994. An interview with Susan M. Tarnowski. *Teaching Music* 2(2): 44-45.

Chapter 13

Aronson, E. 1978. *The jigsaw classroom*. Beverly Hills, CA: Sage.

Clifford, C., and R. Feezell. 1997. *Coaching for character*. Champaign, IL: Human Kinetics.

Council on Physical Education for Children (COPEC). 1992. *Developmentally appropriate physical education practices for children*. Reston, VA: National Association for Sport and Physical Education (NASPE).

Graham, G. 1992. *Teaching children physical education: Becoming a master teacher*. Champaign, IL: Human Kinetics.

Greenberg, P. 1992. How to institute some simple democratic practices pertaining to respect, rights, roots, and responsibilities in any classroom (without losing your leadership position). *Young Children* 47(5): 10-17.

Hellison, D. 1996. Teaching personal and social responsibility in physical education. In *Student learning in physical education: Applying research to enhance instruction*, ed. S. Silverman and C. Ennis, 269-86. Champaign, IL: Human Kinetics.

Johnson, D., and R. Johnson. 1975. *Learning together and alone*. Englewood Cliffs, NJ: Prentice Hall.

Johnson, D., and R. Johnson, E. Holubec, and P. Roy. 1984. *Circles of learning*. Alexandria, VA: Association for Supervision and Development.

Kagan, S. 1992. *Cooperative learning.* San Juan Capistrano, CA: Kagan Cooperative Learning.

Klein, J. 1990. Young children and learning. In *Moving and learning for the young child,* ed. W.J. Stinson, 23-30. Reston, Virginia: National Association for Sport & Physical Education.

Kohn, A. 1992. *No contest: The case against competition.* Boston: Houghton Mifflin.

Lipowitz, S. 1996. Social skills are the foundation. *Teaching Elementary Physical Education* 7(4): 22.

Masser, L.S. 1990. Teaching for affective learning in elementary physical education. *Journal of Physical Education, Recreation and Dance* 67(2): 18-19.

Mercier, R. 1993. Student-centered physical education—Strategies for teaching social skills. *Journal of Physical Education, Recreation and Dance* 64(5): 60-65.

Morris, G. 1980. *Elementary physical education: Toward inclusion.* Salt Lake City: Brighton.

Mosston, M., and S. Ashworth. 1990. *The spectrum of teaching styles: From command to discovery.* New York: Longman.

Orlick, T. 1978. *The cooperative sports and games book.* New York: Pantheon Books.

———. 1982. *The second cooperative sports and games book.* New York: Pantheon Books.

Orlick, T., J. McNally, and T. O'Hara. 1978. Cooperative games: Systematic analysis and cooperative impact. In *Psychological perspectives in youth sports,* ed. F.L. Smoll and R.E. Smith. Washington, DC: Hemisphere.

Pica, R. 1993a. Responsibility and young children—What does physical education have to do with it? *Journal of Physical Education, Recreation and Dance* 64(5): 72-75.

———. 1993b. *Upper elementary children moving & learning.* Champaign, IL: Human Kinetics.

Slavin, R. 1980. *Using student team learning.* Baltimore: The Center for Social Organization of Schools, Johns Hopkins University.

Stiehl, J. 1993. Becoming responsible—Theoretical and practical considerations. *Journal of Physical Education, Recreation and Dance* (May-June): 38-40, 57-59, 70-71.

Weinberg, R., and D. Gould. 1995. *Foundations of sport and exercise psychology.* Champaign, IL: Human Kinetics.

Williams, N.F. 1992. The physical education hall of shame. *Journal of Physical Education, Recreation and Dance* (August): 57-60.

———. 1994. The physical education hall of shame, part II. *Journal of Physical Education, Recreation and Dance* (February): 17-20.

Chapter 14

Banks, J.A. 1988. *Multiethnic education: Theory and practice.* Boston: Allyn & Bacon.

Cohen, G. 1993. *Women in Sport.* Newbury Park, CA: Sage Publications.

Cook Inlet Tribal Council and Johnson O'Malley Program. 1989, 1993, 1995. *Native youth olympics handbook,* Statewide.

Council on Physical Education for Children (COPEC). 1992. *Developmentally appropriate physical education practices for children.* Reston, VA: National Association for Sport and Physical Education (NASPE).

Craft, D. 1994. Strategies for teaching inclusively. *Teaching Elementary Physical Education* 5(5): 8-9.

Davis, R., and T. Davis. 1994. Inclusion and least restrictive environments. *Teaching Elementary Physical Education* 5(5): 1, 4-5.

Depauw, K. 1996. Students with disabilities in physical education. In *Student learning in physical education: Applying research to enhance instruction,* ed. S. Silverman and C. Ennis, 101-24. Champaign, IL: Human Kinetics.

Hall, M.A. 1996. *Feminism and sporting bodies.* Champaign, IL: Human Kinetics.

Hopple, C. 1994. Fairhill Elementary School: An integrated model. *Teaching Elementary Physical Education* 5(5): 14-15.

Hutchinson, G.E. 1995. Gender-fair teaching in physical education. *Journal of Physical Education, Recreation and Dance* 60(2): 23-24.

Lieberman, L.J. 1996. Adapting games, sports and recreation for children and adults who are deaf-blind. *Deaf-Blind Perspectives* 3: 5-8.

Lieberman, L.J., and J.F. Cowart. 1996. *Games for people with sensory impairments.* Champaign, IL: Human Kinetics.

Lowy, S. 1995. A multicultural perspective on planning. *Teaching Elementary Physical Education* 6(3): 14-15.

Mawdsley, R. 1977. Comparison of teacher behaviors in regular and adapted movement classes. PhD diss., Boston University School of Education.

Mohnsen, B. 1997. *Teaching middle school physical education.* Champaign, IL: Human Kinetics.

Nilges, L. 1996. Ingredients for a gender equitable physical education program. *Teaching Elementary Physical Education* 7(5): 28-30.

Sadker, M., and D. Sadker. 1995. *Failing at fairness: How our schools cheat girls*. New York: Simon & Schuster.

Schincariol, L. 1994. Including the physically awkward child. *Teaching Elementary Physical Education* 5(5): 10-11.

Sherrill, C. 1998. *Adapted physical activity, recreation, and sport: Cross disciplinary and lifespan.* 5th ed. Boston: McGraw-Hill.

Singer, A. 1994. Reflections on multiculturalism. *Phi Delta Kappan* 7(4): 284-288.

Slavin, R.E., and R.J. Stevens. 1991. Cooperative learning and mainstreaming. In *The regular education initiative: Alternative perspectives on concepts, issues, and models*, ed. J.W. Lloyd, N.N. Singh, and A.C. Repp, 177-92. Sycamore, IL: Sycamore Press.

Taylor, J., and E. Loovis. 1978. *Measuring effective teacher behavior in adapted physical education.* Paper presented at the Midwest District of the American Alliance for Health, Physical Education, and Recreation. Indianapolis. (ERIC Document Reproduction Service No. ED 156660.)

Tucci, B. 1994. Special needs in the gymnasium: They're all just kids. *Teaching Elementary Physical Education* 5(5): 17-18.

Ulrich, D. 1985. *Test of gross motor development.* Austin, TX: Pro-Ed Publishers.

Vandell, K., and L. Fishbein. 1989. Equitable treatment of girls and boys in the classroom. Washington, DC: American Association of University Women (AAUW).

Vogler, B., and M. Block. 1994. Innovative and adaptive curriculum models for full inclusion. *Teaching Elementary Physical Education* 5(5): 6-7.

Wall, A.E. 1982. Physically awkward children: A motor development perspective. In *Theory and research in learning disabilities*, ed. J.P. Das, R.F. Mulcahy, and A.E. Wall, 253-68. New York: Plenum Press.

Winnick, J.P., ed. 1995. *Adapted physical education and sport.* 2d ed. Champaign, IL: Human Kinetics.

Chapter 15

Block, M.E., L.J. Lieberman, and F. Conner-Kuntz. 1998. Authentic assessment in adapted physical education. *Journal of Physical Education, Recreation and Dance* 69(3): 48-56.

Block, M.E., B. Oberweiser, and M. Bain. 1995. Using classwide peer tutoring to facilitate inclusion of students with disabilities in regular physical education. *The Physical Educator* 52: 47-56.

Delquadri, J., C.R. Greenwood, D. Whorton, J.J. Carta, and R.V. Hall. 1986. Classwide peer tutoring. *Exceptional Children* 52: 535-42.

DePaepe, J.L. 1985. The influence of three least restrictive environments on the content, motor-ALT, and performance of moderately mentally retarded students. *Journal of Teaching Physical Education* 5: 34-41.

Greenwood, C.R., J.J. Carta, and D. Kamps. 1990. Teacher mediated versus peer mediated instruction: A review of educational advantages and disadvantages. In *Children helping children*, ed. H.C. Foot, M.J. Morgan, and R.H. Shute, 177-205. New York: Wiley.

Greenwood, C.R., J. Delquadri, and R.V. Hall. 1984. Opportunity to respond and student academic performance. In *Focus on behavior analysis in education*, ed. W.L. Heward, T.E. Heron, J. Trap-Porter, and D.S. Hill, 58-88. Columbus, OH: Merril.

Greenwood, C.R., B. Terry, C. Arreaga-Mayer, and R. Finney. 1992. The classwide peer tutoring program: Implementation factors moderating student achievement. *Journal of Applied Behavior Analysis* 25: 101-16.

Houston-Wilson, C., J.M. Dunn, H. Van der Mars, and J.A. McCubbin. 1997. The effect of untrained and trained peer tutors on the motor performance of students with developmental disabilities in integrated physical education classes. *Adapted Physical Activity Quarterly.* 14(4): 298-313.

Houston-Wilson, C., L.J. Lieberman, M. Horton, and S. Kasser. 1997. Peer-tutoring: An effective strategy for inclusion. *Journal of Physical Education, Recreation and Dance* 68(6): 39-44.

Lieberman, L.J., J.M. Dunn, H. Van der Mars, and J.A. McCubbin. 1996. The effect of trained hearing peer tutors on the physical activity levels of deaf students in inclusive elementary school physical education classes. PhD diss., Oregon State University.

Lieberman, L.J., J. Newcomer, J.A. McCubbin, and N. Dalrymple. 1997. The effects of cross aged peer tutors on the academic learning time in physical education of students with disabilities in inclusive elementary physical education. *Brazilian International Journal of Adapted Physical Education and Recreation* 4(1): 15-32.

Long, E., L. Irmer, L. Burkett, G. Glasenapp, and B. Odenkirk. 1980. PEOPEL. *Journal of Physical Education and Recreation* 51: 28-29.

Mosston, M., and S. Ashworth. 1990. *Teaching in physical education.* 4th ed. Columbus, OH: Merrill.

Sherrill, C. 1998. *Adapted physical activity, recreation, and sport: Crossdisciplinary and lifespan*. Boston: McGraw-Hill.

Webster, G.E. 1987. Influence of peer tutors upon academic learning time-physical education of mentally handicapped students. *Journal of Teaching in Physical Education* 7: 393-403.

Winnick, J.P., ed. 1995. *Adapted physical education and sport*. 2d ed. Champaign, IL: Human Kinetics.

Chapter 16

Council on Physical Education for Children (COPEC). 1992. *Developmentally appropriate physical education practices for children*. Reston, VA: National Association for Sport and Physical Education (NASPE).

Virgilio, S. 1997. *Fitness education for children: A team approach*. Champaign, IL: Human Kinetics.

Chapter 17

American Law Institute. 1965 (and supplements). *Restatement of the Law (Second) of Torts*. St. Paul, MN: American Law Institute.

Americans With Disabilities Act. 42 U.S.C. 12101 *et seq.* (1994), Pub.L. 101-336 (1990), 104 Stat. 328.

Baley, James A., and David L. Matthews. 1989. *Law and liability in athletics, physical education, and recreation*. Dubuque, IA: Brown.

Carpenter, L. 1995. *Legal concepts in sport: A primer*. Reston, VA: American Alliance for Health, Physical Education, Recreation and Dance.

Dougherty, N., D. Auxter, A. Goldberger, and G. Heinzmann. 1994. *Sport, physical activity, and the law*. Champaign, IL: Human Kinetics.

Herbert, D. 1995. Another heat stroke race victim. *The Sports, Parks, & Recreation Law Reporter* 9(2): 17 and 20.

Mawdley, Ralph D. 1993. Supervisory standard of care for students with disabilities. *Education Law Reporter* 80: 779-91.

Osborne, Allan G. 1997. Making the manifestation determination when disciplining a special education student. *Education Law Reporter* 119: 323-30.

Rabin, Robert L., ed. 1990. *Perspectives on tort law*. 3d ed. Boston: Little, Brown.

Statsky, William P. 1994. *Essentials of Torts*. Minneapolis: West.

Sutliff, M. 1996. Plan activities to avoid injuries. *Teaching Elementary Physical Education* 7(1): 10-11.

Title IX of the Education Amendments of 1972. 20 U.S.C. 1681 *et. seq.* (1994), Pub.L. 920318 (1972) *as amended*, 86 Stat. 373.

Van der Smissen, B. 1990. *Legal liability and risk management practices for public and private entities*. Cincinnati, OH: Anderson.

White, G. Edward. 1985. *Tort Law in America: An Intellectual History*. New York: Oxford University Press.

Chapter 18

Council on Physical Education for Children (COPEC). 1992. *Developmentally appropriate physical education practices for children*. Reston, VA: National Association for Sport and Physical Education (NASPE).

Pica, R. 1991. Face the music: Choosing it and using it. *Teaching Elementary Physical Education* 2(4): 15-17.

———. 1995. *Experiences in movement*. Albany, NY: Delmar.

Purcell, T. 1994. *Teaching children dance: Becoming a master teacher*. Champaign, IL: Human Kinetics.

Schiemer, S. 1996. Equip your students for success. *Teaching Elementary Physical Education* (October): 20-22, vol. 7, issue 5.

South Carolina State Department of Education. 1989. *South Carolina physical education guidelines*. Vol. I (K-6). Columbia, SC: South Carolina State Department of Education.

Chapter 19

Council on Physical Education for Children (COPEC). 1992. *Developmentally appropriate physical education practices for children*. Reston, VA: National Association for Sport and Physical Education (NASPE).

Dansky, J.L., and I.W. Silverman. 1973. Effects of play on associative fluency in preschool-aged children. *Developmental Psychology* 9: 38-43.

———. 1975. Play: A general facilitator of associative fluency. *Developmental Psychology* 11: 104.

Eisenberg, N., and J.D. Harris. 1984. Social competence: A developmental perspective. *School Psychology Review* 13: 267-77.

Eriksen, E. 1956. *Childhood and society*. New York: Norton.

Freud, A. 1971. *Normality and pathology in childhood: Assessments of development*. New York: International Universities Press.

Frost, J. 1992. *Play and playscapes*. Albany, NY: Delmar.

Hannaford, C. 1995. *Smart moves: Why learning is not all in your head*. Arlington, VA: Great Ocean Publishers.

King, S. 1991. Presentation at the Minneapolis Recreation and Park Congress. Minneapolis, MN.

Moore, R.C., S.M. Goltsman, and D.S. Iacofano. 1987. *Play for all guidelines: Planning, design, and management of outdoor play settings for all children*. Berkeley, CA: MIG Communications.

Neuman, E. 1971. *The elements of play*. New York: MSS Information Corporation.

Pepler, D.J., and H.S. Ross. 1981. The effects of play on convergent and divergent problem solving. *Child Development* 52: 1202-10.

Thompson, D., S.D. Hudson, and M.G. Mack. 1997. HELP for playground supervisors. *Teaching Elementary Physical Education* 8(4): 8-9.

U.S. Consumer Product Safety Commission (CPSC). 1994. *Handbook for public playground safety*. (Report No. 325 available free from CPSC, 4330 East West Highway, Bethesda, MD 20814.)

Werner, P. 1983. Playscapes: Children's needs and safety standards. *Dimensions* 11(2): 11-14.

Werner, P., S. Timms, and L. Almond. 1996. Health stops: Practical ideas for health-related exercise in preschool and primary classrooms. *Young Children* 51(6): 48-55.

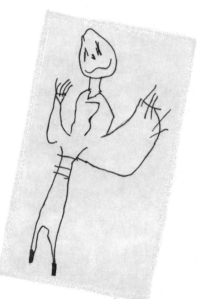

Dillon, 5

Blake, 6

Timmy, 11

Jaime, 5

Appendix

Resource Contacts

Council on Physical Education for Children (COPEC)
[a division of National Association for Sport and Physical Education (NASPE)]
1900 Association Dr.
Reston, VA 22091-1599
1-800-321-0789

Ask for the pamphlet "Developmentally Appropriate Physical Education Practices for Children" ($5).

Handbook for Public Playground Safety
U.S. Consumer Product Safety Commission
Washington, D.C. 20207

American Heart Association National Center
7272 Greenville Avenue
Dallas, Texas 75231
www.americanheart.org

Tennis Associations

USTA New England
181 Wells Ave.
Newton Centre, MA 02159
(617) 964-2030

USTA Eastern Section
550 Mamaroneck Ave., Ste. 505
Harrison, NY 10528
(914) 698-0414

USTA Middle States Section
460 Glennie Circle
King of Prussia, PA 19406
(610) 277-4040

USTA/Mid-Atlantic
2230 George C. Marshall Dr., Ste. E
Falls Church, VA 22043
Phone (703) 560-9480
Fax (703) 560-9505

USTA Southern Section
Spalding Woods Office Park
3850 Holcomb Bridge Rd., Ste. 305
Norcross, GA 30092
(770) 368-8200

USTA/Florida Section
1280 S.W. 36th Ave., Ste. 305
Pompano Beach, FL 33069
Phone (954) 968-3434
Fax (954) 968-3986

Caribbean Tennis Association
P.O. Box 40439
San Juan, PR 00940-0439

USTA/Midwest Section
8720 Castle Creek Pkway, Ste. 329
Indianapolis 46250
(317) 577-5130

USTA Northern Section
1001 W. 98th St., Ste. 101
Bloomington, MN 55431
(612) 887-5001

USTA Missouri Valley Section
801 Walnut, Ste. 100
Kansas City, MO 64106
Toll free (888) 368-8612
In the Kansas City metro area, (816) 472-6882

USTA/Texas Section
2111 Dickson, Ste. 33
Austin, TX 78704
(512) 443-1334

USTA Southwest Section
6240 E. Thomas Rd., Ste. 302
Scottsdale, AZ 85251
Phone (602) 947-9293
Fax (602) 947-1102

Other Sports

United States Badminton Association
One Olympic Plaza
Colorado Springs, CO 80909
719-578-4808

Youth Basketball of America
P.O. Box 3067
Orlando, FL 32802-3067
40-363-0599

U.S. Flag and Touch Football League
7709 Ohio St.
Mentor, OH 44060
216-974-8735

USA Gymnastics
201. S. Capitol, Ste. 300
Indianapolis, IN 46225
317-237-5050

American Youth Soccer Association
5403 W. 138th St.
Hawthorne, CA 90250
310-643-6455

National Softball Association
P.O. Box 23403
Lexington, KY 40523
606-887-4114

USA Table Tennis
One Olympic Plaza
Colorado Springs, CO 80909
719-578-4583

USA Volleyball
3595 E. Fountain Blvd.
Colorado Springs, CO 80910-1740
719-637-8300

Suzanne, 7

Chelsea, 8

Index

About the Contributors

David E. Belka, PhD, has taught elementary physical education for 10 years and college courses in motor development, elementary physical education, and pedagogy for 24 years. David is the author of *Teaching Children Games* and a contributor to the book series on preschool and elementary physical education teaching units written by Bette Logsdon, et al. David has been President of the Ohio AHPERD, served on AAHPERD's committee to select the Elementary Physical Education Teacher of the Year, and supervised more than 500 teaching internships. David lives in Oxford, Ohio, where he is a professor at Miami University.

Eloise M. Elliott, PhD, has 23 years of teaching experience in the field of physical education. She has been teaching at Concord College since 1986. Eloise received her PhD in Curriculum and Instruction–Physical Education Pedagogy from Virginia Polytechnic Institute and State University and her M.A. in Physical Education with a concentration in Safety Education from Salem-Teikyo University. Eloise's articles have appeared in the Journal of Teaching in Physical Education, Teaching Elementary Physical Education, and Teaching Secondary Physical Education. She is a past president of West Virginia AHPERD and a member of the Honor Society of Phi Kappa Phi. Eloise resides in Princeton, West Virginia.

Lauren J. Lieberman, PhD, is an assistant professor in the Department of Physical Education and Sport at the State University of New York at Brockport. She earned her PhD in 1995 in Human Performance with a minor in Movement Studies and Disabilities from Oregon State University. She also taught classes in adapted physical education and coordinated a play-based program for infants and toddlers while at OSU. In 1997 the International Federation of Adapted Physical Activity presented Lieberman with the Dr. Elly D. Friedman Outstanding Young Professional Award. Lieberman is the co-author of *Games for People With Sensory Impairments* with Jim F. Cowart.

Wendy Mustain has taught for more than 15 years and has taught at many levels, including the secondary level, kindergarten through eighth grade, as a graduate assistant at Virginia Tech, and at the university level at California State University in Sacramento, California State University in Chico, and Central Washington University. She received her B.A. in Physical Education and her teaching credential from California State University in Sacramento, her M.S.Ed. in Health and Physical Education from Virginia Polytechnic Institute and State University, and is currently working toward her PhD in Education at Virginia Polytechnic Institute and State University. Wendy has been honored as the "Emerging Professional" by the WSPECW and is a member of AAHPERD, ASCD, and WSPECW. Wendy's articles have appeared in the *Journal of Physical Education, Recreation and Dance* and in *Teaching Elementary Physical Education*.

Rae Pica has taught for 10 years at the University of New Hampshire in the Department of Kinesiology. She is a member of the National Association for the Education of Young Children, the Early Childhood Music and Movement Association, and the American Association for the Child's Right to Play. Rae has written widely on the subject of movement, music, and dance, with articles appearing in Instructor Magazine, Preschool Perspectives, Early Childhood Music, and International Gymnast. She is the author of the *Moving and Learning* series and *Dance Training for Gymnastics*.

Michael Sutliff is an Assistant Professor of Physical Education and Kinesiology at California Polytechnic State University. He earned a D.A. from Middle Tennessee State University. Michael has published over 20 articles on issues related to teaching. He serves as Vice President of Physical Education for the California Association of Health, Physical Education, Recreation, and Dance; and is a member of the American Association of Health, Physical Education, Recreation, and Dance.

Debbie Vigil is a member of the faculty at Jefferson Elementary in Sacramento, California. She has 14 years of elementary physical education teaching experience. Debbie earned her M.S. in Physical Education from California State University at Sacramento and a B.S. in Physical Education from the University of Oregon. She has presented more than 200 workshops and inservices throughout the United States and Europe on such topics as fitness, rhythm and dance, teaching styles, assessment strategies and social skills to assist teachers in implementing quality daily physical education. In 1999 Debbie was named California Teacher of the Year. Debbie is the author of *Collaborative PE: Classroom and PE Teachers Working Together*.

Peter Werner, has more than 30 years' experience as a teacher of physical education for children. He received his PED in physical education from Indiana University in 1971.

Peter teaches educational games, dance, and gymnastics and elementary physical education methods courses at the University of South Carolina, and he regularly spends time in the public schools teaching elementary physical education. For two years Peter chaired the Southern District of the Council on Physical Education for Children (COPEC), and he was the publications coordinator for the National Association for Sport and Physical Education (NASPE) for three years. He is currently working with Steve Sanders as a section editor of integrated curriculum of *Teaching Elementary Physical Education*. Peter has written more than 40 articles and five books, including *Teaching Children Gymnastics* and *Learning Through Movement* and was a co-author on *Interdisciplinary Teaching Through Physical Education*.

Deborah Wolf, PhD, has taught for 12 years at Eastern Illinois University. She received her PhD from the University of Illinois. In 1998 Wolf was presented with a presidential citation for her service to the Illinois Association of Health, Physical Education, Recreation, and Dance. Deborah has authored articles on teacher concerns and physical education. She is also a two-time recipient of Eastern Illinois University's Faculty Excellence Award. Deborah is a member of the American Alliance of Health, Physical Education, Recreation, and Dance, NASPE, the Illinois Association for Professional Preparation in Health, Physical Education, and Recreation.

About the Writer

A former elementary classroom teacher in both American and overseas public and private schools, Bonnie Pettifor holds a Bachelor's in English and a Master of Arts in Education from Washington University in St. Louis, Missouri. Currently she freelance writes for a number of other publishers. Her work includes science and literature units contributed to The Education Center's books and magazines (*Mailbox* and *Bookbag*) as well as two classroom science simulations for Interact of El Cajon, California (*New Atlantis* and *Insect Island*). She has also freelance edited for Human Kinetics for several years. She lives in Urbana, Illinois.